CHICAGO PUBLIC LIBRARY
HAROLD WASHINGTON LIBRARY CENTER

R0011675509

THE CHICAGO PUBLIC LIBRARY

BUSINESS/SCIENCE/TECHNOLOGY
DIVISION

FORM 19

CHILTON'S
REPAIR & TUNE-UP GUIDE
LASER DAYTONA 1984-85

All U.S. and Canadian models of DODGE Daytona and PLYMOUTH Laser, including turbocharged engines

President LAWRENCE A. FORNASIERI
Vice President and General Manager JOHN P. KUSHNERICK
Executive Editor KERRY A. FREEMAN, S.A.E.
Senior Editor RICHARD J. RIVELE, S.A.E.
Editor W. CALVIN SETTLE, JR.

CHILTON BOOK COMPANY
Radnor, Pennsylvania
19089

SAFETY NOTICE

Proper service and repair procedures are vital to the safe, reliable operation of all motor vehicles, as well as the personal safety of those performing repairs. This book outlines procedures for servicing and repairing vehicles using safe, effective methods. The procedures contain many NOTES, CAUTIONS and WARNINGS which should be followed along with standard safety procedures to eliminate the possibility of personal injury or improper service which could damage the vehicle or compromise its safety.

It is important to note that repair procedures and techniques, tools and parts for servicing motor vehicles, as well as the skill and experience of the individual performing the work vary widely. It is not possible to anticipate all of the conceivable ways or conditions under which vehicles may be serviced, or to provide cautions as to all of the possible hazards that may result. Standard and accepted safety precautions and equipment should be used when handling toxic or flammable fluids, and safety goggles or other protection should be used during cutting, grinding, chiseling, prying, or any other process that can cause material removal or projectiles.

Some procedures require the use of tools specially designed for a specific purpose. Before substituting another tool or procedure, you must be completely satisfied that neither your personal safety, nor the performance of the vehicle will be endangered.

Although information in this guide is based on industry sources and is as complete as possible at the time of publication, the possibility exists that the manufacturer made later changes which could not be included here. While striving for total accuracy, Chilton Book Company cannot assume responsibility for any errors, changes, or omissions that may occur in the compilation of this data.

PART NUMBERS

Part numbers listed in this reference are not recommendations by Chilton for any product by brand name. They are references that can be used with interchange manuals and aftermarket supplier catalogs to locate each brand supplier's discrete part number.

SPECIAL TOOLS

Special tools are recommended by the vehicle manufacturer to perform their specific job. Use has been kept to a minimum, but where absolutely necessary, they are referred to in the text by the part number of the tool manufacturer. These tools can be purchased, under the appropriate part number, from Owatonna Tool Company, Owatonna, MN 55060 or an equivalent tool can be purchased locally from a tool supplier or parts outlet. Before substituting any tool for the one recommended, read the SAFETY NOTICE at the top of this page.

ACKNOWLEDGMENTS

The Chilton Book Company wishes to express appreciation to the Chrysler Plymouth Division, Chrysler Motor Corporation, Detroit, Michigan, and the Dodge Division, Chrysler Motors Corporation, Detroit, Michigan for their generous assistance in the preparation of this book.

Copyright © 1985 by Chilton Book Company
All Rights Reserved
Published in Radnor, Pennsylvania 19089, by Chilton Book Company

Manufactured in the United States of America
1234567890   4321098765

Chilton's Repair & Tune-Up Guide: Laser/Daytona 1984–85
ISBN 0-8019-7563-8 pbk.
Library of Congress Catalog Card No. 84-45487

CONTENTS

1 General Information and Maintenance
- 1 How to Use this Book
- 2 Tools and Equipment
- 7 Routine Maintenance and Lubrication

2 Tune-Up and Performance Maintenance
- 32 Tune-Up Procedures
- 32 Tune-Up Specifications

3 Engine and Engine Rebuilding
- 37 Engine Electrical System
- 41 Engine Service and Specifications

4 Emission Controls and Fuel System
- 72 Emission Control System and Service
- 81 Fuel System Service

5 Chassis Electrical
- 106 Accessory Service
- 112 Instrument Panel Service
- 113 Lights, Fuses and Flashers

98 Chilton's Fuel Economy and Tune-Up Tips

6 Clutch and Transaxle
- 115 Manual Transaxle
- 118 Clutch
- 120 Automatic Transaxle

7 Suspension and Steering
- 124 Front Suspension
- 132 Rear Suspension
- 134 Steering

8 Brakes
- 140 Front Brakes
- 146 Rear Brakes
- 151 Brake Specifications

9 Troubleshooting
- 153 Problem Diagnosis

- 186 Mechanic's Data
- 188 Index

162 Chilton's Body Repair Tips

Quick Reference Specifications For Your Vehicle

Fill in this chart with the most commonly used specifications for your vehicle. Specifications can be found in Chapters 1 through 3 or on the tune-up decal under the hood of the vehicle.

Tune-Up

Firing Order _____

Spark Plugs:

    Type _____

    Gap (in.) _____

Point Gap (in.) _____

Dwell Angle (°) _____

Ignition Timing (°) _____

    Vacuum (Connected/Disconnected) _____

Valve Clearance (in.)

    Intake _____ Exhaust _____

Capacities

Engine Oil (qts)

    With Filter Change _____

    Without Filter Change _____

Cooling System (qts) _____

Manual Transmission (pts) _____

    Type _____

Automatic Transmission (pts) _____

    Type _____

Front Differential (pts) _____

    Type _____

Rear Differential (pts) _____

    Type _____

Transfer Case (pts) _____

    Type _____

FREQUENTLY REPLACED PARTS

Use these spaces to record the part numbers of frequently replaced parts.

PCV VALVE	**OIL FILTER**	**AIR FILTER**
Manufacturer _____	Manufacturer _____	Manufacturer _____
Part No. _____	Part No. _____	Part No. _____

General Information and Maintenance

HOW TO USE THIS BOOK

Chilton's Repair & Tune-Up Guide for the Chrysler Laser/Dodge Daytona is intended to help you learn more about the inner workings of your vehicle and save you money on its upkeep and operation.

The first two chapters will be the most used, since they contain maintenance and tune-up information and procedures. Studies have shown that a properly tuned and maintained car can get at least 10% better gas mileage than an out-of-tune car. The other chapters deal with the more complex systems of your car. Operating systems from engine through brakes are covered to the extent that the average do-it-yourselfer becomes mechanically involved. This book will not explain such things as rebuilding the differential for the simple reason that the expertise required and the investment in special tools make this task uneconomical. It will give you the detailed instructions to help you change your own brake pads and shoes, replace points and plugs, and do many more jobs that will save you money, give you personal satisfaction, and help you avoid expensive problems.

A secondary purpose of this book is a reference for owners who want to understand their car and/or their mechanics better. In this case, no tools at all are required.

Before removing any bolts, read through the entire procedure. This will give you the overall view of what tools and supplies will be required. There is nothing more frustrating than having to walk to the bus stop on Monday morning because you were short one bolt on Sunday afternoon. So read ahead and plan ahead. Each operation should be approached logically and all procedures thoroughly understood before attempting any work.

All chapters contain adjustments, maintenance, removal and installation procedures, and repair and overhaul procedures. When repair is not considered practical, we tell you how to remove the part and then how to install the new or rebuilt replacement. In this way, you at least save the labor costs. Backyard repair of such components as the alternator is just not practical.

Two basic mechanic's rules should be mentioned here. One, whenever the left side of the car or engine is referred to, it is meant to specify the driver's side of the car. Conversely, the right side of the car means the passenger's side. Secondly, most screws and bolts are removed by turning counterclockwise, and tightened by turning clockwise.

Safety is always the most important rule. Constantly be aware of the dangers involved in working on an automobile and taking the proper precautions. (See the section in this chapter "Servicing Your Vehicle Safely" and the SAFETY NOTICE on the acknowledgment page.)

Pay attention to the instructions provided. There are 3 common mistakes in mechanical work:

1. Incorrect order of assembly, disassembly or adjustment. When taking something apart or putting it together, doing things in the wrong order usually just costs you extra time; however it CAN break something. Read the entire procedure before beginning disassembly. Do everything in the order in which the instructions say you should do it, even if you can't immediately see a reason for it. When you're taking apart something that is very intricate (for example a carburetor), you might want to draw a picture of how it looks when assembled at one point in order to make sure you get everything back in its proper position. (We will supply exploded views whenever possible.) When making adjustments, especially tune-up adjustments, do them in order; often one adjustment affects another, and you cannot expect even satisfactory results unless each adjustment is

GENERAL INFORMATION AND MAINTENANCE

made only when it cannot be changed by any other.

2. Overtorquing (or undertorquing). While it is more common for overtorquing to cause damage, undertorquing can cause a fastener to vibrate loose causing serious damage. Especially when dealing with aluminum parts, pay attention to torque specifications and utilize a torque wrench in assembly. If a torque figure is not available, remember that if you are using the right tool to do the job, you will probably not have to strain yourself to get a fastener tight enough. The pitch of most threads is so slight that the tension you put on the wrench will be multiplied many, many times in actual force on what you are tightening. A good example of how critical torque is can be seen in the case of spark plug installation, especially where you are putting the plug into an aluminum cylinder head. Too little torque can fail to crush the gasket, causing leakage of combustion gases and consequent overheating of the plug and engine parts. Too much torque can damage the threads, or distort the plug, which changes the spark gap.

There are many commercial products available for ensuring that fasteners won't come loose, even if they are not torqued just right (a very common brand is "Locktite®"). If you're worried about getting something together tight enough to hold, but loose enough to avoid mechanical damage during assembly, one of these products might offer substantial insurance. Read the label on the package and make sure the product is compatible with the materials, fluids, etc. involved before choosing one.

3. Crossthreading. This occurs when a part such as a bolt is screwed into a nut or casting at the wrong angle and forced. Crossthreading is more likely to occur if access is difficult. It helps to clean and lubricate fasteners, and to start threading with the part to be installed going straight in. Then, start the bolt, spark plug, etc. with your fingers. If you encounter resistance, unscrew the part and start over again at a different angle until it can be inserted and turned several turns without much effort. Keep in mind that many parts, especially spark plugs, use tapered threads so that gentle turning will automatically bring the part you're threading to the proper angle if you don't force it or resist a change in angle. Don't put a wrench on the part until it's been turned a couple of turns by hand. If you suddenly encounter resistance, and the part has not seated fully, don't force it. Pull it back out and make sure it's clean and threading properly.

Always take your time and be patient; once you have some experience, working on your car will become an enjoyable hobby.

TOOLS AND EQUIPMENT

Naturally, without the proper tools and equipment it is impossible to properly service your vehicle. It would be impossible to catalog each tool that you would need to perform each or every operation in this book. It would also be unwise for the amateur to rush out and buy an expensive set of tools on the theory that he may need one or more of them at sometime.

The best approach is to proceed slowly, gathering together a good quality set of those tools that are used most frequently. Don't be misled by the low cost of bargain tools. It is far better to spend a little more for better quality. Forged wrenches, 10 or 12 point sockets and fine tooth ratchets are by far preferable to their less expensive counterparts. As any good mechanic can tell you, there are few worse experiences than trying to work on a car or truck with bad tools. Your monetary savings will be far outweighed by frustration and mangled knuckles.

Begin accumulating those tools that are used most frequently; those associated with routine maintenance and tune-up.

In addition to the normal assortment of screwdrivers and pliers you should have the following tools for routine maintenance jobs (your Laser or Daytona uses both SAE and metric fasteners):

1. SAE/Metric wrenches—sockets and combination open end/box end wrenches in sizes from 1/8 in. (3 mm) to 3/4 in. (19 mm); and a spark plug socket (13/16 in.)

If possible, buy various length socket drive extensions. One break in this department is that the metric sockets available in the U.S. will all fit the ratchet handles and extensions you may already have (1/4 3/8 and 1/2 in. drive).

2. Jackstands—for support;
3. Oil filter wrench;
4. Oil filter spout—for pouring oil;
5. Grease gun—for chassis lubrication;
6. Hydrometer—for checking the battery;
7. A container for draining oil;
8. Many rags for wiping up the inevitable mess.

In addition to the above items there are several others that are not absolutely necessary, but handy to have around. These include oil dry, a transmission funnel and the usual supply of lubricants, antifreeze and fluids, although these can be purchased as needed. This is a basic list for routine maintenance, but only if your personal needs and desire can accurately determine your list of tools.

The second list of tools is for tune-ups. While the tools involved here are slightly more sophisticated, they need not be outrageously ex-

GENERAL INFORMATION AND MAINTENANCE

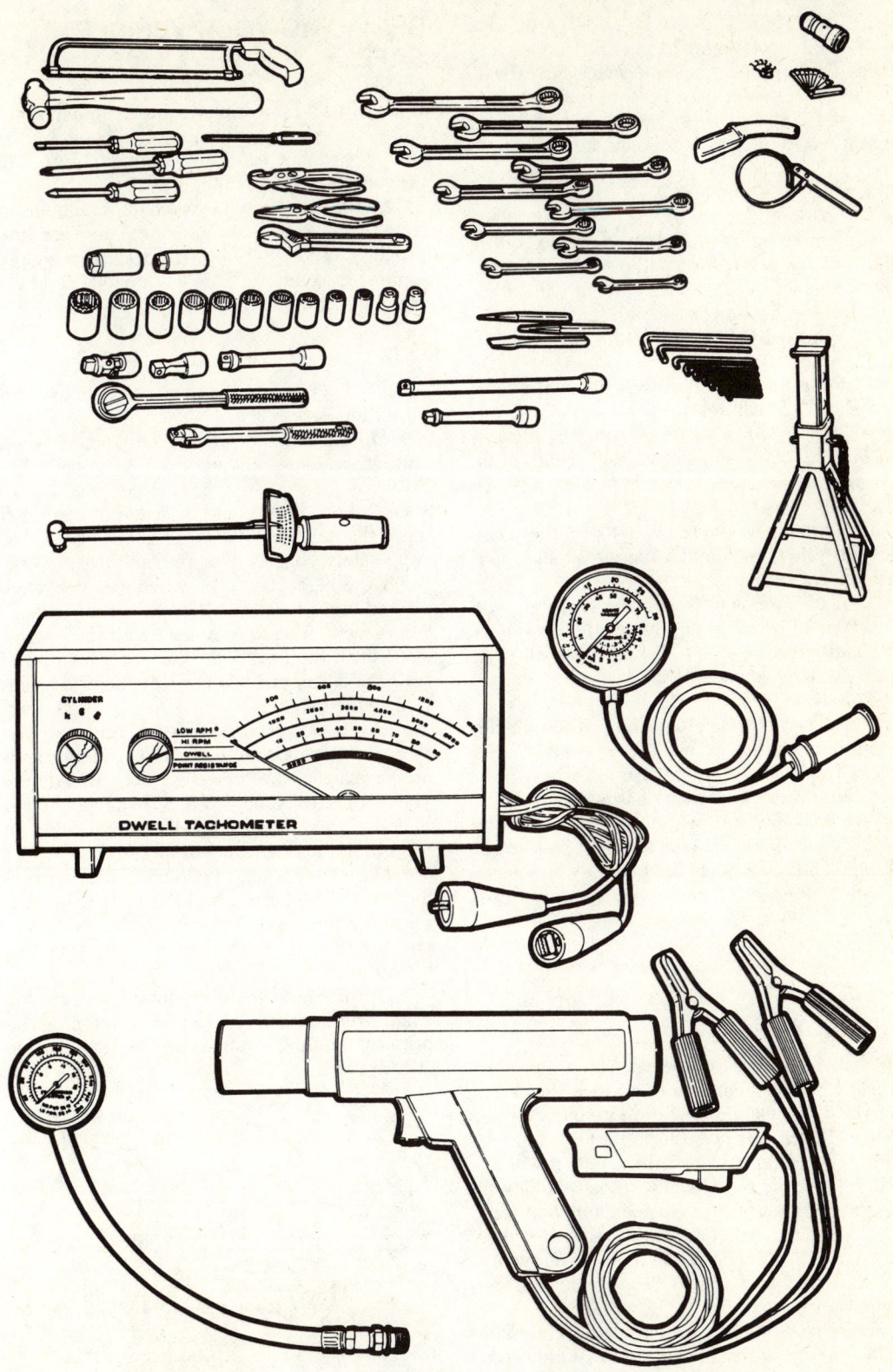

The majority of automotive service can be handled with these tools

4 GENERAL INFORMATION AND MAINTENANCE

pensive. There are several inexpensive tach/dwell meters on the market that are every bit as good for the average mechanic as a $100.00 professional model. Just be sure that it goes to at least 1,200–1,500 rpm on the tach scale and that it works on 4, 6 and 8 cylinder engines. A basic list of tune-up equipment could include:

1. Tach-dwell meter;
2. Spark plug wrench;
3. Timing light (a DC light that works from the car's battery is best, although an AC light that plugs into 110V house current will suffice at some sacrifice in brightness);
4. Wire spark plug gauge/adjusting tools;
5. Set of feeler blades.

Here again, be guided by your own needs. A feeler blade will set the point gap as easily as dwell meter will read dwell, but slightly less accurately. And since you will need a tachometer anyway . . . well, make your own decision.

In addition to these basic tools, there are several other tools and gauges you may find useful. These include:

1. A compression gauge. The screw in type is slower to use, but eliminates the possibility of a faulty reading due to escaping pressure;
2. A manifold vacuum gauge;
3. A test light;
4. An induction meter. This is used for determining whether or not there is current in a wire. These are handy for use if a wire is broken somewhere in a wiring harness.

As a final note, you will probably find a torque wrench necessary for all but the most basic work. The beam type models are perfectly adequate, although the newer click type are more precise.

Special Tools

Normally, the use of special factory tools is avoided for repair procedures, since these are not readily available for the do-it-yourself mechanic. When it is possible to perform the job with more commonly available tools, it will be pointed out, but occasionally, a special tool was designed to perform a specific function and should be used. Before substituting another tool, you should be convinced that neither your safety nor the performance of the vehicle will be compromised.

Some special tools are available commercially from major tool manufacturers. Others can be purchased from Miller Special Tools; Division of Utica Tool Company, 32615 Park Lane, Garden City, Michigan 48135.

SERVICING YOUR VEHICLE SAFELY

It is virtually impossible to anticipate all of the hazards involved with automotive maintenance and service but care and common sense will prevent most accidents.

The rules of safety for mechanics range from "don't smoke around gasoline," to "use the proper tool for the job." The trick to avoiding injuries is to develop safe work habits and take every possible precaution.

Dos

• Do keep a fire extinguisher and first aid kit within easy reach.
• Do wear safety glasses or goggles when cutting, drilling or prying, even if you have 20–20 vision. If you wear glasses for the sake of vision, then they should be made of hardened glass that can serve also as safety glasses, or wear safety goggles over your regular glasses.
• Do shield your eyes whenever you work around the battery. Batteries contain sulphuric acid; in case of contact with the eyes or skin, flush the area with water or a mixture of water and baking soda and get medical attention immediately.
• Do use safety stands for any undercar service. Jacks are for raising vehicles; safety stands are for making sure the vehicle stays raised until you want it to come down. Whenever the vehicle is raised, block the wheels remaining on the ground and set the parking brake.
• Do use adequate ventilation when working with any chemicals. Like carbon monoxide, the asbestos dust resulting from brake lining wear can be poisonous in sufficient quantities.
• Do disconnect the negative battery cable when working on the electrical system. The primary ignition system can contain up to 40,000 volts.

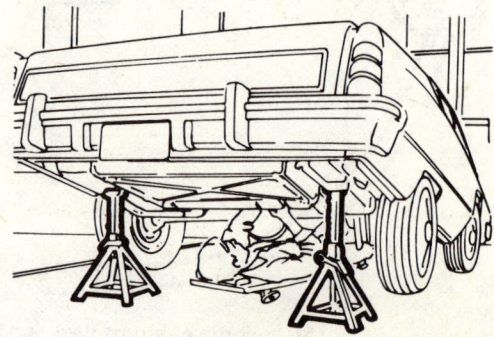

Always use jackstands when working under the car

GENERAL INFORMATION AND MAINTENANCE

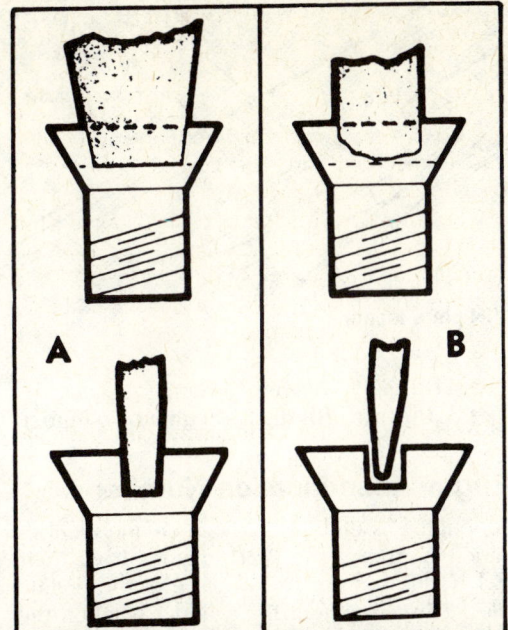

Screwdrivers should be kept in good condition to prevent injury

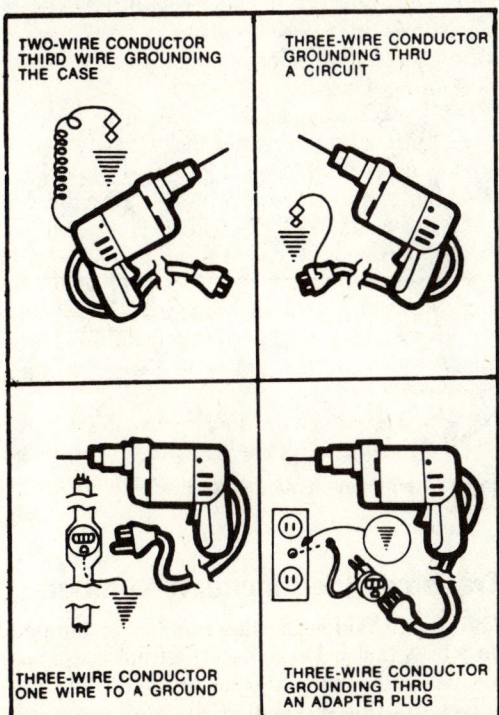

Power tools should always be properly grounded

• Do follow manufacturer's directions whenever working with potentially hazardous materials. Both brake fluid and antifreeze are poisonous if taken internally.
• Do properly maintain your tools. Loose hammerheads, mushroomed punches and chisels, frayed or poorly grounded electrical cords, excessively worn screwdrivers, spread wrenches (open end), cracked sockets, slipping ratchets, or faulty droplight sockets can cause accidents.
• Do use the proper size and type of tool for the job being done.
• Do when possible, pull on a wrench handle rather than push on it, and adjust your stance to prevent a fall.
• Do be sure that adjustable wrenches are tightly adjusted on the nut or bolt and pulled so that the face is on the side of the fixed jaw.
• Do select a wrench or socket that fits the nut or bolt. The wrench or socket should sit straight, not cocked.
• Do strike squarely with a hammer—avoid glancing blows.
• Do set the parking brake and block the drive wheels if the work requires that the engine be running.

Don'ts

• Don't run an engine in a garage or anywhere else without proper ventilation—EVER! Carbon monoxide is poisonous; it takes a long time to leave the human body and you can build up a deadly supply of it in your system by simply breathing in a little every day. You may not realize you are slowly poisoning yourself. Always use power vents, windows, fans or open the garage doors.
• Don't work around moving parts while wearing a necktie or other loose clothing. Short sleeves are much safer than long, loose sleeves and hard-toed shoes with neoprene soles protect your toes and give a better grip on slippery surfaces. Jewelry such as watches, fancy belt buckles, beads or body adornment of any kind is not safe working around a car. Long hair should be hidden under a hat or cap.
• Don't use pockets for toolboxes. A fall or bump can drive a screwdriver deep into your body. Even a wiping cloth hanging from the back pocket can wrap around a spinning shaft or fan.
• Don't smoke when working around gasoline, cleaning solvent or other flammable material.
• Don't smoke when working around the battery. When the battery is being charged, it gives off explosive hydrogen gas.
• Don't use gasoline to wash your hands; there are excellent soaps available. Gasoline may contain lead, and lead can enter the body through a cut, accumulating in the body until you are very ill. Gasoline also removes all the

6 GENERAL INFORMATION AND MAINTENANCE

natural oils from the skin so that bone dry hands will suck up oil and grease.

• Don't service the air conditioning system unless you are equipped with the necessary tools and training. The refrigerant, R-12, is extremely cold and when exposed to the air, will instantly freeze any surface it comes in contact with, including your eyes. Although the refrigerant is normally non-toxic, R-12 becomes a deadly poisonous gas in the presence of an open flame. One good whiff of the vapors from burning refrigerant can be fatal.

HISTORY

The Laser and Daytona models were introduced as the first American-built, front-wheel drive sports car available with a transverse-mounted, turbo-charged 4-cylinder engine.

In designing the new Laser and Daytona sports car models and their components, Chrysler used Computer Aided Design in virtually every department with design responsibility.

The base engine on the Laser and Daytona is Chrysler's 2.2 liter single-point Electronic Fuel Injected powerplant. The optional engine in these models and the standard engine in the Laser XE, Daytona Turbo, and the Daytona Turbo Z is the new Chrysler-engineered 2.2 liter multipoint Electronic Fuel Injected turbocharged powerplant.

SERIAL NUMBER IDENTIFICATION

Vehicle (VIN)

The vehicle identification number (VIN) is located on a plate attached to the upper left-hand corner of the instrument panel visible through the windshield. The complete VIN is also on the Safety Certification label located on the rear facing of the driver's door. An abbreviated form of the VIN is also stamped on a pad on the engine and on the transaxle housing.

All VIN's contain 17 digits coded to reveal the following information:
- 1st digit—Country of Origin
- 2nd digit—Make
- 3rd digit—Type of Vehicle
- 4th digit—Pass Safety System
- 5th digit—Model Type
- 6th digit—Series
- 7th digit—Body Style
- 8th digit—Engine
- 9th digit—Check digit
- 10th digit—Model Year

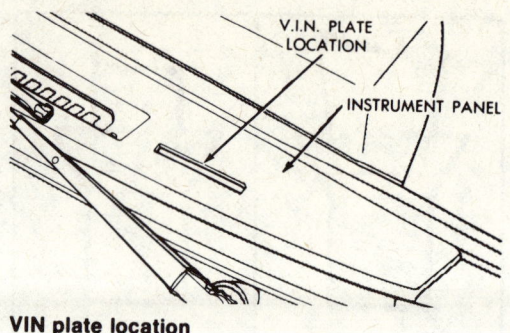

VIN plate location

- 11th digit—Assembly Plant
- 12th thru 17th digit—Sequence Number

Engine Identification Number

All engine assemblies carry an engine identification number. The 2.2L engines have their E.I.N. located on the rear face of the engine block, directly under the cylinder head on the left side of the vehicle.

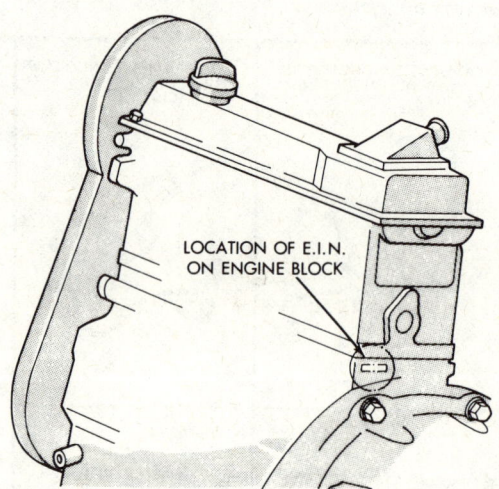

Engine identification number location

Transaxle Identification Number

The transaxle identification number is stamped on a boss that is located on the transaxle housing when the transaxles are installed into the vehicles during production.

Transaxle Serial Number

In addition to the transaxle identification number, each transaxle carries an assembly part number which must be referenced when ordering parts for the transaxle.

On the A525 manual transaxle, the assembly part number is located on a metal tag attached

GENERAL INFORMATION AND MAINTENANCE

1984–1985 V.I.N. Code Chart

Position	Code Options	Interpretation
1	1 = U.S. 2 = Canada	Country of Origin
2	C = Chrysler P = Plymouth	Make
3	3 = Pass. Car	Type of Vehicle
4	B = Manual Seat Belts D = 1–3000 lbs. GVW.	Pass Safety System
5	A = C Laser A = V Daytona	Model
6	1 = Economy 2 = Low 4 = High 5 = Premium 6 = Special	Series
7	4 = 2 door Hatchback	Body Style
8	D = 2.2L EFI E = 2.2L Turbo	Engine
9*	(1 thru 9, 0 or X)	Check Digit
10	E = 1984 F = 1985	Model Year
11	C = Jefferson D = Belvidere F = Newark G = St. Louis 1 X = St. Louis 2	Assembly Plant
12 thru 17	(6 digits)	Sequence Number

*Digit in the 9th position is used for VIN verification

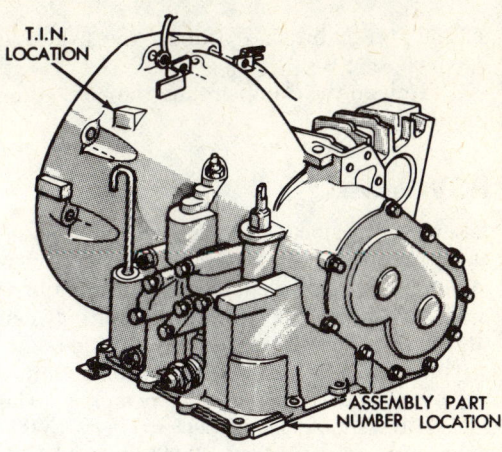

Automatic transaxle number location

to the front side of the transaxle. On the A413 automatic transaxle, the assembly part number is located on a pad just above the oil pan at the rear of the transaxle.

ROUTINE MAINTENANCE

Air Cleaner

The engine air cleaner element should be replaced every 52,500 miles under normal use. If the car is driven in extremely dirty, dusty or sandy areas, the filter element should be inspected at least every 15,000 miles and replaced if necessary.

1. Remove the clamp securing the hose to the throttle body.
2. Release the five clips on the air cleaner. Pull the hose off of the throttle body and lift the cover and the hose off the bottom of the air cleaner.
3. To install, place the new filter element, screen up, into the plastic bottom section of the air filter housing.
4. Place the calmp loosely on the throttle body hose and push the hose on to the throttle body.
5. Align the upper and lower halves of the

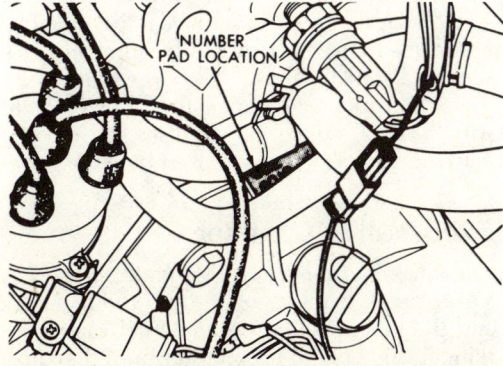

The manual transaxle number is stamped on a pad

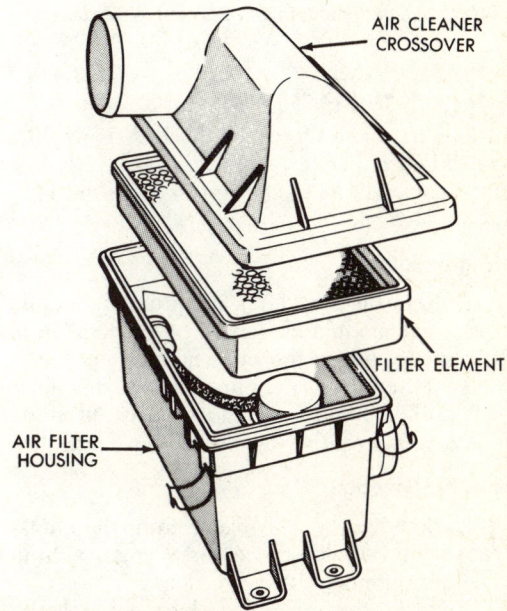

Air cleaner assembly and filter element

8 GENERAL INFORMATION AND MAINTENANCE

air filter assembly and connect the five hold down clips.

6. Tighten the clamp around the hose at the throttle body.

PCV Valve

Lasers and Daytonas are equipped with a closed crankcase ventilation system. The PCV valve is located either in the crankcase vent module or (on turbo engines) in a line running between the cylinder head cover and the throttle body.

This valve must be kept clean for optimum engine performance and fuel economy. The PCV valve should be inspected every 15,000 miles and replaced every 30,000 miles. In extremely dusty conditions or if the car is subjected to excessive idling or short trip operation, the interval should be halved.

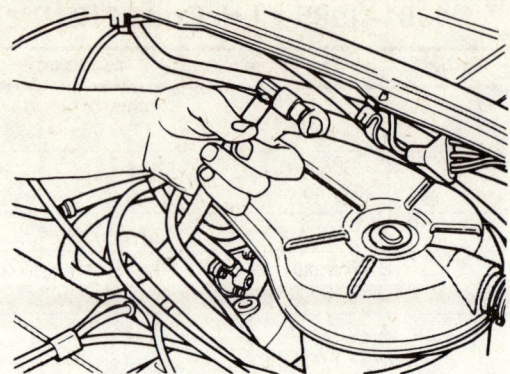

Checking for vacuum at PCV Valve

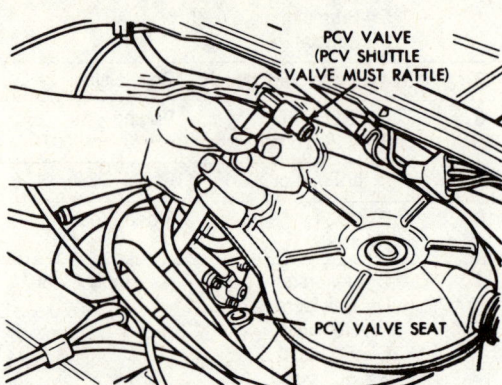

To be considered serviceable, the PCV valve must rattle when shaken

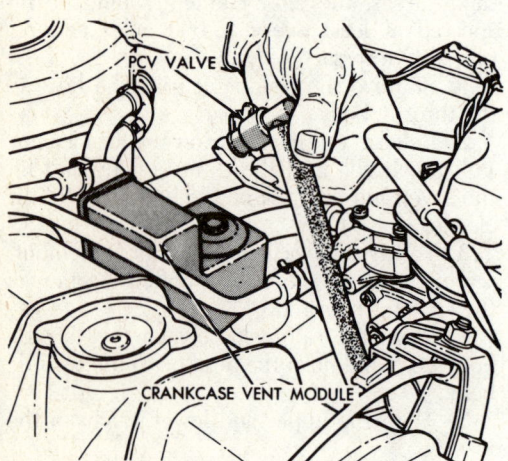

Crankcase vent module and PCV valve location

PCV VALVE INSPECTION

There are 2 ways to check the PCV valve. If a valve fails either test, replace the valve with a new one. DO NOT attempt to clean the PCV valve.

Engine Idling

1. Remove the PCV valve from the crankcase vent module or, (on turbo engines) from the line leading to the air cleaner.
2. If the valve is not plugged, a hissing noise will be heard and a strong vacuum will be felt when you cover the valve with your finger.

Engine Stopped

1. Remove the PCV valve from the crankcase vent module or, (on turbo engines) from the line leading to the air cleaner.
2. Shake the valve; a clicking noise should be plainly audible if the valve is free.

Crankcase Vent Module

The crankcase vent module is located on the cylinder head cover of all nonturbocharged engines.

This module must be kept clean for optimum engine performance and fuel economy. The crankcase vent module should be cleaned and lubricated every 52,500 miles. In extremely dusty conditions or if the car is subjected to excessive idling or short trip operation, the interval should be halved.

To clean the module, remove it from the cylinder head cover and wash the filter in kerosene or a similar solvent. Allow the filter to dry then, lubricate or dampen the filter element with SAE 30 engine oil. Replace the module onto the cylinder head and insert the PCV valve.

Evaporative Canister

The charcoal canister is used on all models to store vapors that evaporate from the fuel tank and the fuel injection system. Fuel vapors are temporarily held in the canister until they may be returned through the intake manifold. The

GENERAL INFORMATION AND MAINTENANCE

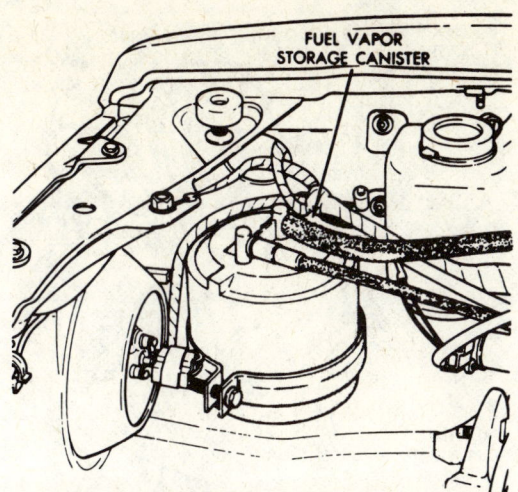

Fuel vapor storage canister

charcoal canister is sealed, maintenance free, and is located in the wheelwell area of the engine compartment.

Battery

Loose, dirty, or corroded battery terminals are a major cause of "no-start." Every 3 months or so, remove the battery terminals and clean them, giving them a light coating of petroleum jelly when you are finished. This will help retard corrosion.

Check the battery cables for signs of wear or chafing and replace any cable or terminal that looks marginal. Battery terminals can be easily cleaned and inexpensive terminal cleaning tools are an excellent investment that will pay for themselves many times over. They can usually

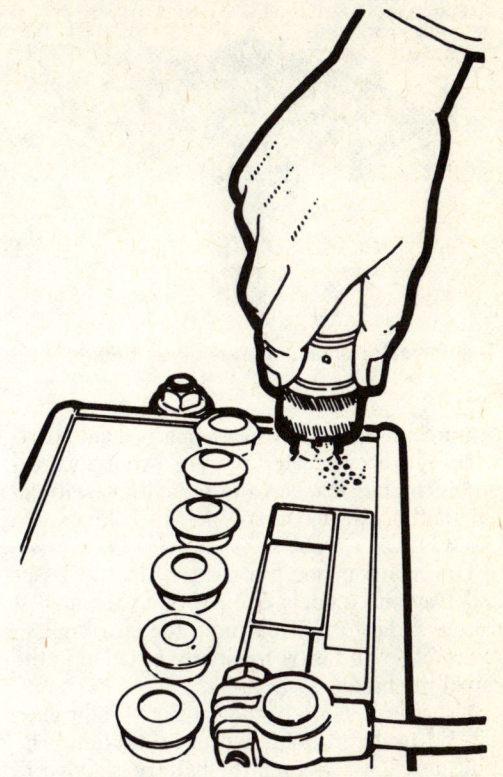

An inexpensive tool easily cleans the battery terminals

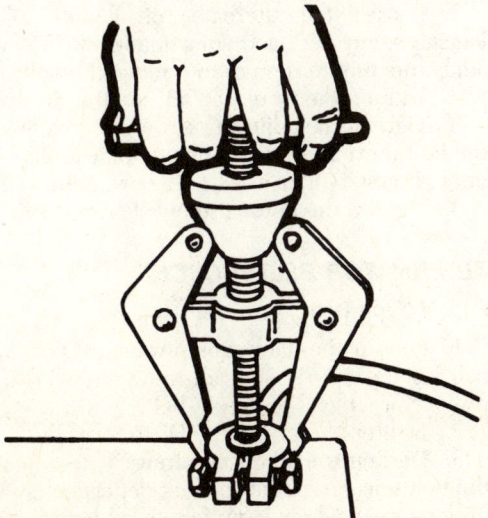

A small puller will easily remove the cable from the terminals

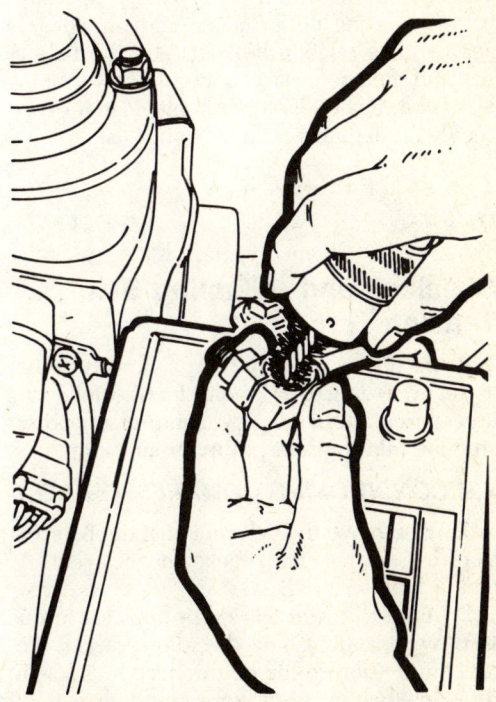

Clean the inside of the terminal clamp

10 GENERAL INFORMATION AND MAINTENANCE

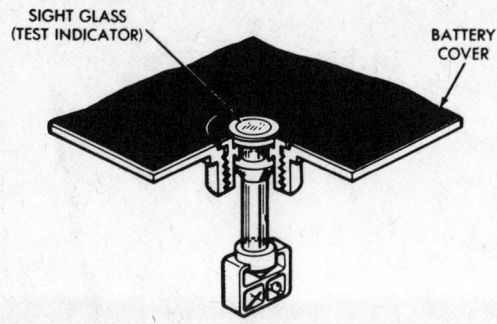

Test indicator on maintenance free battery

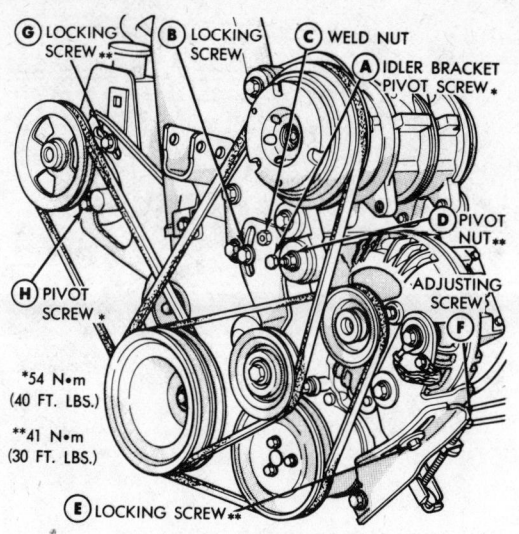

Accessory drive belts—2.2L engine

be purchased from any well-equipped auto parts store. The accumulated white powder and corrosion can be cleaned from the battery with an old toothbrush and a solution of baking soda and water.

The maintenance free battery in the Laser and Daytona models is equipped with a "test charge indicator." This indicator is a built in hydrometer and is permanently installed in the cap of the battery.

Visual inspection of the indicator sight glass will aid in determining battery condition. The indicator shows green if the battery is above 75 to 80 percent of being fully charged and "dark" if it needs recharging. Light yellow means the battery may need replacing.

REPLACEMENT BATTERIES

The cold power rating of a battery measures battery starting performance and provides an approximate relationship between the battery size and the engine size. The cold power rating of a replacement battery should match or exceed your engine size in cubic inches.

BELTS

Checking and Adjusting Belt Tension

Your particular car may have as few as one or as many as four drive belts for the following accessories: alternator, A/C compressor, power steering pump, water pump, or air pump.

AIR CONDITIONING COMPRESSOR BELT

1. To remove the belt or adjust the belt tension, loosen the idler bracket pivot screw "A" and locking screw "B".
2. Adjust the belt tension by applying torque to the weld nut "C" on the idler bracket. Adjust the tension so the belt deflection is 5/16 in. for a new belt or 7/16 in. for a used belt.
3. Retighten in order, first, locking screw "B", then pivot screw "A". Tighten both screws to 40 ft. lbs.

POWER STEERING PUMP BELT

1. From above the engine loosen the locking screw "G".
2. From beneath the vehicle loosen the pivot nut "H".
3. Install a 1/2 in. breaker bar into the slot in the adjusting bracket. Adjust the belt tension so that the belt deflection is 1/4 in. for a new belt or 7/16 in. for a used belt.
4. Retighten in order, first, locking screw "G", then pivot screw "H" and the pivot nut. Tighten both screws to 40 ft. lbs.

ALTERNATOR BELT (CHRYSLER)

1. Loosen the alternator pivot nut "D", locking screw "E", and adjusting screw "F" to adjust the belt tension or to remove the belt.
2. Tighten the pivot nut "D" to 30 ft. lbs.
3. Tighten the adjusting screw "F" to adjust the belt tension so that the belt deflection is 1/8 in. for a new belt or 1/4 in. for a used belt.
4. Tighten the locking screw "E".

ALTERNATOR BELT (BOSCH)
Poly-V Type Belt

1. Loosen the alternator pivot nut "D", T-bolt locking nut "K" and adjusting screw "J" to remove or adjust the Poly-V belt.
2. Tighten the pivot nut "D" to 30 ft. lbs.
3. Tighten the adjusting screw "J" to adjust the belt tension so that the belt deflection is 1/8 in. for a new belt or 1/4 in. for a used belt.
4. Tighten the T-Bolt locking nut to 25 ft. lbs.

GENERAL INFORMATION AND MAINTENANCE

HOW TO SPOT WORN V-BELTS

V-Belts are vital to efficient engine operation—they drive the fan, water pump and other accessories. They require little maintenance (occasional tightening) but they will not last forever. Slipping or failure of the V-belt will lead to overheating. If your V-belt looks like any of these, it should be replaced.

Cracking or weathering

This belt has deep cracks, which cause it to flex. Too much flexing leads to heat build-up and premature failure. These cracks can be caused by using the belt on a pulley that is too small. Notched belts are available for small diameter pulleys.

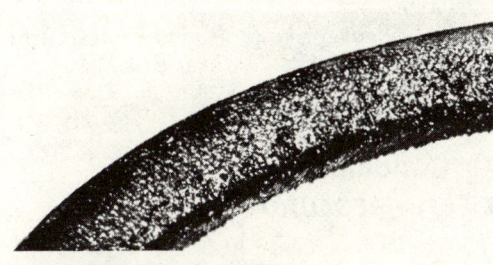

Softening (grease and oil)

Oil and grease on a belt can cause the belt's rubber compounds to soften and separate from the reinforcing cords that hold the belt together. The belt will first slip, then finally fail altogether.

Glazing

Glazing is caused by a belt that is slipping. A slipping belt can cause a run-down battery, erratic power steering, overheating or poor accessory performance. The more the belt slips, the more glazing will be built up on the surface of the belt. The more the belt is glazed, the more it will slip. If the glazing is light, tighten the belt.

Worn cover

The cover of this belt is worn off and is peeling away. The reinforcing cords will begin to wear and the belt will shortly break. When the belt cover wears in spots or has a rough jagged appearance, check the pulley grooves for roughness.

Separation

This belt is on the verge of breaking and leaving you stranded. The layers of the belt are separating and the reinforcing cords are exposed. It's just a matter of time before it breaks completely.

GENERAL INFORMATION AND MAINTENANCE

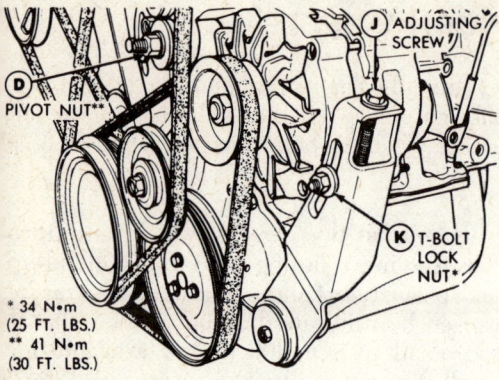

Bosch alternator belt adjusting screw and T-bolt locking nut

AIR PUMP

NOTE: *Be careful not to rotate the camshaft while servicing the air pump. Use the square holes provided in the drive pulley to prevent it from rotating.*

1. Remove the screws and nuts holding the drive pulley in place.
2. Remove the locking bolt "L" and pivot bolt "M" lift the air pump up and out of the way.
3. Install the new drive belt, reposition the air pump and install the pivot bolt "M" and then the locking bolt "L" finger tight.
4. Be certain that the air pump pulley is restrained so that it does not rotate. Adjust the belt tension so that the belt deflection is ³⁄₁₆ in. for a new belt or ¼ in. for a used belt.
5. Tighten the first locking bolt "L" and then pivot bolt "M" to 25 ft. lbs.
6. Reinstall the air pump drive pulley cover.

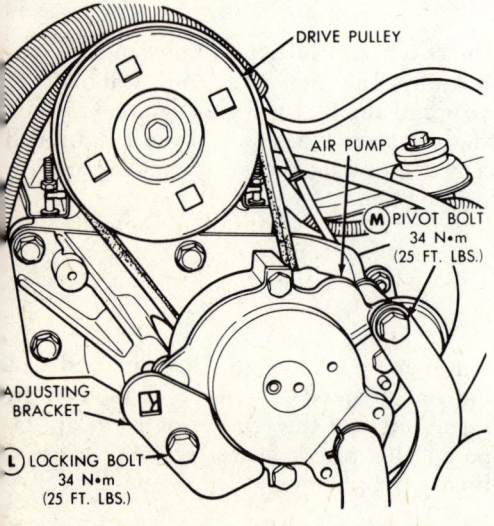

Air pump mounting—2.2L engine

Hoses

Hoses can be removed or installed with pliers or a screwdriver. Some cars use spring type clamps while others use screw type clamps. If spring type clamps are used, it is recommended to remove these with hose clamp pliers to avoid pinching your fingers.

1. Drain the radiator. If the coolant is less than a year old it can be saved and reused.

NOTE: *Before opening the radiator drain cock to drain the radiator, spray some penetrating solvent around the drain cock to be sure it will open with ease.*

2. Remove the hose clamps.
3. Pull the hose off the fitting on the radiator and the engine.
4. Install a new hose. A small amount of soapy water on the inside of the hose end will ease installation.

NOTE: *Radiator hoses should be routed with no kinks and routed as the original.*

5. Refill the cooling system and check the coolant level.

Air Conditioning

SAFETY PRECAUTIONS

There are two particular hazards associated with air conditioning systems and they both relate to refrigerant gas.

First, the refrigerant gas is an extremely cold substance. When exposed to air, it will instantly freeze any surface it comes in contact with, including your eyes. The other hazard relates to fire. Although normally non-toxic, refrigerant gas becomes highly poisonous in the presence of an open flame. One good whiff of the vapor formed by burning refrigerant can be fatal. Keep all forms of fire (including cigarettes) well clear of the air conditioning system.

Any repair work to an air conditioning system should be left to a professional. DO NOT, under any circumstances, attempt to loosen or tighten any fittings or perform any work other than that outlined here.

Checking for Oil Leaks

Refrigerant leaks show up only as oily areas on the various components because the compressor oil is transported around the entire system along with the refrigerant. Look for oily spots on all the hoses and lines, and especially on the hose and tube connections. If there are oily deposits, the system may have a leak, and you should have it checked by a qualified repairman.

NOTE: *A small area of oil on the front of the compressor is normal and no cause for alarm.*

GENERAL INFORMATION AND MAINTENANCE

HOW TO SPOT BAD HOSES

Both the upper and lower radiator hoses are called upon to perform difficult jobs in an inhospitable environment. They are subject to nearly 18 psi at under hood temperatures often over 280°F., and must circulate nearly 7500 gallons of coolant an hour—3 good reasons to have good hoses.

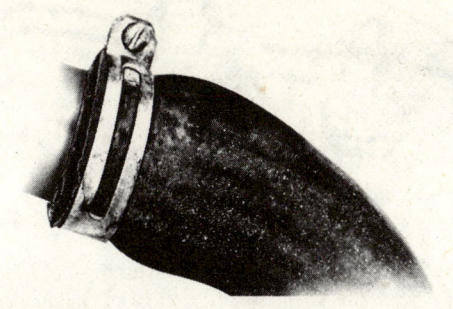

Swollen hose

A good test for any hose is to feel it for soft or spongy spots. Frequently these will appear as swollen areas of the hose. The most likely cause is oil soaking. This hose could burst at any time, when hot or under pressure.

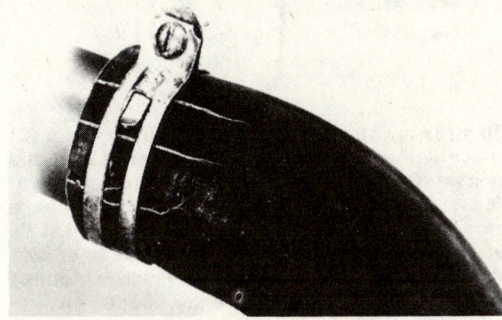

Cracked hose

Cracked hoses can usually be seen but feel the hoses to be sure they have not hardened; a prime cause of cracking. This hose has cracked down to the reinforcing cords and could split at any of the cracks.

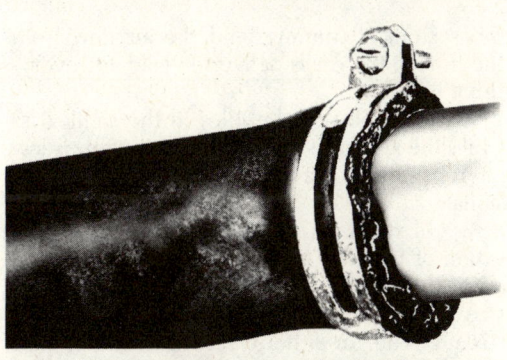

Frayed hose end (due to weak clamp)

Weakened clamps frequently are the cause of hose and cooling system failure. The connection between the pipe and hose has deteriorated enough to allow coolant to escape when the engine is hot.

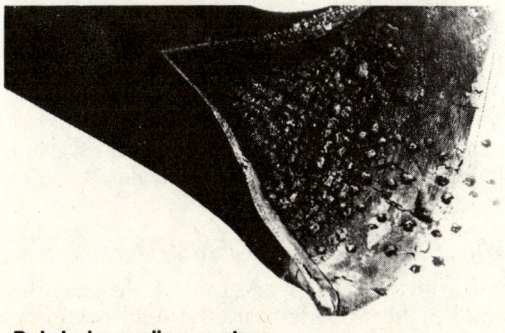

Debris in cooling system

Debris, rust and scale in the cooling system can cause the inside of a hose to weaken. This can usually be felt on the outside of the hose as soft or thinner areas.

GENERAL INFORMATION AND MAINTENANCE

Check the Compressor Belt

Refer to the section in this chapter on "Drive Belts".

Keep the Condenser Clear

Periodically inspect the front of the condenser for bent fins or foreign material (dirt, bugs, leaves, etc.) If any cooling fins are bent, straighten them carefully with needle nose pliers. You can remove any debris with a stiff bristle brush or hose.

Operate the A/C System Periodically

A lot of A/C problems can be avoided by simply running the air conditioner at least once a week, regardless of the season. Simply let the system run for a at least 5 minutes a week (even in the winter), and you'll keep the internal parts lubricated as well as preventing the hoses from hardening.

Refrigerant Level Check

The first order of business when checking the sight glass is to find the sight glass. It is located in the head of the receiver/drier. Once you've found it, wipe it clean and proceed as follows:

1. With the engine and the air conditioning system running, look for the flow of refrigerant through the sight glass. If the air conditioner is working properly, you'll be able to see a continuous flow of clear refrigerant through the sight glass, with perhaps an occasional bubble at very high temperatures.

2. Cycle the air conditioner on and off to make sure what you are seeing is clear refrigerant. Since the refrigerant is clear, it is possible to mistake a completely discharged system for one that is fully charged. Turn the system off and watch the sight glass. If there is refrigerant in the system, you'll see bubbles during the off cycle. If you observe no bubbles when

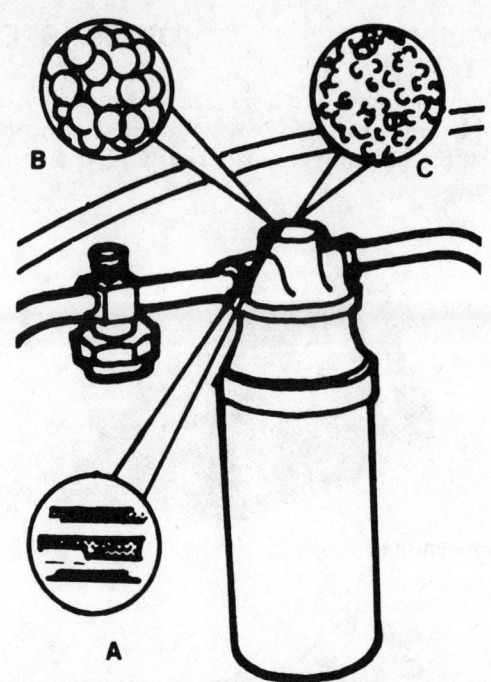

Oil streaks (A), constant bubbles (B) or foam (C) indicate there is not enough refrigerant in the system. Occasional bubbles during initial operation is normal. A clear sight glass indicates a proper charge of refrigerant or no refrigerant at all, which can be determined by the presence of cold air at the outlets in the car. If the glass is clouded with a milky white substance, have the receiver/drier checked professionally

the system is running, and the air flow from the unit in the car is delivering cold air, everything is OK.

3. If you observe bubbles in the sight glass while the system is operating, the system is low on refrigerant. Have it checked by a professional.

4. Oil streaks in the sight glass are an indication of trouble. Most of the time, if you see oil in the sight glass, it will appear as series of streaks, although occasionally it may be a solid stream of oil. In either case, it means that part of the charge has been lost.

Windshield Wipers

Intense heat from the sun, snow and ice, road oils and the chemicals used in windshield washer solvents combine to deteriorate the rubber wiper refills. The refills should be replaced about twice a year or whenever the blades begin to streak or chatter.

WIPER REFILL REPLACEMENT

Normally, if the wipers are not cleaning the windshield properly, only the refill has to be replaced. The blade and arm usually require

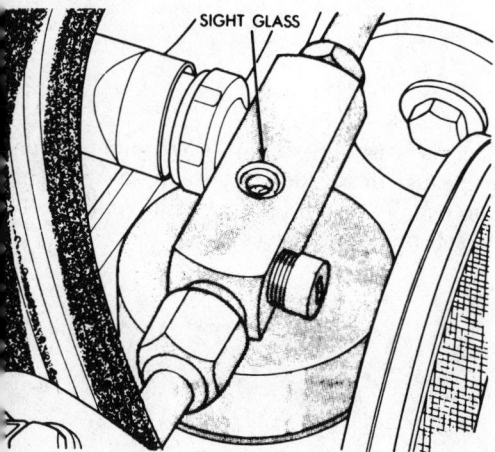

A/C sight glass in the top of the receiver/drier

GENERAL INFORMATION AND MAINTENANCE

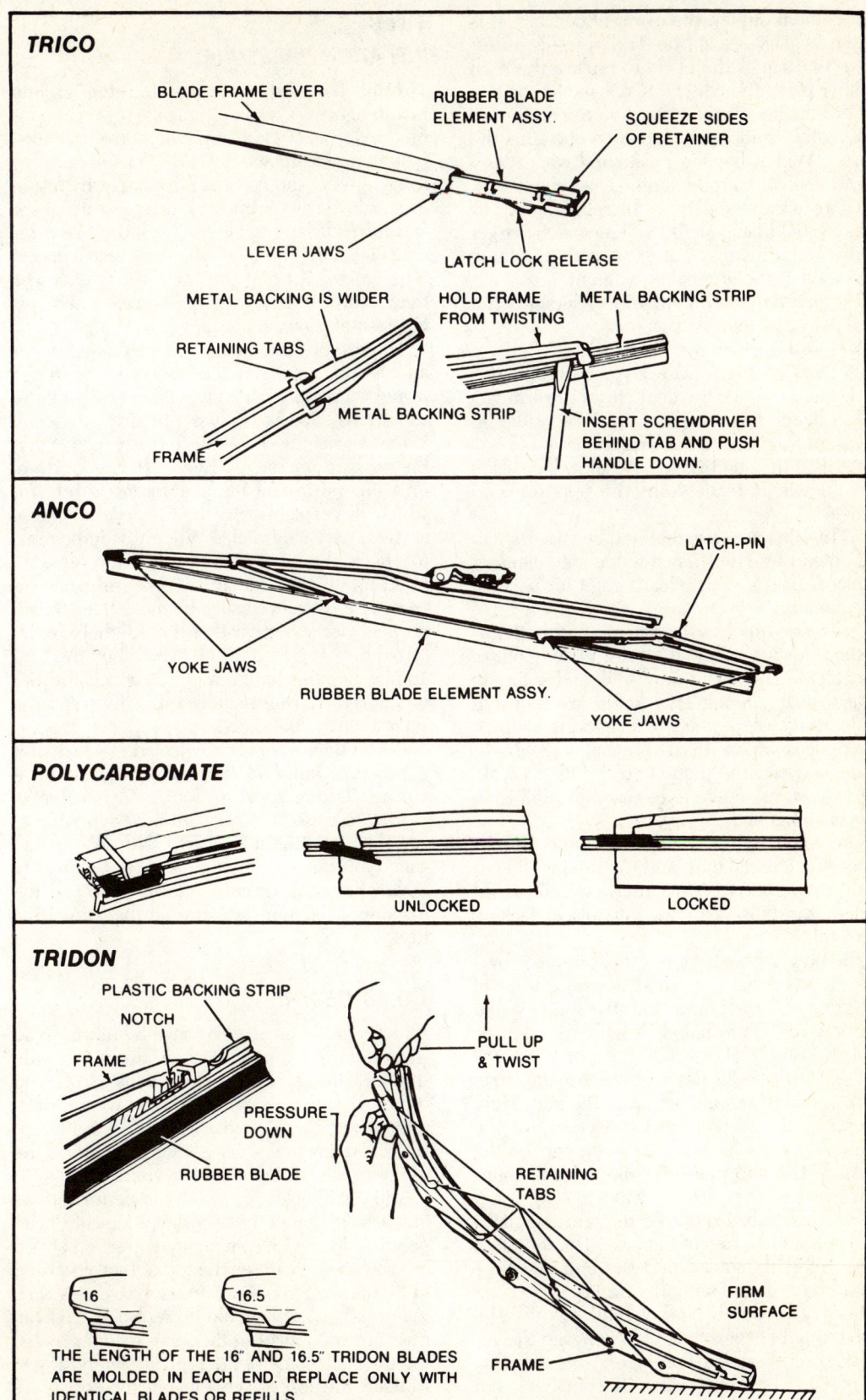

Replacing popular styles of wiper refills

GENERAL INFORMATION AND MAINTENANCE

replacement only in the event of damage. It is only necessary (except on Tridon refills) to remove the arm or the blade to replace the refill (rubber part), though you may have to position the arm higher on the glass. You can do this by turning the ignition switch on and operating the wipers. When they are positioned where they are accessible, turn the ignition switch off.

There are several types of refills and your vehicle could have any kind, since aftermarket blades and arms may not use exactly the same type refill as the original equipment.

The original equipment wiper elements can be replaced as follows:
1. Lift the wiper arm off the glass.
2. Depress the release lever on the center bridge and remove the blade from the arm.
3. Lift the tab and pinch the end bridge to release it from the center bridge.
4. Slide the end bridge from the wiper blade and the wiper blade from the opposite end bridge.
5. Install a new element and be sure the tab on the end bridge is down to lock the element in place. Check each release point for positive engagement.

Most Trico styles use a release button that is pushed down to allow the refill to slide out of the release jaws. The new refill slides in and locks in place. Some Trico refills are removed by locating where the metal backing strip or the refill is wider. Insert a small screwdriver blade between the frame and the metal backing strip. Press down to release the refill from the retaining tab.

The Anco style is unlocked at one end by squeezing 2 metal tabs, and the refill is slid out of the frame jaws. When the new refill is installed, the tabs will click into place, locking the refill.

The polycarbonate type is held in place by a locking lever that is pushed downward out of the groove in the arm to free the refill. When the new refill is installed, it will lock in place automatically.

The Tridon refill has a plastic backing strip with a notch about an inch from the end. Hold the blade (frame) on a hard surface so that the frame is tightly bowed. Grip the tip of the backing strip and pull up while twisting counterclockwise. The backing strip will snap out of the retaining tab. Do this for the remaining tabs until the refill is free of the arm. The length of these refills is molded into the end and they should be replaced with identical types.

No matter which type of refill you use, be sure that all of the frame claws engage the refill. Before operating the wipers, be sure that no part of the metal frame is contacting the windshield.

Tires
INFLATION PRESSURE

Tire inflation is the most ignored item of auto maintenance. Gasoline mileage can drop as much as .8% for every 1 pound per square inch (psi) of under inflation.

Two items should be a permanent fixture in every glove compartment; a tire pressure gauge and a tread depth gauge. Check the tire pressure (including the spare) regularly with a pocket type gauge. Kicking the tires won't tell you a thing, and the gauge on the service station air hose is notoriously inaccurate.

The tire pressures recommended for your car are usually found on the door post or in the owner's manual. Ideally, inflation pressure should be checked when the tires are cool. When the air becomes heated it expands and the pressure increases. Every 10° rise (or drop) in temperature means a difference of 1 psi, which also explains why the tire appears to lose air on a very cold night. When it is impossible to check the tires "cold," allow for pressure build-up due to heat. If the "hot" pressure exceeds the "cold" pressure by more than 15 psi, reduce your speed, load or both. Otherwise internal heat is crated in the tire. When the heat approaches the temperature at which the tire was cured, during manufacture, the tread can separate from the body.

CAUTION: *Never counteract excessive pressure build-up by bleeding off air pressure (letting some air out). This will only further raise the tire operating temperature.*

Before starting a long trip with lots of luggage, you can add about 2–4 psi to the tires to make them run cooler, but never exceed the maximum inflation pressure on the side of the tire.

TREAD DEPTH

All tires made since 1968, have 8 built-in tread wear indicator bars that show up as ½" wide smooth bands across the tire when 1/16" of tread remains. The appearance of tread wear indicators means that the tires should be replaced. In fact, many states have laws prohibiting the use of tires with less than 1/16" tread.

You can check your own tread depth with an inexpensive gauge or by using a Lincoln head penny. Slip the Lincoln penny into several tread grooves. If you can see the top of Lincoln's head in 2 adjacent grooves, the tires have less than 1/16" tread left and should be replaced. You can measure snow tires in the same manner by using the "tails" side of the Lincoln penny. If you can see the top of the Lincoln memorial, it's time to replace the snow tires.

GENERAL INFORMATION AND MAINTENANCE

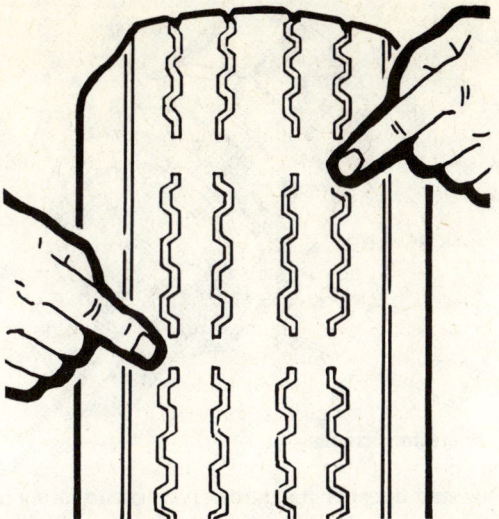

Tire wear indicators appear as 1/2" wide bands when tread is less than 1/16".

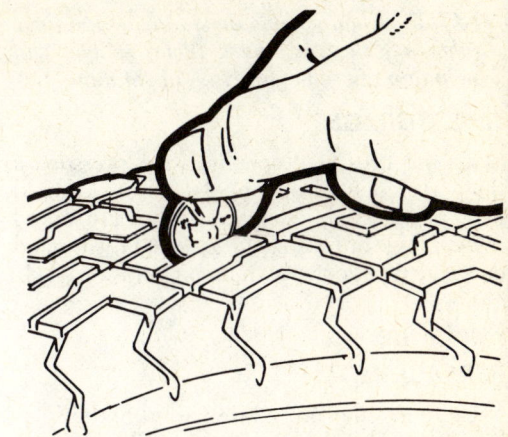

A penny works as well as anything for checking tire tread depth; when you can see the top of Lincoln's head, it's time for a new tire

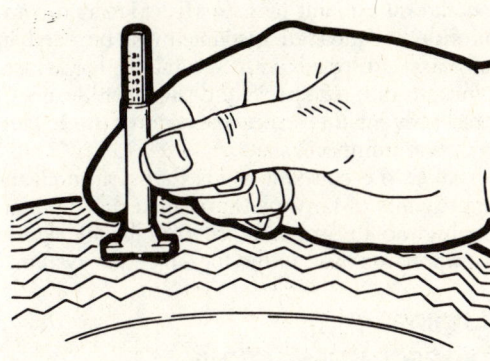

Check tire tread depth with an inexpensive gauge

TIRE ROTATION

Tire wear can be equalized by switching the position of the tires about every 6000 miles. Including a conventional spare in the rotation pattern can give up to 20% more tire life.

CAUTION: *Do not include the new "Spacesaver" rotation pattern.*

There are certain exceptions to tire rotation, however. Studded snow tires should not be rotated, and radials should be kept on the same side of the car (maintain the same direction of rotation). The belts on radial tires get set in a pattern. If the direction of rotation is reversed, it can cause rough ride and vibration.

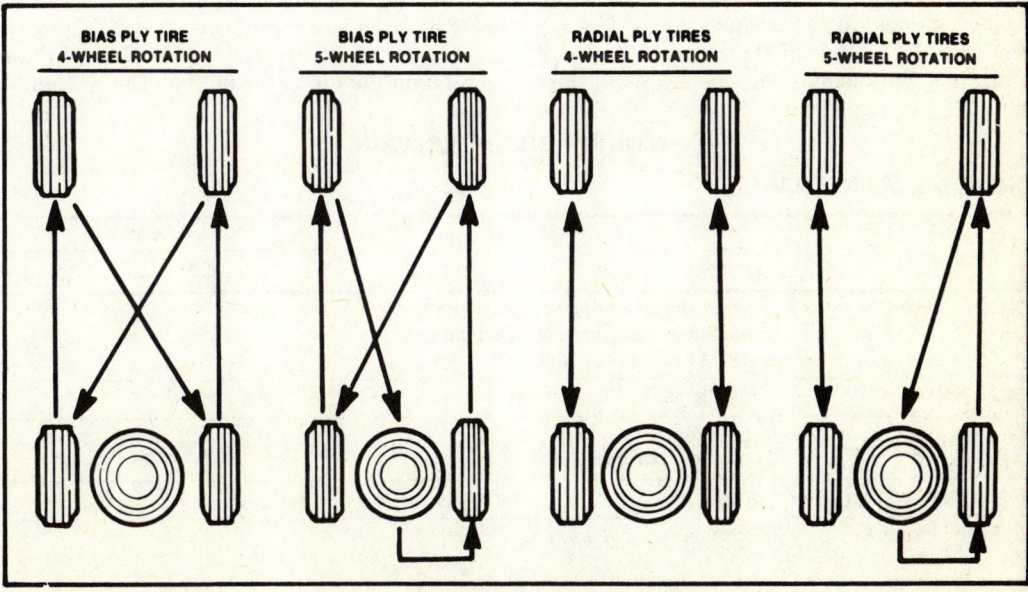

Tire rotation pattern

18 GENERAL INFORMATION AND MAINTENANCE

NOTE: *When radials or studded snows are taken off the car, mark them, so you can maintain the same direction of rotation.*

TIRE STORAGE

Store the tires at proper inflation pressure if they are mounted on wheels. All tires should be kept in a cool, dry place. If they are stored in the garage or basement, do not let them stand on a concrete floor, set them on strips of wood.

Fuel Filter
REPLACEMENT

1. Follow the procedures listed under "Relieving Fuel System Pressure" in Chapter 4.
2. Loosen the outlet clamp on the filter and inlet hose clamp on the rear fuel tube.
3. Wrap a rag around the hoses to absorb fuel. Remove the hoses at the filter and the fuel tube.
4. Loosen the filter retaining screw and slide the filter assembly from the bracket.
5. Slide the new filter assembly into the mounting bracket until the stone shield shoulder contacts the bracket.
6. Position the filter in the bracket and tighten the filter mounting screw.
7. Install the formed outlet hose on the filter outlet fitting and tighten the clamp.
8. Install the inlet hose on the fuel tube and tighten the clamp.

FLUIDS AND LUBRICANTS

Fuel Recommendations

Only gasolines with an octane value of 87 using the $(R+M)/2$ rating method should be used. Turbocharged engines will operate satisfactory

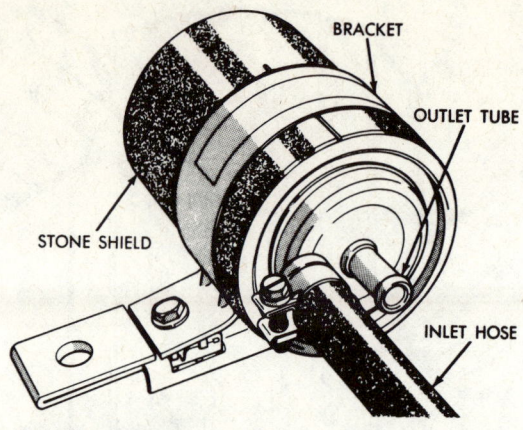

Fuel filter assembly

on gasolines having a miniumn octane rating of 87 $(R+M)/2$, however for increased performance and fuel economy, the use of Premium or Super unleaded gasoline having a minimum octane rating of at least 91 $(R+M)/2$ is recommended. Unleaded gasoline must be used in all cars equipped with a catalytic converter. These cars have specially designed filler necks that prevent the direct insertion of the leaded gasoline pump nozzle.

Avoid the constant use of fuel system cleaning agents. Many of these materials contain highly active solvents that will deteriorate components used in the fuel injection system.

Engine
OIL RECOMMENDATIONS

Oils are classified according to standards established by the Society of Automotive Engineers (SAE), and the American Petroleum Institute (API).

Oil classifications made by SAE and API are found on the top of the oil can. The SAE grade

Maintenance Intervals
GENERAL MAINTENANCE

		\multicolumn{6}{c}{Miles—in thousands}
		7.5	15	22.5	30	37.5	45
Cooling System	Drain, flush and refill at 36 months or 52,500 miles. Subsequent drain, flush and refill every 24 months or 30,000 miles						
Brake Hoses	Inspect for leaks & deterioration	*	*	*	*	*	*
Brake Linings	Inspect front Inspect rear brakes			* *			* *
Rear wheel bearings	Inspect			*			*
Steering Linkage & Tie Rod Ends	Lubricate every 3 years or				*		
Drive Shaft Boots	Inspect for Leaks or Deterioration	*	*	*	*	*	*

GENERAL INFORMATION AND MAINTENANCE

Maintenance Intervals (continued)

EMISSION CONTROL SYSTEM MAINTENANCE

		Miles—in thousands					
		7.5	15	22.5	30	37.5	45
Engine Oil							
(wo/turbocharger)	Change every 12 months or	*	*	*	*	*	*
(w/turbocharger)	Change every 6 months or	*	*	*	*	*	*
Engine Oil Filter							
(wo/turbocharger)	Replace every second oil Change 12 months or			*		*	*
(w/turbocharger)	Replace every oil change, 6 months or		*	*	*	*	*
Spark Plugs	Replace			*		*	*
Drive Belts	Inspect and adjust tension, replace as necessary			*		*	*
Crankcase Vent Module	Clean and Lubricate every 52,500 miles						
PCV Valve	Inspect			*			
	Replace				*		
Air Filter	Replace every 52,500 miles						
Fuel Filter	Replace	*		*		*	

SEVERE SERVICE MAINTENANCE

	Miles—in thousands															
	3	6	9	12	15	18	21	24	27	30	33	36	39	42	45	48
Brake Linings (Front & Rear) Inspect			*			*			*			*			*	
Rear Wheel Bearings Inspect			*			*			*			*			*	
Constant Velocity Joints	Inspect every oil change															
Engine Oil Change every 3 months or	*	*	*	*	*	*	*	*	*	*	*	*	*	*	*	*
Engine Oil Filter																
(wo/turbocharger)	Replace every second oil															
(w/turbocharger)	Replace every oil change															
Ball Joints	Inspect at every oil change															
Automatic Transmission Fluid and Filter Change & adjust bands					*					*					*	
Steering Linkage & Tie Rod Ends Lubricate every 18 months or						*				*					*	
Air Filter Inspect and replace if required					*					*					*	
Manual Transmission Fluid Change and clean pan magnet						*				*					*	

20 GENERAL INFORMATION AND MAINTENANCE

Capacities Chart

Year	Engine	Crankcase Includes Filter (qt)	Transaxle (qts) Manual	Transaxle (qts) Auto ①	Power Steering (pts)	Fuel Tank (gal)	Cooling System (qt) w/AC	Cooling System (qt) wo/AC
1984–85	2.2L	4	2.3	4	2.5	14	9	9
	2.2L Turbo	5	2.3	4	2.5	14	9	9

① Total refill is 8.9 qts.

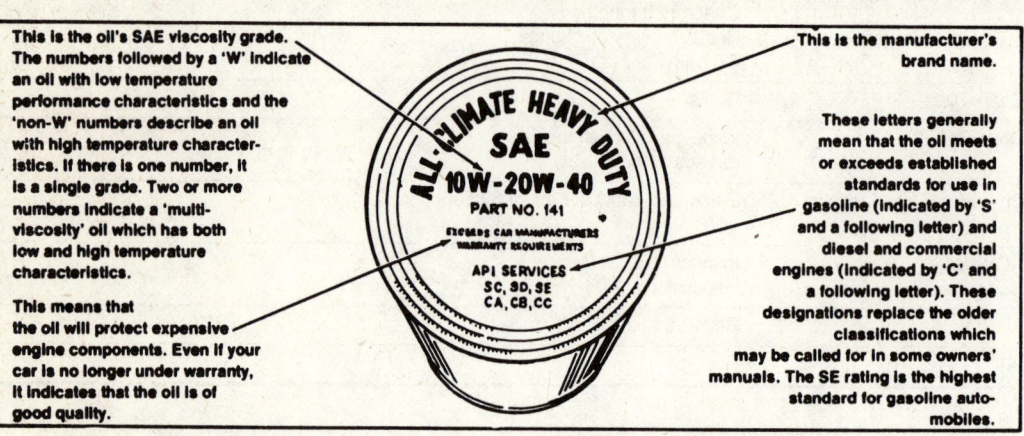

The top of the oil can will tell you all you need to know about the oil

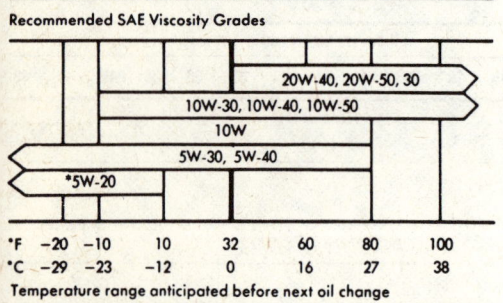

Oil viscosity chart

OIL LEVEL CHECK

The engine oil dipstick is located on the radiator side of the engine. Engine oil level should be checked weekly as a matter of course. Always check the oil with the car on level ground and after the engine has been shut off for about five minutes.

The oil level may read at the top of the FULL range after the car has been standing for several hours. When the engine is started, the level will drop, due to oil passages filling, but the level should never be allowed to remain below the ADD mark.

1. Remove the dipstick and wipe it clean.
2. Reinsert the dipstick.
3. Remove the dipstick again. The oil level should be between the two marks. The difference between the marks is one quart.

number indicates the viscosity of engine oils. SAE 10W-40, for example, is a good all-temperature motor oil suitable for use in the winter.

The API classification system defines oil performance in terms of usage. Oils designed for service "SF/CC" may be used in both non-turbocharged and turbocharged engines. However a higher quality oil designed for service "SF/CD" is recommended for turbocharged engines. These engine oils contain sufficient chemical additives to provide maximum engine protection.

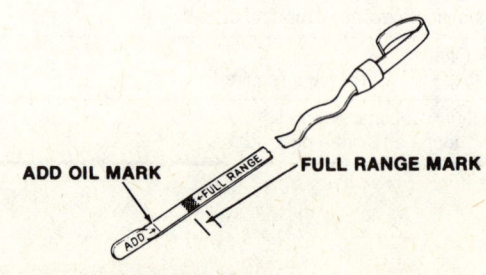

Engine oil dipstick markings

GENERAL INFORMATION AND MAINTENANCE

4. Add oil through the capped opening on the top of the valve cover. Select oil of the proper viscosity.

CHANGING ENGINE OIL AND FILTER

Under normal service, the engine oil and filter should be changed every 12 months or 7,500 miles for non-turbocharged engines, 6 months or 3,000 miles for turbocharged engines, whichever comes first.

Under the following conditions, change the engine oil and filter every 3 months or 3,000-miles, whichever comes first.

- Frequent driving in dusty conditions
- Frequent trailer pulling
- Extensive idling
- Frequent short trip driving (less than 10 miles)
- More than 50% operation at sustained high speeds (over 70 mph).

NOTE: *Drain the engine oil when the engine is at normal operating temperature. DO NOT overfill the crankcase. This will cause aeration in the oil system and loss of oil pressure.*

To change the oil, the vehicle should be on a level surface at normal operating temperature. This ensures that you will drain away the foreign matter in the oil, which will not happen if the oil is cold. Oil which is slightly dirty when drained is a good sign. This means that the contaminants are being drained away and not being left behind to form sludge.

You should have available some means to support the car safely, a wrench to fit the drain plug, a filter wrench, motor oil, a drain pan and some rags.

1. Jack up the front of the car and support it on jackstands.
2. Position the drain pan under the drain plug, which is located at the rear of the oil pan.
3. Loosen, but do not remove the drain plug. Cover your hand with a heavy rag and slowly unscrew the drain plug. Pushing the plug against the threads in the oil pan will prevent hot oil from running down your arm. As the drain plug comes to the end of the threads, quickly pull it away and allow all of the oil to drain into the pan.
4. When all of the oil has been drained, replace the drain plug and tighten it.

NOTE: *Be sure to dispose of the old oil in an environmentally safe manner.*

5. Remove the oil filter. It should be loosened with a suitable oil filter wrench. Once the filter is loose, cover your hand with a thick rag and spin it off by hand.
6. Coat the rubber gasket on a new filter with clean engine oil and install the new filter. Tighten it by hand until the gasket contacts the mounting base and then ¾–1 turn further.

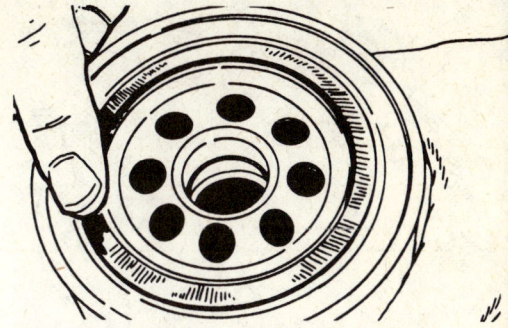
Coat the new oil filter gasket with clean oil

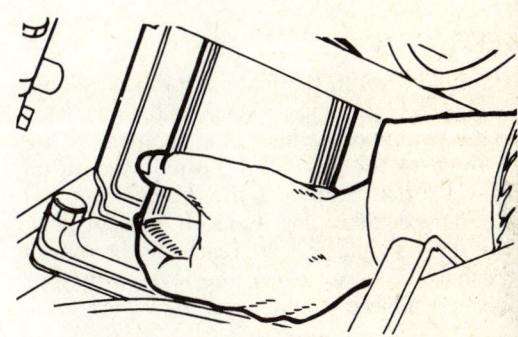
Install the new oil filter by hand

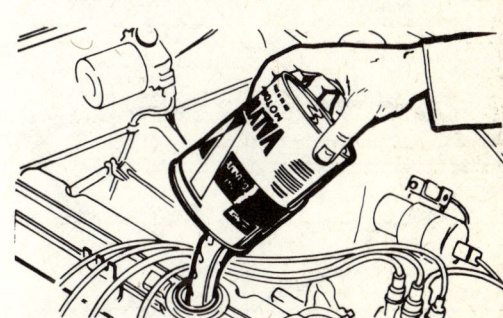
Add oil through the capped opening in the cylinder head cover

7. Refill the engine with 4 quarts (non-turbo engines) or 5 quarts (turbo-charged engines) of fresh oil of the proper viscosity according to the anticipated temperatures before the next oil change.
8. Run the engine for a few minutes and check the oil level.

Manual Transaxle

FLUID RECOMMENDATION

If the manual transaxle used in the Laser and Daytona models requires the addition of fluid, use only fluids of the type labeled "Dexron® II" automatic transmission fluid.

GENERAL INFORMATION AND MAINTENANCE

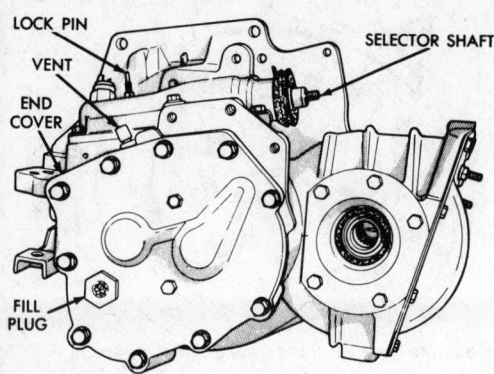

Manual transaxle filler plug

LEVEL CHECK

The fluid level in the manual transaxle should be checked twice a year. Maintain the fluid level to the bottom of the filler plug opening.

To check the fluid level, position the car on a level surface and clean the dirt from around the transaxle filler plug. Remove the filler plug. The level should at least reach the bottom of the hole. You can check the level with your finger or a piece of bent wire.

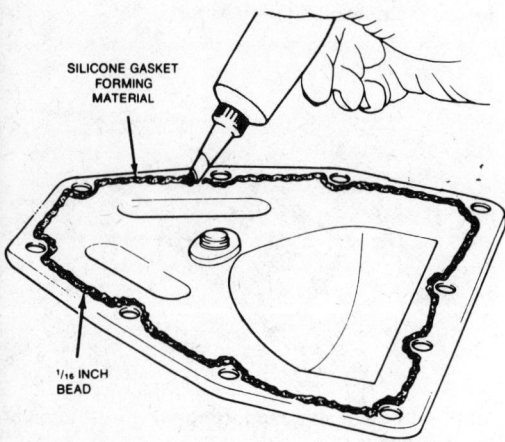

Form a silicone gasket as shown

DRAIN AND REFILL

Under normal conditions, the manula transaxle fluid will never need changing. Rare circumstances, such as the fluid becoming contaminated with water or if the vehicle is operated at sustained high speeds during hot weather, will necessitate fluid replacement.

To change the transaxle fluid:
1. Jack up the car and support it safely on stands.
2. Slide the drain pan under the transaxle.
3. Remove the pan cover on the side of the differential and allow the transaxle fluid to drain.

Clean the magnet and the inside surface of the pan cover with a clean, dry cloth.
4. Using RTV silicone sealer, form a gasket around the sealing edge of the differential pan cover and replace the cover.
5. Refill the transaxle to the bottom of the filler hole with Dexron® II automatic transmission fluid.

Automatic Transaxle

FLUID RECOMMENDATION

If the automatic transaxle used in the Laser and Daytona models requires the addition of fluid, use only fluids of the type labeled "Dexron® II" automatic transmission fluid.

LEVEL CHECK

The automatic transaxle and differential are contained in the same housing, the differential oil sump is integral with the transmission oil sump. The transmission does not have a conventional filler tube, but is filled, instead, through the dipstick hole in the case. There is no drain plug in the transmission pan or in the toruqe converter.

The fluid level should be checked every 6 months when the engine and transmission fluid are warmed to normal operating temperature.
1. Position the car on a level surface.

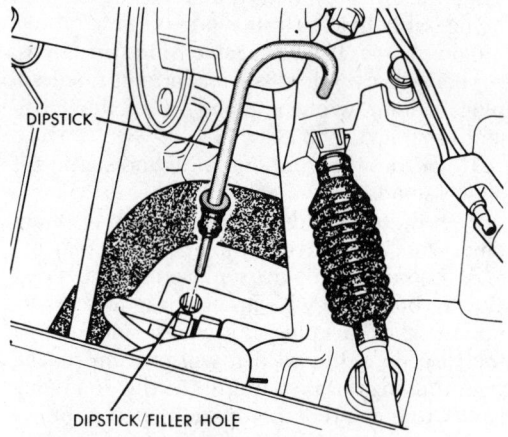

Automatic transaxle dipstick location

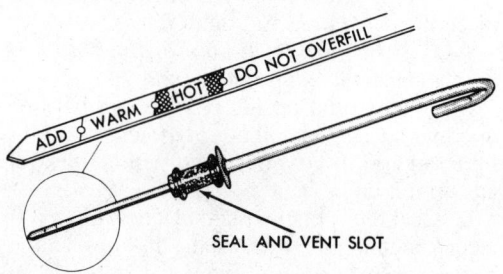

Automatic transaxle dipstick markings

GENERAL INFORMATION AND MAINTENANCE

2. Start the engine and allow it to idle for at least 60 seconds.
3. Apply the parking brake.
4. Shift the gear selector through each gear momentarily and return the lever to PARK.
5. Remove the dipstick and wipe it clean.
6. Reinstall the dipstick and remove it again. If the fluid is hot, the reading should be in the crosshatched area marked "HOT" (between the two upper holes in the dipstick). If the fluid is warm, the fluid level should be in the pebbled area marked "WARM" between the two lower holes in the dipstick.
7. If the fluid level checks low, add the sufficient amount of Dexron® II automatic transmission fluid to bring the level to within the marks indicated for the appropriate temperature.
8. Reinstall the dipstick and be sure it is properly seated. This is the only seal that prevents water or dirt from entering the transmission from the filler opening.

DRAIN AND REFILL

NOTE: *RTV silicone sealer is used in place of a pan gasket on the automatic transaxle.*

Chrysler recommends no fluid or filter changes during the normal service life of the car. Severe usage requires a fluid and filter change every 15,000 miles. Severe usage is defined as:
  a. more than 50% heavy city traffic during hot weather above 90°F.
  b. police, taxi or commercial operation or trailer towing.

When changing the fluid, only Dexron® II fluid should be used. A filter change should be performed at every fluid change.

1. Raise the vehicle and support it on jackstands.
2. Place a large container under the pan, loosen the pan bolts and tap at one corner to break it loose. Drain the fluid.
3. When the fluid is drained remove the pan bolts.
4. Remove the retaining screws and replace the filter. Tighten the screws to 40 inch pounds.
5. Clean the fluid pan and magnet, peel off the old RTV silicone sealer and install the pan, using a 1/8 inch bead of new RTV sealer. Always run the sealer bead inside the bolt holes. Tighten the pan bolts to 11–13 ft. lbs.
6. Pour four quarts of Dexron® II fluid through the filler tube.
7. Start the engine and idle for at least 2 minutes. Set the parking brake and move the selector through each position, ending in PARK.
8. Add sufficient fluid to bring the level to the FULL mark on the dipstick. The level should be checked in PARK, with the engine at normal operating temperature.

Cooling System

The cooling system should be inspected, flushed, and refilled with fresh coolant at the end of the first 3 years and every 2 years thereafter. If the coolant is left in the too long, it loses its ability to prevent rust and corrosion; if the coolant has too much water, it won't protect against freezing.

The pressure cap should be looked at for signs of age or deterioration. Fan belt and other drive belts should be inspected and adjusted to the proper tension.

Hose clamps should be tightened, and soft or cracked hoses replaced. Damp spots, or accumulations of rust or dye near hoses, water pump or other areas, indicate possible leakage, which must be corrected before filling the system with fresh coolannt.

FLUID RECOMMENDATION

Chrysler recommends the use of a high quality ethylene glycol base antifreeze with a silicate inhibitor, or an antifreeze containing the Alugard 340-2 inhibitor system. Failure to use the proper antifreeze could cause radiator cloging and engine overheating. DO NOT mix different brands of antifreeze, use plain water in the cooling system or use alcohol based antifreeze. DO NOT use additional rust inhibitors or antirust additives, as they may not be compatible with the coolant and may clog the radiator.

When adding coolant or refilling the system, a minimum of 50% solution of ethylene glycol antifreeze and water should be used. If temperatures below −37°F are anticipated, higher concentrations (not to exceed 70% are required).

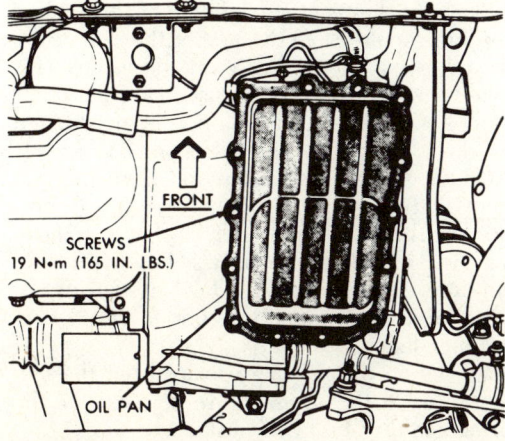

Automatic transaxle oil pan

24 GENERAL INFORMATION AND MAINTENANCE

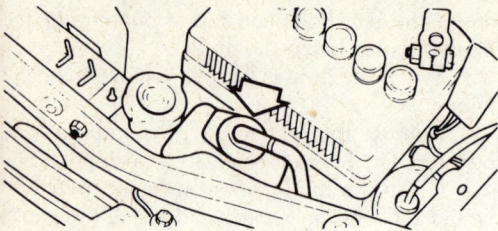

Coolant reserve bottle location

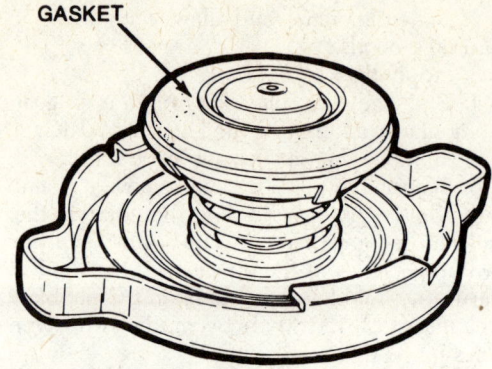

Check the radiator cap gasket

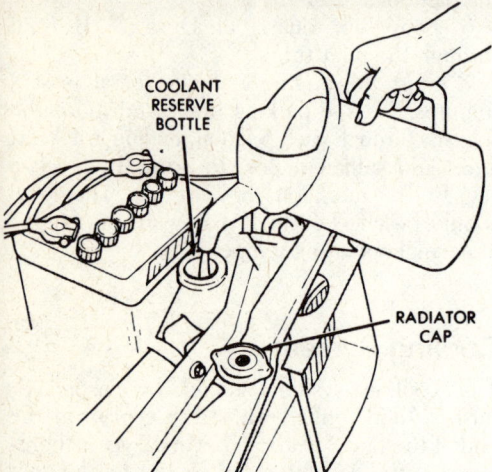

Add coolant to the coolant reserve bottle

COOLANT LEVEL CHECK

The coolant reserve system provides a quick visual method for checking the coolant level. With the engine idling, and warmed to the normal operating temperature, the level of the coolant in the overflow bottle should be between the "MAX" and "MIN" marks. Under normal conditions there is no need to remove the radiator cap except for checking the coolant freeze point or for replacing the coolant with new antifreeze. When additional coolant is needed to maintain the proper level, it should be added to the coolant overflow bottle. DO NOT overfill the overflow bottle.

CHECK THE RADIATOR CAP

While you are checking the coolant level, check the radiator for a worn or cracked gasket. If the cap doesn't seal properly, fluid will be lost and the engine will overheat.

Worn caps should be replaced with a new one.

CLEAN THE RADIATOR OF DEBRIS

Periodically clean any debris—leaves, paper, insects, etc.—from the radiator fins. Pick the large pieces off by hand. The smaller pieces can be washed away with water pressure from a hose.

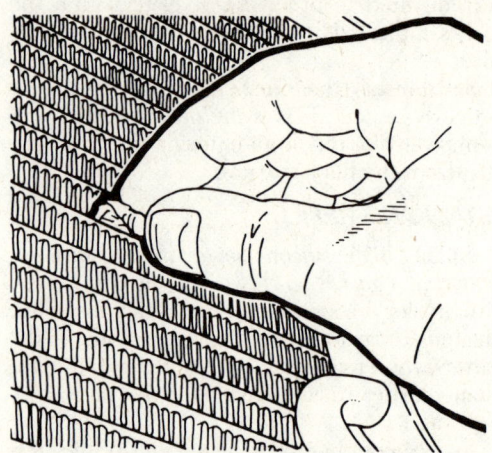

Remove debris from the radiator cooling fins

Carefully straighten any bent radiator fins with a pair of needle nosed pliers. Be careful—the fins are very soft. Don't wiggle the fins back and forth too much. Straighten them once and try not to move them again.

DRAIN AND REFILL THE COOLING SYSTEM

Complete draining and refilling of the cooling system should be performed at the end of the first 3 years and every 2 years thereafter. This will remove accumulated rust, scale and other deposits. If the system solution being drained is dirty or rusty or contains a considerable amount of sediment, clean and flush the system with a reliable cooling system cleaner. Follow this with a thorough rinsing to remove all the deposits and chemicals. Discard the old antifreeze solution and refill using a quality antifreeze as described above under "Fluid Recommendation".

1. Drain the existing coolant from the system. Move the temperature selector for the heater to the "Full On" position.

2. Without removing the radiator pressure

GENERAL INFORMATION AND MAINTENANCE

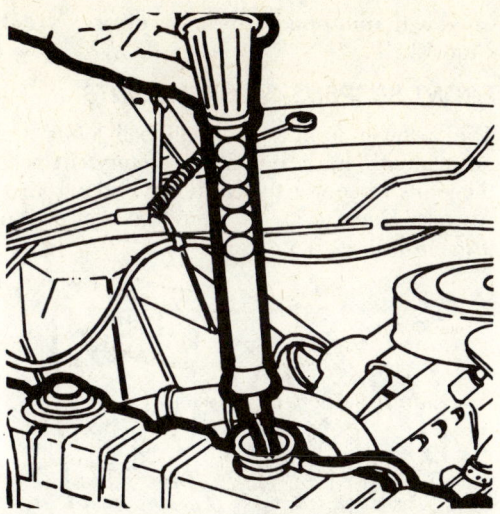

Check the anti-freeze protection

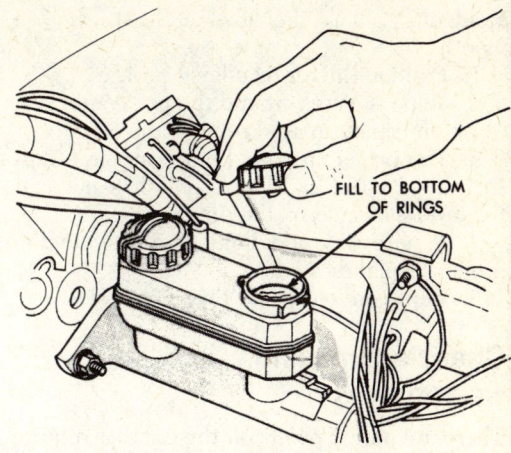

Checking the brake master cylinder level

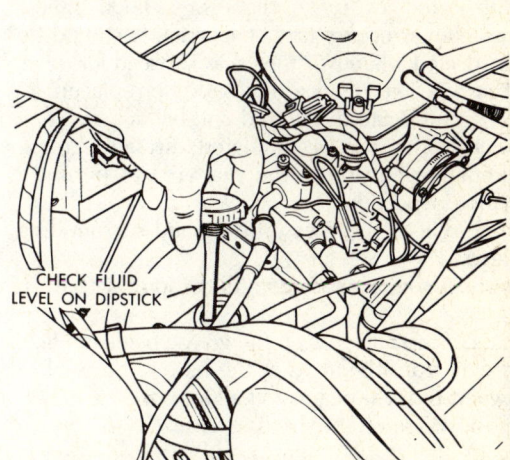

Checking the power steering fluid reservoir

cap and with the system not under pressure open the radiator drain petcock.

3. After the coolant overflow tank has drained remove the radiator pressure cap and remove the plug on the water box near the thermostat housing.

4. Close the radiator petcock, add coolant to the radiator until it reaches the plug hole in the water box. Install and tighten the plug. Continue adding coolant up to the radiator pressure cap seat.

5. Install the radiator pressure cap, start the engine and run until the upper hose feels not, stop the engine and if necessary add more coolant to completely fill the radiator.

CAUTION: *Be careful when removing the radiator cap to avoid the release of hot coolant or steam. Place a heavy rag over the radiator cap, turn the cap counter-clockwise to the first stop, allow any pressure to release through the overflow tube, then press the cap down turn counter-clockwise and remove the cap.*

6. Add the same mixture of antifreeze to the reservoir tank and bring it to a level between the "MIN" and "MAX" marks.

NOTE: *To maintain this level in the reservoir tank, it may be necessary to add coolant to the reserve tank after a couple of warmups because air is generally trapped in the cooling system when the system is filled.*

Brake Master Cylinder
FLUID RECOMMENDATION

Only brake fluid conforming to DOT 3 should be used in the brake system. Use only brake fluid that has been stored in a tightly closed container, which is to ensure against contamination with foreign matter or moisture.

LEVEL CHECK

The brake fluid level should be checked every 6 months.

1. Wipe the area around the master cylinder clean.

2. Remove the master cylinder cap(s). If necessary, add brake fluid to bring the level to the bottom of the split rings in the master cylinder.

Power Steering Reservoir
FLUID RECOMMENDATION

Chrysler recommends the use of only MOPAR Power Steering Fluid or its equivalent. DO NOT USE AUTOMATIC TRANSMISSION FLUID.

LEVEL CHECK

The power steering reservoir fluid level should be checked with the engine OFF to prevent

26 GENERAL INFORMATION AND MAINTENANCE

accidents. Check the level at least every 6 months.
1. Position the car on a level surface.
2. Wipe the area around the power steering reservoir cap clean asnd remove the cap.
3. The power steering pump cap has a dipstick attached. Fluid level should be kept at the level indicated on the dipstick.
4. If necessary add fluid to restore to the proper level indicated.
5. Replace the cap and tighten in place.

Chassis Greasing
TIE-ROD ENDS

There are only 2 points on the car that require periodic greasing. The tie-rod end ball joints are semi-permanently lubricated and should be lubricated every 3 years or 30,000 miles, whichever occurs first. These joints should be inspected whenever the car is serviced for other reasons. Damaged seals should be replaced.

To lubricate the tie-rod end ball joints:
1. Clean the accumulated dirt and grease from the outside of the seal area to permit a close inspection.
2. Clean the grease fitting and surrounding area.
3. Using a grease gun fill the joint with fresh grease.
4. Stop filling when the grease begins to flow freely from the areas at the base of the seal or when the seal begins to balloon.
5. Wipe off the excess grease.

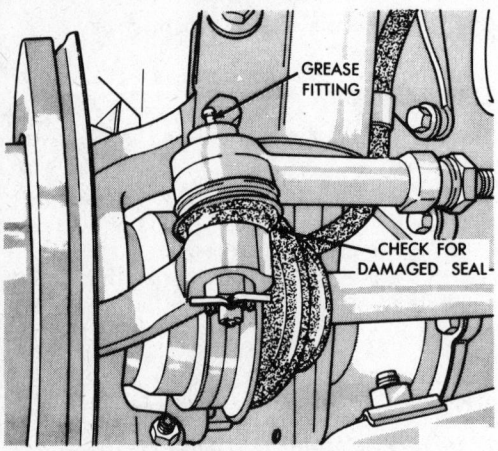

Tie-rod end grease fitting location

STEERING SHAFT SEAL

The steering shaft seal where the steering shaft passes through the dash is lubricated at manufacture. If the seal becomes noisy when the steering shaft is turned, it should be relubri-

cated with multi-purpose chassis grease, NLGI Grade 2 EP.

FRONT SUSPENSION BALL JOINTS

The 2 lower front suspension ball joints are permanently lubricated at the factory. Inspect the joints whenever the car is serviced for other reasons. Damaged seals should be replaced to prevent leakage of grease.

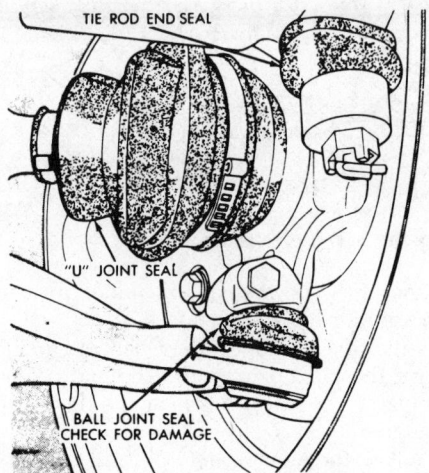

Check ball joints for damaged seals

CLUTCH CABLE

If the clutch cable begins to make odd noises or if the effort to depress the clutch becomes excessive, lubricate the clutch cable ball end with multipurpose chassis grease NLGI Grade 2 EP.

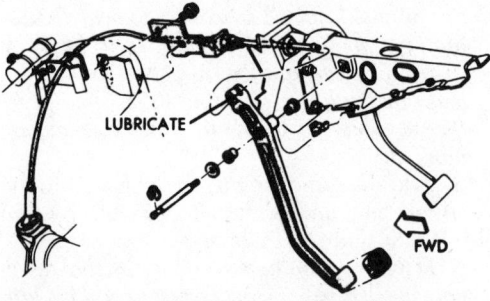

Lubricate the ball end of the clutch cable

FLOORSHIFT CONTROL LINKAGE

The gearshift control linkage should be lubricated whenever the shifting effort becomes excessive or if the linkage exhibits a rattling noise. Use a multi-purpose grease NLGI Grade 2 EP.

DRIVESHAFT U-JOINTS

The car has 4 constant velocity U-joints. No periodic lubrication is required, but the joint

GENERAL INFORMATION AND MAINTENANCE

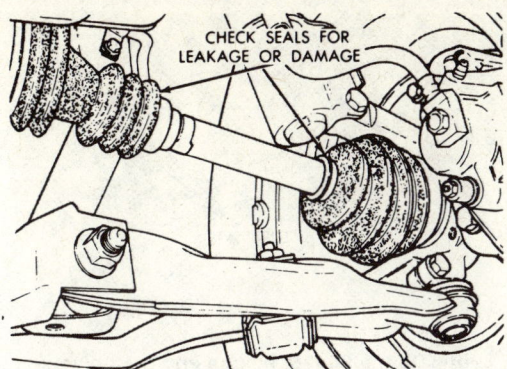

Inspect U-joint seals for leakage

seals should be inspected for damage or leakage whenever the car is serviced. If damage is found, replace the U-joint boot and seal and fill with fresh grease immediately. Failure to do so will eventually require complete replacement of the constant velocity joint.

PARTS REQUIRING NO LUBRICATION

Some components are permanently lubricated. Some parts will be adversely affected by lubricants. In particular, rubber bushings should not be lubricated, since it will destroy their frictional characteristics. Parts that should not be lubricated are:
- Air pumps
- Alternator bearings
- Drive belts
- Fan idler belt pulley
- Front wheel bearings
- Idler arm assembly
- Rubber bushings
- Starter bearings
- Suspension strut bearing
- Throttle control cable
- Throttle linkage
- Water pump bearings

Body Lubrication

Operating mechanisms of the body should be inspected, cleaned and lubricated as necessary. This will provide maximum protection against rust and wear.

Prior to lubricating wipe the parts clean of dirt and old lubricant. When Lubriplate® is specified, use a smooth, white body lubricant of NLGI Grade 1. When Door-Ease® is specified, use a stainless, wax-type lubricant.

HOOD LATCH AND RELEASE

Apply Lubriplate®, or the equivalent to all the pivot and sliding contact areas. Work the lubricant into the latch mechanism. Apply a thin film of the same lubricant to the safety catch.

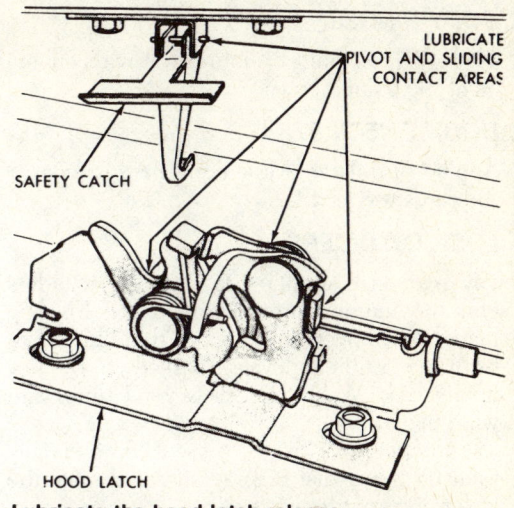

Lubricate the hood latch release

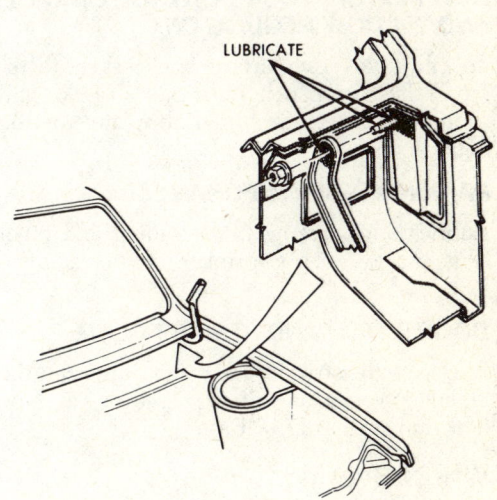

Lubricate the hood hinges

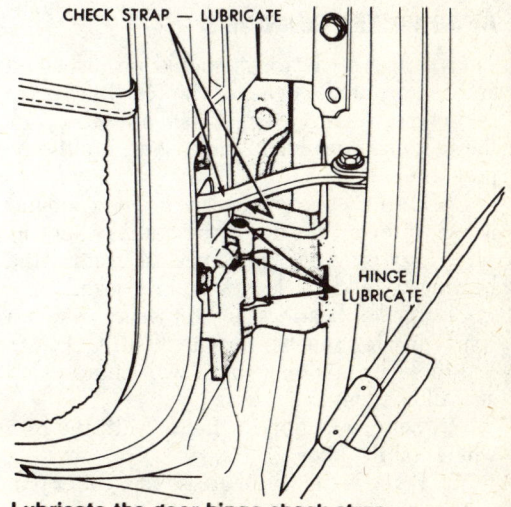

Lubricate the door hinge check strap

28 GENERAL INFORMATION AND MAINTENANCE

BODY HINGES
These parts should be lubricated with engine oil at the points shown.

DOOR CHECK STRAPS
Apply Lubriplate® or the equivalent whenever the car is serviced.

LOCK CYLINDERS
Pay particular attention to the lock cylinders ehn the temperature is around the freezing mark. When necessary, apply a thin film of Lubriplate®, or the equivalent directly to the key in the lock. Work the lock several times and wipe the key dry.

Another alternative is to use a commercially available spray that is sprayed directly into the lock to prevent freezing.

DOOR LATCH, LOCK CONTROL LINKAGE AND WINDOW REGULATOR
To lubricate these parts it is necessary to remove the trim panel. Lubricate all pivot and sliding contact areas with Lubriplate® or the equivalent.

PARKING BRAKE MECHANISM
Lubricate all parking brake sliding and pivot contact areas with Lubriplate® or the equivalent.

DOOR LATCH AND STRIKER PLATE
Lubricate the striker plate contact area and the ratchet pivot areas with a stainless, wax type lubricant such as Door Ease®.

Wheel Bearings
FRONT WHEEL BEARINGS
The front wheel bearings are permanently sealed and require no periodic lubrication.

REAR WHEEL BEARINGS
The rear wheel bearings should be inspected and relubricated whenever the rear brakes are serviced or at least every 30,000 miles. Repack the bearings with high temperature multi-purpose grease.

Check the lubricant to see if it is contaminated. If it contains dirt or has a milky appearance indicating the presence of water, the bearings should be cleaned and repacked.

Clean the bearings in kerosene, mineral spirits or other suitable cleaning fluid. DO NOT dry them by spinning them with compressed air. Allow them to air dry.

1. Raise and support the car with the rear wheels off the floor.
2. Remove the wheel grease cap, cotter pin, nut-lock and bearing adjusting nut.

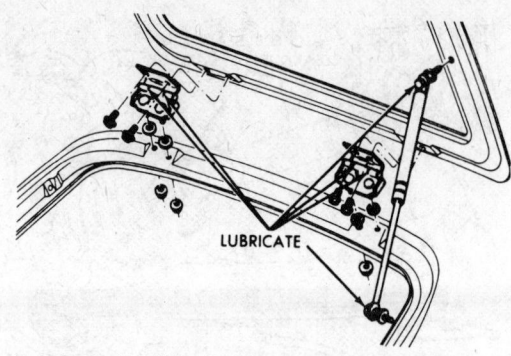

Lubricate the liftgate hinges and prop pivots

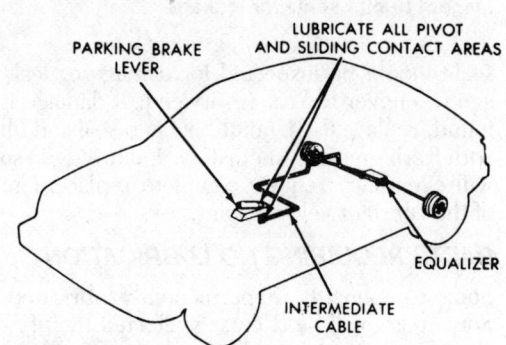

Lubricate the parking brake

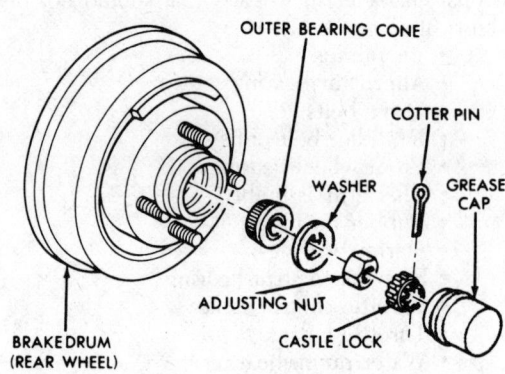

Exploded view of rear wheel bearing

3. Remove the thrust washer and bearing.
4. Remove the drum from the spindle.
5. Thoroughly clean the old lubricant from the bearings and hub cavity. Inspect the bearing rollers for pitting or other signs of wear. Light discoloration is normal.
6. Repack the bearings with high temperature multi-purpose EP grease and add a small amount of new grease to the hub cavity. Be sure to force the lubricant between all the rollers in the bearing.
7. Install the drum on the spindle after coating the polished spindle surfaces with wheel bearing lubricant.
8. Install the outer bearing cone, thrust washer and adjusting nut.

GENERAL INFORMATION AND MAINTENANCE 29

JUMP STARTING A DEAD BATTERY

The chemical reaction in a battery produces explosive hydrogen gas. This is the safe way to jump start a dead battery, reducing the chances of an accidental spark that could cause an explosion.

Jump Starting Precautions

1. Be sure both batteries are of the same voltage.
2. Be sure both batteries are of the same polarity (have the same grounded terminal).
3. Be sure the vehicles are not touching.
4. Be sure the vent cap holes are not obstructed.
5. Do not smoke or allow sparks around the battery.
6. In cold weather, check for frozen electrolyte in the battery.
7. Do not allow electrolyte on your skin or clothing.
8. Be sure the electrolyte is not frozen.

Jump Starting Procedure

1. Determine voltages of the two batteries; they must be the same.
2. Bring the starting vehicle close (they must not touch) so that the batteries can be reached easily.
3. Turn off all accessories and both engines. Put both cars in Neutral or Park and set the handbrake.
4. Cover the cell caps with a rag—do not cover terminals.
5. If the terminals on the run-down battery are heavily corroded, clean them.
6. Identify the positive and negative posts on both batteries and connect the cables in the order shown.
7. Start the engine of the starting vehicle and run it at fast idle. Try to start the car with the dead battery. Crank it for no more than 10 seconds at a time and let it cool off for 20 seconds in between tries.
8. If it doesn't start in 3 tries, there is something else wrong.
9. Disconnect the cables in the reverse order.
10. Replace the cell covers and dispose of the rags.

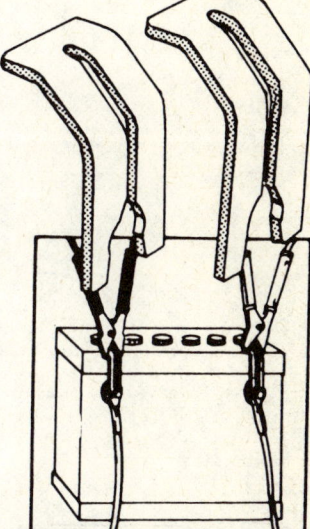

Side terminal batteries occasionally pose a problem when connecting jumper cables. There frequently isn't enough room to clamp the cables without touching sheet metal. Side terminal adaptors are available to alleviate this problem and should be removed after use.

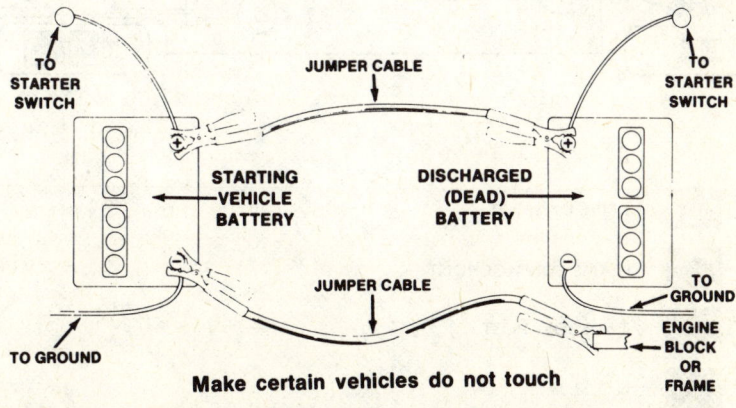

Make certain vehicles do not touch

This hook-up for negative ground cars only

30 GENERAL INFORMATION AND MAINTENANCE

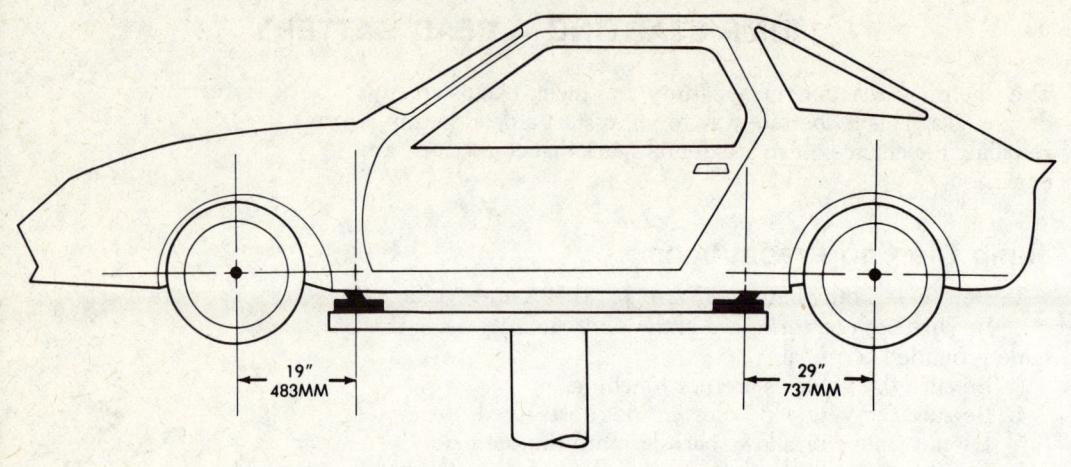

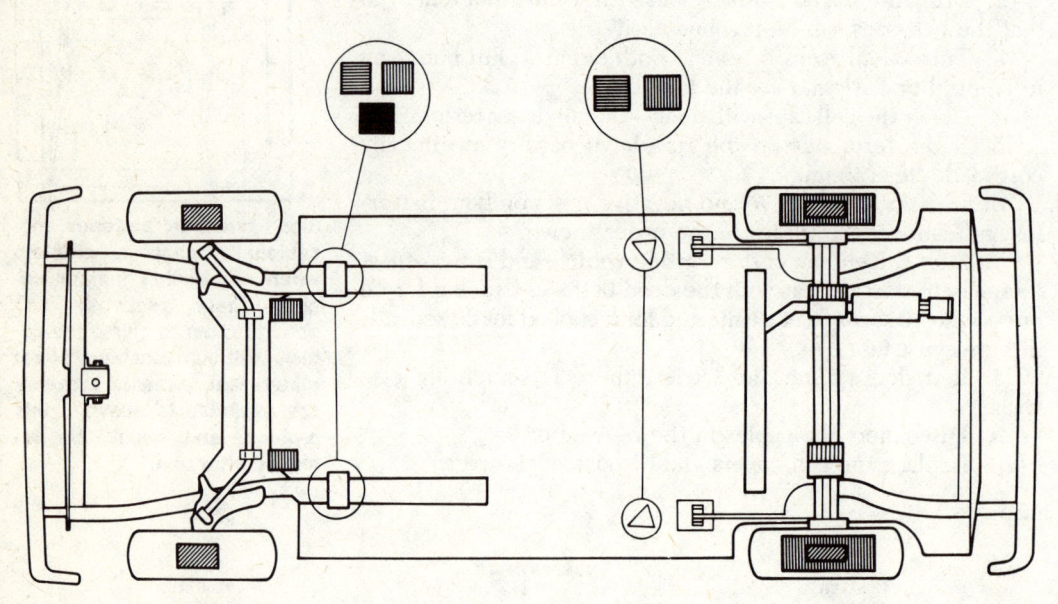

DRIVE ON HOIST

FRAME CONTACT HOIST

TWIN POST HOST

FLOOR JACK

Jacking and hoisting locations

GENERAL INFORMATION AND MAINTENANCE

9. Tighten the adjusting nut to 20–25 ft. lbs. while rotating the wheel.

10. Back off the adjusting nut to completely release the preload from the bearing.

11. Tighten the adjusting nut finger-tight.

12. Position the nut-lock with one pair of slots in line with the cotter pin hole. Install the cotter pin.

13. Clean and install the grease cap and wheel.

14. Lower the car.

PUSHING AND TOWING

If your car is equipped with a manual transaxle, it may be push started in an extreme emergency, but there is the possibility of damaging bumpers and/or fenders of both cars. Make sure the bumpers of both cars are evenly matched. Depress the clutch pedal, select Second or Third gear, and switch the ignition On. When the car reaches a speed of approximately 10 or 15 mph, release the clutch to start the engine. DO NOT ATTEMPT TO PUSH START AN AUTOMATIC LASER OR DAYTONA.

Manual transaxle models may be flat-towed short distances. Attach tow lines to the towing eye on the front suspension or the left or right bumper bracket at the rear. Flat-towing automatic transaxle models is not recommended more than 15 miles at more than 30 mph, and this is only in an emergency. Cars equipped with the automatic should be towed from the rear when the front wheels are on towing dollies.

If you plan on towing a trailer, don't exceed 1000 lbs (trailer without brakes). DO NOT tow a trailer with a car equipped with a turbocharged engine. Towing a trailer with an automatic equipped car places an extra load on the transmission and a few items should be made note of here. Make doubly sure that the transmission fluid is at the correct level. Change the fluid more frequently if you're doing much trailer towing. Start out in 1 or 2 and use the lower ranges when climbing hills. After-market transmission coolers are available which greatly ease the load on your automatic transmission and one should be considered if you often pull a trailer.

JACKING

Floor jacks can be used to raise the car at the locations shown. In addition front hoist points are located at the center of the front crossmember.

NOTE: *Raise the vehicle only until the tire just clears the surface. Minimum tire lift provides maximum stability.*

Jack receptacles or locator pins, are located on each side of the body. Do not use these lift points as bearing points for a floor jack.

Tune-Up and Performance Maintenance

TUNE-UP PROCEDURES

The procedures listed here are intended as specific procedure. More general procedures are given in Chapter 9, Troubleshooting.

Neither tune-up nor troubleshooting can be considered independently, since each has a direct bearing on the other.

An engine tune-up is a service designed to restore the maximum capability of power, performance, economy and reliability in an engine, and, at the same time, assure the owner of a complete check and more lasting results in efficiency and trouble-free performance. Engine tune-up becomes increasingly important each year, to ensure that pollutant levels are in compliance with federal emissions standards.

It is advisable to follow a definite and thorough tune-up procedure. Tune-up consists of three separate steps: Analysis, the process of determining whether normal wear is responsible for performance loss, and whether parts require replacement or service; Parts Replacement or Service; and Adjustment, where engine adjustments are returned to the original factory specifications.

The extent of an engine tune-up is usually determined by the length of time since the previous service, although the type of driving and general mechanical conditioning of the engine must be considered. Specific maintenance should also be performed at regular intervals, depending on operating conditions.

Troubleshooting is a logical sequence of procedures designed to lead the owner or service man to the particular cause of trouble. The troubleshooting chapter of this manual is general in nature, yet specific enough to locate the

Tune-Up Specifications

Part numbers listed in this reference are not recommendations by Chilton for any product by brand name. They are references that can be used with interchange manuals and after market supplier catalogs to locate each brand supplier's discrete part number.

NOTE: *When analyzing compression test results, look for uniformity among cylinders rather than specific pressures. The lowest reading cylinder should be within 20% of the highest.*

Year	Engine	Spark Plugs Orig Type	Gap (in.)	Ignition Timing (deg) ▲ Man Trans	Auto Trans	Intake Valve Opens (deg) ■	Fuel Pump Pressure (psi)	Idle Speed (rpm) ▲ Man Trans	Auto Trans	Valve Lash (in.) ▲ Intake	Exhaust
'84	2.2L	RN12YC	.035	6B	6B	16	36–97	850	750	Hyd.	Hyd.
	2.2L Turbo	RN12YC	.035	12B	12B	10	73–122	950	950	Hyd.	Hyd.
'85	2.2L	RN12YC	.035	12B	12B	16	36–97	850	750	Hyd.	Hyd.
	2.2L Turbo	RN12YC	.035	12B	12B	10	73–122	950	950	Hyd.	Hyd.

NOTE: *The underhood specifications sticker often reflects tune-up specification changes made in production. Sticker figures must be used if they disagree with those in this chart.*
▲ See text for procedure
■ Before Top Dead Center

TUNE-UP AND PERFORMANCE MAINTENANCE

problem. Service usually comprises two areas; diagnosis and repair. While the apparent cause of trouble, in many cases, is worn or damaged parts, performance problems are less obvious. The first job is to locate the problem and cause. Once the problem has been isolated, refer to the appropriate section for repair, removal or adjustment procedures.

It is advisable to read the entire chapter before beginning a tune-up, although those who are more familiar with tune-up procedures may wish to go directly to the instructions.

Spark Plugs

A typical spark plug consists of a metal shell surrounding a ceramic insulator. A metal electrode extends downward through the center of the insulator and protrudes a small distance. Located at the end of the plug and attached to the side of the outer metal shell is the side electrode. The side electrode bends in at a 90° angle so that its tip is even with, and parallel to, the tip of the center electrode. The distance between these two electrodes (measured in thousandths of an inch) is called the spark plug gap. The spark plug in no way produces a spark but merely provides a gap across which the current can arc. The coil produces anywhere from 20,000 to 40,000 volts which travels to the distributor where it is distributed through the spark plug wires to the spark plugs. The current passes along the center electrode and jumps the gap to the side electrode, and, in so doing, ignited the air/fuel mixture in the combustion chamber.

SPARK PLUG HEAT RANGE

Spark plug heat range is the ability of the plug to dissipate heat. The longer the insulator (or the farther it extends into the engine), the hotter the plug will operate; the shorter the insulator the cooler it will operate. A plug that absorbs little heat and remains too cool will quickly accumulate deposits of oil and carbon since it is not hot enough to burn them off. This leads to plug fouling and consequently to misfiring. A plug that absorbs too much heat will have no deposits, but, due to the excessive heat, the electrodes will burn away quickly and in some instances, preignition may result. Preignition takes place when plug tips get so hot that they glow sufficiently to ignite the fuel/air mixture before the actual spark occurs. This early ignition will usually cause a pinging during low speeds and heavy loads.

The general rule of thumb for choosing the correct heat range when picking a spark plug is: if most of your driving is long distance, high speed travel, use a colder plug; if most of your driving is stop and go, use a hotter plug. Original equipment plugs are compromise plugs, but most people never have occasion to change their plugs from the factory-recommended heat range.

REPLACING SPARK PLUGS

A set of spark plugs usually requires replacement after about 10,000 miles on cars with conventional ignition systems and after about 20,000 to 30,000 miles on cars with electronic ignition, depending on your style of driving. In normal operation, plug gap increased about 0.001 in. for every 1,000–2,500 miles. As the gap increased, the plug's voltage requirement also increases. It requires a greater voltage to jump the wider gap and about two or three times as much voltage to fire a plug at high speeds than at idle.

When you're removing spark plugs, you should work on one at a time. Don't start by removing the plug wires all at once, because unless you number them, they may become mixed up. Take a minute before you begin and

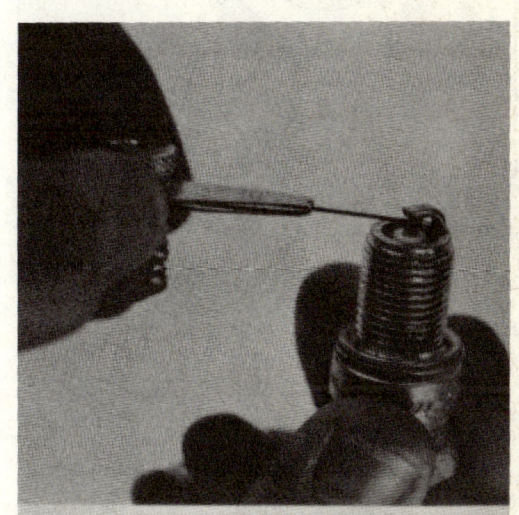

Check the spark plug gap with a round feeler gauge

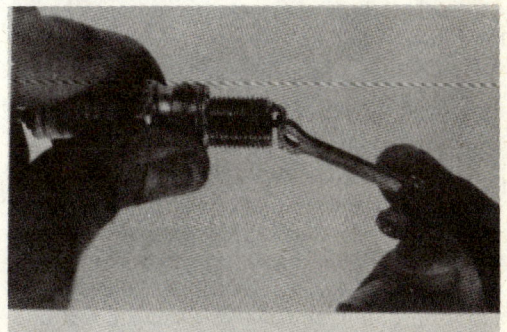

Bend the outer electrode to adjust the plug gap

34 TUNE-UP AND PERFORMANCE MAINTENANCE

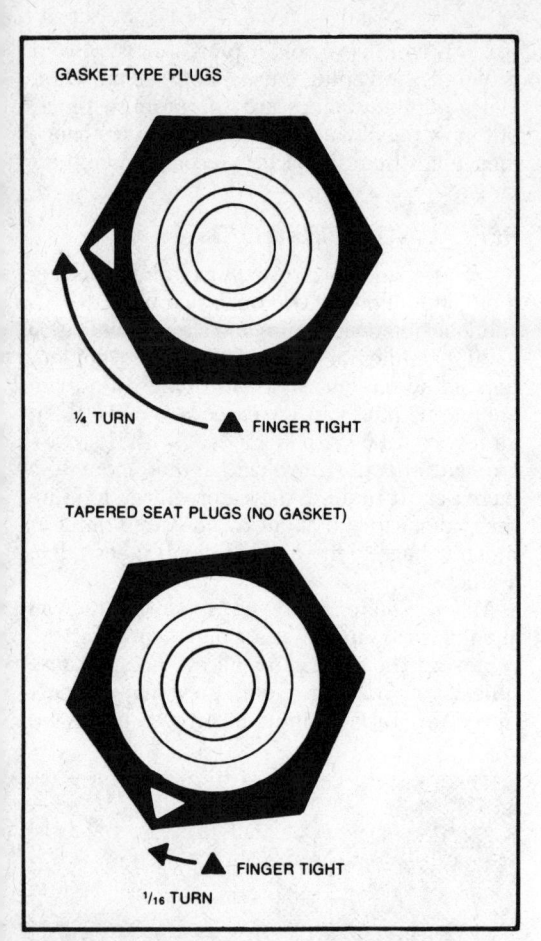

Tighten the plugs as shown in the absence of a specified torque

number the wires with tape. The best location for numbering is near where the wires come out of the cap.

1. Twist the spark plug boot and remove the boot and wire from the plug. Do not pull on the wire itself as this will ruin the wire.
2. If possible, use a brush or rag to clean the area around the spark plug. Make sure that all the dirt is removed so that none will enter the cylinder after the plug is removed.
3. Remove the spark plug using the proper size socket. Turn the socket counterclockwise to remove the plug. Be sure to hold the socket straight on the plug to avoid breaking the plug, or pounding off the hex on the plug.
4. Once the plug is out, check it against the plugs shown in the color section to determine engine condition. This is crucial since plug readings are vital signs of engine condition.
5. Use a round wire feeler gauge to check the plug gap. The correct size gauge should pass through the electrode gap with a slight drag. If you're in doubt, try one size smaller and one larger. The smaller gauge should go through easily while the larger one shouldn't go through at all. If the gap is incorrect, use the electrode bending tool on the end of the gauge to adjust the gap. When adjusting the gap, always bend the side electrode. The center electrode is non-adjustable.
6. Squirt a drop of penetrating oil on the threads of the new plug and install it. Don't oil the threads too heavily. Turn the plug in clockwise by hand until it is snug.
7. When the plug is finger tight, tighten it with a wrench. If you don't have a torque wrench, tighten the plug as shown.
8. Install the plug boot firmly over the plug. Proceed to the next plug.

CHECKING AND REPLACING SPARK PLUG CABLES

CAUTION: *Never pull the wires from the distributor cap. The wires are retained in the cap by means of internal clips in the wire towers. To remove a wire, first remove the distributor cap, then squeeze the clips ends together while gently removing the wire from the cap. Failure to follow this procedure will damage the core of the wire.*

Chrysler recommends that the wires not be removed from the cap for any reason other than replacement of a damaged wire or a wire that shows too much resistance.

Visually inspect the spark plug cables for burns, cuts, or breaks in the insulation. Check the spark plug boots and the nipples on the distributor cap and coil. Replace any damaged wiring. If no physical damage is obvious, the wires can be checked with an ohmmeter for excessive resistance. (See the tune-up and troubleshooting section).

When installing a new set of spark plug cables, replace the cables one at a time so there will be no mixup. Start by replacing the longest cable first. Install the boot firmly over the spark plug. Route the wire exactly the same as the original. Insert the nipple firmly into the tower on the distributor cap. Repeat the process for each cable.

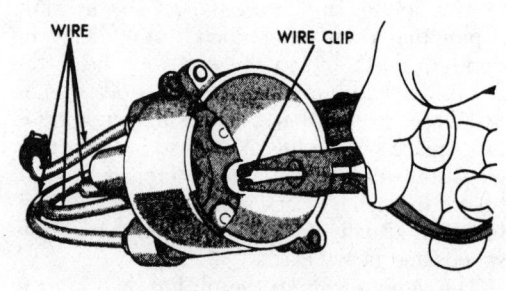

Removing spark plug wires from distributor cap

TUNE-UP AND PERFORMANCE MAINTENANCE

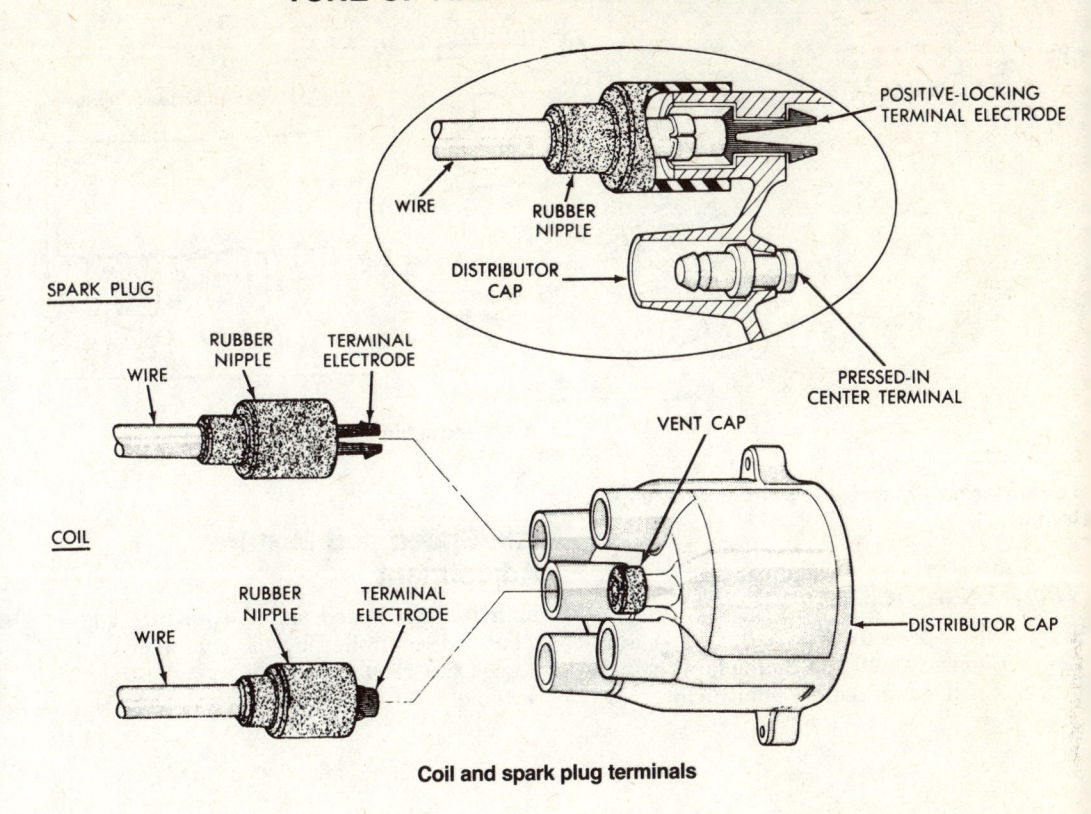

Coil and spark plug terminals

FIRING ORDER

To avoid confusion, replace spark plug wires or spark plugs one at a time.

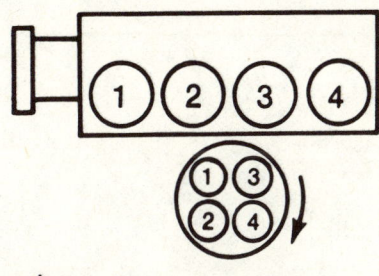

2.2L engine

Ignition Timing Adjustments

The engine is timed on No. 1 cylinder which is on the left-hand side of the car, facing the car.

1. Connect a timing light according to the manufacturer's instructions.
2. Connect a tachometer to the engine, making sure the selector is turned to the proper location.
3. Run the engine to normal operating temperature.
4. Disconnect and reconnect the water temperature sensor connector (located on the thermostat housing). The loss of power light on the dash should come on and stay on. The engine rpm should be within specifications.
5. Aim the timing light at the timing hole in the bell housing.
6. If necessary, loosen the distributor hold down bolt and adjust the timing to specifications.
7. Shut off the engine, disconnect and reconnect the positive battery quick disconnect. Start the vehicle, the loss of power light on the dash should now be off. Shut the engine off.
8. Check, and if necessary adjust, the idle speed.

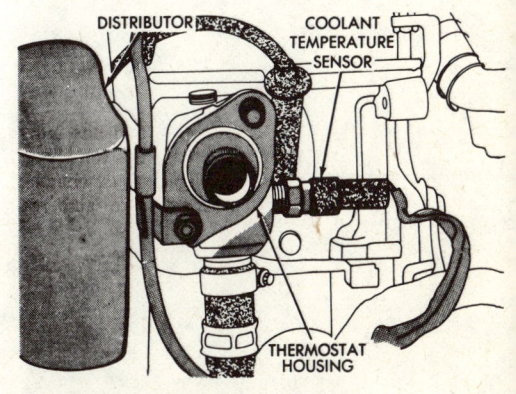

Coolant temperature sensor location

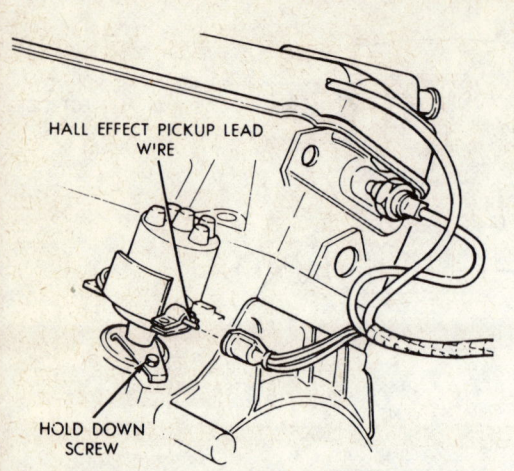

TUNE-UP AND PERFORMANCE MAINTENANCE

Loosen the distributor hold-down bolt to adjust the timing

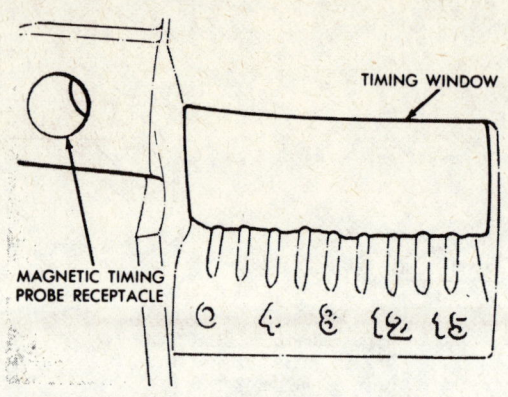

A-525 and automatic transaxle timing marks

Valve Lash Adjustment

The 2.2L Turbocharged and Non-Turbocharged engines both use hydraulic valve adjusters which do not require adjustment.

Idle Speed and Mixture Adjustment

Both the idle speed and the mixture adjustments are controlled by the computer on the Lasaer and Daytona models, no adjustment is possible.

Engine and Engine Rebuilding

3

ENGINE ELECTRICAL

Chrysler Corporation Electronic Fuel Injection Engine Control Electronics

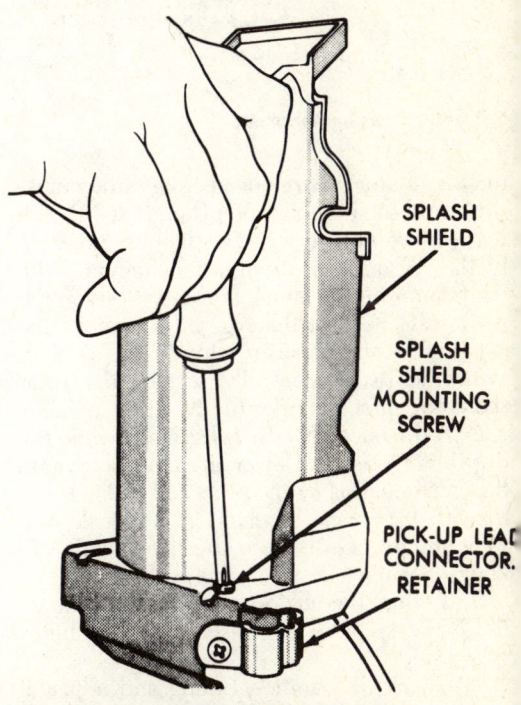

TROUBLESHOOTING

The distributor and ignition system on the Laser and Daytona models, both the multi-point fuel injection (turbocharged models) and the single-point fuel injection (non-turbocharged models) are controlled by the same computers as the fuel system. For an explanation of operation and troubleshooting procedures please refer to Chapter 4 under "Fuel Injection".

Distributor

CAUTION: *Never pull the wires from the distributor cap. The wires are retained in the cap by means of internal clips in the wire towers. To remove a wire, first remove the distributor cap, then squeeze the clips ends together while gently removing the wire from the cap. Failure to follow this procedure will damage the core of the wire.*

Chrysler recommends that the wires not be removed from the cap for any reason other than replacement of a damaged wire or a wire that shows too much resistance.

REMOVAL AND INSTALLATION

1. Disconnect the distributor pickup lead wire at the harness connector and remove the splash shield.
2. Remove the distributor cap.
3. Rotate the engine crankshaft until the rotor is pointing toward the cylinder block. Make a mark on the block at this point for installation reference.
4. Remove the distributor holddown screw.
5. Carefully lift the distributor from the engine. The shaft will move slightly as the distributor is removed.

To install the distributor:

1. If the engine has been cranked over while

ENGINE AND ENGINE REBUILDING

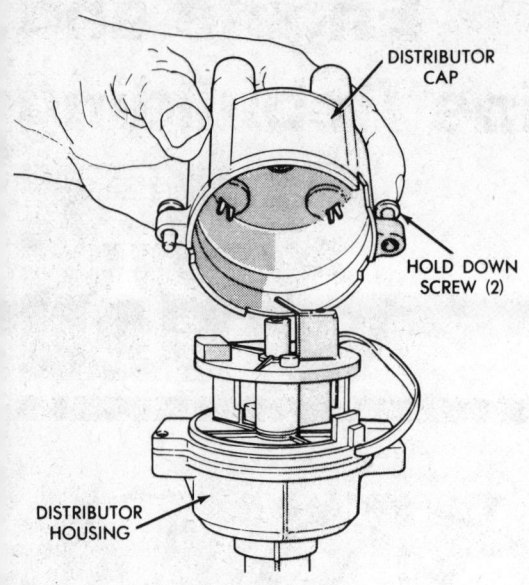

Removing or installing distributor cap

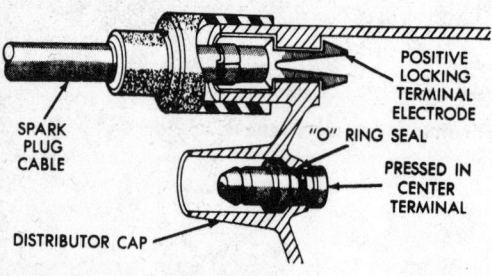

Coil and spark plug terminals

the distributor was removed, rotate the crankshaft until the number one piston is at TDC on the compression stroke. This will be indicated by the "0" mark on the flywheel aligning with the pointer on the clutch housing. Position the rotor just ahead of the No. 1 terminal of the cap and lower the distributor in the engine. With the distributor fully seated, the rotor should be directly under the No. 1 terminal.

2. If the engine was not disturbed while the distributor was out, lower the distributor into the engine, engaging the gears and making sure the gasket is properly seated in the block. The rotor should line up with the mark made before removal.

3. Tighten the holddown screw and connect the harness connector. Install the distributor splash shield.

4. Check the ignition timing and adjust if necessary.

Alternator

A conventional alternator is used on the Laser and Daytona models. It has six built in rectifiers which convert AC current to DC current. Current at the output terminal of the alternator is DC. The main components of the alternator are: the rotor, stator, rectifiers, end shields, brushes, bearings, and the Poly-Vee drive pulley and fan.

ALTERNATOR PRECAUTIONS

To prevent damage to the alternator and regulator, the following precautions should be taken when working with the electrical system.

1. Never reverse the battery connections.
2. Booster batteries for starting must be connected properly—positive-to-positive and negative-to-negative.
3. Disconnect the battery cables before using a fast charger; the charger has a tendency to force current through the diodes in the opposite direction for which they were designed. This burns out the diodes.
4. Never use a fast charger as a booster for starting the vehicle.
5. Never disconnect the voltage regulator while the engine is running.
6. Avoid long soldering times when replacing diodes or transistors. Prolonged heat is damaging to AC generators.
7. Do not use test lamps of more than 12 volts (V) for checking diode continuity.
8. Do not short across or ground any of the terminals on the AC generator.
9. The polarity of the battery, generator, and regulator must be matched and considered before making any electrical connections within the system.
10. Never operate the alternator on an open circuit. Make sure that all connections within the circuit are clean and tight.
11. Disconnect the battery terminals when performing any service on the electrical system. This will eliminate the possibility of accidental reversal of polarity.
12. Disconnect the battery ground cable if arc welding is to be done on any part of the car.

REMOVAL AND INSTALLATION

1. Disconnect the battery ground cable.
2. Disconnect the alternator wiring terminals from the rear of the alternator. Remove the wiring retainer nut and remove the retainer from the alternator.
3. Loosen the alternator adjustment bracket nut, move the alternator and remove the drive belt.
4. Remove the alternator adjusting bolt assembly.
5. Support the alternator, remove the pivot bolt and lift out the unit.
6. Reverse the procedure for installation.

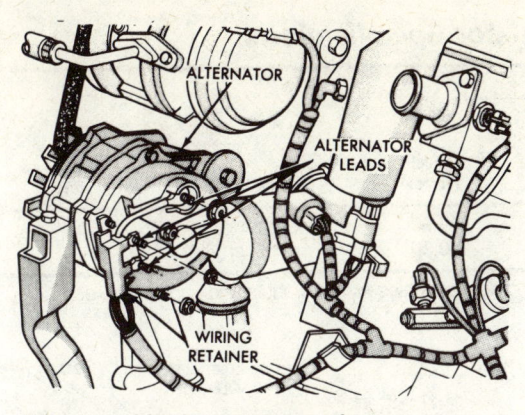

ENGINE AND ENGINE REBUILDING 39

Refer to Chapter 1 for proper belt tightening procedures.

Voltage Regulator

The electronic voltage regulator is contained within the engine electronics Power module and Logic module computer. It regulates the vehicle electrical system voltage by limiting the output voltage that is generated by the alternator. This is accomplished by controlling the amount of current that is allowed to pass through the alternator field winding.

TESTING

The voltage regulator used on the Laser and Daytona models is controlled by the same computers as the fuel system. For an explanation of operation and troubleshooting procedures please refer to Chapter 4 under "Fuel Injection".

Starter

The starter is an overrunning clutch drive type with a solenoid mounted on the starter motor. Two different manufacturer starters are used, built by Bosch and Nippondenso for manual and automatic transaxle applications. Removal and installation procedures are the same for all units. Starters used on the 2.2L Turbo engine use a heat shield and an additional mounting bracket.

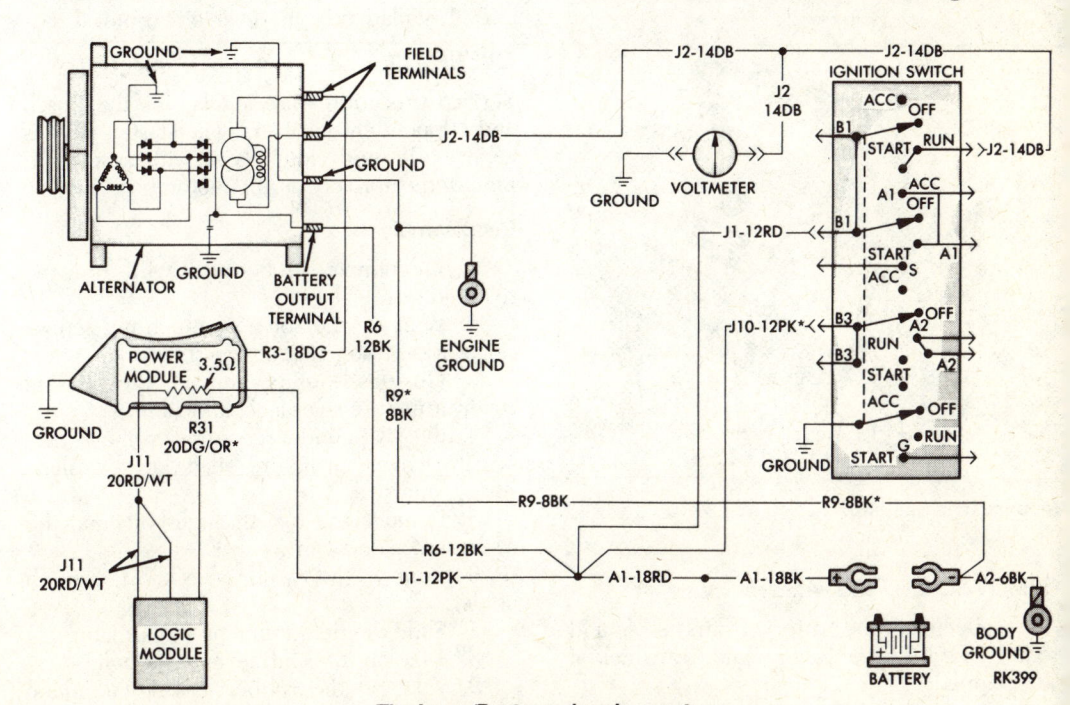

Alternator wiring harness connections

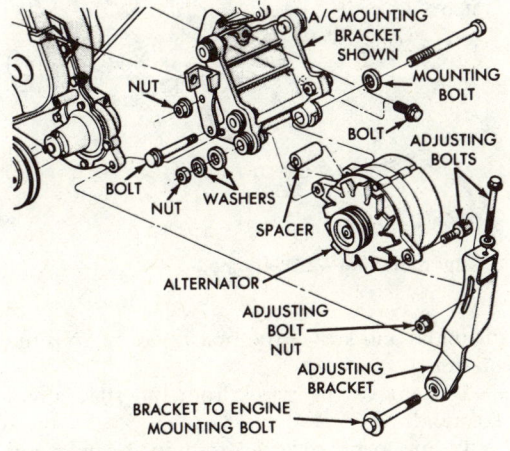

Alternator mounting

The Laser/Daytona charging system

40 ENGINE AND ENGINE REBUILDING

Alternator and Regulator Specifications

Year	Alternator Manufacturer	Field Current @ 12v (amps)	Output (amps)	Regulator ① Manufacturer	Volts @ 75°F
1984–85	Chrysler	2.5–5.0	40/90	Chrysler	13.9
	Bosch	2.5–5.0	40/90	Chrysler	14.1

① The electronic voltage regulator is contained within the engine electronics Power module and Logic module.

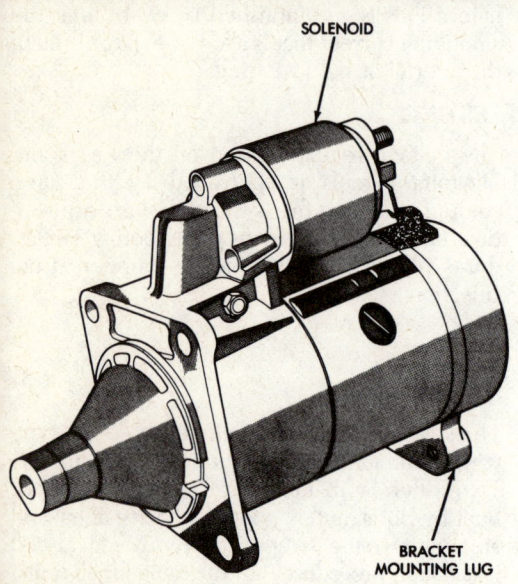

Bosch Starter

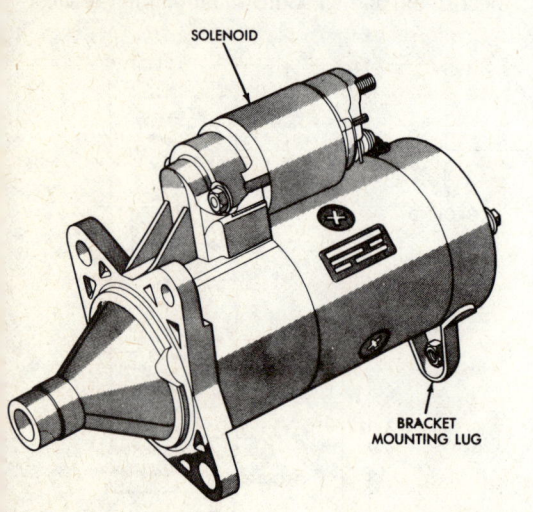

Nippondenso Starter

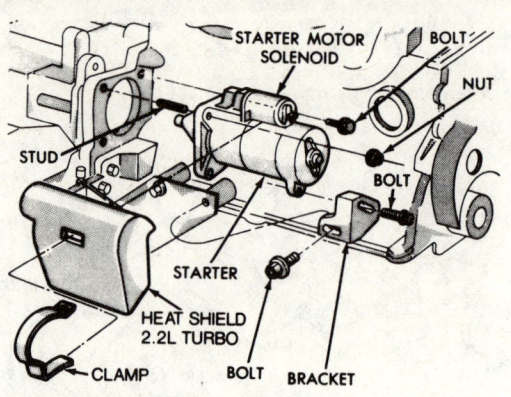

Starter mounting—2.2L engine

REMOVAL AND INSTALLATION

1. Disconnect the battery ground cable and remove the heatshield clamp and heat shield if so equipped.
2. Loosen the air pump tube at the exhaust manifold and swivel the bracket away from the starter.
3. Remove the wires from the starter and solenoid.
4. Support the starter, remove the bolts and lift the unit out from the flywheel housing.
5. Installation is the reverse of removal.

OVERHAUL

Service procedures are similar for the Bosch and Nippondenso starters. The starter drive is an over-running clutch type with a solenoid mounted externally on the motor.

Disassembly

1. Disconnect the field coil wire from the solenoid terminal.
2. Remove the solenoid mounting screws and work the solenoid off the shift fork.
3. On Bosch units, remove the bearing cover, armature shaft lock, and shim.
4. On Nippondenso units, remove the bearing cover, armature shaft lock, washer, spring, and seal.
5. Remove the two through-bolts and the commutator end frame cover.
6. Remove the two brushes and the brush holder.
7. Slide the field frame off the armature.
8. Take out the shift lever pivot bolt.
9. Take off the rubber gasket and metal plate.

ENGINE AND ENGINE REBUILDING 41

10. Remove the armature assembly and shift lever from the drive end housing.

11. Press the stop collar off the snap-ring. Remove the snap-ring, stop collar, and clutch.

Inspection

1. Brushes that are worn more than one-half the length of new brushes, or are oil-soaked, should be replaced.

2. DO NOT immerse the starter clutch unit in cleaning solvent. Solvent will wash the lubricant from the clutch.

3. Place the drive unit on the armature shaft and, while holding the armature, rotate the pinion. The drive pinion should rotate smoothly in one direction only. The pinion may not rotate easily. If the clutch does not function properly, or if the pinion is worn, chipped, or burred, replace the unit.

Assembly

1. Lubricate the armature shaft splines with motor oil.

2. Install the clutch, stop collar, and lock ring on the armature.

3. Place the armature assembly and shift fork in the drive end housing. Install the shift lever pivot bolt.

4. Install the rubber gasket and metal plate.

5. Slide the field frame into position. Install the brush holder and brushes.

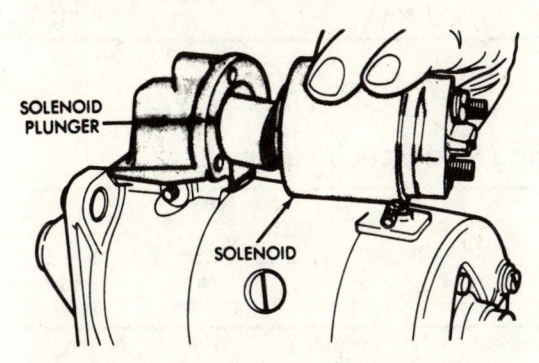

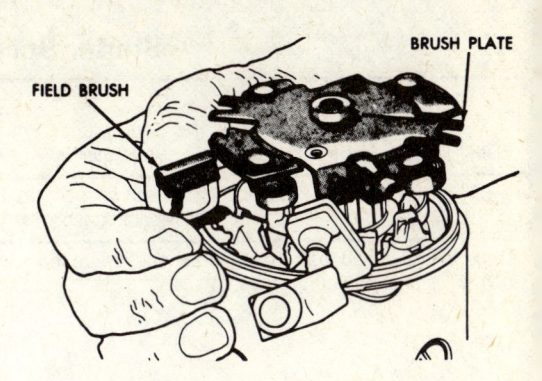

Brush assembly

6. Position the commutator end frame cover and install the through bolts.

7. On the Bosch starter, install the shim and armature shaft lock. Check that the end play is 0.05–0.3mm (0.002–0.012 in.). Install the bearing cover.

8. On the Nippondenso starter, install the seal, spring, washer, armature shaft lock, and bearing cover.

9. Assemble the solenoid to the shift fork and install the mounting screws.

10. Connect the field coil wire to the solenoid.

Battery

The battery is located conventionally, under the hood. It can be easily removed by disconnecting the battery cables and removing the hold-down bolts from the battery tray. Coat the terminals with a small amount of petroleum jelly after installation.

ENGINE MECHANICAL

The 2.2 Liter displacement engine is a four cylinder, overhead camshaft design powerplant with a cast iron block and an aluminum cylinder head. The cast iron crankshaft is supported by five main bearings. No vibration dampener is used. The iron camshaft also has five bearing journals and there are flanges at the rear of the journal to control the camshaft end play. Sintered iron timing sprockets are mounted on both the camshaft and crankshaft which are driven by the timing belt. The timing belt also drives the accessory shaft, housed in the forward-facing side of the block. The accessory shaft, in turn drives the oil pump and the distributor. The engine oil filter is attached to the base located at the left front of the block, toward the front of the car. The intake manifold is cast aluminum and the exhaust manifold is cast iron, both of which face the rear of the vehicle. The

Solenoid removal (automatic transaxle shown)

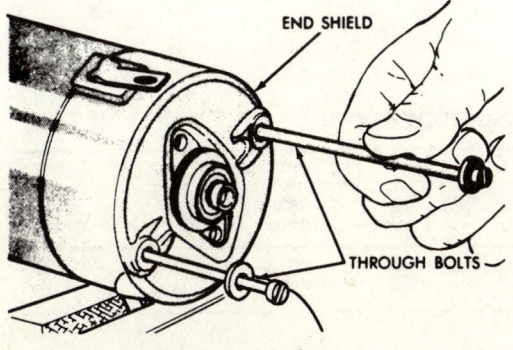

Removing starter through bolts

42 ENGINE AND ENGINE REBUILDING

Starter Specifications

Year	Engine	Trans.	Manufacturer	Load Test* Amps	Load Test* Volts	Load Test* Torque (ft. lb.)	No-Load Test Amps	No-Load Test Volts	No-Load Test RPM
84–85	2.2	All	Bosch or Nippondenso	120–160	12	—	47	11	6600

*To perform the load test, the engine should be up to operating temperature. Extremely heavy oil or tight engine will increase starter amperage draw.

General Engine Specifications

Year	Engine	Fuel System Type	Horsepower @ rpm	Torque ft. lb. @ rpm	Bore x Stroke	Comp. Ratio	Oil Press. (psi) @ 2000 rpm
1984	2.2L	E.F.I.	99 @ 5600	121 @ 3200	3.44 x 3.62	9.0	50
	2.2L Turbo	E.F.I.	142 @ 5600	160 @ 3600	3.44 x 3.62	8.1	50
1985	2.2L	E.F.I.	99 @ 5600	121 @ 3200	3.44 x 3.62	9.0	50
	2.2L Turbo	E.F.I.	146 @ 5600	168 @ 3600	3.44 x 3.62	8.1	50

Valve Specifications

Engine	Seat Angle (deg)	Face Angle (deg)	Spring Test Pressure (lbs. @ in.)	Spring Installed Height (in.)	Stem to Guide Clearance (in.) Intake	Stem to Guide Clearance (in.) Exhaust	Stem Diameter (in.) Intake	Stem Diameter (in.) Exhaust
2.2L	45	45	168–182 @1.22	1.59	.001–.003	.002–.004	.312–.313	.311–.312

Crankshaft and Connecting Rod Specifications

Engine	Crankshaft Main Bearing Journal Dia.	Crankshaft Main Bearing Oil Clearance	Crankshaft Shaft End Play	Crankshaft Thrust on No.	Connecting Rod Journal Dia.	Connecting Rod Oil Clearance	Connecting Rod Side Clearance
2.2L	2.362–2.363	.0003–.0031 ①	.002–.007	3	1.968–1.969	.0008–.0034	.005–.013

① Turbo charged engines: .0004–.0023 in.

Piston and Ring Specifications

Year	Engine	Ring Gap Top Compr.	Ring Gap Bottom Compr.	Ring Gap Oil Control	Ring Side Clearance Top Compr.	Ring Side Clearance Bottom Compr.	Ring Side Clearance Oil Control	Piston Clearance
1984–85	2.2L	.011–.021 ①	.011–.021 ②	.015–.055	.0015–.0031	.0015–.0037	.008 max	.0005–.0015

① Turbo charged engines: .010–.020 in.
② Turbo charged engines: .009–.018 in.

ENGINE AND ENGINE REBUILDING   43

Torque Specifications
(ft. lbs.)

Engine	Cyl. Head	Conn. Rod	Main Bearing	Crankshaft Bolt	Flywheel	Camshaft Cap Bolts	Camshaft Sprocket Bolts
2.2L	45 ①	40 ②	30 ②	50	65	14	65

① Tighten in four steps: 30 ft. lbs.; 45 ft. lbs.; 45 ft. lbs. again; then a ¼ turn more.
② Tighten to specified torque, then a ¼ turn more.

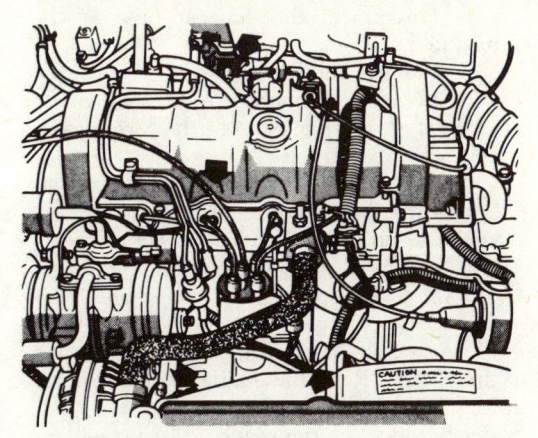

Remove the indicated electrical connections before removing the engine

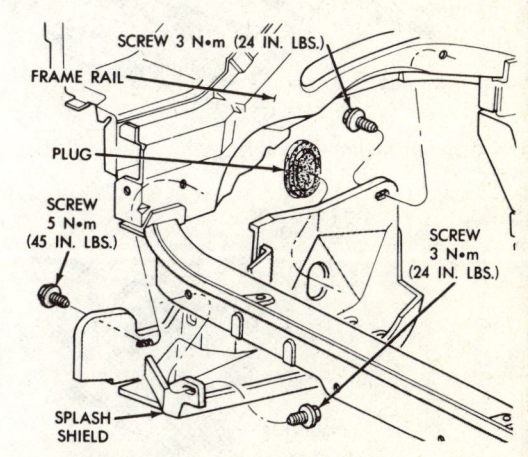

Removing the right inner splash shield

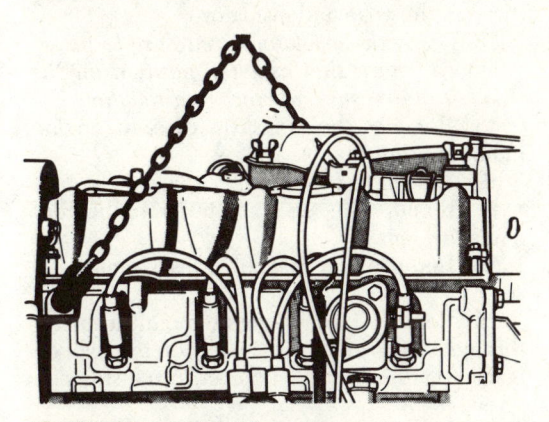

Attaching the engine lifting sling

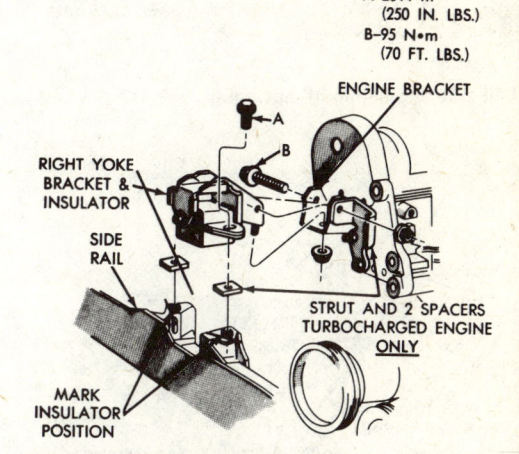

Right side engine mount assembly

distributor, spark plugs, and oil filter are all located on the foreward-facing side of the engine.

Engine Removal

1. Disconnect the battery.
2. Mark the hood hinge outline and remove the hood.
3. Drain the cooling system.
4. Remove the radiator hoses and remove the radiator and shroud assembly.
5. Remove the air cleaner and hoses.
6. On cars equipped with air conditioning, the compressor does not have to be disconnected. Remove it from its bracket and position it out of the way. Securing it with a piece of wire is the best method.

NOTE: *On A/C cars do not disconnect any hoses from the A/C system. Disconnect the compressor from the bracket with the hoses attached.*

7. Remove the power steering pump and position it out of the way.
8. Drain the engine oil and remove the oil filter.

ENGINE AND ENGINE REBUILDING

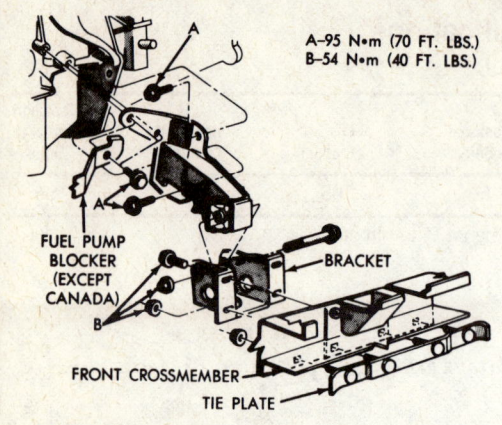

A—95 N•m (70 FT. LBS.)
B—54 N•m (40 FT. LBS.)

Front engine mount assembly

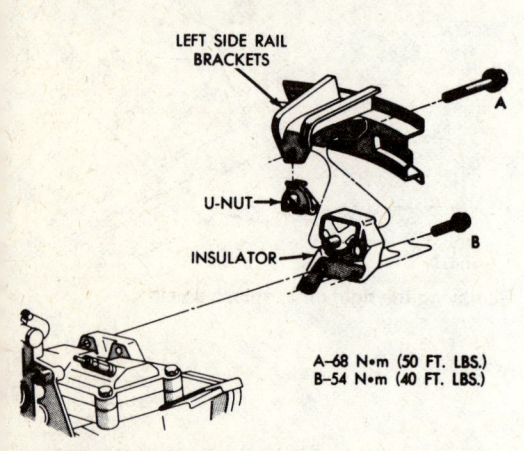

A—68 N•m (50 FT. LBS.)
B—54 N•m (40 FT. LBS.)

Left side engine mount assembly

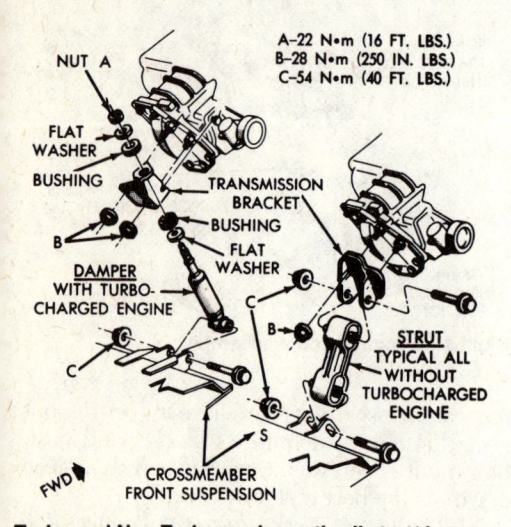

A—22 N•m (16 FT. LBS.)
B—28 N•m (250 IN. LBS.)
C—54 N•m (40 FT. LBS.)

Turbo and Non-Turbo engine anti-roll strut/damper

9. Disconnect all the wiring from the engine and alternator.
10. Disconnect the fuel line, heater hose and the accelerator cable.
11. Remove the alternator.
12. On Manual Transaxle models:
   a. Disconnect the clutch cable.
   b. Remove the transaxle case lower cover.
   c. Disconnect the exhaust pipe at the manifold.
   d. Remove the starter.
   e. Install a transaxle holding fixture to support the transaxle when the engine is removed.
13. On Automatic Transaxle models:
   a. Disconnect the exhaust pipe at the manifold.
   b. Remove the starter.
   c. Remove the transaxle case lower cover.
   d. Mark the flex plate to the torque converter for reassembly.
   e. Attach a "C" clamp on the front bottom of the torque converter housing to prevent the torque converter from coming out.
   f. Install a transaxle holding fixture to support the transaxle when the engine is removed.
14. Attach a lifting fixture and a shop crane to the engine. Raise the engine slightly to take up the weight of the engine.
15. Remove the right inner splash shield.
16. Remove the ground strap.
17. To raise the engine remove the long bolts through the yoke and insulator.
NOTE: *If the insulator screws are to be removed, mark the insulator position on the side rail to insure an exact reinstallation.*
18. Remove the transaxle case to engine mounting screws.
19. Disconnect the clutch cable.
20. Remove the screw and nut from the front engine mount.
21. Remove the manual transaxle anti roll strut.
22. Remove the left engine mount insulator through bolt (from the inside of the wheelhouse) or the insulator bracket to transmission screws.
23. Lift the engine out of the vehicle.

Engine Installation

1. Carefully lower the engine into place and loosely install all the mounting bolts. When all the mounting bolts have been hand tightened, then torque each to 40 ft. lbs.
2. Install the transaxle case to the engine and torque the mounting bolts to 70 ft. lbs.
3. Remove the engine sling and the transaxle holding fixture.
4. Install the ground strap.
5. Install the right inner splash shield.
6. Install the starter.
7. Connect the exhaust pipe to the manifold.
8. On manual transaxle models, install the

ENGINE AND ENGINE REBUILDING 45

lower case cover and connect the clutch cable.

9. On automatic transaxle models, remove the "C" clamp from the torque converter housing. Align the flex plate to the torque converter, install the mounting screws and tighten to 40 ft. lbs.

10. Reinstall the power steering pump and alternator.

12. Connect the fuel line, heater hose and the accelerator cable.

13. Connect all wiring.

14. Install the oil filter and refill the engine crankcase with the proper oil to the correct level.

15. If equipped with air conditioning, reinstall the A/C compressor.

16. Reinstall the air cleaner and hoses.

17. Install the radiator and hoses.

18. Fill the cooling system.

19. Install the hood.

20. Connect the battery.

21. Start the engine and run it to normal operating temperature.

22. Adjust the transmission linkage if necessary.

Rocker Arm/Camshaft Cover
REMOVAL AND INSTALLATION

1. Separate the crankcase ventilator hose from the PCV module.

2. Depress the retaining clip on the PCV module, turn the module counterclockwise and remove it from the cylinder head cover taking care not to damage the module of the cylinder head cover during the removal.

3. Remove the ten screws that retain the cover to the cylinder head and remove the cover.

4. To install, clean the cylinder head cover and its mating surface on the cylinder head thoroughly.

5. Depress the retaining clip on the PCV module, turn the module clockwise and install the PCV module into the cylinder head cover,

Camshaft cover—2.2L engine

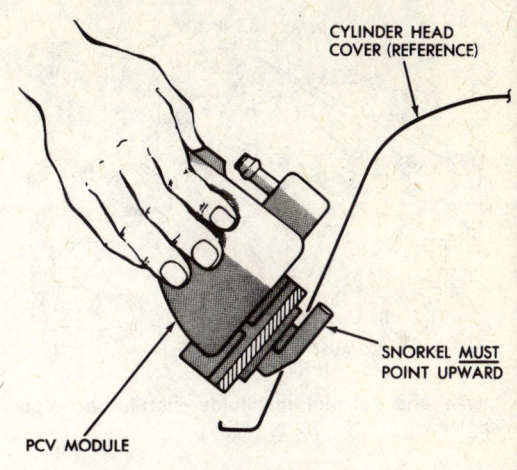

PCV module removal and installation

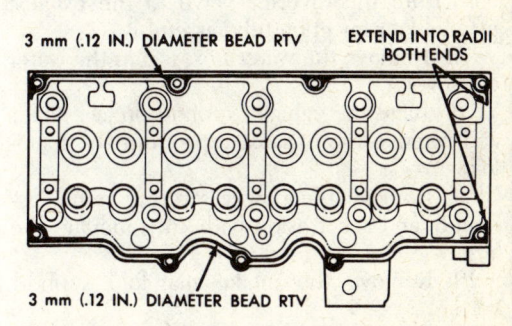

RTV gasket material application for the camshaft cover

check to see that the snorkle is positioned so that the open end is facing up. The snorkle should not be free to rotate.

6. Apply RTV gasket sealer in a continuous bead approximately 1/8 in. in diameter as shown in the illustration.

7. Install the ten screws that retain the cover to the cylinder head and tighten to 105 inch lbs.

8. Connect the crankcase ventilator hose to the PCV module.

Intake and Exhaust Manifolds
REMOVAL AND INSTALLATION
Non-turbocharged Engines

1. Drain the cooling system.

2. Remove the air cleaner assembly including the throttle body adaptor, hose and air cleaner box with the support bracket.

3. Disconnect the accelerator linkage, throttle body electrical connector and vacuum hoses.

4. Loosen the power steering pump and remove the belt.

5. Remove the power brake vacuum hose from the intake manifold.

6. On Canadian cars, remove the coupling

46 ENGINE AND ENGINE REBUILDING

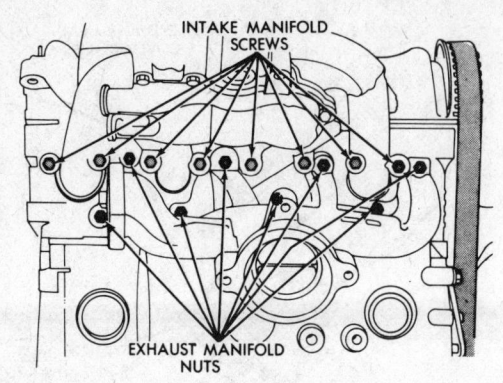

Intake and exhaust manifolds—non-turbocharged engines

hose from the diverter valve to the exhaust manifold air injection tube assembly.

7. Remove the water hoses from the water crossover.

8. Raise the vehicle, support on jackstands and remove the exhaust pipe from the manifold.

9. Remove the power steering pump assembly and set it aside without removing the hoses.

10. Remove the intake manifold support bracket.

11. Remove the EGR tube.

12. On Canadian cars, remove the four air injection tube bolts and the air injection tube assembly.

13. Remove the intake manifold retaining bolts. Lower the vehicle and remove the intake manifold.

14. Remove the exhaust manifold retaining bolts and remove the exhaust manifold.

15. Discard the old gaskets and clean the gasket surfaces.

16. To Install: Place a new intake/exhaust manifold gasket in position, set the exhaust manifold in place. Apply anti-seize compound to the threads, install the torque the retaining nuts starting at the center and progressing outward in both directions. Repeat this procedure until all screws are at 200 inch lbs.

17. Set the intake manifold in place. Raise the vehicle and torque the retaining screws starting at the center and progressing outward in both directions. Repeat this procedure until all screws are at 200 inch lbs.

18. The remaining procedures are reverse of the installation, steps 1 thru 12.

Turbocharged Engines

NOTE: *The cylinder head on the turbocharged engine must be removed in order to remove the intake and exhaust manifolds.*

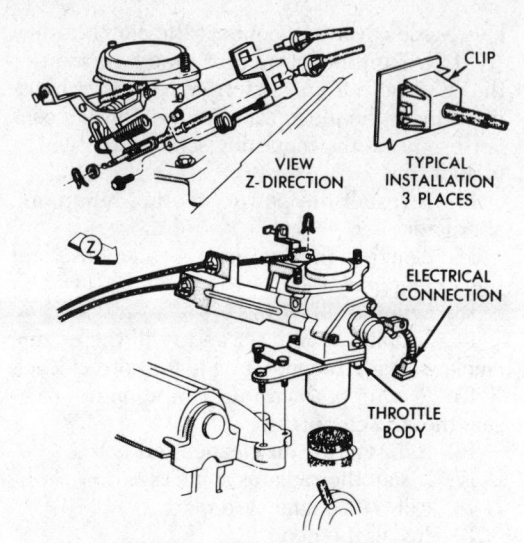

Accelerator linkage and throttle body—2.2L Turbocharged engine

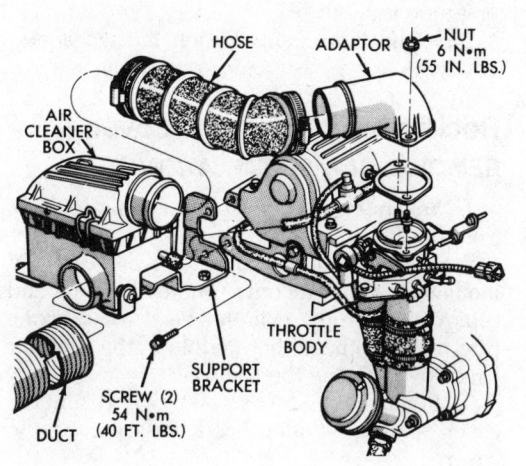

Air cleaner, hoses and throttle body—2.2L Turbocharged engine

1. Disconnect the battery and drain the cooling system.

2. Disconnect the exhaust pipe at the articulated joint and disconnect the electrical connections on the Oxygen sensor.

3. Remove the turbocharger to block support bracket.

4. Loosen the oil drain return tube connector hose clamps. Move the tube down on the block fitting.

5. Disconnect the turbocharger coolant inlet tube at the cylinder block and disconnect the tube support bracket.

6. Remove the air cleaner assembly including the throttle body adaptor, hose and air cleaner box with the support bracket.

7. Disconnect the accelerator linkage, throttle body electrical connector and vacuum hoses.

ENGINE AND ENGINE REBUILDING

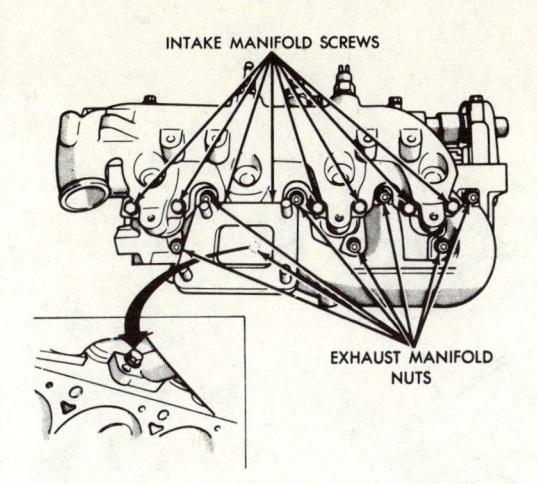

Intake and exhaust manifolds—2.2L Turbocharged engine

8. Relocate the fuel rail assembly: Remove the four bracket to intake manifold screws and the two bracket to heat shield retaining clips and lift and secure the fuel rail, (with the injectors, wiring harness, and fuel lines intact) up out of the way.

9. Disconnect the turbocharger oil feed line at the oil sending unit tee.

10. Disconnect the upper radiator hose from the thermostat housing.

11. Remove the cylinder head with the manifolds and turbocharger attached as an assembly, refer to "Cylinder Head Removal and Installation" in this chapter for procedures.

12. With the assembly located on a bench, loosen the turbocharger discharge hose end clamp, remove the 3 throttle body to intake manifold screws and remove the throttle body assembly.

NOTE: *DO NOT Disturb the Center Deswirler Retaining Clamp*

13. Disconnect the turbocharger coolant return tube at the water box and the retaining bracket on the cylinder head.

14. Remove the screws retaining the heat shield to the intake manifold and remove the heat shield.

15. Remove the 4 nuts attaching the turbocharger to the exhaust manifold and remove the turbocharger.

16. Remove the intake and exhaust manifold screws and remove the manifolds.

17. Discard the old gaskets and clean the gasket surfaces.

18. To Install: Place a new intake/exhaust manifold gasket in position, set the exhaust manifold in place. Apply anti-seize compound to the threads, install and torque the retaining nuts starting at the center and progressing outward in both directions. Repeat this procedure until all screws are at 200 in. lbs.

19. Connect the turbocharger outlet to the intake manifold inlet tube and position the turbocharger in place on the exhaust manifold, apply anti-seize compound to the threads and torque the retaining nuts to 40 ft. lbs. Tighten the connector tube clamps to 30 inch lbs.

20. Install the coolant return tube into the water box connector and tighten the tube nut to 30 ft. lbs. Install the tube support bracket to the cylinder head.

21. Install the heat shield to the intake manifold and tighten the three attaching screws to 105 inch lbs.

22. Install the throttle body air horn into the turbocharger inlet tube and install the three throttle body to intake manifold screws to 250 inch lbs. Tighten the tube clamp to 30 inch lbs.

23. Install the cylinder head assembly, refer to "Cylinder Head Removal and Installation" in this chapter for procedures.

24. Reconnect the turbocharger oil feed line to the oil sending unit tee and bearing housing, if it was disconnected. Torque the tube nuts to 125 inch lbs.

25. Install the air cleaner assembly and reconnect the vacuum lines and accelerator cables.

26. Reposition the fuel rail, install and tighten the 4 bracket screws to 250 inch lbs. and install the 2 air shield retaining clips.

27. Connect the turbocharger inlet coolant tube to the cylinder block. Tighten the tube nut to 30 ft. lbs. Install the tube support bracket.

28. Install the turbocharger housing to block support bracket, and install the screws finger tight. Tighten the block screws first to 40 ft. lbs. then, tighten the screw to turbocharger housing to 20 ft. lbs.

29. Reposition the drain back hose connector and tighten the hose clamps. Reconnect the exhaust pipe.

30. Connect the upper radiator hose to the thermostat housing. Tighten the hose clamp to 35 inch lbs.

31. Refill the cooling system.

Turbocharger

REMOVAL AND INSTALLATION

1. Disconnect the battery and drain the cooling system.

2. Disconnect the exhaust pipe at the articulated joint and disconnect the electrical connections on the Oxygen sensor.

3. Remove the turbocharger to block support bracket.

4. Loosen the oil drain return tube connector hose clamps. Move the tube down on the block fitting.

5. Disconnect the turbocharger coolant in-

48 ENGINE AND ENGINE REBUILDING

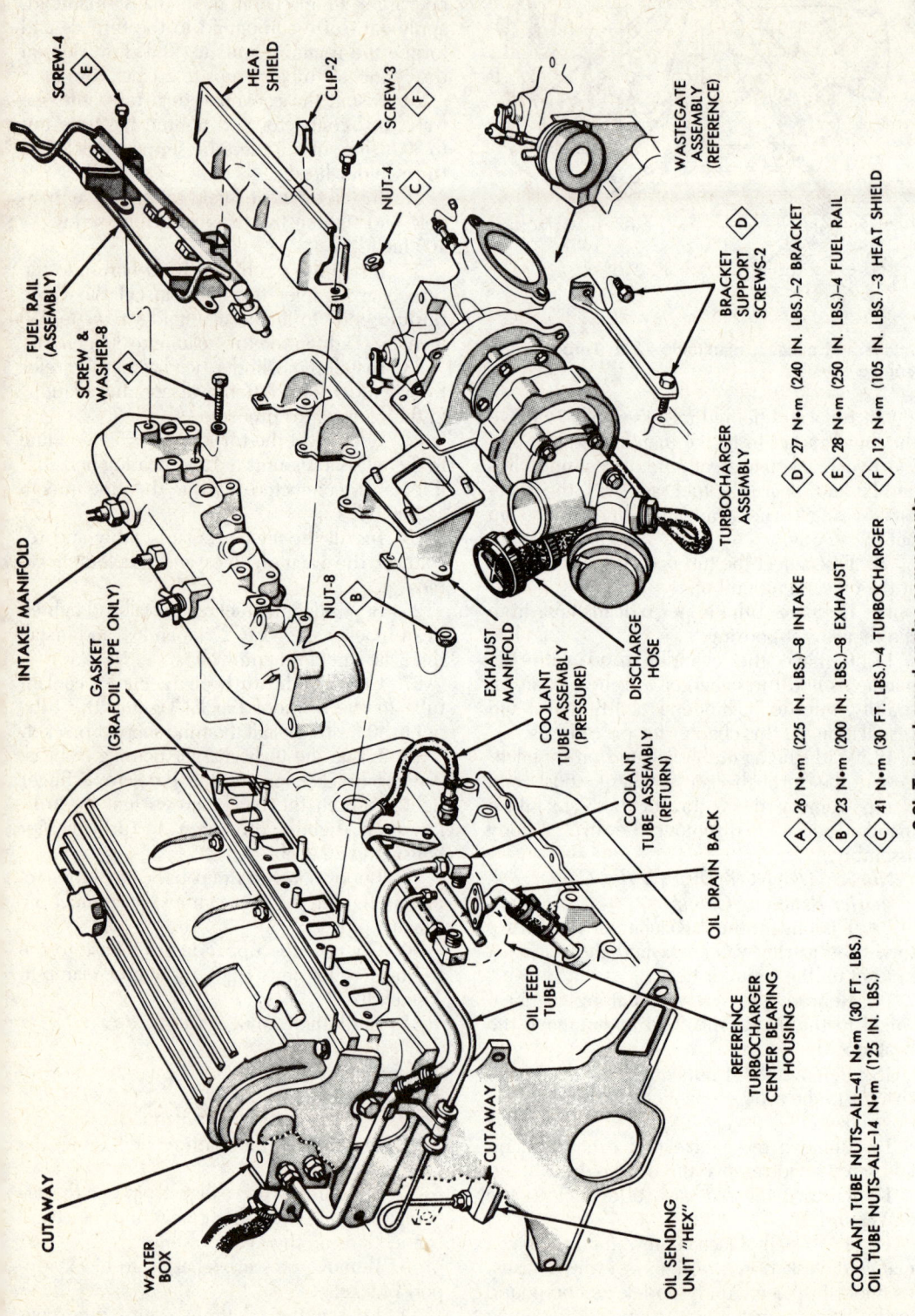

2.2L Turbocharged engine components

A) 26 N•m (225 IN. LBS.)–8 INTAKE
B) 23 N•m (200 IN. LBS.)–8 EXHAUST
C) 41 N•m (30 FT. LBS.)–4 TURBOCHARGER
D) 27 N•m (240 IN. LBS.)–2 BRACKET
E) 28 N•m (250 IN. LBS.)–4 FUEL RAIL
F) 12 N•m (105 IN. LBS.)–3 HEAT SHIELD

COOLANT TUBE NUTS–ALL 41 N•m (30 FT. LBS.)
OIL TUBE NUTS–ALL 14 N•m (125 IN. LBS.)

ENGINE AND ENGINE REBUILDING

let tube at the cylinder block and disconnect the tube support bracket.

6. Remove the air cleaner assembly including the throttle body adaptor, hose and air cleaner box with the support bracket.

7. Disconnect the accelerator linkage, throttle body electrical connector and vacuum hose.

8. Loosen the throttle body to turbocharger inlet hose clamps.

9. Remove the three throttle body to intake manifold attaching screws and remove the throttle body.

10. Loosen the turbocharger discharge hose end clamps.

NOTE: *DO NOT Disturb the Center Deswirler Retaining Clamp*

11. Relocate the fuel rail assembly: Remove the one hose retainer bracket screw and the four bracket to intake manifold screws and the two bracket to heat shield retaining clips and lift and secure the fuel rail, (with the injectors, wiring harness, and fuel lines intact) up out of the way.

12. Disconnect the oil feed line from the turbocharger bearing housing.

13. Remove the screws retaining the heat shield to the intake manifold and remove the heat shield.

14. Disconnect the coolant return hose assembly from the turbocharger and to the water box. Remove the tube support bracket from the cylinder head and remove the assembly.

15. Remove the 4 nuts attaching the turbocharger to the exhaust manifold and remove the turbocharger assembly by lifting it off the exhaust manifold studs, push downward towards the passenger side of the unit, up and out of the engine compartment.

16. To install reverse the removal procedures, paying special attention to the fastener torque values and any special instructions that follow.

17. Reposition the turbocharger assembly on the exhaust manifold studs. Making sure that the turbocharger discharge tube is in position between the intake manifold and the turbocharger.

18. Apply anti-seize compound to the threads and torque the nuts to 30 ft. lbs.

19. Torque the oil feed line tube nuts to the sending unit hex tee and the turbocharger center housing to 125 inch lbs. Install and tighten the support bracket screw.

20. Tighten the three heat shield to intake manifold screws to 105 inch lbs.

21. Tighten the coolant tube nuts to 30 ft. lbs. and install the bracket screw.

22. Tighten the four fuel rail bracket to intake manifold retaining screws to 250 inch lbs. Reinstall the shield to bracket clips.

23. Tighten the discharge hose clamp to 35 inch lbs.

24. Tighten the three throttle body to intake manifold screws to 250 inch lbs.

25. Tighten the throttle body hose clamps to 35 inch lbs.

26. Reconnect the accelerator linkage, electrical connector and vacuum hoses.

27. Tighten the two hose adapter to throttle body screws to 55 inch lbs. and the air cleaner box support bracket screws to 40 ft. lbs.

28. Tighten the coolant tube nut to block connector to 30 ft. lbs.

29. Reposition the oil drain back hose and tighten the clamps to 30 inch lbs.

30. Install the turbocharger-to-block support bracket and install the screws finger tight. Tighten the block screw first to 40 ft. lbs., then tighten the screw to turbocharger housing to 20 ft. lbs.

31. Tighten the articulated ball joint shoulder bolts to 250 inch lbs.

32. Refill the cooling system.

Cylinder Head
REMOVAL AND INSTALLATION

1. Disconnect the negative battery terminal.
2. Drain the cooling system.
3. Remove the air cleaner assembly.
4. Disconnect all lines, hoses and wires from the head, manifold and fuel injection.
5. Disconnect the accelerator linkage.
6. Remove the distributor cap.
7. Disconnect the exhaust pipe.
8. Remove throttle body adaptor, hose and air cleaner box with the support bracket.
9. Remove the intake and exhaust manifolds.
10. Remove the upper portion of the front cover.
11. Turn the engine by hand until all gear timing marks are aligned.
12. Loosen the drive belt tensioner and slip the belt off the camshaft gear.
13. If equipped with air conditioning, remove the compressor from the mounting brackets and support it out of the way with wires. Remove the mounting brackets from the head.
14. Remove the valve cover, gaskets and seals.
15. Remove head bolts in reverse order of tightening sequence.
16. Lift off the head and discard the gasket.
17. Installation is the reverse of removal.

ENGINE AND ENGINE REBUILDING

ENGINE OVERHAUL

Most engine overhaul procedures are fairly standard. In addition to specific parts replacement procedures and complete specifications for your individual engine, this chapter also is a guide to accepted rebuilding procedures. Examples of standard rebuilding practice are shown and should be used along with specific details concerning your particular engine.

Competent and accurate machine shop services will ensure maximum performance, reliability and engine life. Procedures marked with the symbol shown above should be performed by a competent machine shop, and are provided so that you will be familiar with the procedures necessary to a successful overhaul.

In most instances it is more profitable for the do-it-yourself mechanic to remove, clean and inspect the component, buy the necessary parts and deliver these to a shop for actual machine work.

On the other hand, much of the rebuilding work (crankshaft, block, bearings, pistons, rods, and other components) is well within the scope of the do-it-yourself mechanic.

Tools

The tools required for an engine overhaul or parts replacement will depend on the depth of your involvement. With a few exceptions, they will be the tools found in a mechanic's tool kit (see Chapter 1). More in-depth work will require any or all of the following:
• a dial indicator (reading in thousandths) mounted on a universal base
  • micrometers and telescope gauges
  • jaw and screw-type pullers
  • scraper
  • valve spring compressor
  • ring groove cleaner
  • piston ring expander and compressor
  • ridge reamer
  • cylinder hone or glaze breaker
  • Plastigage®
  • engine stand

Use of most of these tools is illustrated in this chapter. Many can be rented for a one-time use from a local parts jobber or tool supply house specializing in automotive work.

Occasionally, the use of special tools is called for. See the information on Special Tools and the Safety Notice in the front of this book before substituting another tool.

Inspection Techniques

Procedures and specifications are given in this chapter for inspecting, cleaning and assessing the wear limits of most major components. Other procedures such as Magnaflux and Zyglo can be used to locate material flaws and stress cracks. Magnaflux is a magnetic process applicable only to ferrous materials. The Zyglo process coats the material with a flourescent dye penetrant and can be used on any material. Check for suspected surface cracks can be more readily made using spot check dye. The dye is sprayed onto the suspected area, wiped off and the area sprayed with a developer. Cracks will show up brightly.

Overhaul Tips

Aluminum has become extremely popular for use in engines, due to its low weight. Observe the following precautions when handling aluminum parts:
• Never hot tank aluminum parts (the caustic hot-tank solution will eat the aluminum)
• Remove all aluminum parts (identification tag, etc.) from engine parts prior to hot-tanking.
• Always coat threads lightly with engine oil or anti-seize compounds before installation, to prevent seizure.
• Never over-torque bolts or spark plugs, especially in aluminum threads.

Stripped threads in any component can be repaired using any of several commercial repair kits (Heli-Coil, Microdot, Keenserts, etc.)

When assembling the engine, any parts that will be in frictional contact must be pre-lubed to provide lubrication at initial start-up. Any product specifically formulated for this purpose can be used, but engine oil is not recommended as a pre-lube.

When semi-permanent (locked, but removable) installation of bolts or nuts is desired, threads should be cleaned and coated with Loctite® or other similar, commercial non-hardening sealant.

ENGINE AND ENGINE REBUILDING

Repairing Damaged Threads

Several methods of repairing damaged threads are available. Heli-Coil® (shown here), Keenserts® and Microdot® are among the most widely used. All involve basically the same principle—drilling out stripped threads, tapping the hole and installing a prewound insert—making welding, plugging and oversize fasteners unnecessary.

Two types of thread repair inserts are usually supplied—a standard type for most Inch Coarse, Inch Fine, Metric Coarse and Metric Fine thread sizes and a spark plug type to fit most spark plug port sizes. Consult the individual manufacturer's catalog to determine exact applications. Typical thread repair kits will contain a selection of prewound threaded inserts, a tap (corresponding to the outside diameter threads of the insert) and an installation tool. Spark plug inserts usually differ because they require a tap equipped with pilot threads and a combined reamer/tap section. Most manufacturers also supply blister-packed thread repair inserts separately in addition to a master kit containing a variety of taps and inserts plus installation tools.

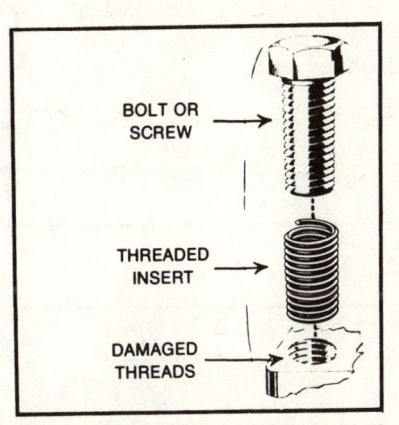

Before effecting a repair to a threaded hole, remove any snapped, broken or damaged bolts or studs. Penetrating oil can be used to free frozen threads; the offending item can be removed with locking pliers or with a screw or stud extractor. After the hole is clear, the thread can be repaired, as follows:

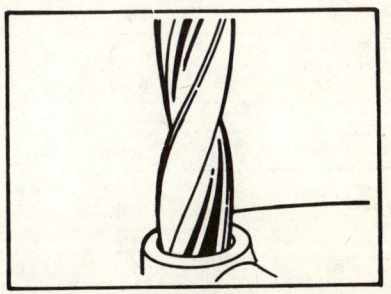

Drill out the damaged threads with specified drill. Drill completely through the hole or to the bottom of a blind hole

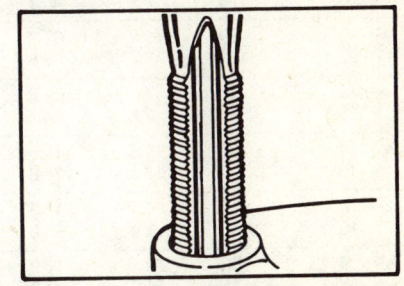

With the tap supplied, tap the hole to receive the thread insert. Keep the tap well oiled and back it out frequently to avoid clogging the threads

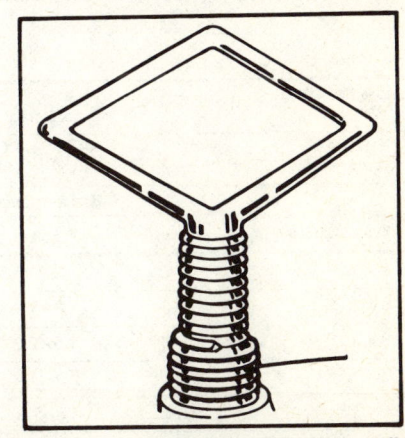

Damaged bolt holes can be repaired with thread repair inserts

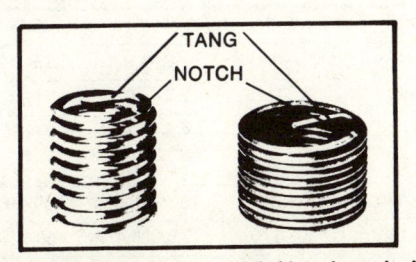

Standard thread repair insert (left) and spark plug thread insert (right)

Screw the threaded insert onto the installation tool until the tang engages the slot. Screw the insert into the tapped hole until it is ¼–½ turn below the top surface. After installation break off the tang with a hammer and punch

ENGINE AND ENGINE REBUILDING

Standard Torque Specifications and Fastener Markings

In the absence of specific torques, the following chart can be used as a guide to the maximum safe torque of a particular size/grade of fastener.
- There is no torque difference for fine or coarse threads.
- Torque values are based on clean, dry threads. Reduce the value by 10% if threads are oiled prior to assembly.
- The torque required for aluminum components or fasteners is considerably less.

U.S. Bolts

SAE Grade Number	1 or 2			5			6 or 7		
Number of lines always 2 less than the grade number.									
Bolt Size (inches)—(Thread)	Maximum Torque			Maximum Torque			Maximum Torque		
	Ft./Lbs.	Kgm	Nm	Ft./Lbs.	Kgm	Nm	Ft./Lbs.	Kgm	Nm
¼ — 20 — 28	5 6	0.7 0.8	6.8 8.1	8 10	1.1 1.4	10.8 13.6	10	1.4	13.5
5/16 — 18 — 24	11 13	1.5 1.8	14.9 17.6	17 19	2.3 2.6	23.0 25.7	19	2.6	25.8
3/8 — 16 — 24	18 20	2.5 2.75	24.4 27.1	31 35	4.3 4.8	42.0 47.5	34	4.7	46.0
7/16 — 14 — 20	28 30	3.8 4.2	37.0 40.7	49 55	6.8 7.6	66.4 74.5	55	7.6	74.5
½ — 13 — 20	39 41	5.4 5.7	52.8 55.6	75 85	10.4 11.7	101.7 115.2	85	11.75	115.2
9/16 — 12 — 18	51 55	7.0 7.6	69.2 74.5	110 120	15.2 16.6	149.1 162.7	120	16.6	162.7
5/8 — 11 — 18	83 95	11.5 13.1	112.5 128.8	150 170	20.7 23.5	203.3 230.5	167	23.0	226.5
¾ — 10 — 16	105 115	14.5 15.9	142.3 155.9	270 295	37.3 40.8	366.0 400.0	280	38.7	379.6
7/8 — 9 — 14	160 175	22.1 24.2	216.9 237.2	395 435	54.6 60.1	535.5 589.7	440	60.9	596.5
1 — 8 — 14	236 250	32.5 34.6	318.6 338.9	590 660	81.6 91.3	799.9 849.8	660	91.3	894.8

Metric Bolts

Relative Strength Marking	4.6, 4.8			8.8		
Bolt Markings						
Bolt Size Thread Size x Pitch (mm)	Maximum Torque			Maximum Torque		
	Ft./Lbs.	Kgm	Nm	Ft./Lbs.	Kgm	Nm
6 x 1.0	2–3	.2–.4	3–4	3–6	.4–.8	5–8
8 x 1.25	6–8	.8–1	8–12	9–14	1.2–1.9	13–19
10 x 1.25	12–17	1.5–2.3	16–23	20–29	2.7–4.0	27–39
12 x 1.25	21–32	2.9–4.4	29–43	35–53	4.8–7.3	47–72
14 x 1.5	35–52	4.8–7.1	48–70	57–85	7.8–11.7	77–110
16 x 1.5	51–77	7.0–10.6	67–100	90–120	12.4–16.5	130–160
18 x 1.5	74–110	10.2–15.1	100–150	130–170	17.9–23.4	180–230
20 x 1.5	110–140	15.1–19.3	150–190	190–240	26.2–46.9	160–320
22 x 1.5	150–190	22.0–26.2	200–260	250–320	34.5–44.1	340–430
24 x 1.5	190–240	26.2–46.9	260–320	310–410	42.7–56.5	420–550

ENGINE AND ENGINE REBUILDING

CHECKING ENGINE COMPRESSION

A noticeable lack of engine power, excessive oil consumption and/or poor fuel mileage measured over an extended period are all indicators of internal engine wear. Worn piston rings, scored or worn cylinder bores, blown head gaskets, sticking or burnt valves and worn valve seats are all possible culprits here. A check of each cylinder's compression will help you locate the problems.

As mentioned in the "Tools and Equipment" section of Chapter 1, a screw-in type compression gauge is more accurate than the type you simply hold against the spark plug hole, although it takes slightly longer to use. It's worth it to obtain a more accurate reading. Follow the procedures below for gasoline and diesel-engined cars.

Gasoline Engines

1. Warm up the engine to normal operating temperature.
2. Remove all spark plugs.

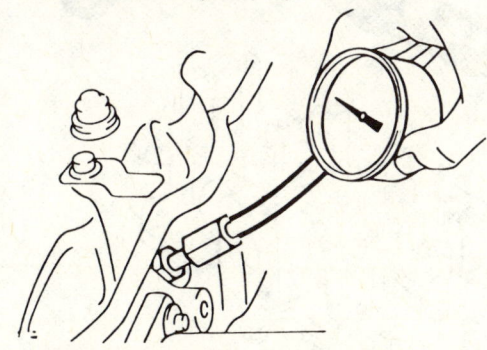

The screw-in type compression gauge is more accurate

3. Disconnect the high-tension lead from the ignition coil.
4. On carbureted cars, fully open the throttle either by operating the carburetor throttle linkage by hand or by having an assistant "floor" the accelerator pedal. On fuel-injected cars, disconnect the cold start valve and all injector connections.
5. Screw the compression gauge into the No. 1 spark plug hole until the fitting is snug.
NOTE: *Be careful not to crossthread the plug hole. On aluminum cylinder heads use extra care, as the threads in these heads are easily ruined.*
6. Ask an assistant to depress the accelerator pedal fully on both carbureted and fuel-injected cars. Then, while you read the compression gauge, ask the assistant to crank the engine two or three times in short bursts using the ignition switch.
7. Read the compression gauge at the end of each series of cranks, and record the highest of these readings. Repeat this procedure for each of the engine's cylinders. Compare the highest reading of each cylinder to the compression pressure specifications in the "Tune-Up Specifications" chart in Chapter 2. The specs in this chart are maximum values.

A cylinder's compression pressure is usually acceptable if it is not less than 80% of maximum. The difference between each cylinder should be no more than 12–14 pounds.

8. If a cylinder is unusually low, pour a tablespoon of clean engine oil into the cylinder through the spark plug hole and repeat the compression test. If the compression comes up after adding the oil, it appears that that cylinder's piston rings or bore are damaged or worn. If the pressure remains low, the valves may not be seating properly (a valve job is needed), or the head gasket may be blown near that cylinder. If compression in any two adjacent cylinders is low, and if the addition of oil doesn't help the compression, there is leakage past the head gasket. Oil and coolant water in the combustion chamber can result from this problem. There may be evidence of water droplets on the engine dipstick when a head gasket has blown.

Diesel Engines

Checking cylinder compression on diesel engines is basically the same procedure as on gasoline engines except for the following:
1. A special compression gauge adaptor suitable for diesel engines (because these engines have much greater compression pressures) must be used.
2. Remove the injector tubes and remove the injectors from each cylinder.
NOTE: *Don't forget to remove the washer underneath each injector; otherwise, it may get lost when the engine is cranked.*

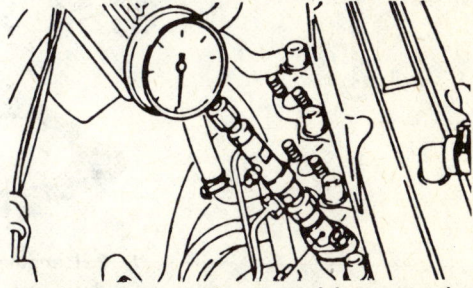

Diesel engines require a special compression gauge adaptor

3. When fitting the compression gauge adaptor to the cylinder head, make sure the bleeder of the gauge (if equipped) is closed.
4. When reinstalling the injector assemblies, install new washers underneath each injector.

54 ENGINE AND ENGINE REBUILDING

2.2L engine cylinder head

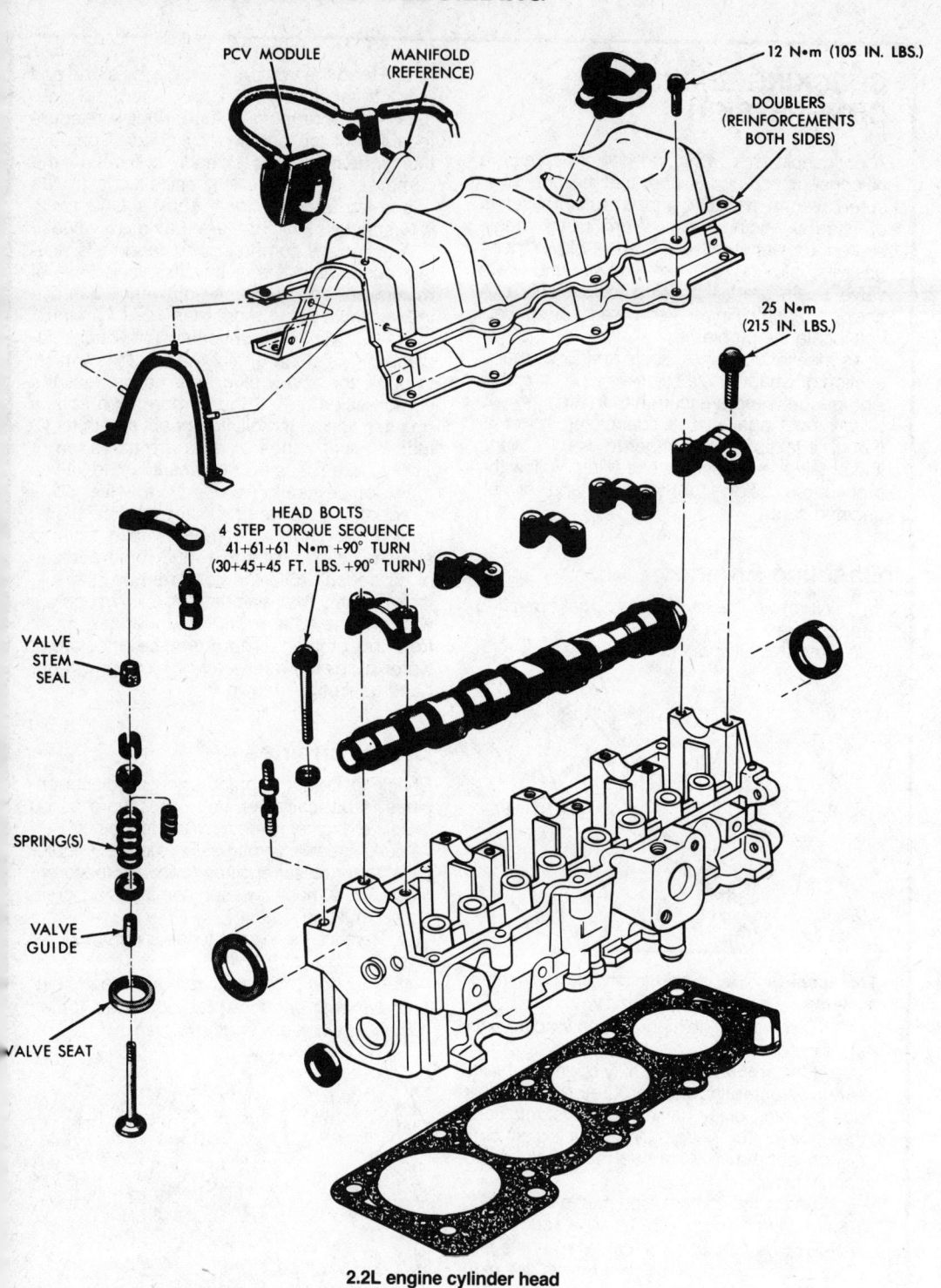

Make certain all gasket surfaces are thoroughly cleaned and are free of deep nicks or scratches. Always use new gaskets and seals. Never reuse a gasket or seal, even if it looks good. When position the head on the block, insert bolts 8 and 10 (see illustration) to align the head. Tighten bolts in the order shown to specifications. Make sure all timing marks are aligned before installing the drive belt. The drive belt is correctly tensioned when it can be twisted

ENGINE AND ENGINE REBUILDING

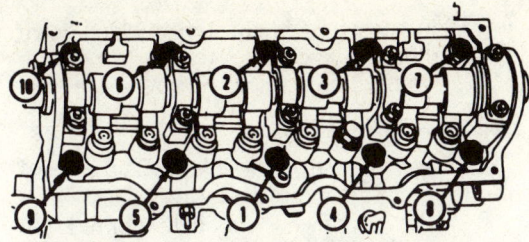

2.2L cylinder head bolt tightening sequence

90° with the thumb and index finger midway between the camshaft and the intermediate shaft.

CLEANING AND INSPECTION

NOTE: *With the cylinder head removed from the engine, the rocker arm assemblies and camshaft removed, the valves, valve springs and the valve stem oil seals can now be serviced.*

Since the machining of valve seats and valves, and the insertion of new valve guides or valve seats may tax the experience and equipment resources of the car owner, it is suggested that the cylinder head be taken to an automotive machine shop for rebuilding.

1. Remove the cylinder head from the car engine (see Cylinder Head Removal). Place the head on a workbench and remove any manifolds that are still connected. Remove all rocker arm assembly parts, if still installed and the camshaft (see Camshaft Removal).
2. Turn the cylinder head over so that the mounting surface is facing up and support evenly on wooden blocks.
3. Use a scraper and remove all of the gasket material and carbon stuck to the head mounting surface. Mount a wire carbon removal brush in an electric drill and clean away the carbon on the valve heads and head combustion chambers.

CAUTION: *When scraping or decarbonizing the cylinder head, take care not to damage or nick the gasket mounting surface or combustion chamber.*

4. Number the valve heads with a permanent felt-tipped marker for cylinder location.

RESURFACING

If the cylinder head is warped resurfacing, by an automotive machine shop, will be required. After cleaning the gasket surface, place a straightedge across the mounting surface of the head. Using feeler gauges, determine the clearance at the center and along the lengths of both diagonals. If warpage exceeds .003 inches in a six inch span, or .006 over the total length the cylinder head must be resurfaced.

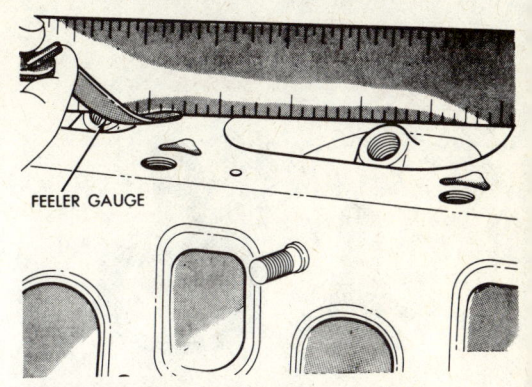

FEELER GAUGE

Checking cylinder head flatness—typical

Valves and Springs

VALVE ADJUSTMENT

The 2.2L Turbocharged and Non-Turbocharged engines both use hydraulic valve adjusters which do not require adjustment.

REMOVAL AND INSTALLATION

1. Remove the rocker arm cover.
2. For each rocker arm, rotate the cam until the base circle is in contact with the rocker arm.
3. Depress the valve spring using tool 4682 or equivalent and slide the rocker arm out. Label all rocker arms so that they may be reassembled in their original order.
4. Remove the hydraulic lash adjusters.
5. Rotate the crankshaft so that the cylinder is at TDC with the intake and exhaust valves closed.
6. With an airline adapter and an air hose installed into the spark plug hole, apply 90–120 psi of air pressure.
7. Using tool 4682 or equivalent compress the valve spring and remove the valve locks.
8. Remove the valve spring.

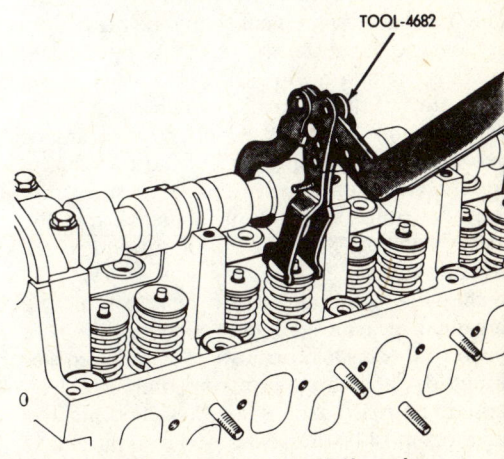

TOOL-4682

Compressing the valve spring—2.2L engine

ENGINE AND ENGINE REBUILDING

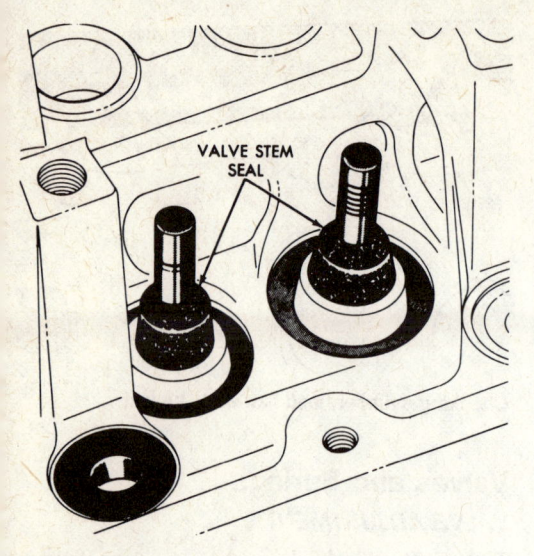

Installing valve stem seals—2.2L engine

9. Remove the seal by pulling side-to-side with a pair of long nose pliers.
10. To install, install the spring seat on each guide.
11. Place a protective cap over the end of the valve, or wrap the lock grooves with tape to prevent the edges of the valve from damaging the oil seals.
12. Install the new valve stem seals on all of the valves. The seals should be pushed firmly and squarely over the valve guide and down until it bottoms out.

NOTE: *When using tool 4682 the valve locks can become dislocated. Check to be certain that both locks are in position after removing the tool.*

13. Install the valve springs and retainers. Compress the valve spring with tool 4682 or equivalent, only enough to install the locks, being careful not to misalign the direction of compression.
14. Check the installed spring height of the springs. This measurement should be made from the lower edge of the spring to its upper edge, not including the spring seat.
15. Install the rocker arms and adjusters in their original locations. Check the clearance between the projecting ears of the rocker arm and the valve spring retainers. At least .020 in. clearance must be present, if necessary, the rocker arm ears may have to be ground to obtain this clearance.
16. Check the dry lash. Dry lash is the amount of clearance that exists between the base circle of the installed camshaft and the rocker arm pad when the adjuster is completely collapsed. Dry lash should be .024–.060 in. The adjusters must be drained to perform this check. Refill the adjuster before final assembly and allow 10 minutes for the adjusters to bleed down before rotating the cam.
17. Reinstall the rocker arm cover.

VALVE INSPECTION

1. Clean the valves thoroughly and discard burned, warped, or cracked valves.
2. If the valve face is only lightly pitted, the valve may be refaced to an angle of 45° by a qualified machine shop.
3. Measure the valve stem for wear at various points and check it against the specifications shown in the "Valve Specifications" chart.

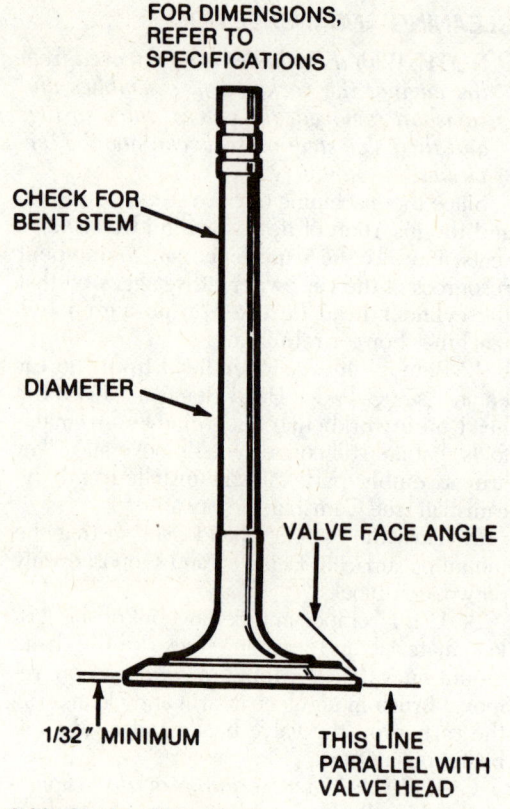

Critical valve dimensions

VALVE REFACING

Using a valve grinder, resurface the valves according to the specifications given in the "Valve Specifications" chart.

NOTE: *The valve face angle is not always identical to the valve sat angle.*

A minimum margin of 1/32 in. should remain after grinding the valve. The valve stem top should also be squared and resurfaced, by placing the stem in the V-block of the grinder, and turning it while pressing lightly against the grinding wheel.

ENGINE AND ENGINE REBUILDING 57

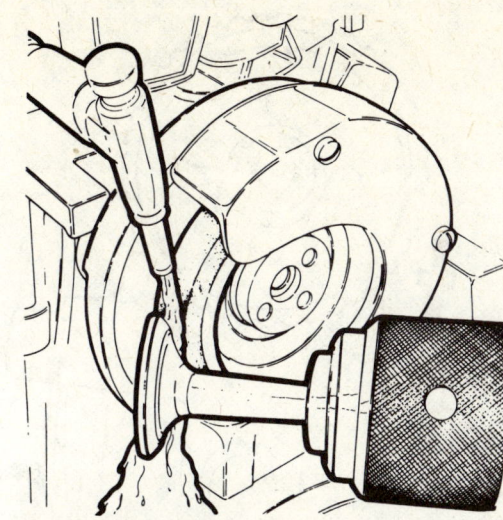

Valve grinding by machine

CHECK SPRINGS

Whenever the valves have been removed for inspection, reconditioning or replacement, the valve springs should be tested. To test the spring tension you will need special tool C-647 or equivalent. Place the spring over the stud on the table and lift the compressing lever to set the tone device. Pull on the torque wrench until a ping is heard. Take a reading on the torque wrench at this instant. Multiply this reading by two. The resulting specification is the spring load at the test length. Refer to the "Valve Specifications" chart for specifications. Inspect each valve spring for squareness with a steel square and a surface plate, test the springs from both ends. If the spring is more than 1/16 out of square, replace the spring.

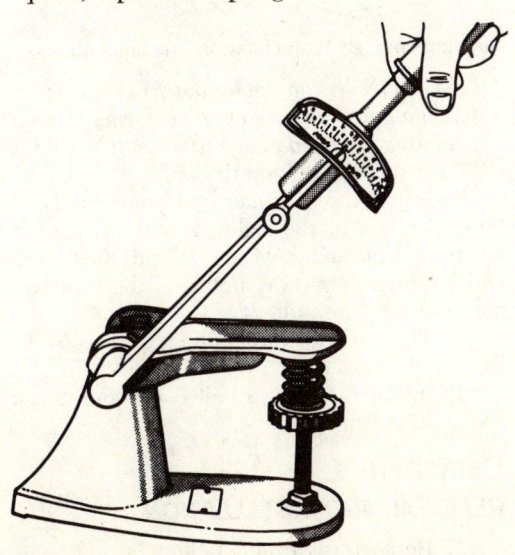

Testing the valve spring pressure with special tool C-647

Valve Guides
REMOVAL AND INSTALLATION

Valve guides are replaceable, but they should not be replaced in a cylinder head in which the valve seats cannot be refaced.

Worn guides should be pressed out from the combustion chamber side and new guides pressed in as far as they will go.

NOTE: *Service guides have a shoulder. Once the guide is seated, do not use more than 1 ton pressure or the guide could break.*

Valve Seats
REMOVAL AND INSTALLATION

Valve seats can be refaced if they are worn or burned, but the correction angle and seat width must be maintained. If not, the cylinder head must be replaced.

Intake valve seats should be ground to a 45° angle and the valve margin should not be less than 0.02 in. Check the valve stem diameter.

Exhaust valves are sodium filled and should not be ground by machine. Use lapping compound and lap by hand. Valve margin should be at least 0.02 in. Check the stem diameter. The exhaust valve seat should be ground to a 45° angle.

Intake the exhaust valves are available with stems 0.020 in. shorter than production valves. If the seats are cut too much during repairs, these shorter valves should be installed to allow the use of proper sized valve adjusting discs.

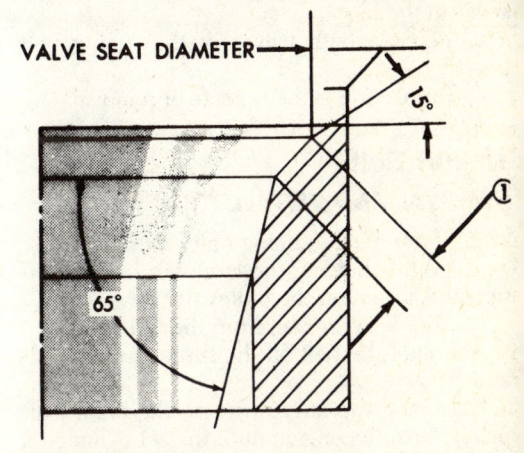

Refacing the valve seats, dimension (1) is 2.00mm (0.079 in.)

Timing Cover
REMOVAL AND INSTALLATION

1. Loosen the alternator mounting bolts, pivot the alternator and remove the drive belt.

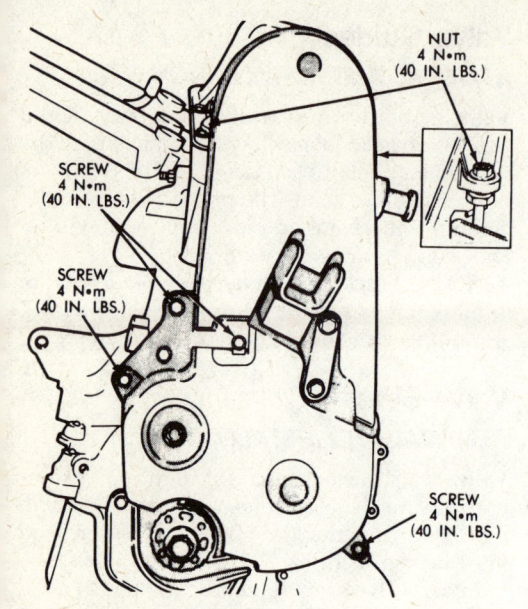

58 ENGINE AND ENGINE REBUILDING

Timing belt cover—2.2L engine

Aligning the camshaft timing marks

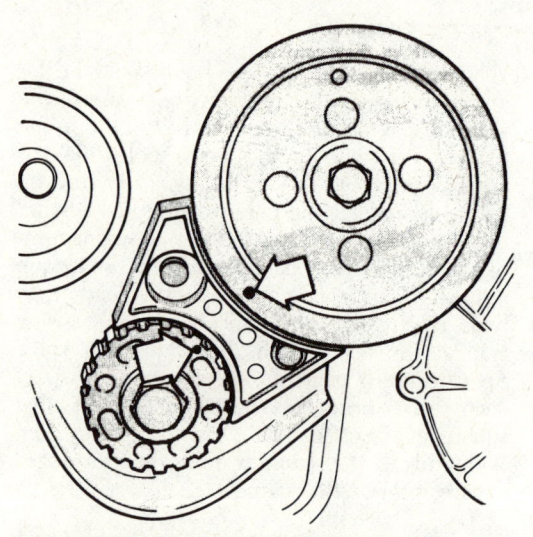

Aligning crankshaft and intermediate shaft marks

2. Do the same thing with the air conditioning compressor.
3. Remove the power steering pump locking screws. Remove the pivot bolt and nut and remove the drive belt.
4. Remove the screws retaining the water pump pulley and lay the pulley aside. Remove the bolts retaining the crankshaft pulley and remove the pulley.
5. Remove the nuts holding the cover to the cylinder head. Remove the screws holding the cover to the block.
6. Remove both halves of the timing belt cover.
7. Installation is the reverse of removal.

Timing Belt
REMOVAL AND INSTALLATION

1. Remove the timing belt cover.
2. While holding the large hex on the tension pulley, loosen the pulley nut.
3. Remove the belt from the tensioner.
4. Slide the belt off the three toothed pulleys.
5. Using the larger bolt on the crankshaft pulley, turn the engine until the #1 cylinder is at TDC of the compression stroke. At this point the valves for the #1 cylinder will be closed and the timing mark will be aligned with the pointer on the flywheel housing. Make sure that the marks on the cam sprocket and cylinder head are aligned.
6. Check that the mark in the crankshaft pulley aligns with the dot mark on the intermediate shaft.

CAUTION: *If the timing marks are not perfectly aligned, poor engine performance and probable engine damage will result!*

7. Install the belt on the pulleys.
8. Adjust the tensioner by turning the large tensioner hex to the right. Tension is correct when the belt can be twisted 90° with the thumb and forefinger, midway between the camshaft and intermediate pulleys.
9. Tighten the tensioner locknut to 32 ft. lb.
10. Install the timing belt cover and check the ignition timing.

Camshaft
REMOVAL AND INSTALLATION

1. Remove the timing belt.
2. Mark the rocker arms for installation identification.

ENGINE AND ENGINE REBUILDING

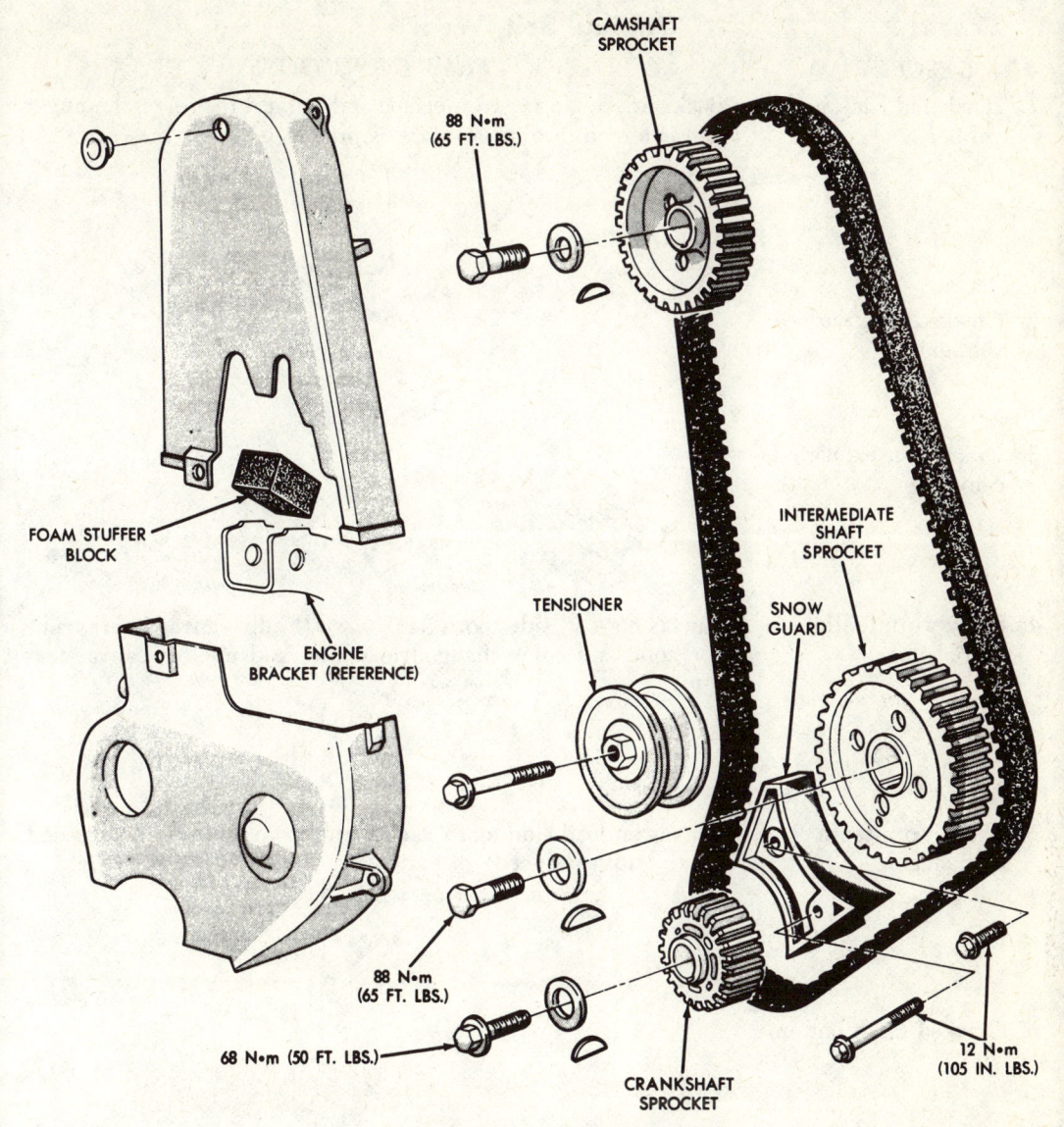

Camshaft belt drive assembly—2.2L engine

3. Loosen the camshaft bearing capnuts several turns each.

4. Using a wooden or rubber mallet, rap the rear of the camshaft a few times to break it loose.

5. Remove the capnuts and caps being very careful that the camshaft does not cock. Cocking the camshaft could cause irreparable damage to the bearings.

6. Check all oil holes for blockage.

7. Install the bearing caps with #1 at the timing belt end and #5 at the transmission end. Caps are numbered and have arrows facing forward. Cap nut torque is 14 ft. lb.

8. Apply RTV silicone gasket material as per the accompanying picture.

9. Install the bearing caps before the seals are installed.

10. The rest of the procedure is the reverse of disassembly.

CAMSHAFT ENDPLAY CHECK

1. Move the camshaft as far forward as possible.

2. Install a dial indicator as per the accompanying picture.

3. Zero the indicator, push the camshaft backward, then forward as far as possible and record the play. Maximum play should be .006 in.

60 ENGINE AND ENGINE REBUILDING

Timing Belt Wear

DESCRIPTION	FLAW CONDITIONS
1. Hardened back surface rubber	Back surface glossy. Non-elastic and so hard that even if a finger nail is forced into it, no mark is produced.
2. Cracked back surface rubber	
3. Cracked or exfoliated canvas	
4. Badly worn teeth (initial stage)	Canvas on load side tooth flank worn (Fluffy canvas fibers, rubber gone and color changed to white, and unclear canvas texture)
5. Badly worn teeth (last stage)	Canvas on load side tooth flank worn down and rubber exposed (tooth width reduced)
6. Cracked tooth bottom	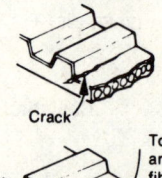
7. Missing tooth	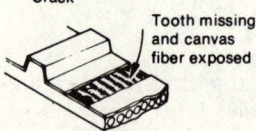
8. Side of belt badly worn	
9. Side of belt cracked	NOTE: *Normal belt should have clear-cut sides as if cut by a sharp knife.*

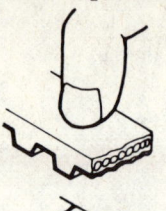

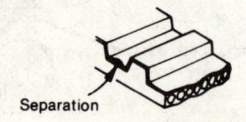

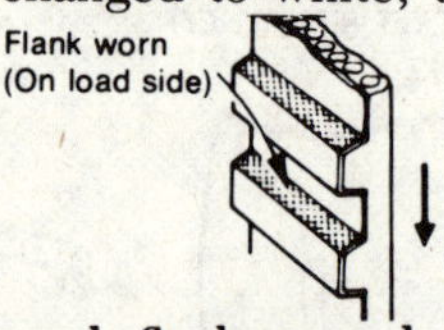

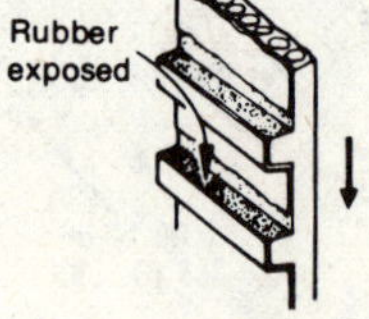

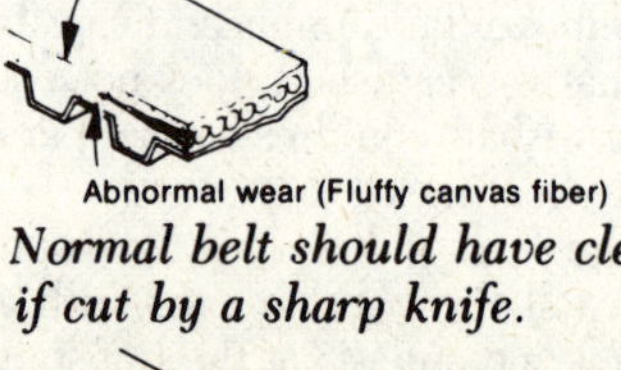

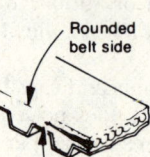

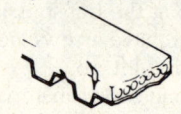

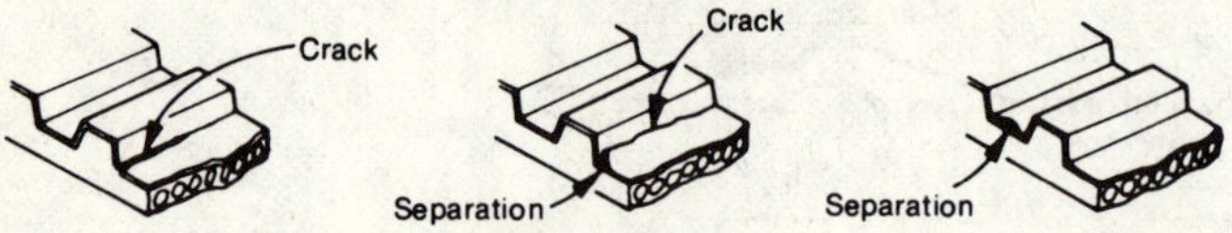

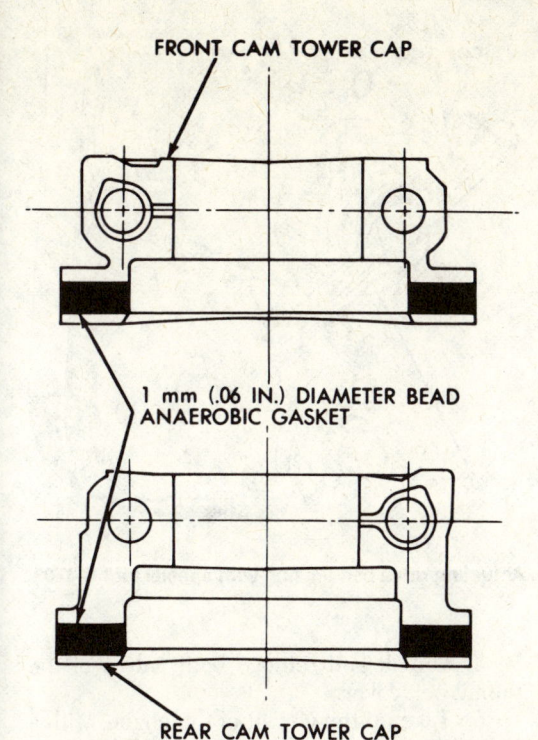

ENGINE AND ENGINE REBUILDING

2.2L engine camshaft tower cap showing sealer location

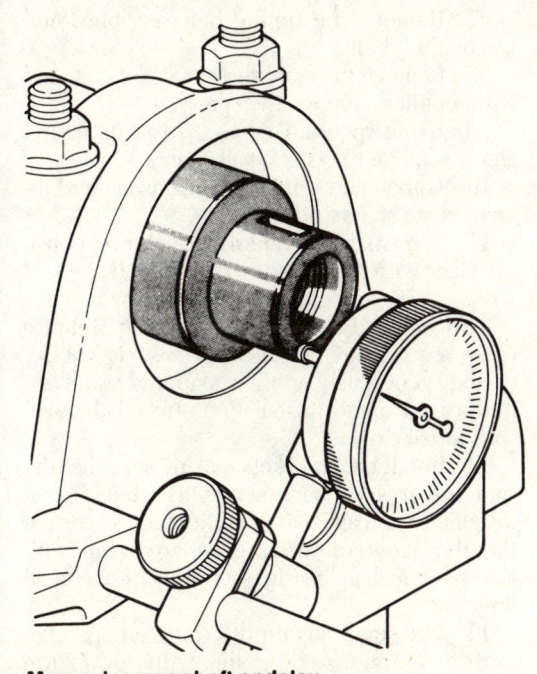

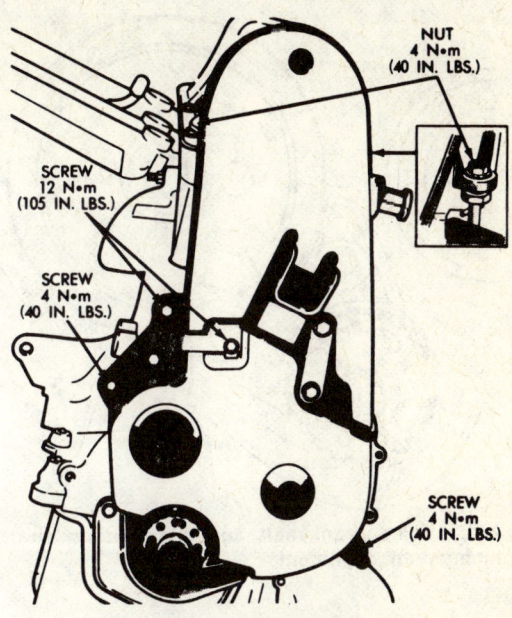

2.2L engine front cover installation

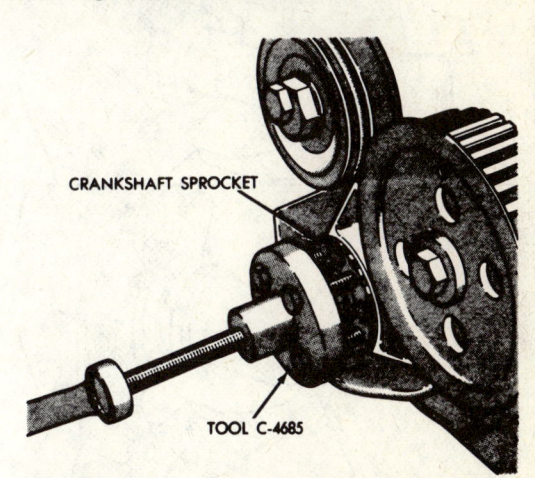

2.2L engine crankshaft sprocket removal

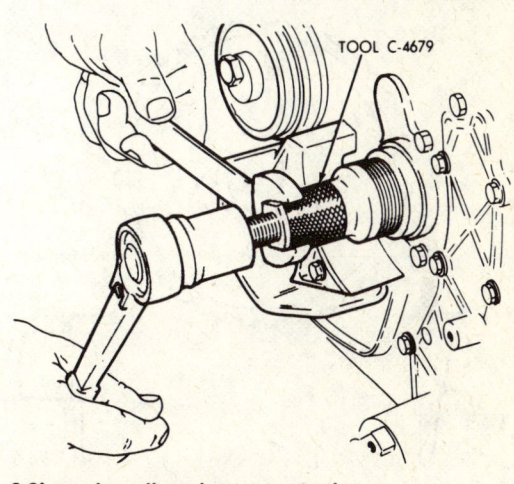

Measuring camshaft endplay

2.2L engine oil seal remover tool

Timing Sprockets and Oil Seal
REMOVAL AND INSTALLATION

1. Raise and support the car on jackstands.
2. Remove the right inner splash shield.
3. Remove the crankshaft pulley.

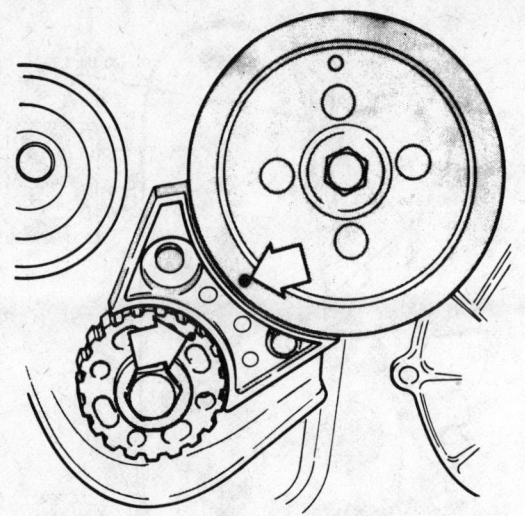

ENGINE AND ENGINE REBUILDING

2.2L engine crankshaft and intermediate shaft timing mark alignment

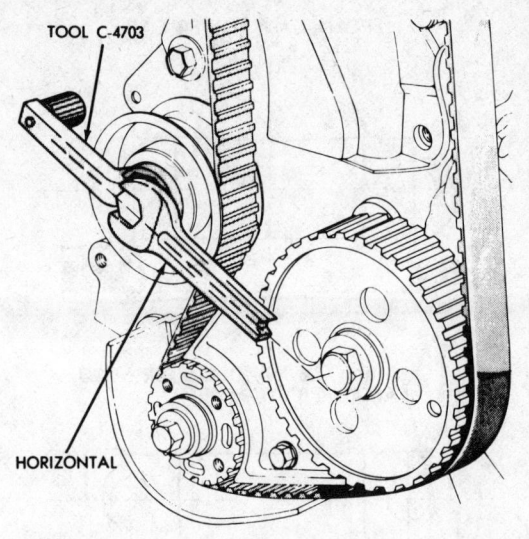

Adjusting drive belt tension with special tool C-4703

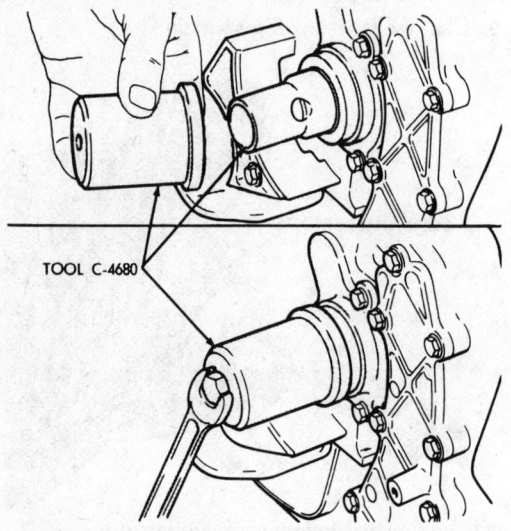

Installing the shaft seal on any of the 2.2L engine shafts

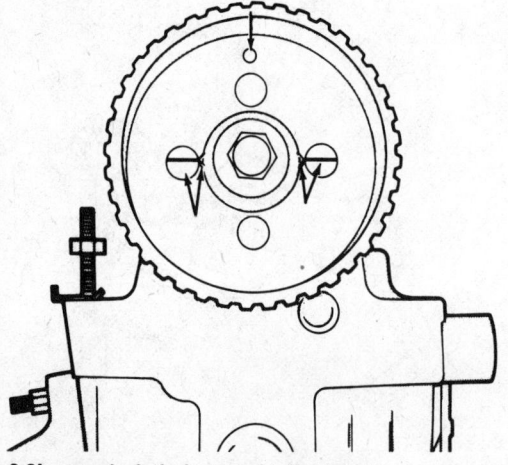

2.2L camshaft timing mark alignment

4. Unbolt and remove both halves of the timing belt cover.
5. Take up the weight of the engine with a jack.
6. Remove the right engine mount bolt and raise the engine slightly.
7. Remove the timing belt tensioner and remove the belt.
8. Remove the crankshaft sprocket bolt, and with a puller, remove the sprocket.
9. Using special Tool C-4679 or its equivalent, remove the crankshaft seal.
10. Unbolt and remove the camshaft and intermediate shaft sprockets.
11. To install the crankshaft seal, first polish the shaft with 400 grit emery paper. If the seal has a steel case, lightly coat the outer diameter of the seal with Loctite Stud N' Bearing Mount® or its equivalent. If the seal case is rubber coated, generously apply a soap and water solution to facilitate installation. Install the seal with a seal driver.
12. Install the sprockets making sure that the timing marks are aligned as illustrated. When installing the camshaft sprocket, make certain that the arrows on the sprocket are in line with the #1 camshaft bearing cap-to-cylinder head line.
13. The small hole in the camshaft sprocket must be at the top and in line with the vertical center line of the engine.
14. Rotate the engine two full revolutions and recheck timing mark positioning.
15. Install the belt.
16. Rotate the engine to the #1 piston TDC position.
17. Install the belt tensioner and place tool C-4703 on the large hex nut.

ENGINE AND ENGINE REBUILDING 63

18. Reset the belt tension so that the axis of the tool is about 15° off of horizontal.

19. Turn the engine clockwise two full revolutions to #1 TDC.

20. Tighten the tensioner locknut using a weighted tool C-4703 as shown in the illustration. Torques: Timing belt cover bolts, 105 inch lbs.; Camshaft sprocket bolt, 65 ft. lbs.; Crankshaft sprocket bolt, 50 ft. lbs; Intermediate shaft sprocket bolt, 65 ft. lbs.

Piston and Connecting Rods

REMOVAL AND INSTALLATION

1. Follow the instructions under "Cylinder Head" removal and "Timing Belt" removal.

2. Remove the oil pan as described later in this chapter.

3. This procedure is much easier performed with the engine out of the car.

4. Pistons should be removed in the order: 1-3-4-2. Turn the crankshaft until the piston to be removed is at the bottom of its stroke.

5. Place a cloth on the head of the piston to be removed and, using a ridge reamer, remove the deposits from the upper end of the cylinder bore.

NOTE: *Never remove more than 1/32 in. from the ring travel area when removing the ridges.*

6. Mark all connecting rod bearing caps so that they may be returned to their original locations in the engine. The connecting rod caps

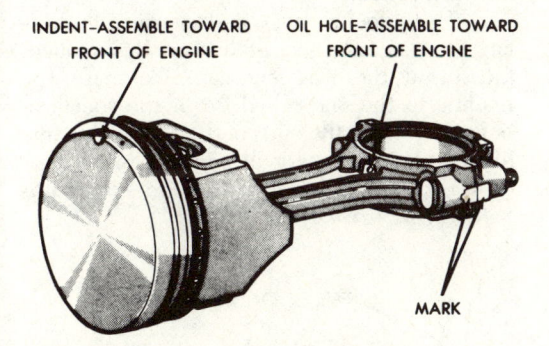

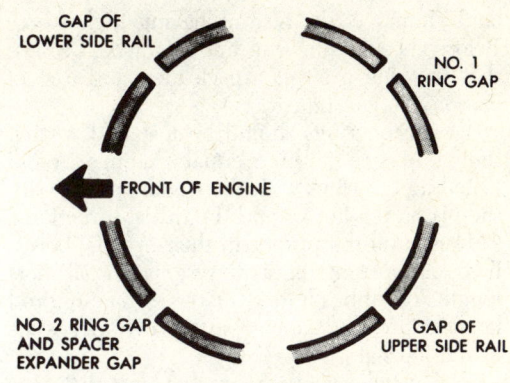

2.2L piston ring gap positioning

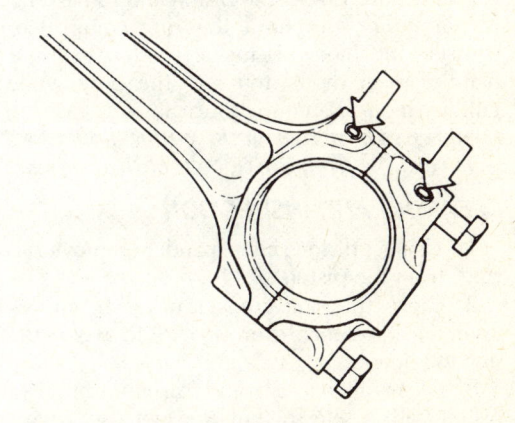

Connecting rod match marks

2.2L engine piston and connecting rod

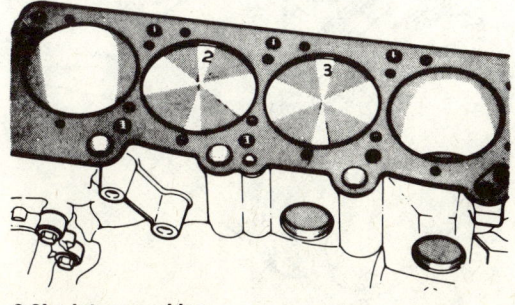

2.2L piston marking

are marked with rectangular forge marks which must be mated during assembly and be installed on the intermediate shaft side of the engine. Mark all pistons so they can be returned to their original cylinders.

CAUTION: *Don't score the cylinder walls or the crankshaft journal.*

7. Using an internal micrometer, measure the bores across the thrust faces of the cylinder and parallel to the axis of the crankshaft at a minimum of four equally spaced locations. The bore must not be out-of-round by more than 0.005 in. and it must not taper more than 0.010 in. Taper is the difference in wear between two bore measurements in any cylinder.

8. If the cylinder bore is in satisfactory condition, place each ring in the bore in turn and square it in the bore with the head of the piston. Measure the ring gap. If the ring gap is greater than the limit, get a new ring. If the ring gap is less than the limit, file the end of the ring to obtain the correct gap.

9. Check the ring side clearance by installing rings on the piston, and inserting a feeler gauge of the correct dimension between the ring and the lower land. The gauge should slide freely around the ring circumference without binding. Any wear will form a step on the lower

ENGINE AND ENGINE REBUILDING

land. Remove any pistons having high steps. Before checking the ring side clearance, be sure that the ring grooves are cleaned and free of carbon, sludge, or grit.

10. Piston rings should be installed so that their ends are at three equal spacings. Avoid installing the rings with their ends in line with the piston pin bosses and the thrust direction.

11. Install the pistons in their original bores, if you are reusing the same pistons. Install short lengths of rubber hose over the connecting rod bolts to prevent damage to the cylinder walls or rod journal.

12. Install a ring compressor over the rings on the piston. Lower the piston and rod assembly into the bore until the ring compressor contacts the block. Using a wooden hammer handle, push the piston into the bore while guiding the rod onto the journal.

NOTE: *The arrow on the piston should face toward the front (drive bolt) of the engine.*

CLEANING AND INSPECTION

1. Using a piston ring expander, remove the rings from the piston.
2. Clean the ring grooves using an appropriate cleaning tool, exercise care to avoid cutting too deeply.
3. Clean all varnish and carbon from the piston with a safe solvent. Do not use a wire brush or caustic solution on the pistons.
4. Inspect the pistons for scuffing, scoring, cracks, pitting or excessive ring groove wear. If wear is evident, the piston must be replaced.
5. Have the piston and connecting rod assembly checked by a machine shop for correct alignment, piston pin wear and piston diameter. If the piston has "collapsed" it will have to be replaced or knurled to restore original diameter. Connecting rod bushings replacement, piston pin fitting and piston changing can be handled by the machine shop.

CYLINDER BORE

Check the cylinder bore for wearing using a telescope gauge and a micrometer, measure the cylinder bore diameter perpendicular to the piston pin at a point 2½ inches below the top of the engine block. Measure the piston skirt perpendicular to the piston pin. The difference between the two measurements is the piston clearance. If the clearance is within specifications, finish honing or glaze breaking is all that is required. If clearance is excessive a slightly oversize piston may be required. If greatly oversized, the engine will have to be bored and .010 inch or larger oversized pistons installed.

PISTON PINS

The pin connecting the piston and connecting rod is press fitted. If too much free play devel-

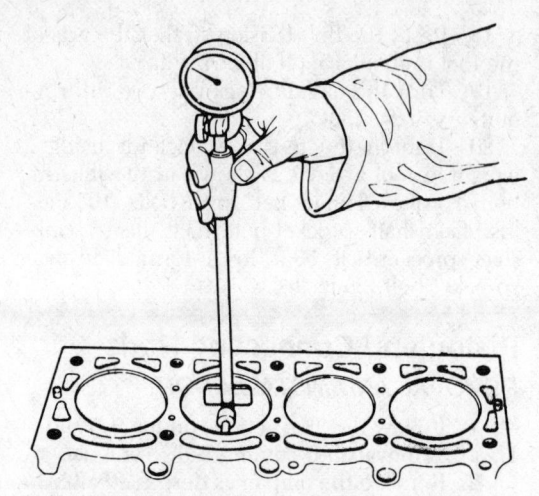

Checking the cylinder bore with a bore gauge

ops take the piston assemblies to the machine shop and have oversize pins installed. Installing new rods or pistons requires the use of a press—have the machine shop handle the job for you.

Fitting and Positioning Piston Rings

1. Take the new piston rings and compress them, one at a time into the cylinder that they will be used in. Press the ring about one inch below the top of the cylinder block using an inverted piston.
2. Use a feeler gauge and measure the distance between the ends of the ring, this is called, measuring the ring end-gap. Compare the reading to the one called for in the specifications table. File the ends of the ring with a fine file to obtain necessary clearance.

NOTE: *If inadequate ring end-gap is utilized ring breakage will result.*

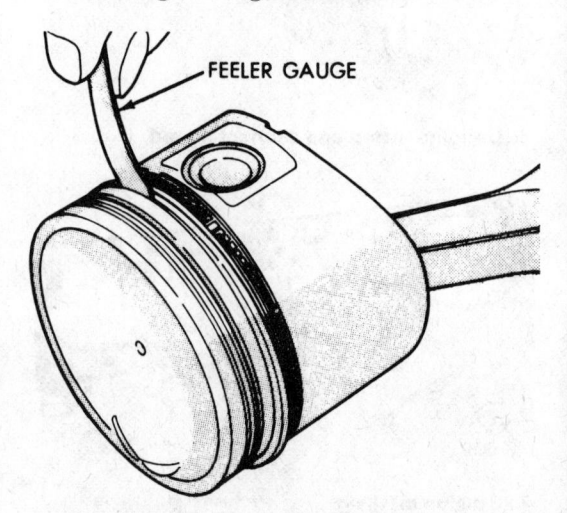

Checking the piston ring side clearance

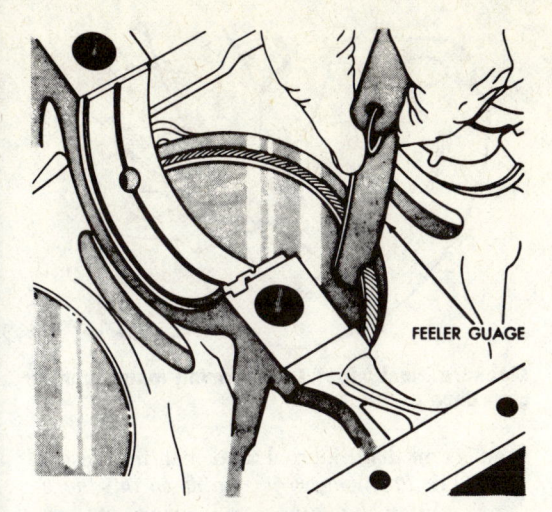

ENGINE AND ENGINE REBUILDING 65

from the butted end of the control but on the opposite side from the lower rail.

7. Install the two compression rings.

8. Consult the illustration with piston ring set instruction sheet for ring positioning, arrange the rings as shown, install a ring compressor and insert the piston and rod assembly into the engine.

Crankshaft and Bearings

1. Rod bearings can be installed when the pistons have been removed for servicing (rings etc.) or, in most cases, while the engine is still in the car. Bearing replacement, however, is far easier with the engine out of the car and disassembled.

2. For in car service, remove the oil pan, spark plugs and front cover if necessary. Turn the engine until the connecting rod to be serviced is at the bottom of it's travel. Remove the bearing cap place two pieces of rubber hose over the rod cap bolts and push the piston and rod assembly up the cylinder bore until enough room is gained for bearing insert removal. Take care not to push the rod assembly up too far or the top ring will engage the cylinder ridge or come out of the cylinder and require head removal for reinstallation.

3. Clean the rod journal, connecting rod end and the bearing cap after removing the old bearing inserts. Install the new inserts in the rod and bearing cap, lubricate them with oil. Position the rod over the crankshaft journal and install the rod caps. Make sure the cap and rod

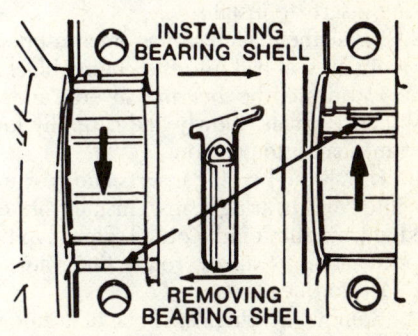

Checking the piston ring end gap

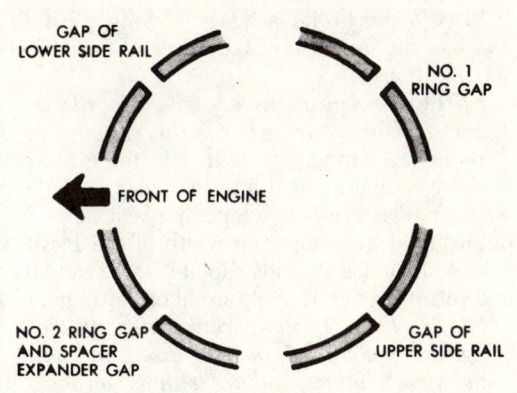

Piston ring end gap positioning

3. Inspect the ring grooves on the piston for excessive wear or taper. If necessary have the grooves recut for use with a standard ring and spacer. The machine shop can handle the job for you.

4. Check the ring groove by rolling the new piston ring around the groove to check for burrs or carbon deposits. If any are found, remove with a fine file. Hold the ring in the groove and measure side clearance with a feeler gauge. If clearance is excessive, spacer(s) will have to be added.

NOTE: *Always add spacers above the piston ring.*

5. Install the rings on the piston, lower ring first using a ring installing tool. Consult the instruction sheet that comes with the rings to be sure they are installed with the correct side up. A mark on the ring usually faces upward.

6. When installing oil rings, first, install the ring in the groove. Hold the ends of the ring butted together (they must not overlap) and install the bottom rail (scraper) with the end about one inch away from the butted end of the control ring. Install the top rail about an inch away

Remove or install the upper bearing insert using a roll-out pin

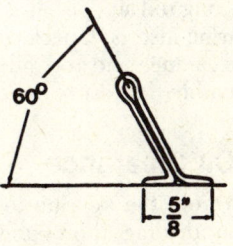

Home-made bearing roll-out pin

numbers match, torque the rod nuts to specifications.

4. Main bearings may be replaced while the engine is still in the car by "rolling" them out and in.

5. Special roll-out pins are available from automotive parts houses or can be fabricated from a cotter pin. The roll out pin fits in the oil hole of the main bearing journal. When the crankshaft is rotated opposite the direction of the bearing lock tab, the pin engages the end of the bearing and "rolls" out the insert.

6. Remove main bearing cap and roll out upper bearing insert. Remove insert from main bearing cap. Clean the inside of the bearing cap and crankshaft journal.

7. Lubricate and roll upper insert into position, make sure the lock tab is anchored and the insert is not "cocked". Install the lower bearing insert into the cap; lubricate and install on the engine. Make sure the main bearing cap is installed facing in the correct direction and torque to specifications.

8. With the engine out of the car. Remove the intake manifold, cylinder head, front cover, timing gears and/or chain, oil pan, oil pump and flywheel.

9. Remove the piston and rod assemblies. remove the main bearing caps after marking them for position and direction.

10. Remove the crankshaft bearing inserts and rear main oil seal. Clean the engine block and cap bearing saddles. Clean the crankshaft and inspect for wear. Check the bearing journals with a micrometer for out-of-round condition and to determine what size rod and main bearing inserts to install.

11. Install the main bearing upper inserts and rear main oil seal half into the engine block.

12. Lubricate the bearing inserts and the crankshaft journals. Slowly and carefully lower the crankshaft into position.

13. Install the bearing inserts and rear main seal into the bearing caps, install the caps working from the middle out. Troque cap bolts to specification in stages, rotate the crankshaft after each torque stage.

14. Remove bearing caps, one at a time and check the oil clearance with Plastigage®. Reinstall if clearance is within specifications. Check the crankshaft end-play, if within specifications install connecting rod and piston assemblies with new rod bearing inserts. Check connecting rod bearing oil clearance and rod side play, if correct and assemble the rest of the engine.

Bearing Oil Clearance

Remove cap from the bearing to be checked. Using a clean, dry rag, thoroughly clean all oil

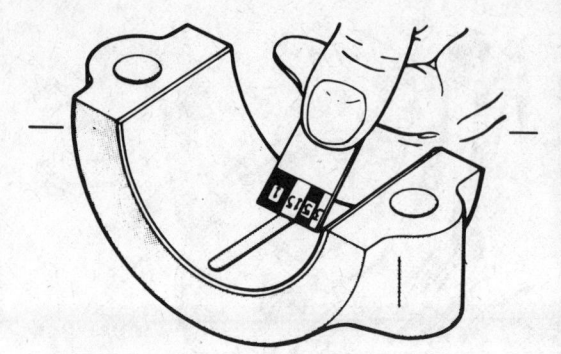

Measure Plastigage® to determine main bearing clearance

from crankshaft journal and bearing insert.
NOTE: *Plastigage® is soluble in oil; therefore, oil on the journal or bearing could result in erroneous readings.*

Place a piece of Plastigage® along the full width of the insert, reinstall cap, and torque to specifications.

NOTE: *Specifications are given in the engine specifications earlier in this chapter.*

Remove bearing cap, and determine clearance by comparing width of Plastigage® to the scale on Plastigage envelope. Journal taper is determined by comparing width of the Plastigage® strip near its ends. Rotate crankshaft 90° and retest, to determine journal eccentricity.

NOTE: *Do not rotate crankshaft with Plastigage® installed. If bearing insert and journal appear intact, and are within tolerances, no further main bearing service is required. If bearing or journal appear defective, cause of failure should be determined before replacement.*

Crankshaft End-Play/Connecting Rod Side Play

Place a pry bar between a main bearing cap and crankshaft casting taking care not to damage any journals. Pry backward and forward measure the distance between the thrust bearing (center main 3) and crankshaft with a feeler gauge. Compare reading with specifications. If too great a clearance is determined, a larger thrust bearing or crank machine may be required. Check with an automotive machine shop for their advice.

Connecting rod clearance between the rod and crankthrow casting can be checked with a feeler gauge. Pry the rod carefully to one side as far as possible and measure the distance on the other side of the rod.

Crankshaft Repairs

If a journal is damaged on the crankshaft, repair is possible by having the crankshaft ma-

ENGINE AND ENGINE REBUILDING

chined, after removal from engine to a standard undersize. Consult the machine shop for their advice.

Oil Pan
REMOVAL AND INSTALLATION
1. Drain the oil pan.
2. Support the pan and remove the attaching bolts.
3. Lower the pan and discard the gaskets.
4. Clean all gasket surfaces thoroughly and install the pan using RTV sealer.
5. Torque the pan bolts to 17 ft. lbs.
6. Refill the pan, start the engine, and check for leaks.

Oil Pump
REMOVAL AND INSTALLATION
1. Remove the oil pan.
2. Remove the two pump mounting bolts.
3. Pull the oil pump down and out of the engine.
4. Installation is the reverse of removal. Torque pump mounting bolts to 9 ft.

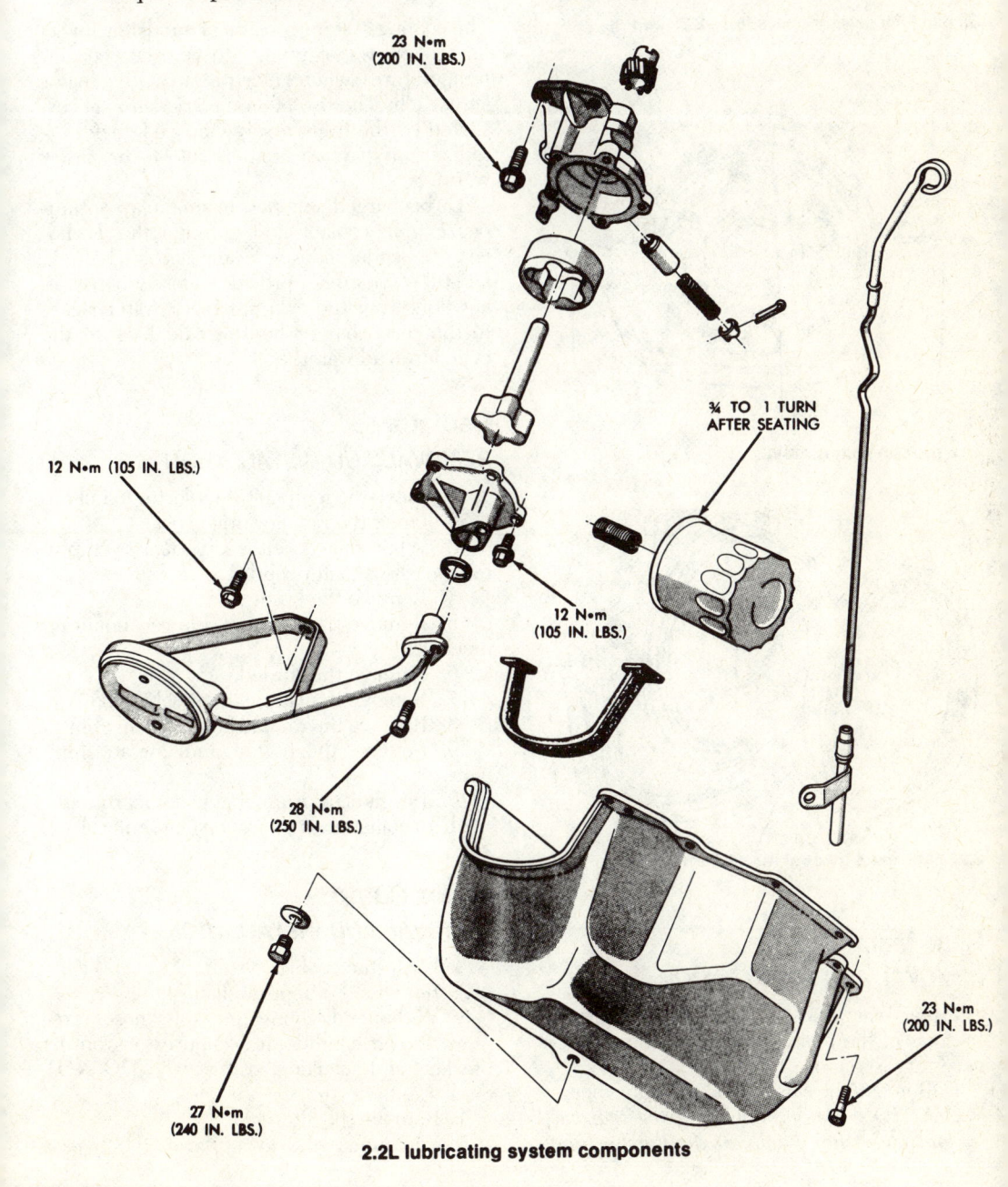

2.2L lubricating system components

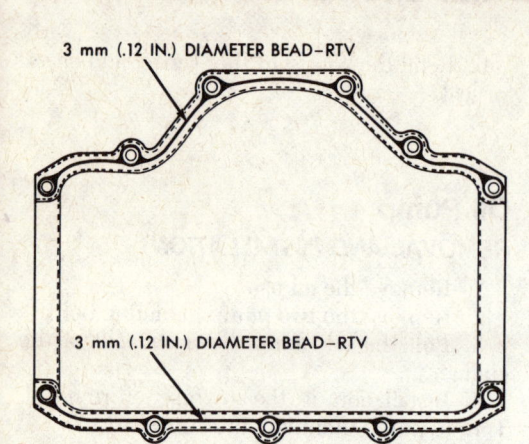

68 ENGINE AND ENGINE REBUILDING

Oil pan RTV sealer application—2.2L engine

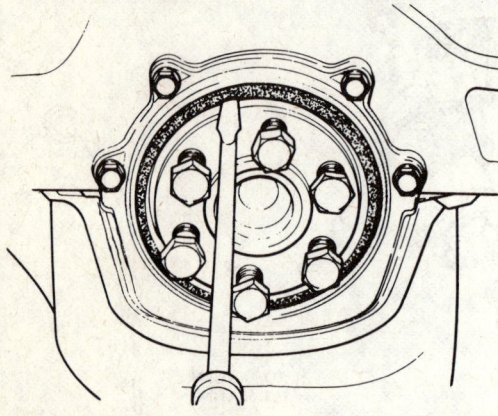

2.2L rear oil seal removal

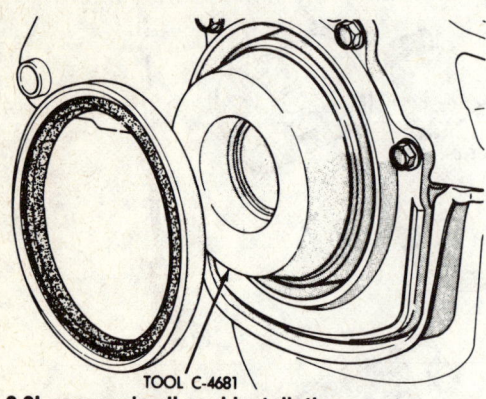

2.2L rear main oil seal installation

Rear Main Seal
REMOVAL AND INSTALLATION

The rear main seal is located in a housing on the rear of the block. To replace the seal it is necessary to remove the engine.

1. Remove the transmission and flywheel.
   CAUTION: *Before removing the transmission, align the dimple on the flywheel with the pointer on the flywheel housing. The transmission will not mate with the engine during installation unless this alignment is observed.*
2. Very carefully, pry the old seal out of the support ring with a suitable tool.
3. Coat the new seal with clean engine oil and press it into place with a flat piece of metal. Take great care not to scratch the seal or crankshaft.
4. Install the flywheel and transmission.

ENGINE COOLING

The cooling system consists of a radiator, overflow tank, water pump, thermostat, coolant temperature switch, electric fan and radiator fan switch. The use of an electric fan is necessitated by the transversely mounted engine. A radiator bypass system is used for faster warmup.

Turbocharged engines maintain a continuous engine coolant flow through the Turbocharger bearing housing water jacket. The hose and tube assemblies provide a closed loop coolant flow from the cylinder block water jacket to the turbocharger housing and back to the cylinder head waterbox.

Radiator
REMOVAL AND INSTALLATION

1. Move the temperature selector to full on.
2. Open the radiator drain cock.
3. When the coolant reserve tank is empty, remove the radiator cap.
4. Remove the hoses.
5. Remove the upper and lower mounting brackets.
6. Remove the shroud.
7. Remove the fan motor attaching bolts.
8. Remove the top radiator attaching bolts.
9. Remove the bottom radiator attaching bolts.
10. Lift radiator from engine compartment.
11. Installation is the reverse of removal.

Water Pump
REMOVAL AND INSTALLATION

1. Drain the cooling system.
2. Remove the upper radiator hose.
3. Without disconnecting any hoses, remove the air conditioning compressor from its brackets and set it out of the way. DO NOT discharge the system.
4. Remove the alternator.
5. Disconnect the lower hose, the bypass

ENGINE AND ENGINE REBUILDING 69

Cooling system operation

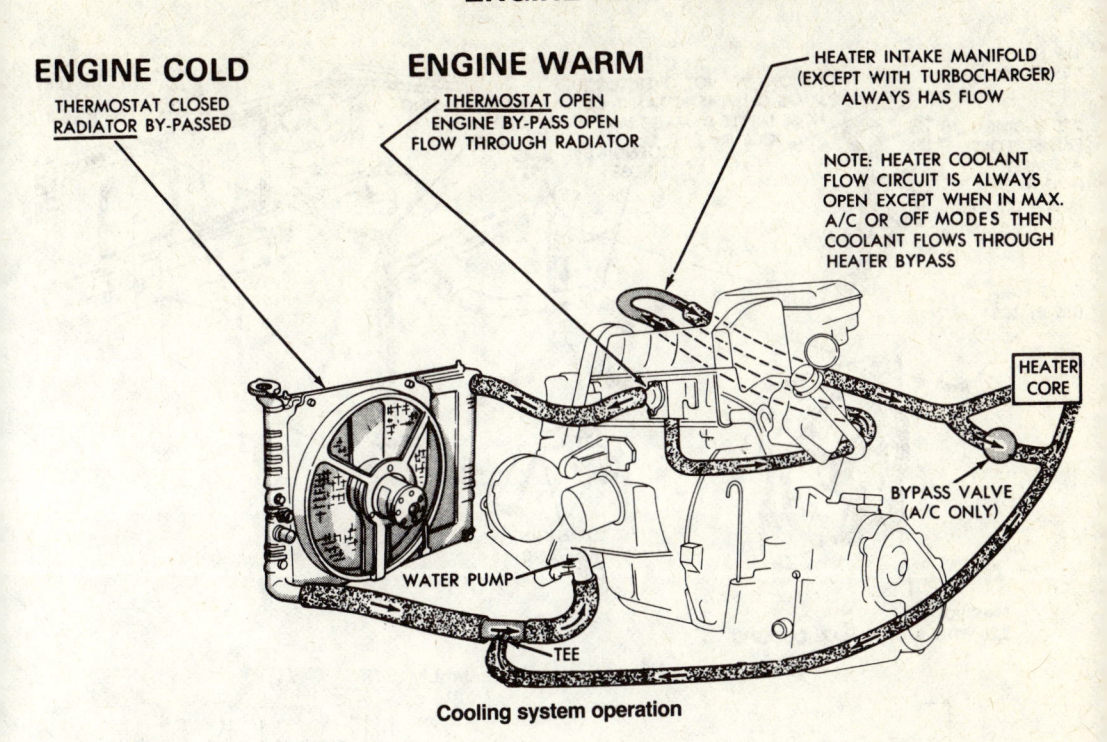

hose and then, unbolt and remove the water pump.

6. Installation is the reverse of removal. Torque the three upper bolts to 20 ft. lbs.; the lower bolt to 50 ft. lbs.

Thermostat

REMOVAL AND INSTALLATION

1. Drain the cooling system to a level below the thermostat.
2. Remove the hose(s) from the thermostat housing.
3. Remove the thermostat housing.
4. Remove the thermostat and discard the gasket. Clean the gasket surfaces thoroughly.
5. Using a new gasket, position the thermostat and install the housing and bolts. Make sure that the thermostat is seated properly.
6. Refill the cooling system.

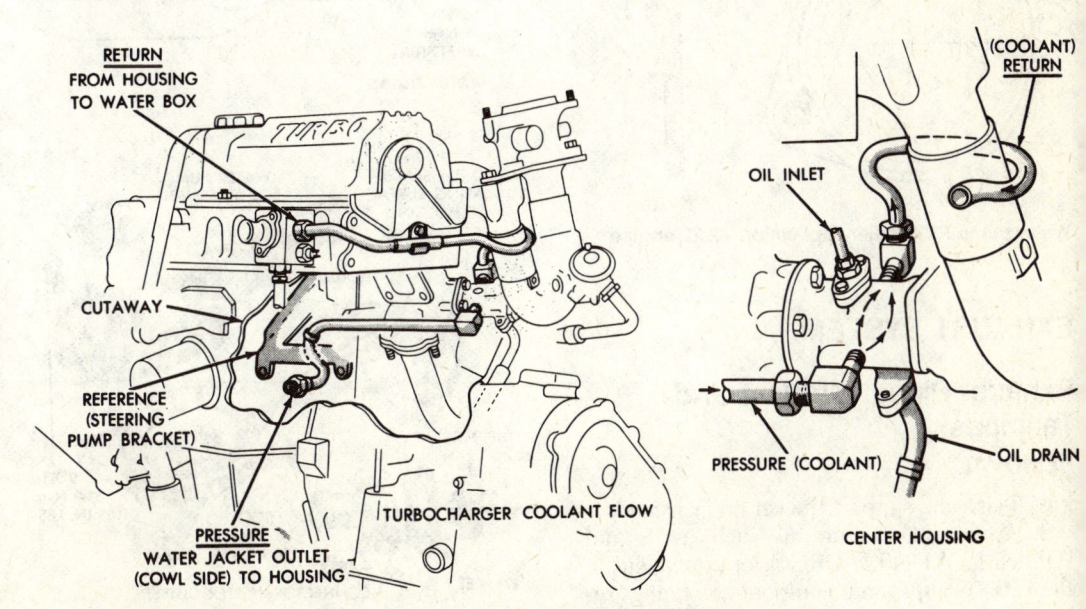

Coolant routing for the turbocharger (bearing) housing

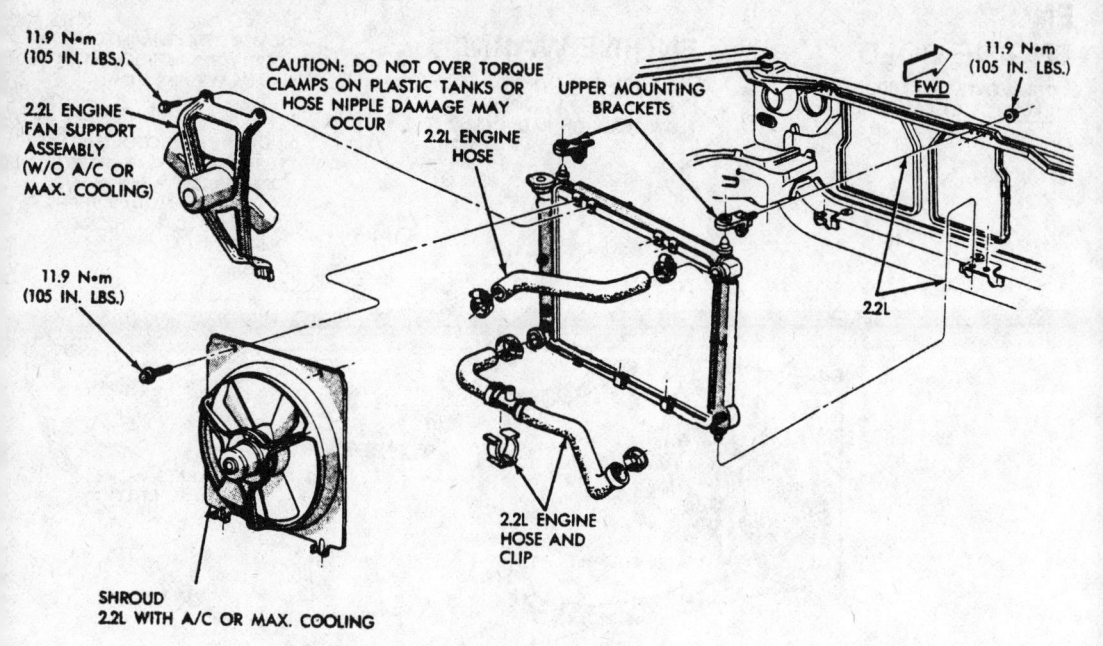

70 ENGINE AND ENGINE REBUILDING

Radiator and electric fan assembly

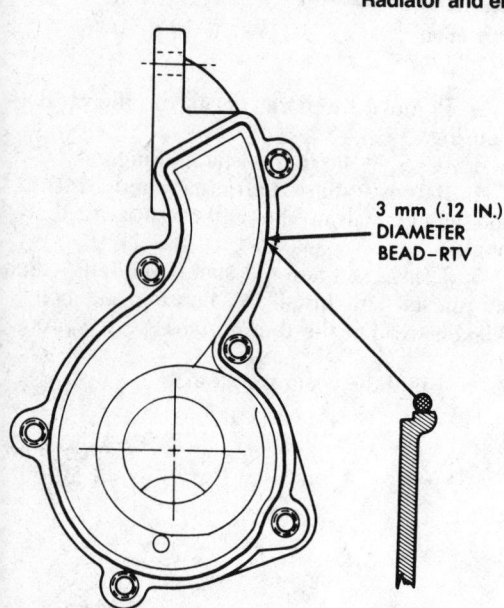

Water pump RTV sealer application—2.2L engine

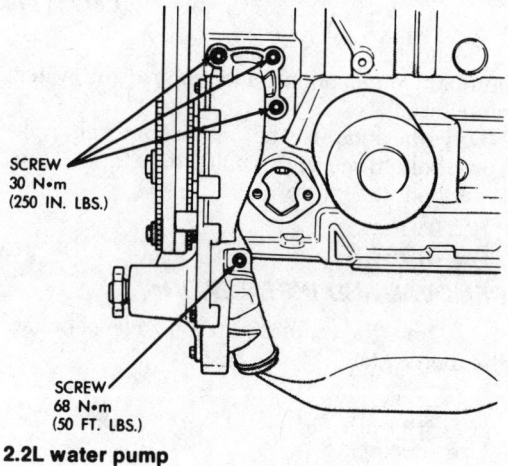

2.2L water pump

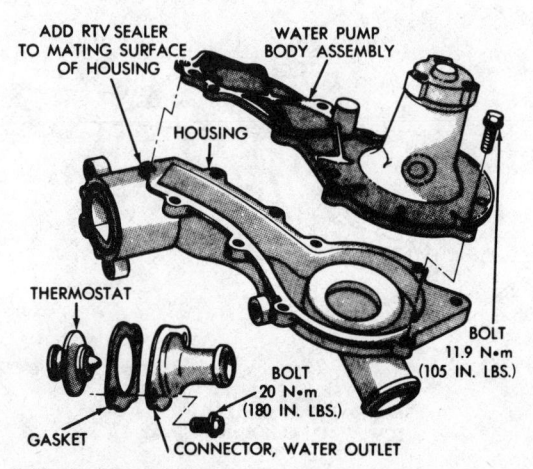

2.2L thermostat and water pump

EXHAUST SYSTEM

Exhaust Pipes, Mufflers and Tailpipes

REMOVAL

1. Raise and support the car on jackstands.
2. Apply penetrating oil such as Liquid Wrench®, WD-40®, CRC®, or equivalent to all nuts, clamps and components being removed. Let stand while the penetrants act.

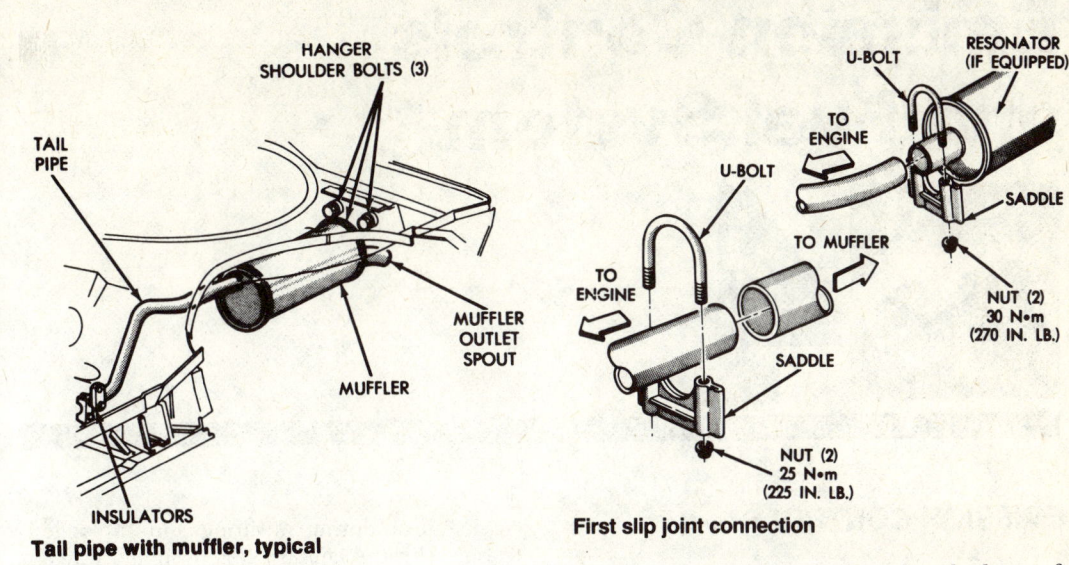

ENGINE AND ENGINE REBUILDING 71

Tail pipe with muffler, typical

First slip joint connection

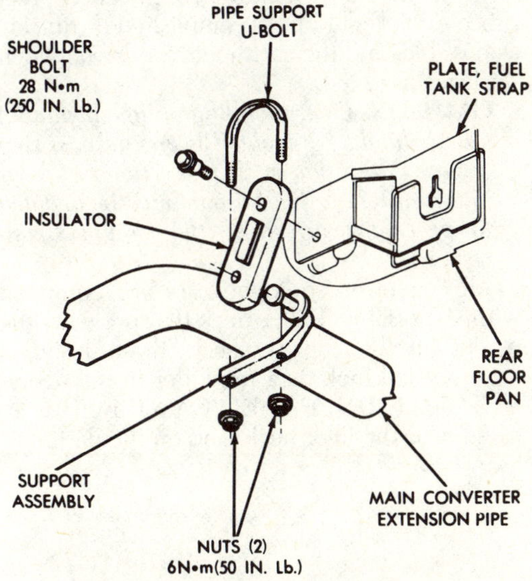

3. If the tail pipe is integral with the muffler, (most original pipes), cut the tail pipe close to the muffler with a hacksaw or pipe cutter.
4. Remove all clamps and supports from the exhaust system to aid in proper alignment of components when installing aftermarket parts.
5. When removing the tail pipe, raise and support the rear of the car to take the weight off of the springs and to provide clearance for parts removal.
6. Thoroughly clean the mating ends of all parts with a wire brush, making sure that they are free of rust, dirt and scale. Discard all worn, rusted or broken clamps and insulators.

INSTALLATION

1. Assemble all parts, clamps, supports and insulators loosely, to provide for proper alignment.
2. Beginning at the front of the system, align and clamp each part maintaining proper clearance between parts and body members.
3. Tighten all clamps and supports.

Underfloor converter extension pipe support

Proper exhaust system clearance chart

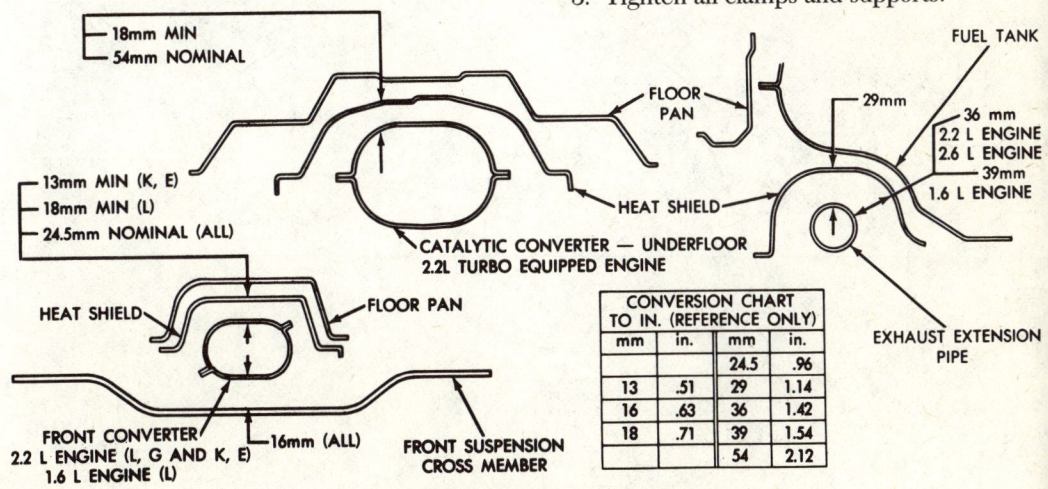

CONVERSION CHART TO IN. (REFERENCE ONLY)				
mm	in.	mm	in.
		24.5	.96
13	.51	29	1.14
16	.63	36	1.42
18	.71	39	1.54
		54	2.12

Emission Controls and Fuel System 4

EMISSION CONTROLS

Several different systems are used on each car. Most require no service and those which may require service also require sophisticated equipment for testing purposes. Following is a brief description of each system.

Catalytic Converter

Two catalysts are used in a small one located just after the exhaust manifold and a larger one located under the car body. Catalysts promote complete oxidation of exhaust gases through the effect of a platinum coated mass in the catalyst shell. Two things act to destroy the catalyst, functionally: excessive heat and leaded gas. Excessive heat during misfiring and prolonged testing with the ignition system in any way altered is the most common occurrence. Test procedures should be accomplished as quickly as possible, and the car should be driven when misfiring as noted.

CAUTION: *Operation of any type including idling should be avoided if engine misfiring occurs. Alteration or deterioration of the ignition system or fuel system must be avoided to prevent overheating the catalytic converter.*

All converter equipped cars are equipped with a special fuel filler neck that prevents the use of any filler nozzle except those designed for unleaded fuel. As a reminder to the operator, a decal "UNLEADED GASOLINE" is located near the filler neck, and on the dash.

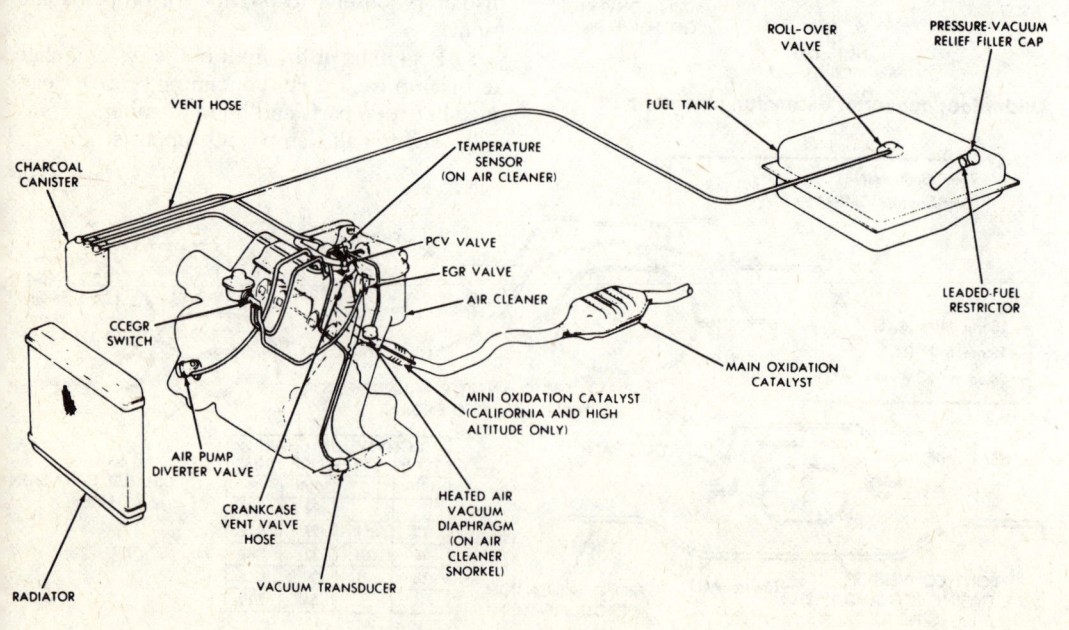

Emission control system

EMISSION CONTROLS AND FUEL SYSTEM

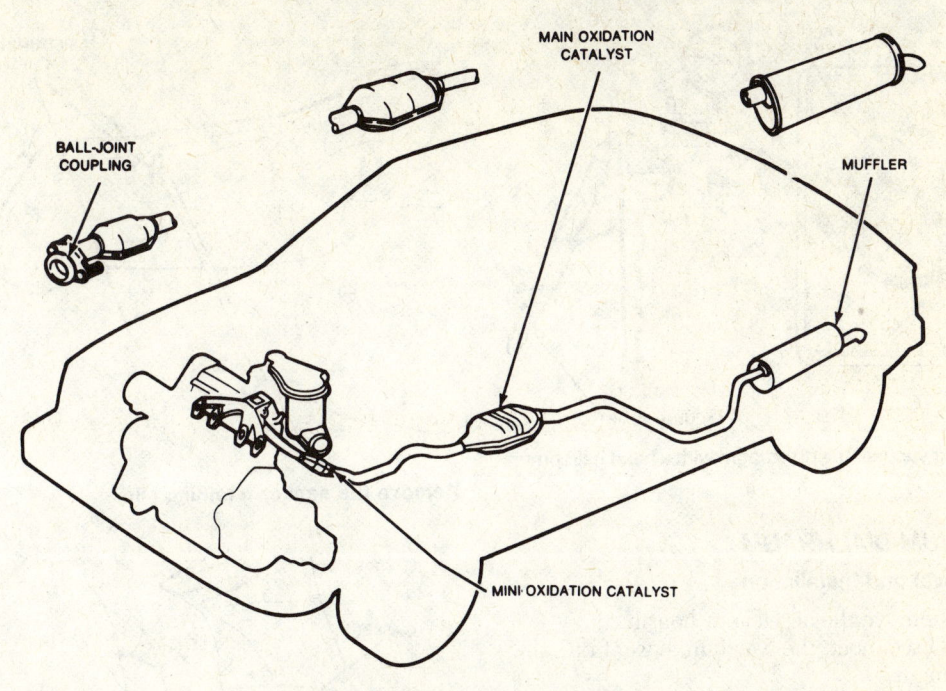

Exhaust system with catalytic converter

Heated Air Inlet System

All engines are equipped with a vacuum device located in the air cleaner intake. A small door is operated by a vacuum diaphragm and a thermostatic spring. When the air temperature outside is 40°F or lower, the door will block off air entering from outside and allow air channeled from the exhaust manifold area to enter the intake. This air is heated by the hot manifold. At 65°F or above, the door fully blocks off the heated air. At temperatures in between, the door is operated in intermediate positions. During acceleration the door is controlled by engine vacuum to allow the maximum amount of air to enter the carburetor.

TESTING THE SYSTEM

To determine if the system is functioning properly, use the following procedures.

1. Make sure all vacuum hoses and the flexible pipe from the heat stove are in good condition.
2. On a cold engine and the outside air temperature less than 50°F, the heat control door in the air cleaner snorkel should be up on the up or "Heat Off" position.
4. Remove the air cleaner. Allow it to cool to 50°F, or less, Using a hand vacuum pump, apply 20 in./Hg to the sensor. The door in the air cleaner snorkel should be in the up or "Heat On" position. If not, check the vacuum diaphragm.
5. To test the diaphragm, use a hand vacuum pump to apply about 20 in./Hg to the diaphragm. It should not leak down more than 10 in./Hg in 3 minutes. The door should not lift from the snorkel at less than 2 in./Hg, and be in the full up position with no more than 4 in./Hg.
6. If these conditions in Step 6 are not met, replace the diaphragm and repeat the checks in Steps 2 and 3. If the vacuum diaphragm performs properly, but proper temperature is not maintained, replace the sensor and repeat the checks in Steps 2 and 3.

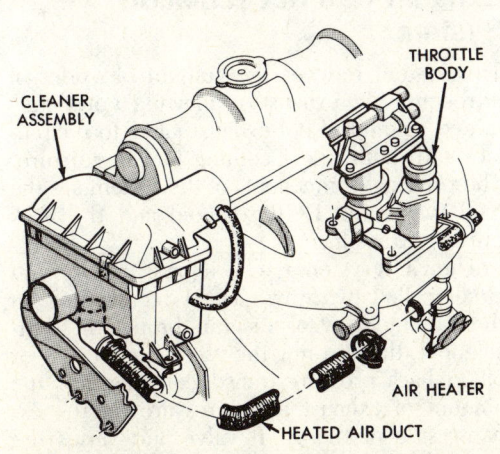

Heated air inlet system—2.2L engine with single point fuel injection

74 EMISSION CONTROLS AND FUEL SYSTEM

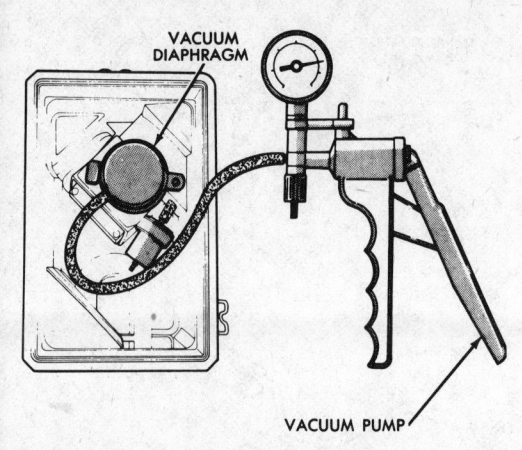

Testing vacuum the diaphragm with a hand held pump

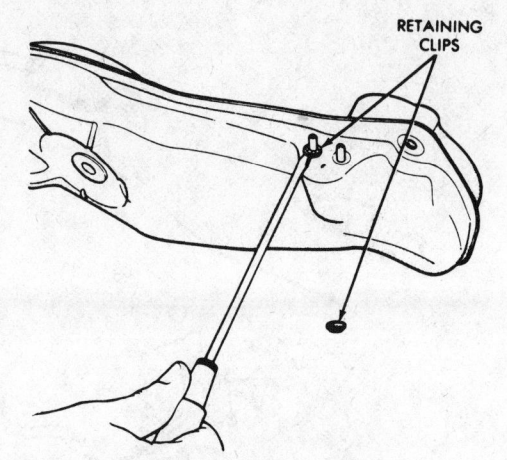

Remove the sensor retaining clip

Install the gasket and sensor

VACUUM DIAPHRAGM
Removal and Installation

1. Remove the air cleaner housing.
2. Disconnect the vacuum hose from the diaphragm.
3. Drill through the metal (welded) tab and tip the diaphragm slightly forward to disengage the lock. Rotate the diaphragm counterclockwise.
4. When the diaphragm is free, slide the complete assembly to one side and remove the operating rod from the heat control door.
5. With the diaphragm removed, check the door for freedom of operation. When the door is raised, it should fall freely when released. If not, check the snorkel walls for interference, or check the hinge pin.
6. Insert the operating rod into the heat control door. Position the diaphragm tangs in the openings in the snorkel and turn clockwise until the lock is engaged.
7. Apply 9 in. of vacuum to the diaphragm hose nipple and check to be sure the heat control door operates freely.
   CAUTION: *Manually operating the heat control door could cock the operating rod and restrict proper operation of the system.*
8. Assemble the air cleaner and install it on the car. Test the operation.

SENSOR
Removal and Installation

1. Remove the air cleaner housing.
2. Disconnect the vacuum hoses from the sensor and remove the retainer clips. Discard the old clips; new ones are supplied with a new sensor.
3. Remove the sensor and gasket.
4. Install a new gasket and sensor. Hold the sensor in place and install new retainer clips. Be sure the gasket forms a tight air seal. Do not attempt to adjust the sensor.

Exhaust Gas Recirculation System

This system reduces the amount of oxides of nitrogen in the exhaust by allowing a predetermined amount of hot exhaust gases to recirculate and dilute the incoming fuel/air mixture. The principal components of the system are the EGR valve the EGR solenoid and the back pressure transducer.

The EGR system is a back pressure type and is controlled two ways. The Logic Module in the computer controls vacuum through the EGR solenoid, thus turning the vacuum circuit on or off. A back pressure transducer measures the amount of exhaust back pressure on the exhaust side of the EGR valve and varies the strength of the vacuum signal applied to the EGR valve. The Logic Module in the com-

EMISSION CONTROLS AND FUEL SYSTEM 75

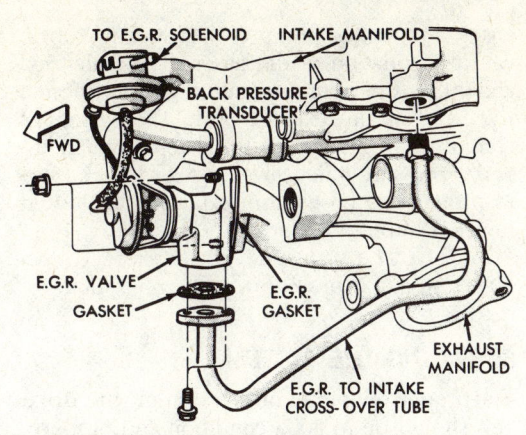

Single point fuel injection—EGR mounting

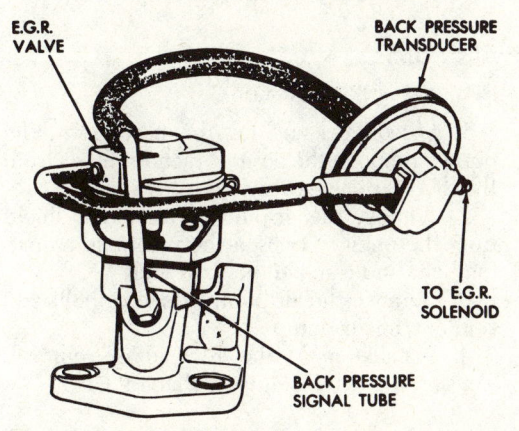

EGR valve and back pressure transducer—single point fuel injection

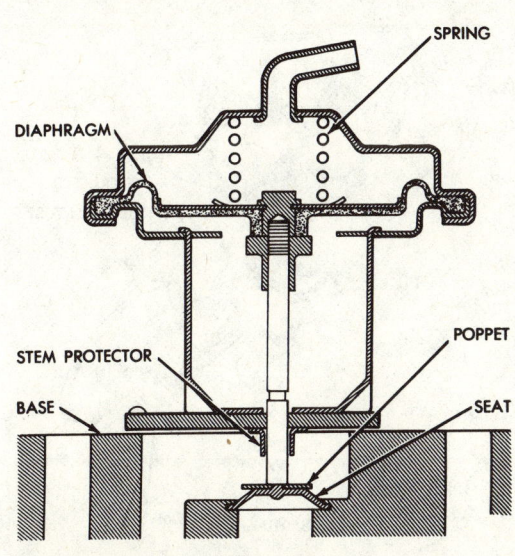

Cut-away view of the EGR valve

puter will prevent the EGR valve from operating by turning the EGR solenoid off at idle, wide open throttle or when the engine temperature falls below 70°F. The back pressure transducer adjusts the signal to the EGR valve to provide programed amounts of Exhaust Gas Recirculation under all other conditions.

The EGR solenoid is controlled by the Logic Module in the computer. When the engine temperature is below 70°F, the Logic Module energizes the solenoid by grounding it. This closes the solenoid and prevents ported vacuum from reaching the EGR valve. When the predetermined temperature is reached, the Logic Module will turn off the ground for the solenoid de-energizing it. Once the solenoid is de-enerized, ported vacuum from the throttle body will pass through to the EGR valve. At idle and wide open throttle the solenoid is energized which prevents EGR operation.

TESTING THE SYSTEM
EGR Valve

1. Inspect all hose connections between the intake manifold and EGR valve.
2. Check the valve with the engine warmed and running.
3. Allow the engine to idle in Neutral for 70 seconds, with the throttle closed. Abruptly accelerate the engine to about 2000 rpm, but not more than 3000 rpm.
4. Visible movement of the EGR valve stem should occur during this operation. Movement can be seen by the position of the groove on the EGR valve stem. You may have to repeat the operation several times to definitely ascertain movement.

Inspect the EGR valve for deposits, particularly around the poppet and seat area. If the deposits amount to more than a thin film, the valve should be cleaned. Apply a liberal amount of manifold heat control valve solvent to the poppet and seat area and allow the deposits to soften. Open the valve with an external vacuum source and remove the deposits, with a suitable sharp tool.

CAUTION: *During the cleaning operation, do not spill solvent on the valve diaphragm or it will cause failure of the diaphragm. Do not push on the diaphragm to operate the valve; use an external vacuum source.*

An alternate procedure to this messy operation is to simply replace the valve if it is extremely clogged.

CCEGR Valve

This valve is mounted in the thermostat housing and is color coded yellow for its calibrated temperature of 120–130°F. During warm-up, when engine coolant temperature exceeds 125°F, the valve opens, allowing vacuum to reach the EGR valve, causing recirculation of exhaust gasses.

76 EMISSION CONTROLS AND FUEL SYSTEM

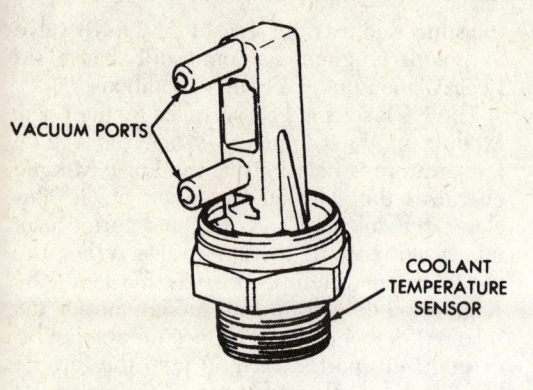

CCEGR valve

1. Remove the valve from the housing.
2. Place in an ice bath below 40°F. so that the threaded portion of the valve is covered.
3. Connect a hand vacuum pump to the valve nipple corresponding to the yellow stripe hose. Apply 10 in. vacuum. There should be no more than 1 in. drop in vacuum in one (1) minute. If the vacuum reading falls off, the valve should be replaced.

Air Injection System

This systems job is to reduce carbon monoxide and hydrocarbons to required levels. The system adds a controlled amount of air to exhaust gases, via an air pump and induction tubes, causing oxidation of the gases. The California and other American cars, introduces air through the head at the exhaust port. The system is composed of an air pump, a combination diverter/pressure-relief valve, hoses, a check valve to protect the hoses from exhaust gas, and an injection tube.

NOTE: *The system is not noiseless. A certain squeal is present in pump operation.*

SERVICING THE SYSTEM

For proper operation of the system, the drive belt should be in good condition and properly tensioned. The air pump is not a serviceable item; if necessary, it should be replaced.

AIR PUMP

Removal and Installation

1. Disconnect and tag the hoses from the pump. Remove the air and vacuum hoses from the diverter valve or switch relief valve.
2. Remove the air pump drive pulley shield from the engine. Loosen the pivot and adjusting bolts and remove the drive belt.
3. Remove the air pump attaching bolts and remove the air pump.
4. Installation is the reverse of removal. Tension the drive belt (see Chapter 1).

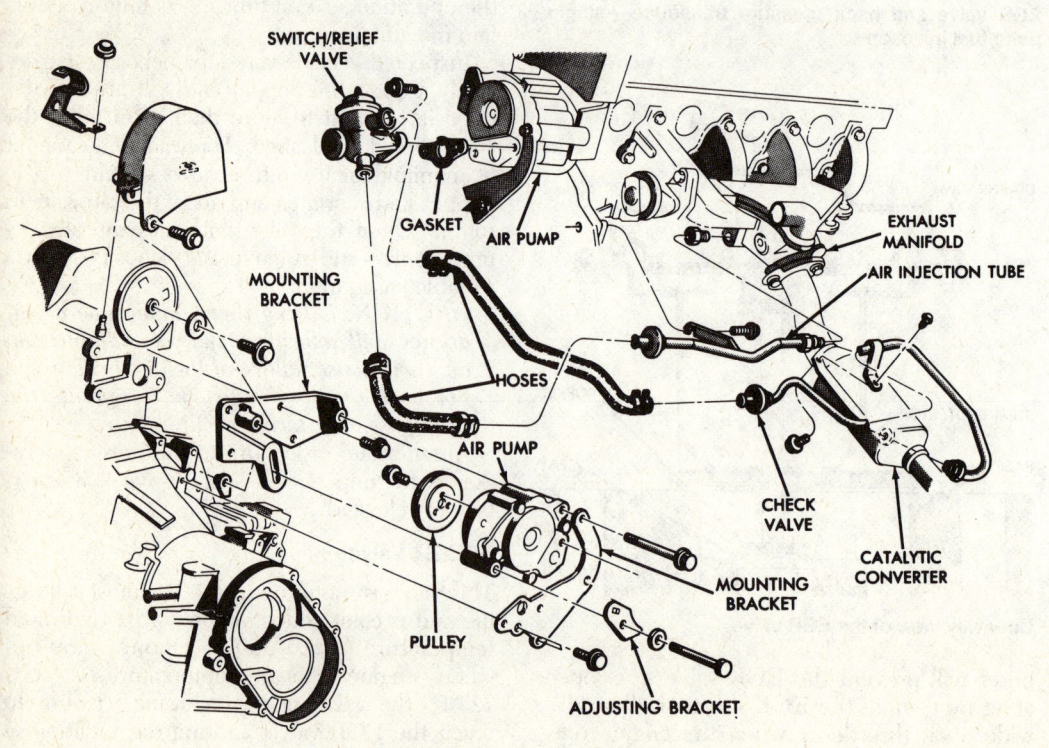

Air injection system—typical

EMISSION CONTROLS AND FUEL SYSTEM

EGR Diagnosis

NOTE: *All tests must be made with fully warm engine running continuously for at least two minutes*

Condition	Possible Cause	Correction
EGR valve stem does not move on system test.	(a) Check, leaking disconnected or plugged hoses. (b) Defective EGR valve.	(a) Verify correct hose connections and leak check and confirm that all hoses are open. If defective hoses are found, replace hose harness. (b) Disconnect hose harness from EGR valve. Connect external vacuum source, 10 in./Hg or greater, to valve diaphragm while checking valve movement. If no valve movement occurs, replace valve. If valve opens, approx. 1/8" travel, clamp off supply hose to check for diaphragm leakage. Valve should remain open 30 seconds or longer. If leakage occurs, replace valve. If valve is satisfactory, evaluate control system.
EGR valve stem does not move on system test, operates normally on external vacuum source.	(a) Defective thermal control valve. (b) Defective control system—Plugged passages.	(a) Disconnect CCEGR valve and bypass the valve with a short length of 3/16" tubing. If normal movement of the EGR valve is restored, replace the thermal valve. (b) Ported Vacuum Control System: Remove carburetor and inspect port (slot type) in throttle bore and associated vacuum passages in carburetor throttle body including limiting orifice at hose end of passages. Use suitable solvent to remove deposits and check for flow with light air pressure. Normal operation should be restored to ported vacuum control EGR system.
Engine will not idle, dies out on return to idle or idle is very rough or slow. EGR valve open at idle.	(a) Control system defective.	(a) Disconnect hose from EGR valve and plug hose. If idle is unsatisfactory, replace EGR valve. If idle is still unsatisfactory, install a vacuum gauge on ported signal tap and observe gauge for vacuum reading. If vacuum signal is greater than 1 inch/Hg, check idle set (refer to Carburetor, Engine Idle Check and Set Procedure). If vacuum is ok, remove carburetor, Group 14, Fuel System, and check linkage and throttle blades for binding.
Engine will not idle, does out on return to idle or idle is rough or slow. EGR valve closed at idle.	(a) High EGR valve leakage in closed position.	(a) If removal of vacuum hose from EGR valve does not correct rough idle, remove EGR valve and inspect to insure that poppet is seated. Clean deposits if necessary or replace EGR valve if found defective.

DIVERTER VALVE
Removal and Installation

Servicing the diverter valve is limited to replacement. If the valve fails it will become extremely noisy. If air escapes from the silencer at idle speed, either the diverter valve or the relief valve has failed and the entire valve assembly should be replaced.

1. Remove the air and vacuum hoses.
2. Remove the 2 screws holding the diverter valve to the mounting flange and remove the valve.
3. Remove the old gasket.
4. Installation is the reverse of removal. Use a new gasket and connect the hoses properly.

78 EMISSION CONTROLS AND FUEL SYSTEM

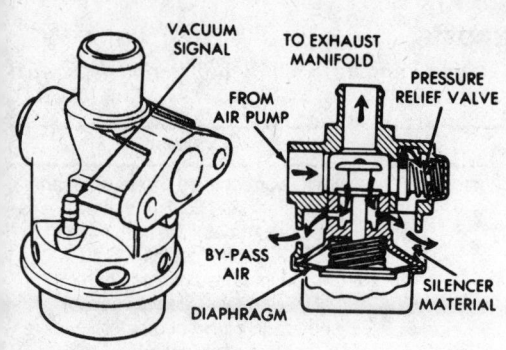

AIR pump diverter valve

SWITCH/RELIEF VALVE

The switch/relief valve is not serviceable. If vacuum is applied to the valve and the air injection is not upstream, or if the air injection is both upstream and downstream, the valve is defective and should be replaced. The relief valve has failed if air escapes from the silencer while the engine is at idle.

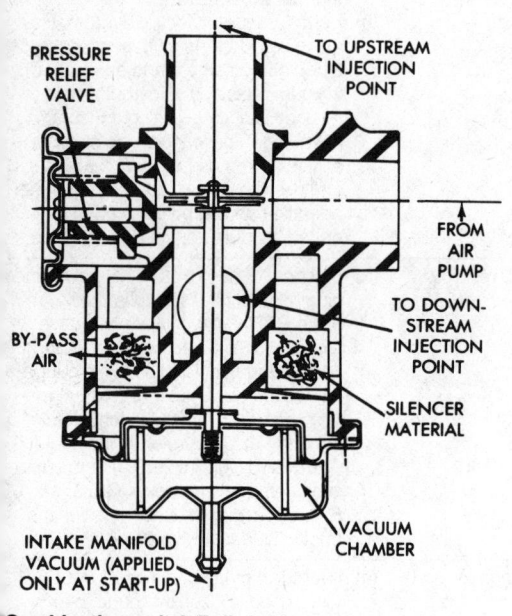

Combination switch/Relief valve

Removal and Installation

1. Remove the hoses from the valve.
2. Remove the screws securing the valve to the air pump.
3. Remove the gasket material from the pump mounting flange and relief valve.
4. Installation is the reverse of removal.

CHECK VALVE

The check valve is not repairable; if necessary to service it, replace it with a new one. The valve can be tested by removing the hose from the valve inlet tube. If exhaust gases escape from the inlet tube the valve has failed. If the tube nut joint is leaking, retorque the nut to 25–35 ft. lbs. If the adapter to the exhaust manifold joint is leaking, retorque the connection to a maximum of 40 ft. lbs.

REMOVAL AND INSTALLATION

1. Release the clamp and disconnect the air hose from the check valve.
2. Remove the tube nut holding the injection tube to the exhaust manifold.
3. Loosen the starter motor attaching bolt and remove the injection tube from the engine.
4. Remove the catalyst injection tube attaching tube from the catalyst flange and remove the injection tube from the exhaust system.
5. Installation is the reverse of removal.

Canadian Cars

1. Release the clamp and remove the air hose from the check valve inlet.
2. On A/C cars, remove the air conditioning compressor from the mount.
   CAUTION: *Do not disconnect any A/C system hoses.*
3. Remove the 4 isolated rubber compressor mounting bracket bolts and the compressor-to-cylinder head bolt. Set the compressor aside and keep it upright.
4. Drain the cooling system to a level below the thermostat housing.
5. Remove the housing from the bypass hose.
6. Remove the 4 hollow bolts holding the injection tube assembly to the cylinder head.
7. Install the injection tube assembly on the cylinder head. The 4 copper washers must be used between the tube assembly and the cylinder head.
8. Install the 4 hollow bolts with copper washers between each bolt and the injection tube assembly. The washers must be used. Torque the bolts to 20 ft. lbs.
9. Install the thermostat housing and connect the bypass hose.
10. On engines with A/C, reinstall the compressor. Adjust the drive belt (see Chapter 1).
11. Reconnect the air hose to the check valve inlet.
12. Refill the cooling system (see Chapter 1).

Air Aspirator System

The air aspirator system uses exhaust pressure pulses to draw air into the exhaust system. This reduces carbon monoxide (CO) and hydrocar-

EMISSION CONTROLS AND FUEL SYSTEM

Air Pump Diagnosis

Condition	Possible Cause	Correction
Excessive belt noise	(a) Loose belt. (b) Seized pump.	(a) Tighten belt (see Chapter 1). (b) Replace pump.
Excessive pump noise, chirping	Insufficient break-in.	Recheck for noise after 1600 km. (1000 miles) of operation.
Excessive pump noise, chirping, rumbling, or knocking	(a) Leak in hose. (b) Loose hose. (c) Hose touching other engine parts. (d) Diverter valve or switch/relief valve inoperative. (e) Check valve inoperative. (f) Pump mounting fasteners loose. (g) Pump failure	(a) Locate source of leak using soap solution and correct. (b) Reassemble and replace or tighten hose clamp. (c) Adjust hose position. (d) Replace diverter valve or switch/relief valve. (e) Replace check valve. (f) Tighten mounting screws as specified. (g) Replace pump.
No air supply (accelerate engine to 1500 rpm and observe rpm and observe air flow from hoses. If the flow increases as the rpm's increase, the pump is functioning normally. If not, check possible cause.	(a) Loose drive belt. (b) Leaks in supply hose. (c) Leak at fitting(s). (d) Diverter valve or switch/relief valve leaking. (e) Diverter valve inoperative. (f) Check valve inoperative.	(a) Tighten to specifications. (b) Locate leak and repair or replace as required. (c) Tighten or replace clamps. (d) If air is expelled through diverter exhaust with vehicle at idle, replace diverter valve or switch/relief valve. (e) Usually accompanied by backfire during deceleration. Replace diverter valve. (f) Replace check valve.
Air supply upstream with no vacuum applied to switch/relief valve.	Switch/relief valve inoperative.	Replace switch/relief valve.

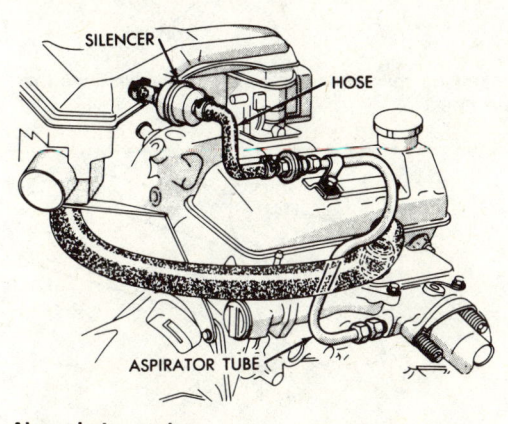

Air aspirator system

bon (HC) emissions. It draws fresh air from the clean side of the air cleaner past a one-way diaphragm in the aspirator valve. The diaphragm opens to allow fresh air to mix with exhaust gasses during negative pressure pulses. If pressure pulses are positive, the diaphragm closes, which prevents exhaust gasses from entering the air cleaner. The air aspirator is most effective at idle and slightly off idle where negative pressure pulses are greatest.

The aspirator valve utilizes exhaust pressure pulsation to draw clean air from the inside of the air cleaner into the exhaust system. The function is to reduce HC (hydrocarbon) emissions. It is located in a tube between the exhaust manifold and the air cleaner.

TESTING THE SYSTEM

To determine if the air aspirator valve has failed, disconnect the hose from the aspirator inlet. With the engine idling in Neutral, vacuum exhaust pulses can be felt at the aspirator inlet. If hot exhaust gas is escaping from the aspirator inlet, the valve has failed and should be replaced.

ASPIRATOR VALVE

Removal and Installation

1. Disconnect the air hose from the aspirator valve inlet and unscrew the valve from the aspirator tube assembly.
2. Installation is the reverse of Removal. Replace the hose if it has hardened.

ASPIRATOR TUBE ASSEMBLY

Removal and Installation

1. Disconnect the air hose from the aspirator valve inlet.
2. Remove the nut securing the aspirator tube assembly to the engine.

EMISSION CONTROLS AND FUEL SYSTEM

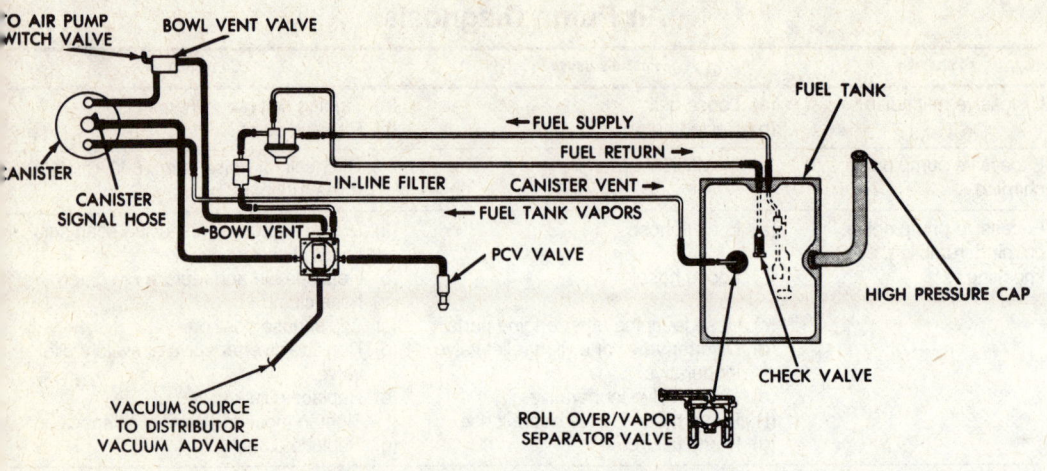

Fuel evaporative control system schematic

3. Remove the aspirator tube.
4. Installation is the reverse of removal. Tighten the tube nut to 25–35 ft. lbs.

Evaporation Control System

This system prevents the release of gasoline vapors from the fule tank and the carburetor into the atmosphere. The system is vacuum operated and draws the fumes into a charcoal canister where they are temporarily held until they are drawn into the intake manifold for burning. For proper operation of the system and to prevent gas tank failure, the lines should never be plugged, and no other cap other than the one specified should be used on the fuel tank filler neck.

The Evaporation Control System should not require service other than replacement of the charcoal canister filter. All hoses should be inspected and replaced if cracked or leaking. Any loss of fuel or vapor from the filler cap would indicate one of the following conditions:
1. Poor seal between cap and filler neck,
2. Malfunction of fuel cap release valve,
3. Plugged vent line roll-over valve in the fuel tank, or
4. Plugged vapor vent lines between fuel tank and charcoal canister.

FUEL TANK ROLL-OVER VALVE AND LIQUID VAPOR SEPARATOR VALVE

Removal and Installation

1. Remove the fuel tank.
2. Wedge the blade of a suitable pry bar between the rubber grommet and the support rib on the fuel tank.
NOTE: *Chrysler recommends the use of 2 screwdrivers for this operation. Before performing this operation with screwdrivers, read the Safety Notice on the acknowledgements page of this book and read the section in Chapter 1 concerning Safety.*

3. Use a second screwdriver as a support and pry the valve and grommet from the tank.
CAUTION: *Do not pry between the valve and grommet.*

4. To remove the grommet from the valve,

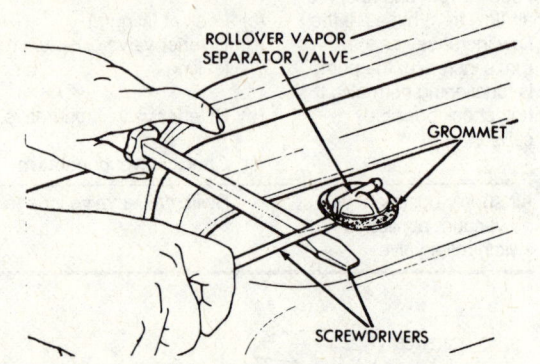

Removing rollover/vapor separation valve from the fuel tank

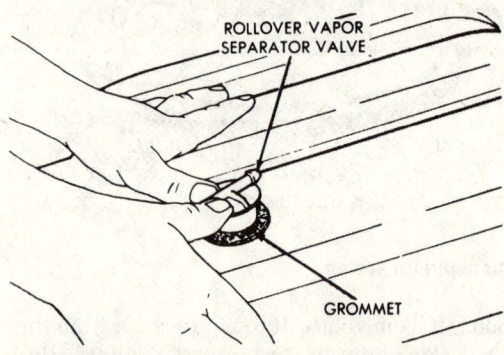

Installing the rollover/vapor separator valve

EMISSION CONTROLS AND FUEL SYSTEM

place the valve upright on a flat surface and push down on the grommet.

5. Install the rubber grommet in the fuel tank and work it around the curled lip.

6. Lubricate the grommet with engine oil and twist the valve down into the grommet.

7. Install the fuel tank.

FUEL SYSTEM

NOTE: *The following fuel system section contains complete information for both the Multi-port fuel injection system used on the turbocharged 2.2L Laser/Daytona models, and the Throttle body injection system used on the non-turbocharged 2.2L Laser/Daytona models. Procedures within this section may be too complex and/or require special tools not readily available to the average weekend/do-it-yourselfer mechanic. However in the interest of making this manual as complete as possible they have been included.*

Chrysler Multi-Port Electronic Fuel Injection Turbocharged Engines

The turbocharged multi-point Electronic Fuel Injection system combines an electronic fuel and spark advance control system with a turbocharged intake system. At the center of this system is a digital pre-programmed computer known as a Logic Module that regulates ignition timing, air-fuel ratio, emission control devices and idle speed. This component has the ability to update and revise its programming to meet changing operation conditions.

Various sensors provide the input necessary for the Logic Module to correctly regulate fuel flow at the fuel injectors. These include the Manifold Absolute Pressure, throttle Position, Oxygen Feedback, Coolant Temperature, Charge Temperature, and Vehicle Speed Sensor. In addition to the sensors, various switches also provide importnant information. These include the Transmission Neutral-Safety, Heated Backlite, Air Conditioning, and the Air Conditioning Clutch Switches.

Inputs to the Logic Module are converted into signals sent to the Power Module. These signals cause the Power Module to change either the fuel flow at the injector or ignition timing or both. The Logic Module tests many of its own input and output circuits. If a fault is found in a major circuit, this information is stored in the Logic Module. Information on this fault can be displayed to a technician by means of the instrument panel power loss lamp or by connecting a diagnostic readout and observing a numbered display code which directly relates to a general fault.

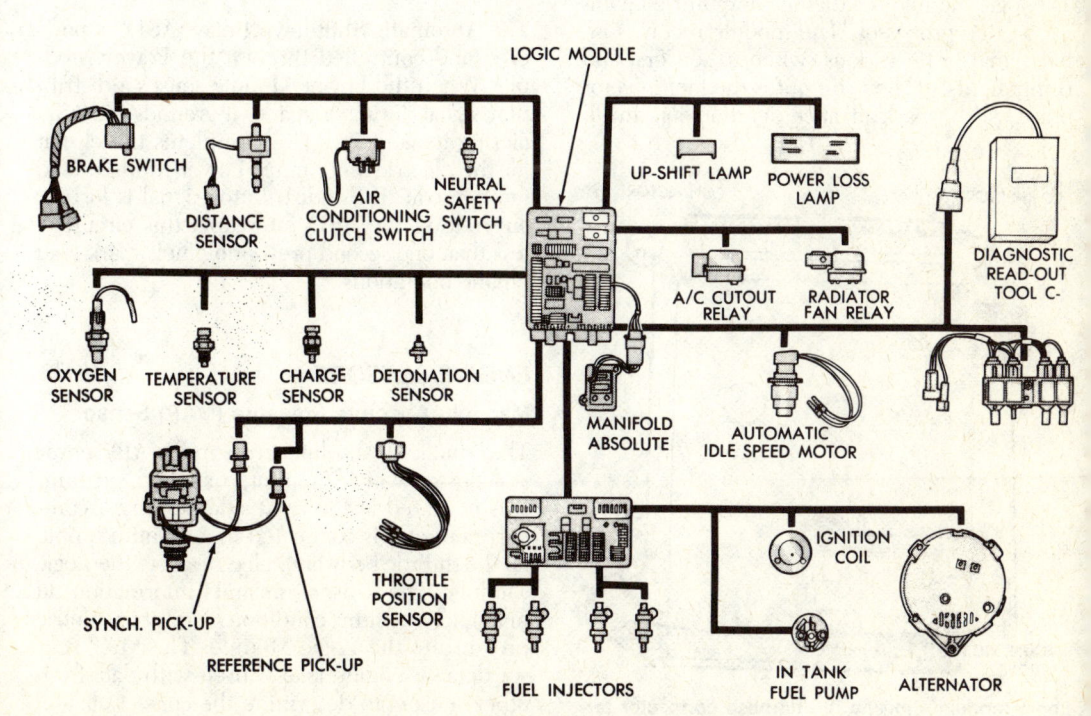

Components, multi-point fuel injection system

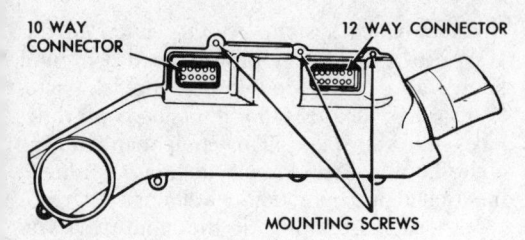

82 EMISSION CONTROLS AND FUEL SYSTEM

Power module and connectors

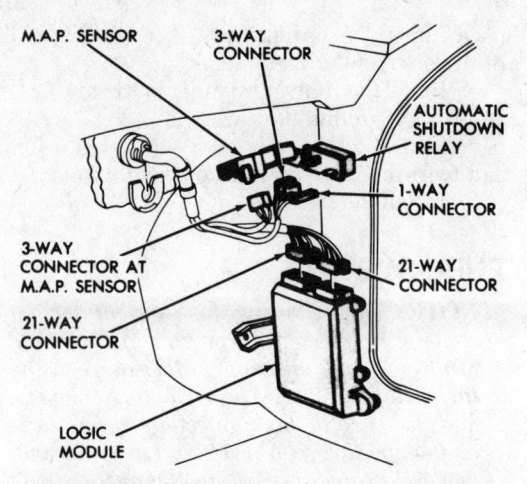

Logic module, components and harness connectors located inside the cowl on the passenger's compartment

ELECTRONIC CONTROL SYSTEM

Power Module

The Power Module contains the circuits necessary to power the ignition coil and the fuel injector. These are high current devices and their power supply has been isolated to minimize any "electrical noise" reaching the Logic Module. The Power Module also energizes the Automatic Shut Down (ASD) Relay which activates the fuel pump, ignition coil, and the Power Module itself. The module also receives a signal from the distributor. In the event of no distributor signal, the ASD relay is not activated and power is shut off from the fuel pump and ignition coil. The Power Module contains a voltage converter which reduces battery voltage to a regulated 8.0V output. This 8.0V output powers the distributor and also powers the Logic Module.

Logic Module

The logic module is a digital computer containing a microprocessor. The module receives input signals from various switches, sensors, and components. It then computes the fuel injector pulse width, spark advance, ignition coil dwell, idle speed, and purge and EGR solenoid cycles from this information. The Logic Module tests many of its own input and output circuits. If a fault is found in a major system, this information is stored in the Logic Module.

Information on this fault can be displayed to a technician by means of flashing lamp on the instrument panel or by connecting a diagnostic readout tool and reading a numbered display code which relates to a general fault.

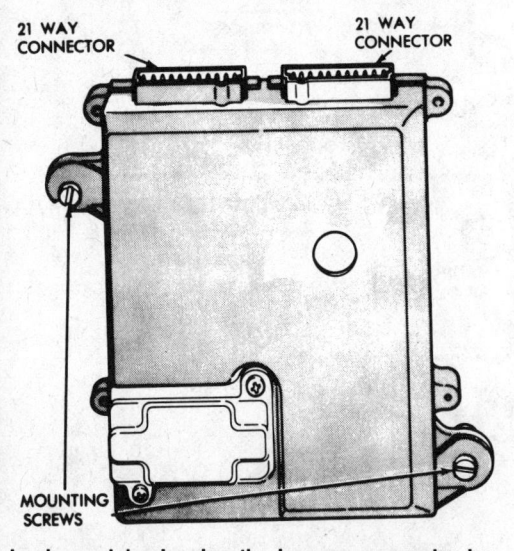

Automatic Shutdown Relay (ASD)

The Automatic Shutdown Relay (ASD) is powered and controlled through the Power Module. When the Power Module senses a distributor signal during cranking, it grounds the ASD closing its contacts. This completes the circuit for the electric fuel pump, Power Module, and ignition coil. If the distributor signal is lost for any reason the ASD interrupts this circuit in less than one second preventing fuel, spark, and engine operations.

ENGINE SENSORS

Manifold Absolute Pressure (MAP) Sensor

The Manifold Absolute Pressure (MAP) sensor is a device which monitors manifold vacuum. It is mounted in the right side passenger compartment and is connected to a vacuum nipple on the throttle body and, electrically to the Logic Module. The sensor transmits information on manifold vacuum conditions and barometric pressure to the Logic Module. The MAP sensor data on engine load is used with data from other sensors to determine the correct air-fuel mixture.

Logic module showing the harness connector terminals

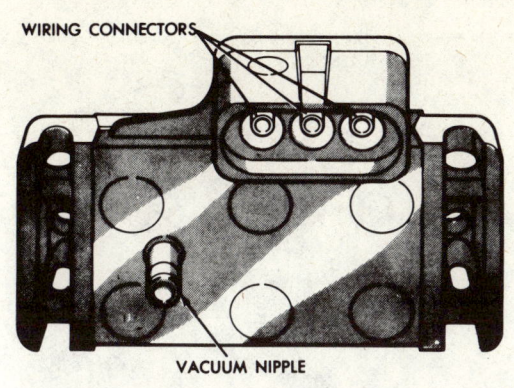

EMISSION CONTROLS AND FUEL SYSTEM

Manifold absolute pressure sensor (MAP)

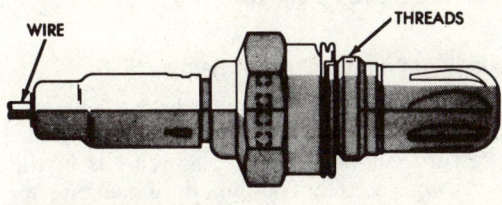

Oxygen sensor—typical

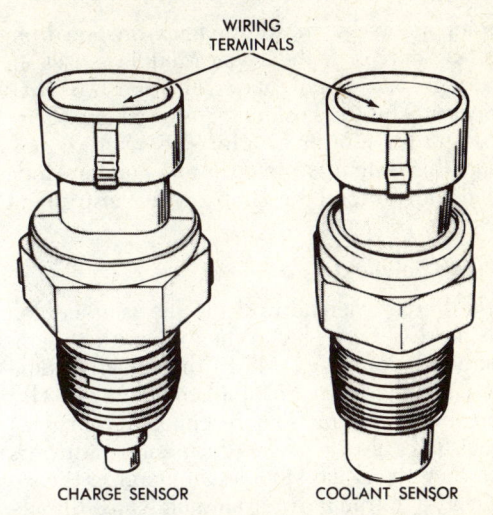

Charge and coolant sensors—typical, wiring terminal may vary

Oxygen Sensor (O² Sensor)

The Oxygen Sensor (O² Sensor) is a device which produces an electrical voltage when exposed to the oxygen present in the exhaust gasses. The sensor is mounted in the exhaust manifold and must be heated by the exhaust gasses before producing the voltage. When there is a large amount of oxygen present (lean mixture), the sensor produces a low voltage. When there is a lesser amount present (rich mixture) it produces a higher voltage. By monitoring the oxygen content and converting it to electrical voltage, the sensor acts as a rich-lean switch. The voltage is transmitted to the Logic Module. The Logic Module signals the Power Module to trigger the fuel injector. The injector changes the mixture.

Charge Temperature Sensor

The Charge Temperature Sensor is a device mounted in the intake manifold which measures the temperature of the air-fuel mixture. This information is used by the logic module to determine engine operating temperature and engine warm-up cycles in the event of a Coolant Temperature Sensor failure.

Coolant Temperature Sensor

The Coolant Temperature Sensor is a device which monitors coolant temperature (which is the same as engine operating temperature). It is mounted in the thermostat housing. This sensor provides data on engine operating temperature to the Logic Module. This data along with data provided by the Charge Tempera-

ture Switch allows the Logic Module to demand slightly richer air-fuel mixtures and higher idle speeds until normal operating temperatures are reached. The sensor is a variable resistor with a range of −60°F to 300°F.

SWITCHES AND SOLENOIDS

Various switches provide information to the Logic Module. These include the Neutral Safety, Air Conditioning Clutch, and Brake Light switches. If one or more of these switches is sensed as being in the on position, the Logic Module signals the Automatic Idle Speed Motor to increase idle speed to a scheduled rpm. With the air conditioning on and the throttle blade above a specific angle, the wide open throttle cut-out relay prevents the air conditioning clutch from engaging until the throttle blade is below this angle.

Power Loss Lamp

The Power Loss Lamp comes on each time the ignition key is turned on and stays on for a few seconds as a bulb test. If the Logic Module receives an incorrect signal or no signal from either the Coolant Temperature Sensor, Manifold Absolute Pressure Sensor, or the Throttle Positon Sensor, the Power Loss Lamp on the instrument panel is illuminated. This is a warning that the logic module has gone into Limp in Mode in an attempt to keep the system operational. It signals an immediate need for service. The Power Loss can also be used to display fault codes. Cycle the ignition switch on, off, on, off, within five seconds and any fault codes stored in the Logic Module will be displayed.

Limp In Mode is the attempt by the logic Module to compensate for the failure of certain

84 EMISSION CONTROLS AND FUEL SYSTEM

components by substituting information from other sources. If the Logic Module senses incorrect data or no data at all from the MAP Sensor, Throttle Position Sensor, Charge Temperature Sensor or Coolant Temperature Sensor, the system is placed into Limp In Mode and the Power Loss lamp on the instrument panel is activated.

Purge Solenoid

The Purge Solenoid works in the same fashion as the EGR solenoid. When engine temperature is below 62°C (145°F) the Logic Module grounds the Purge Solenoid energizing it. This prevents vacuum from reaching the charcoal canister valve. When this temperature is reached the Logic Module de-energizes the solenoid by turning the ground off. Once this occurs vacuum will flow to the canister purge valve and purge fuel vapors through the throttle body.

Exhaust Gas Recirculation Solenoid

The EGR solenoid is operated by the Logic Module. When engine temperature is below 21°C (70°F), the Logic Module energizes the solenoid by grounding it. This closes the solenoid and prevents ported vacuum from reaching the EGR valve. When the prescribed temperature is reached, the logic module will turn off the ground for the solenoid de-energizing it. Once the solenoid is de-energized, ported vacuum from the throttle body will pass through to the EGR valve. At idle and wide open throttle the solenoid is energized which prevents EGR operation.

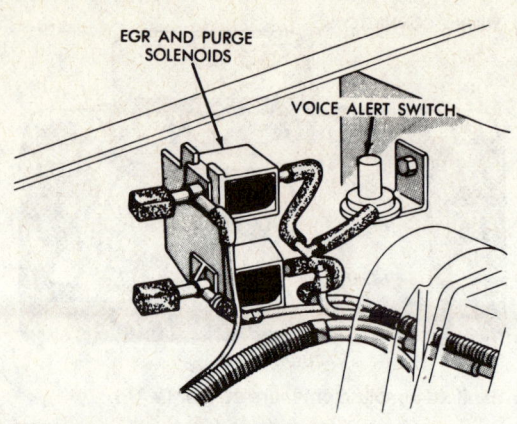

EGR and canister purge solenoids

Air Conditioning Cut Out Relay

The air conditioning cut out relay is electrically in series with the cycling clutch switch and low pressure cut out switch. This relay is in the normally closed (on) position during engine operation. When the Logic Module senses wide open throttle through the Throttle Position Sensor, it will energize the relay, open its contacts, and prevent air conditioning clutch engagement.

FUEL CONTROL SYSTEM

Throttle Body

The throttle body assembly replaces a conventional carburetor air intake system and is connected to both the turbocharger and the intake manifold. The throttle body houses the Throt-

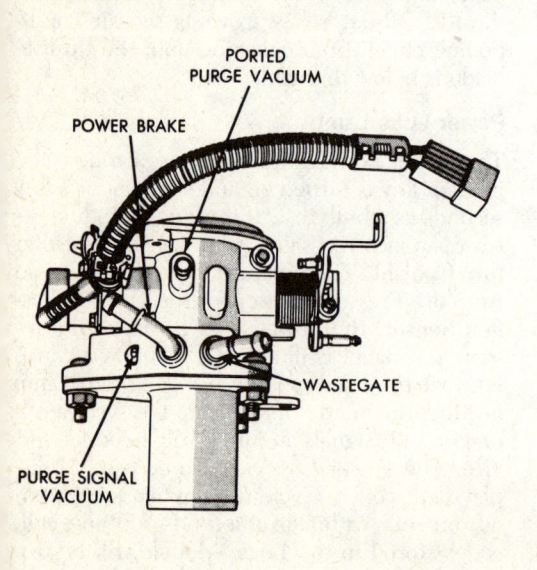

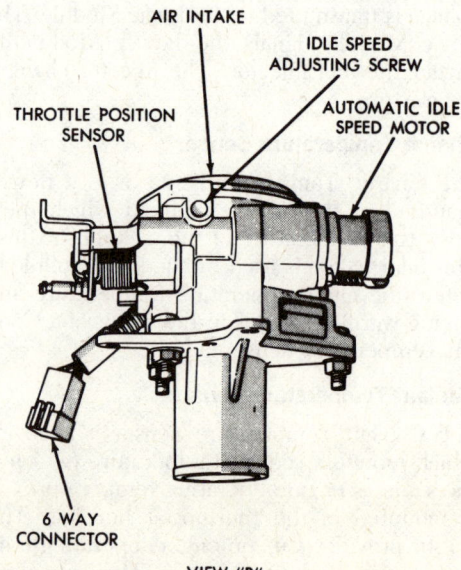

Throttle body assembly—multi-point fuel injection system

EMISSION CONTROLS AND FUEL SYSTEM

tle Position Sensor and the Automatic Idle Speed Motor. Air flow through the throttle body is controlled by a cable operated throttle blade located in the base of the throttle body.

Fuel Supply Circuit

Fuel is pumped to the fuel rail by an electrical pump which is mounted in the fuel tank. The pump inlet is fitted with a filter to prevent water and other contaminents from entering the fuel supply circuit. Fuel pressure is controlled to a preset level above intake manifold pressure by a pressure regulator which is mounted near the fuel rail. The regulator uses intake manifold pressure at the vacuum tee as a reference.

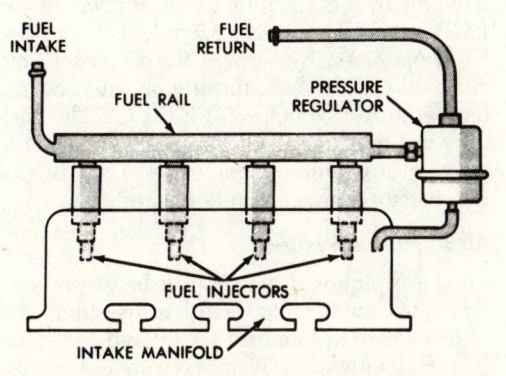

Fuel supply system—multi-point fuel injection system

Fuel Injectors and Fuel Rail Assembly

The four fuel injectors are retained in the fuel rail by lock rings. The rail and injector assembly is then bolted in position with the injectors inserted in the recessed holes in the intake manifold. The Fuel Injector is an electric solenoid powered by the Power Module but, controlled by the Logic Module. The Logic Module, based on ambient, mechanical, and sensor input, determines when and how long the Power Module should operate the injector. When an electric current is supplied to the injector, the armature and pintle move a short distance against a spring, opening a small orifice. Fuel is supplied to the inlet of the injector by the fuel pump, then passes through the injector, around the pintle, and out of the orifice. Since the fuel is under high pressure a fine spray is developed in the shape of a hollow cone. The injector, through this spraying action, atomizes the fuel and distributes it into the air entering the combustion chamber.

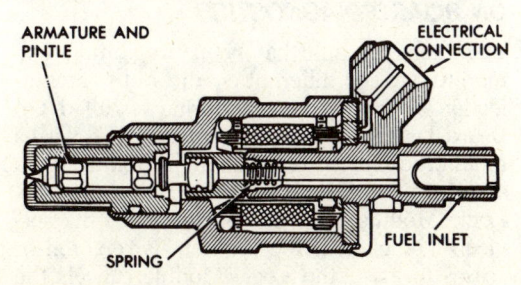

Fuel Pressure Regulator

The pressure regulator is a mechanical device located downstream of the fuel injector on the throttle body. Its function is to maintain a constant 53 psi (380kPa) across the fuel injector tip. The regulator uses a spring loaded rubber diaphragm to uncover a fuel return port. When the fuel pump becomes operational, the fuel flows past the injector into the regulator and is restricted from flowing any further by the blocked return port. When fuel pressure reaches 53 psi (380kPa), it pushes on the diaphragm, compressing the spring, and uncovers the fuel return port. The diaphragm and spring will constantly move from an open to closed position to keep the fuel pressure constant. An assist to the spring loaded diaphragm comes from vacuum in the throttle body above the throttle blade. As venturi vacuum increases less pressure is required to supply the same amount of fuel into the air flow. The vacuum assists in opening the fuel port during high vacuum conditions. This fine tunes the fuel pressure for all operating conditions.

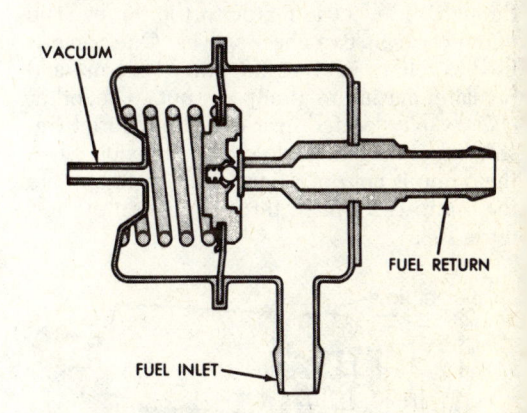

Fuel pressure regulator

Throttle Position Sensor (TPS)

The Throttle Position Sensor (TPS) is an electric resistor which is activated by the movement of the throttle shaft. It is mounted on the throttle body and senses the angle of the throttle body and senses the angle of the throttle blade opening. The voltage that the sensor produces increases or decreases according to the throttle blade opening. This voltage is transmitted to the Logic Module where it is used along with data from other sensors to ad-

Fuel injector—cross-section

EMISSION CONTROLS AND FUEL SYSTEM

just the air-fuel ratio to varying conditions and during acceleration, deceleration, idle, and wide open throttle operations.

Automatic Idle Speed (AIS) Motor

The Automatic Idle Speed Motor (AIS) is operated by the Logic Module. Data from the Throttle Position Sensor, Speed Sensor, Coolant Temperature Sensor, and various switch operations, (Electric Backlite, Air Conditioning, Safety/Neutral, Brake) are used by the Logic Module to adjust engine idle to an optimum during all idle conditions. The AIS adjusts the air portion of the air-fuel mixture through an air bypass on the back of the throttle body. Basic (no load) idle is determined by the minimum air flow through the throttle body. The AIS opens or closes off the air bypass as an increase or decrease is needed due to engine loads or ambient conditions. The Logic Module senses an air/fuel change and increases or decreases fuel proportionally to change engine idle. Deceleration die out is also prevented by increasing engine idle when the throttle is closed quickly after a driving (speed) condition.

Fuel Pump

The fuel pump used in this system is a positive displacement, roller vane immersible pump with a permanent magnet electric motor. The fuel is drawn in through a filter sock and pushed through the electric motor to the outlet. The pump contains two check valves. One valve is used to relieve internal fuel pump pressure and regulate maximum pump output. The other check valve, located near the pump outlet, restricts fuel movement to either direction when the pump is not operations. Voltage to operate the pump is supplied through the Auto Shutdown Relay.

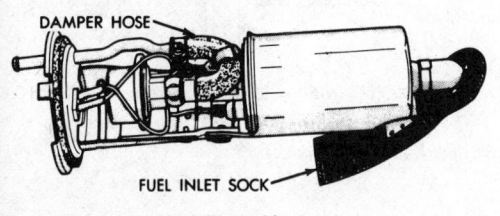

Fuel pump assembly (in-tank)

Fuel Reservoir

The fuel pump is mounted within a fuel reservoir in the fuel tank. The purpose of the reservois is to provide fuel at the pump intake during all driving conditions, especially those when low fuel levels are present. The fuel return line directs fuel into a cup on the side of the reservoir. The stream of fuel coming into this cup creates a low pressure area and causes additional fuel from the main tank to flow into the reservoir. This combination of return fuel and fuel from the main tank keeps the reservoir full even when the fuel level is below the reservoir walls.

Exhaust Gas Recirculation (EGR)

The Exhaust Gas Recirculation system is a back pressure type and is controlled two ways. The Logic Module controls vacuum through the EGR solenoid, turning the vacuum circuit on or off. A back pressure transducer measures the amount of exhaust back pressure on the exhaust side of the EGR valve and varies the strength of the vacuum signal applied to the EGR valve. The Logic Module will prevent EGR operation by turning the EGR solenoid off at idle, wide open throttle or when engine temperature falls below 70°F (21°C). The back pressure transducer adjusts the EGR signal to provide programmed amounts of Exhaust Gas Recirculation under all other conditions.

Air Aspirator System

The air aspirator system uses exhaust pressure pulses to draw air into the exhaust system. This reduces carbon monoxide (CO) and hydrocarbon (HC) emissions. It draws fresh air from the clean side of the air cleaner past a one-way diaphragm in the aspirator valve. The diaphragm opens to allow fresh air to mix with exhaust gasses during negative pressure pulses. If pressure pulses are positive, the diaphragm closes, which prevents exhaust gasses from entering the air cleaner. The air aspirator is most effective at idle and slightly off idle where negative pressure pulses are greatest.

On-Car Service

NOTE: *Most complaints that may occur with turbocharged multi-point Electronic Fuel Injection can be traced to poor wiring or hose connections. A visual check will help spot these faults and save unnecessary test and diagnosis time.*

ON BOARD DIAGNOSTICS

The Logic Module has been programmed to monitor several different circuits of the fuel injection system. This monitoring is called On Board Diagnosis. If a problem is sensed with a monitored circuit, often enough to indicate an actual problem, its Fault Code is stored in the Logic Module for eventual display to the service technician. If the problem is repaired or ceases to exist, the Logic Module cancels the Fault Code after 30 ignition key on/off cycles.

EMISSION CONTROLS AND FUEL SYSTEM

Fault Codes

When a fault code appears (either by flashes of the power loss lamp or by watching the diagnostic readout—Tool C-4805 or equivalent), it indicates that the Logic Module has recognized an abnormal signal in the system. Fault codes indicate the results of a failure do not always identify the failed component.

CODE 11 indicates a problem in the distributor circuit. This code appears if the Logic Module has not sensed a distributor signal since the battery was reconnected.

CODE 12 indicates a problem in the stand-by memory circuit. This code appears if direct memory feed to the logic Module is interrupted.

CODE 13 indicates a problem in the MAP sensor pneumatic system. This code appears if the MAP sensor vacuum level does not change between start and start/run transfer speed (500–600 rpm).

CODE 14 indicates a problem in the MAP sensor electrical system. This code appears if the map sensor signal is either too low (below .02 volts) or too high (above 4.9 volts).

CODE 15 indicates a problem in the vehicle Speed Sensor circuit. This code appears if engine speed is at idle and speed sensor indicates less than 2 mph. This code is valid only if it is sensed while moving.

CODE 21 indicates a problem in the O_2 feedback circuit. This code appears if engine temperature is above 170°F (77°C), engine speed is above 1500 rpm, and there has been no O_2 signal for more than 5 seconds.

CODE 22 indicates a problem in the coolant temperature circuit. This appears if the temperature sensor indicates an improbable temperature or a temperature that changes too fast to be real.

CODE 23 indicates a problem in the charge temperature circuit. This code appears if the charge temperature is an improbable temperature that changes too fast to be real.

CODE 24 indicates a problem in the Throttle Position Sensor circuit. This code appears if the sensor signal is either below .16 volts or above 4.7 volts.

CODE 25 indicates a problem in the Automatic Idle Speed system. This code appears if the proper voltage from the AIS system is not present. An open motor or harness will not activate this code.

CODE 31 indicates a problem in the Canister Purge Solenoid circuit. This code appears when the proper voltage at the purge solenoid is not present (open or shorted system).

CODE 32 indicates a problem in the Power Loss Lamp circuit. This code appears if proper voltage to the Power Loss Lamp is not present (open or shorted system).

CODE 33 indicates a problem in the Air Conditioning Wide Open Throttle Cut Out Relay circuit. This code appears if the proper voltage at the EGR Solenoid is not present (open or shorted).

CODE 34 indicates a problem in the EGR Solenoid circuit. This code appears if proper voltage at the EGR Solenoid is not present (open or shorted).

CODE 35 indicates a problem in the Fan Relay circuit. This code appears if the radiator fan is either not operating or operating at the wrong time.

CODE 41 indicates a problem in the Charging System. This code appears if battery voltage from the Automatic Shut Down Relay is below 11.75 volts.

CODE 42 indicates a problem in the Automatic Shut Down Relay (ASD) circuit. This code appears if during cranking, battery voltage from the ASD relay is not present for at least 1/3 second after the first distributor pulse or, after engine stall, battery voltage is not off within 3 seconds after last distributor pulse.

CODE 43 indicates a problem in the interface circuit. This code appears if the anti-dwell or injector control signal is not present between the Logic Module and Power Module.

CODE 44 indicates a problem in the logic Module. This code appears if an incorrect PROM has been installed in the Logic Module.

CODE 45 indicates a problem in the Overboost Shut Off circuit. This code appears if MAP sensor electrical signal rises above 10 psi boost.

CODE 51 indicates a problem in the closed loop fuel system. This code appears if during closed loop conditions, the O_2 signal is either low or high for more than 2 minutes.

CODE 52 indicates a problem in the Logic Module. This code appears if an internal failure exists in the Logic Module.

CODE 53 indicates a problem in the Logic Module. This code appears if an internal failure exists in the Logic Module.

CODE 54 indicates a problem in the Synchronization pick-up circuit. This code appears, if at start/run transfer speed, the reference pick-up signal is present but the synchronization pick-up signal is missing at the Logic Module.

CODE 55 indicates message complete. This code appears after all fault codes are displayed.

CODE 88 indicates start of message. This code appears at start of fault code messages. This code only appears on Readout Tool C-4805, or equivalent, and may also be used for switch check.

EMISSION CONTROLS AND FUEL SYSTEM

SYSTEM TESTS
Obtaining Fault Codes
1. Connect Diagnostic Readout Box Tool C-4805, or equivalent, to the diagnostic connector located in the engine compartment near the passenger side strut tower.
2. Start the engine if possible, cycle the transmission selector and the A/C switch if applicable. Shut off the engine.
3. Turn the ignition switch on, off, on, off, on. Within 5 seconds record all the diagnostic codes shown on the diagnostic readout box tool, observe the power loss lamp on the instrument panel the lamp should light for 2 seconds then go out (bulb check).

Switch Test
After all codes have been shown and has indicted Code 55 end of message, actuate the following component switches. The digital display must change its numbers when the switch is activated and released:
- Brake Pedal
- Gear Shift Selector park, reverse, park.
- A/C Switch (if applicable).
- Electric Backlite Switch (if applicable).

Actuator Test Mode (ATM)
1. Remove coil wire from cap and place ¼ in. from a ground.
   CAUTION: *Coil wire must be ¼ in. or less from ground or power module damage may result.*
2. Remove air cleaner hose from throttle body.
3. Press the ATM button on the diagnostic readout box tool and observe the following:
- 3 sparks from the coil wire to ground
- 2 AILS motor movement (1 open 1 close) you must listen carefully for AIS operation.
- With the ATM button still depressed, install a jumper wire between pins 2 and 3 of the gray distributor synch. connector. Listen for the click which indicates one set of injectors has been activated. Remove jumper wire and second set of injectors will be activated. Reconnect distributor connector.

4. The ATM capability is canceled 5 minutes after the ignition switch is turned on. To reinstate this capability, cycle the ignition on and off three times ending in the on position.
5. When the ATM button is pressed, fault Code 42 is generated because the ASD relay is by passed. Do not use this code for diagnostics after ATM operation.
6. The ATM test will check 3 categories of operation:
- When coil fires three times.
   a. Coil operational
   b. Logic Module portion operational
   c. Power Module portion operational
   d. Interface between Power Module and Logic Module is working.
- AIS is operational
- Injector fuel pulse into Throttle Body:
   a. Fuel injector operational
   b. Fuel pump operational
   c. Fuel lines intact.
7. The Electronic Fuel Injection system must be evaluated using all the information found in the systems test:
- Start/No Start
- Fault Codes
- Loss of Power Lamp on or off (limp in)
- ATM Results:
   Spark yes/no
   Fuel yes/no
   AIS movement yes/no

Once this information is found it will be easier to determine what circuit to look at for further testing.

Idle Speed Adjustment
Before adjusting the idle on an electronic fuel injected vehicle the following items must be checked:
   a. AIS motor has been checked for operation.
   b. Engine has been checked for vacuum or EGR leaks.
   c. Engine timing has been checked and set to specifications.
   d. Coolant temperature sensor has been checked for operation.
1. Install a tachometer.
2. Warm up engine to normal operating temperature (accessories off).
3. Shut engine off and disconnect radiator fan.
4. Disconnect Throttle Body 6-way connector. Remove the brown with white tracer AIS wire from the connector and reconnect connector.
5. Start engine with transaxle selector in park or neutral.
6. Apply 12 volts to AIS brown with white tracer wire. This will drive the AIS fully closed and the idle should drop.
7. Disconnect then reconnect coolant temperature sensor.
8. With transaxle in neutral, idle speed should be 775 [+ −] 25 (700 [+ −] 25 green engine).
9. If idle is not to specifications adjust idle air bypass screw.
10. If idle will not adjust down, check for vacuum leaks, AIS motor damage, throttle body damage, or speed control cable adjustment.

EMISSION CONTROLS AND FUEL SYSTEM

Ignition Timing Adjustment

1. Connect a power timing light to the number one cylinder, or a magnetic timing unit to the engine. (Use a 10° degree offset when required).
2. Connect a tachometer to the engine and turn selector to the proper cylinder position.
3. Start engine and run until operating temperature is reached.
4. Disconnect and reconnect the water temperature sensor connector on the thermostat housing. The loss of power lamp on the dash must come on and stay on. Engine rpm should be within emission label specifications.
5. Aim power timing light at timing hole in bell housing or read the magnetic timing unit.
6. Loosen distributor and adjust timing to emission label specifications if necessary.
7. Shut engine off, disconnect and reconnect positive battery quick disconnect. Start vehicle, the loss of power lamp should be off.
8. Shut engine off, disconnect and reconnect positive battery quick disconnect. Start vehicle, the loss of power lamp should be off.
9. Shut engine off, then turn ignition on, off, on, off, on. Fault codes should be cleared with 88-51-55 shown.

Relieving Fuel System Pressure

The F.F.I fuel system is under a constant pressure of approximately 53 psi (380 kPa). Before servicing the fuel tank, fuel pump, fuel lines, fuel filter, or fuel components of the throttle body the fuel pressure must be released as follows:

1. Loosen gas cap to release any in tank pressure.
2. Remove wiring harness connector from any injector.
3. Ground one injector terminal with a jumper.
4. Connect a jumper wire to second terminal and touch battery positive post for no longer than 10 seconds.
5. Remove jumper wires.
6. Continue fuel system service.

Fuel System Pressure Test

CAUTION: *Fuel system pressure must be released each time a fuel hose is to be disconnected.*

1. Remove fuel intake hose from throttle body and connect fuel system pressure testers C-3292, and C-4749, or equivalent, between fuel filter hose and throttle body.
2. Start engine. If gauge reads 380 kPa = 14, Pa (53 psi = 2 psi) pressure is correct and no further testing is required. Reinstall fuel hose using a new original equipment type clamp and torque to 10 inch lbs. (1 Nm).
3. If fuel pressure is below specifications, install tester between fuel filter hose and fuel line.
4. Start engine. If pressure is now correct, replace fuel filter. If no change is observed, gently squeeze return hose. If pressure increased, replace pressure regulator. If no change is observed, problem is a plugged pump filter sock or defective fuel pump.
5. If pressure is above specifications, remove fuel return hose from pressure regulator end. Connect a substitute hose and place other end of hose in clean container. Start engine. If pressure is now correct check for restricted fuel return line. If no change is observed, replace fuel regulator.

Component Removal

Mechanical malfunctions are more difficult to diagnose with the EFI system. The Logic Module has been programmed to compensate for some mechanical malfunctions such as incorrect cam timing, vacuum leaks, etc. If engine performance problems are encountered, and no fault codes are displayed, the problem may be mechanical rather than electrical.

THROTTLE BODY

When servicing the fuel portion of the throttle body it will be necessary to bleed fuel pressure before opening any hoses. Always reassemble throttle body components with new O-rings and seals where applicable. Never use lubricants on O-rings or seals, damage may result. If assembly of components is difficult use water to aid assembly. Use care when removing fuel hoses to prevent damage to hose or hose nipple. Always use new hose clamps of the correct type when reassembling and torque hose clamps to 10 inch lbs. (1 Nm). Do not use aviation-style clamps on this system or hose damage may result.

NOTE: *It is not necessary to remove the throttle body from the intake manifold to perform component disassembly. If fuel system hoses are to be replaced, only hoses marked EFI/EFM may be used.*

Removal and Installation

1. Disconnect negative battery cable.
2. Remove air cleaner to throttle body screws, loosen hose clamp and remove air cleaner adaptor.
3. Remove accelerator, speed control, and transmission kickdown cables and return spring.
4. Remove throttle cable bracket from throttle body.

EMISSION CONTROLS AND FUEL SYSTEM

5. Disconnect 6 way connector.
6. Disconnect vacuum hoses from throttle body.
7. Loosen throttle body to turbocharger hose clamp.
8. Remove throttle body to intake manifold screws.
9. Remove throttle body.
10. Reverse the above procedure for installation.

THROTTLE POSITION SENSOR

Removal and Installation

1. Disconnect negative battery cable and 6-way throttle body connector.
2. Remove 2 screws mounting throttle position sensors to throttle body.
3. Unclip wiring clip from convoluted tube and remove mounting bracket.
4. Lift throttle position sensor off throttle shaft and remove O-ring.
5. Pull the 3 wires of the throttle position sensor from the convoluted tubing.
6. Look inside the 6-way throttle body connector and lift a locking tab with a small screwdriver for each T.P.S. wire blade terminal. Remove each blade from connector. (Not wiring position for reassembly.)
7. Insert each wire blade terminal into throttle body connector. Make sure wires are inserted into correct locations.
8. Insert wires from throttle position sensor into convoluted tube.
9. Install throttle position sensor and new O-ring with mounting bracket to throttle body. Torque screws to 20 inch lbs. (2Nm).
10. Install wiring clips to convoluted tube.
11. Connect 6 way connector and battery cable.

AUTOMATIC IDLE SPEED MOTOR

Removal and Installation

1. Disconnect negative battery cable and 6-way throttle body connector.
2. Remove 2 screws that mount the A.I.S. to its adaptor. (Do not remove the clamp on the A.I.S. or damage will result.)
3. Remove wiring clips and rove the two A.I.S. wires from the 6-way throttle body connector. Lift each locking tab with a small screwdriver and remove each blade terminal. (Note wiring position for reassembly).
4. Lift A.I.S. from its adaptor.
5. Remove the 2 O-rings on the A.I.S. carefully.
6. Install 2 new O-rings on A.I.S.
7. Carefully work A.I.S. into its adaptor.

8. Install 2 mounting screws and torque to 20 inch lbs. (2Nm).
9. Route A.I.S. wiring to 6-way connector and install each wire blade terminal into the connector. Make sure wires are inserted in correct locations.
10. Install wiring clips to convoluted rube.
11. Connect 6 way connector and battery cable.

AUTOMATIC IDLE SPEED MOTOR ASSEMBLY

Removal and Installation

1. Disconnect negative battery cable and 6-way throttle body connector.
2. Remove 2 screws on back of throttle body from A.I.S. adaptor.
3. Remove wiring clips and remove the two A.I.S. wires from the 6-way throttle body connector. Lift each locking tab with a small screwdriver and remove each blade terminal. (Note wiring position for reassembly).
4. Carefully pull the assembly from the rear of the throttle body. The O-ring at the top and seal at the bottom may fall off adaptor.
5. Remove O-ring and seal.
6. Place a new O-ring and seal on adaptor.
7. Carefully position assembly onto back of throttle body (make sure seals stay in place) insert screws and torque to 65 inch lbs. (7 Nm).
8. Route A.I.S. wiring to 6-way connector and install each wire blade terminal into the connector. Make sure wires are inserted in correct locations.
9. Connect wiring clips, 6-way connector, and battery cable.

OXYGEN SENSOR

Removal and Installation

Removing the oxygen sensor from the exhaust manifold may be difficult if the sensor was overtorqued during installation. Use Tool C-4589, or equivalent, to remove the sensor. The threads in the exhaust manifold must be cleaned with an 18mm x 1.5 6E tap. If the same sensor is to be reinstalled, the threads must be coated with an antiseize compound, such as Loctite® 771–64 or equivalent. New sensors are packaged with anti-seize compound on the threads and no additional compound is required. Sensors must be torqued to 20 ft. lbs. (27Nm).

FUEL FILTER

Removal and Installation

1. Follow the procedures listed under "Relieving Fuel System Pressure."
2. Loosen the outlet clamp on the filter and inlet hose clamp on the rear fuel tube.

EMISSION CONTROLS AND FUEL SYSTEM   91

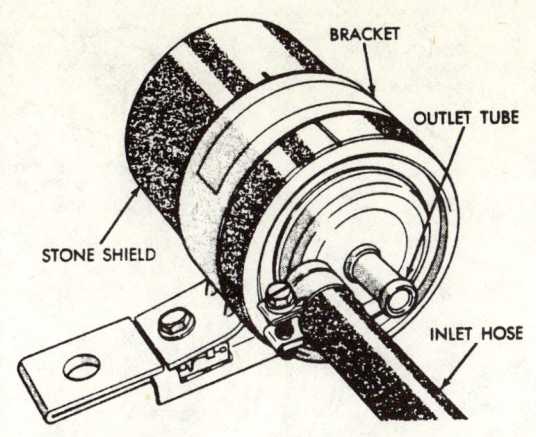

Fuel filter assembly

3. Wrap a rag around the hoses to absorb fuel. Remove the hoses at the filter and the fuel tube.
4. Loosen the filter retaining screw and slide the filter assembly from the bracket.
5. Slide the new filter assembly into the mounting bracket until the stone shield shoulder contacts the bracket.
6. Position the filter in the bracket and tighten the filter mounting screw.
7. Install the formed outlet hose on the filter outlet fitting and tighten the clamp.
8. Install the inlet hose on the fuel tube and tighten the clamp.

Fuel Pump

Removal and Installation

NOTE: *It is necessary to remove the fuel tank from the vehicle in order to remove the fuel pump. Follow the fuel tank removal procedure.*

1. Using a hammer and a non-metallic punch carefully tap the lock ring counter clockwise to release the pump.
2. Remove the fuel pump and O-ring seal from the tank.
3. To install: Wipe the seal area of the tank clean and place a new O-ring seal in position on the pump.
4. Before installing the pump check the condition of the filter on the end of the suction tube. Replace if necessary.
5. Position the fuel pump in the tank with the locking ring.
6. Using a hammer and a non-metallic punch drive the ring around clockwise to lock the pump in place.
CAUTION: *Use extreme care when installing the pump as overtightening could cause the pump to leak.*
7. Install the fuel tank.

FUEL TANK

Removal and Installation

1. Follow the procedures listed under "Relieving Fuel System Pressure".
2. Disconnect the negative battery cable.
3. Remove the fuel filler cap.
4. Remove the screws that secure the fuel filler tube to the quarter panel.
5. Raise the car and support on jackstands.
6. Remove the draft tube cap on the sending unit and connect a fuel siphon hose and siphon the fuel from the tank.
7. Disconnect the wiring and fuel lines from the tank.
NOTE: *Place rags over the lines when disconnecting to catch any fuel left in the system.*
8. Using a transmission jack or equivalent, support the fuel tank and remove the retaining nuts and straps.
9. Lower the tank slightly and carefully work the filler tube from the tank.
10. Lower the tank and disconnect the vapor separator rollover valve hose. Remove the tank and insulator pad from the car.
11. To install: Position the fuel tank on the transmission jack or equivalent. Connect the vapor separator, roll over valve hose and position the insulator pad on the fuel tank.
CAUTION: *Be certain the vapor vent hose is clipped to the tank and not pinched between the tank and the floor pan during the installation.*

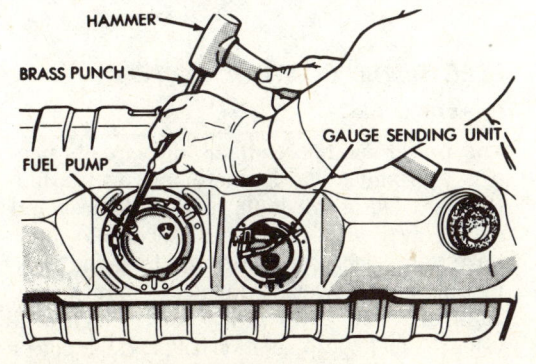

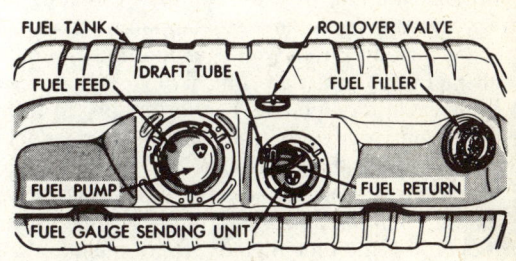

Removing the fuel pump assembly

Fuel tank and components

EMISSION CONTROLS AND FUEL SYSTEM

Fuel tank assembly

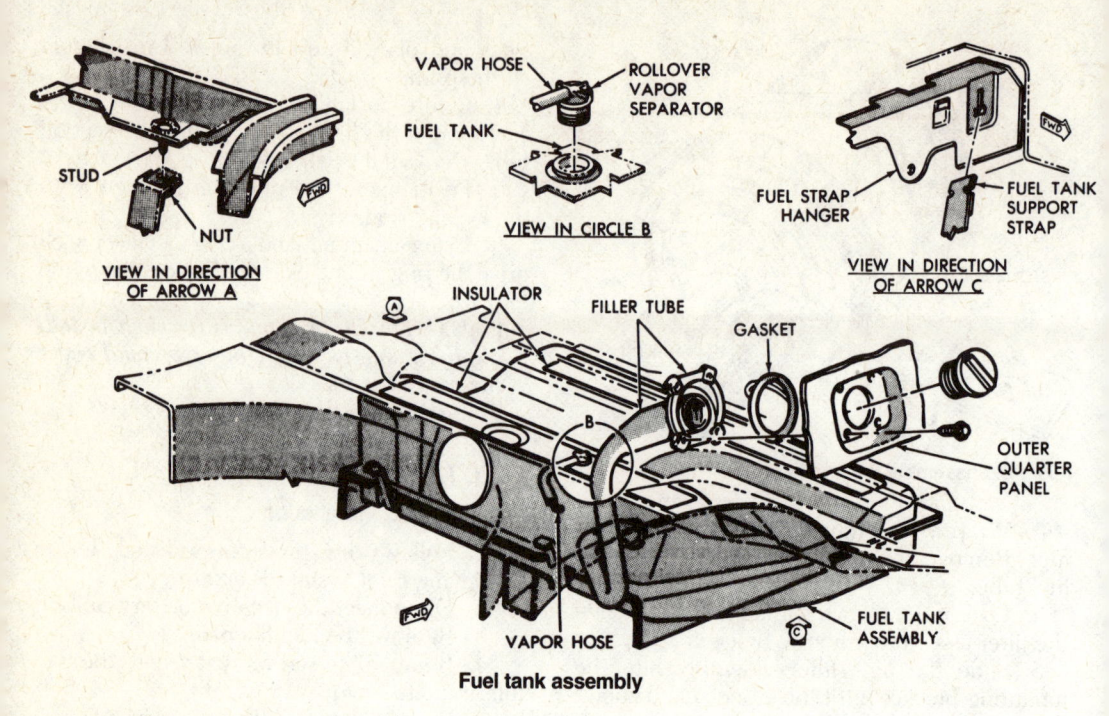

12. Raise the tank into position and carefully work the filler tube into the tank.
13. Tighten the strap nut to 250 inch lbs.
CAUTION: *Be certain the straps are not twisted or bent before or after tightening the strap nuts.*
14. Connect the lines, draft tube cap, and wiring. Use new hose clamps.
15. Lower the car and tighten the filler tube to quarter panel.
16. Fill the fuel tank, connect the battery. Start and run the car.
17. Check for any leaks at the hose connections.

Chrysler Throttle Body Injection System—Non-Turbocharged Engines

This electronic fuel injection system is a computer regulated single point fuel injection system that provides precise air/fuel ratio for all driving conditions. At the center of this system is a digital preprogrammed computer known as a logic module that regulates ignition timing, air-fuel ratio, emission control devices and idle speed. The component has the ability to update and revise its programming to meet changing operating conditions.

Various sensors provide the input necessary for the logic module to correctly regulate the fuel flow at the fuel injector. These include the manifold absolute pressure, throttle-position, oxygen feedback, coolant temperature, charge temperature and vehicle speed sensors. In addition to the sensor, various switches also provide important information. These include the neutral-safety, heated back like, air conditioning, air conditioning clutch switches, and an electronic idle switch.

All inputs to the logic module are converted into signals sent to the power module. These signals cause the power module to change either the fuel flow at the injector or ignition timing or both.

The logic module tests many of its own input and output circuit. If a fault is found in a major system this information is stored in the logic module. Information on this fault can be displayed to a technician by means of a flashing light emitting diode (LED) or by connecting a diagnostic read out and reading a numbered display code which directly relates to specific fault.

ELECTRONIC CONTROL SYSTEM
Power Module

The power module contains the circuits necessary to power the ignition coil and the fuel injector. These are high current devices and their power supply has been isolated to minimize any "electrical noise" reaching the logic module. The power module also energizes the automatic shut down (ASD) relay which activates the fuel pump, ignition coil, and the power module itself. The module also receives a sig-

EMISSION CONTROLS AND FUEL SYSTEM 93

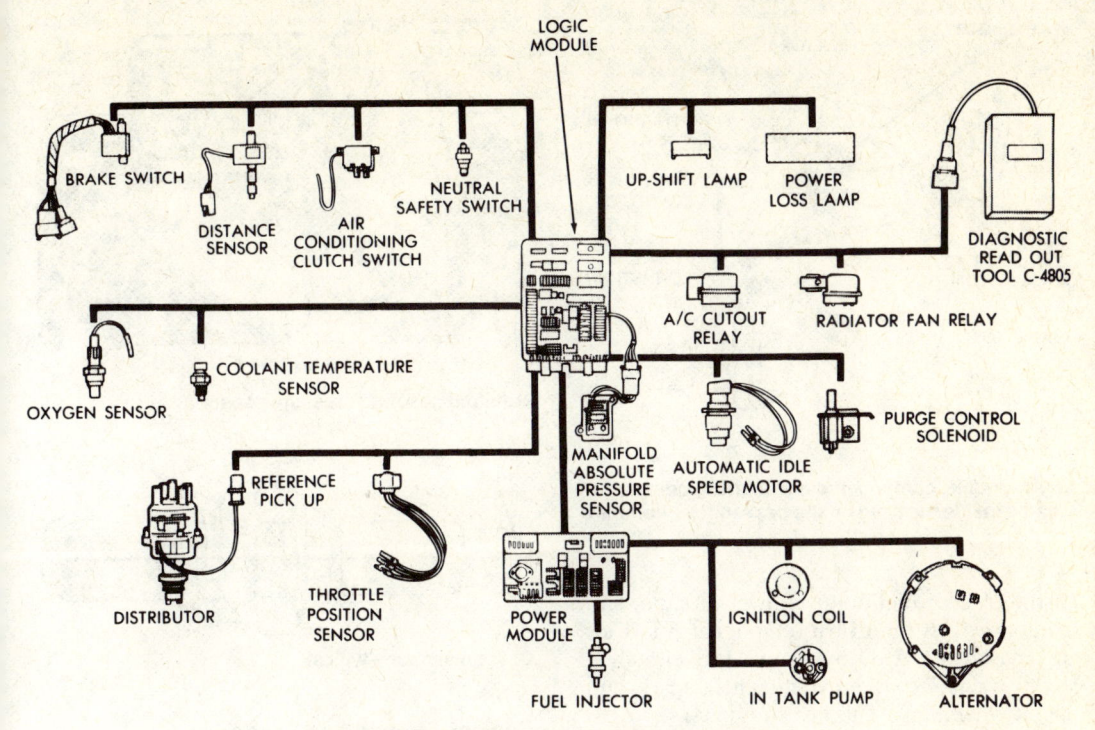

Components, Single-Point fuel injection system

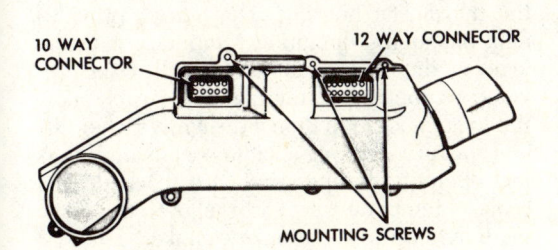

Power module and connectors

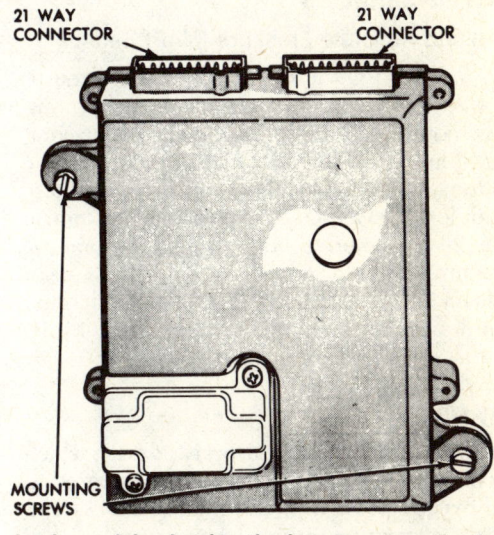

Logic module showing the harness connector terminals

nal from the distributor and sends this signal to the logic. In the event of no distributor signal, the ASD relay is not activated and power is shut off from the fuel pump and ignition coil. The power module contains a voltage converter which reduces battery voltage to a regulated 8.0V output. This 8.0V output powers the distributor and also powers the logic module.

Logic Module

The logic module is a digital computer containing a microprocessor. The module receives input signals from various switches, sensors, and components. It then computes the fuel injector pulse width, spark advance, ignition coil dwell, automatic idle speed actuation, and purge, and EGR control solenoid cycles.

The logic module tests many of its own input and output circuits.

If a fault is found in a major system, this information is stored in the logic module. Information on this fault can be displayed to a technician by means of a flashing light emitting diode (LED) or by connecting a diagnostic read out and reading a numbered display code which directly relates to a specific fault.

When the power module senses a distributor signal during cranking, it grounds the ASD closing its contacts. This completes the circuit

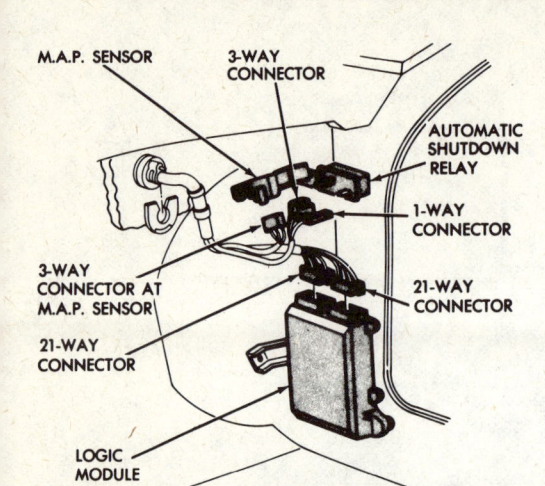

94 EMISSION CONTROLS AND FUEL SYSTEM

Logic module, components and harness connectors located inside the cowl on the passenger's compartment

Manifold absolute pressure sensor (MAP)

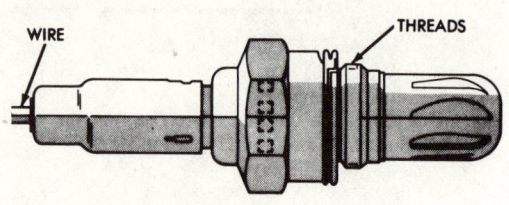

Oxygen sensor—typical

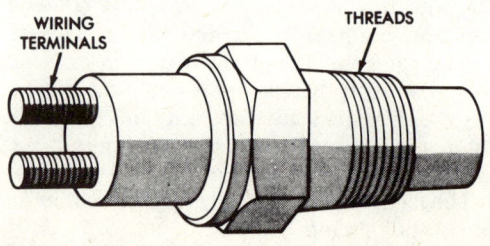

Coolant sensor—typical, wiring terminal may vary

for the electric fuel pump, power module, and ignition coil. If the distributor signal is lost for any reason the ASD interrupts this circuit in less than one second preventing fuel, spark, and engine operations. This fast shutdown serves as a safety feature in the event of an accident.

ENGINE SENSORS

Manifold Absolute Pressure (MAP) Sensor

The manifold absolute pressure (MAP) sensor is a device which monitors manifold vacuum. It is mounted in the right side passenger compartment and is connected to a vacuum nipple on the throttle body and, electrically to the logic module. The sensor transmits information on manifold vacuum conditions and barometric pressure to the logic module. The MAP sensor data on engine load is used with data from other sensors to determine the correct air-fuel mixture.

Oxygen Sensor

The oxygen sensor (02 sensor) is a device which produces an electrical voltage when exposed to the oxygen present in the exhaust gases. The sensor is mounted in the exhaust manifold and must be heated by the exhaust gases before producing the voltage. When there is a large amount of oxygen present (lean mixture), the sensor produces a low voltage. When there is a lesser amount present (rich mixture) it produces a higher voltage. By monitoring the oxygen content and converting it to electrical voltage, the sensor acts as a rich-lean switch. The voltage is transmitted to the logic module. The logic module signals the power module to trigger the fuel injector. The injector changes the mixture.

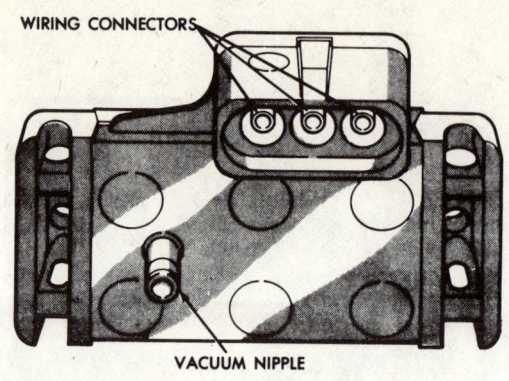

Coolant Temperature Sensor

The coolant temperature sensor is mounted in the thermostat housing. This sensor provides data on engine operating temperature to the logic module. This data along with data provided by the charge temperature switch allow the logic module to demand slightly richer air-fuel mixtures and higher idle speeds until normal operating temperatures are reached. The coolant temperature sensor allows the logic module to act as an automatic choke.

Charge Temperature Sensor

The charge temperature sensor is a device mounted in the intake manifold which measures the temperature of the air-fuel mixture. This information is used by the logic module to determine engine operating temperature and engine warm-up cycles in the event of a coolant temperature sensor failure.

Switch Input

Various switches provide information to the logic module. These include the idle, neutral safety,

EMISSION CONTROLS AND FUEL SYSTEM 95

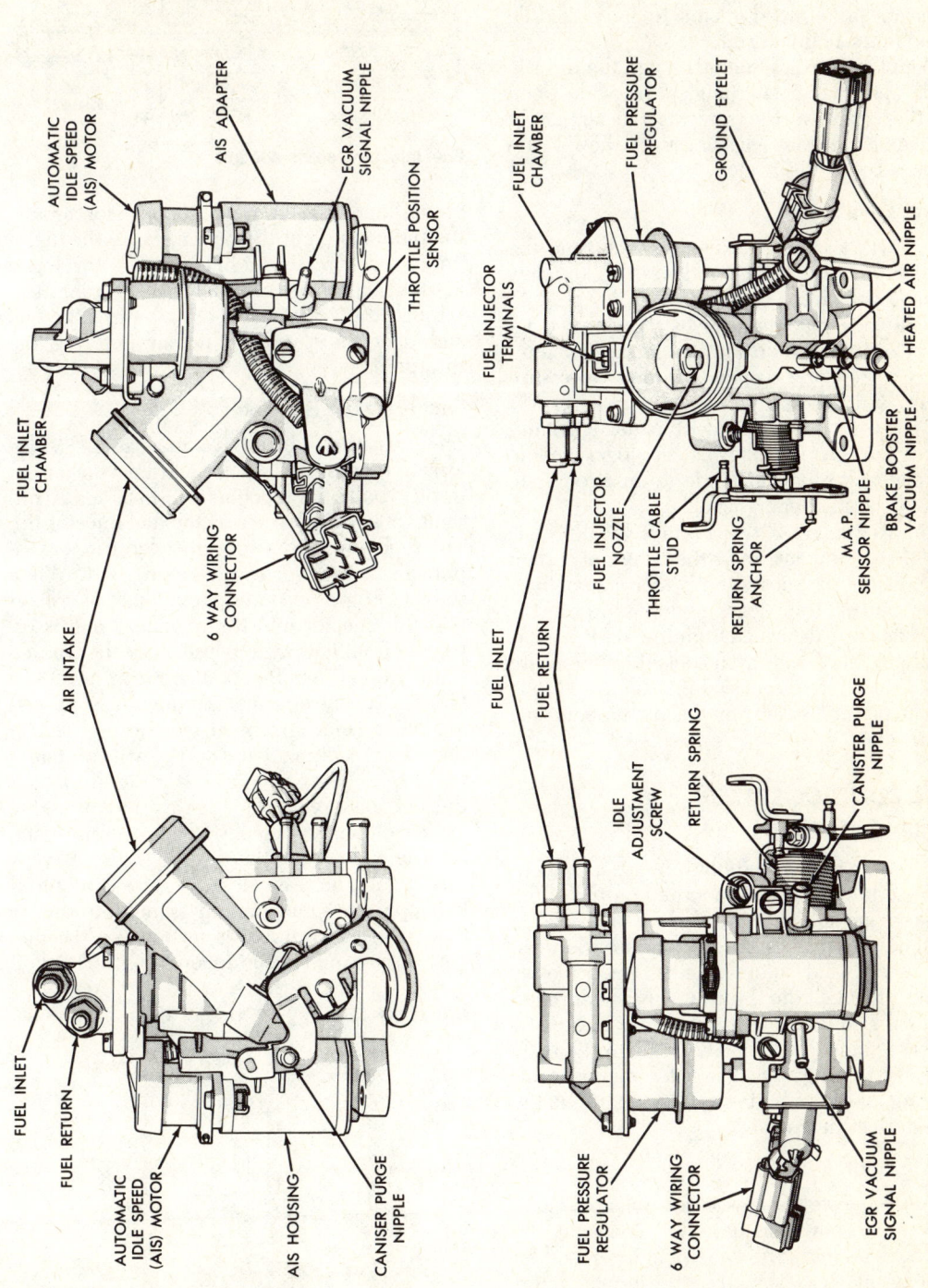

Throttle body assembly—single-point fuel injection system

EMISSION CONTROLS AND FUEL SYSTEM

electric backlite, air conditioning, air conditioning clutch, and brake light switches. If one or more of these switches is sensed as being in the on position, the logic module signals the automatic idle speed motor to increase idle speed to a scheduled rpm.

With the air conditioning on and the throttle blade above a specific angle, the wide open throttle cut-out relay prevents the air conditioning clutch from engaging until the throttle blade is below this angle.

Power Loss Lamp

The power loss lamp comes on each time the ignition key is turned on and stays on for a few seconds as a bulb test.

If the logic module receives an incorrect signal or no signal from either the coolant temperature sensor, manifold absolute pressure sensor, or the throttle position sensor, the power loss lamp on the instrument panel is illuminated. This is a warning that the logic module has gone into limp in mode in an attempt to keep the system operational.

Limp in mode is the attempt by the logic module to compensate for the failure of certain components by substituting information from other sources. If the logic module senses incorrect data or no data at all from the MAP sensor, throttle position sensor on coolant temperature sensor, the system is placed into Limp in Mode and the power loss lamp on the instrument panel activated.

FUEL CONTROL SYSTEM

Throttle Body

The throttle body assembly replaces a conventional carburetor and is mounted on top of the intake manifold. The throttle body houses the fuel injector, pressure regulator, throttle position sensor, and automatic idle speed motor. Air flow through the throttle body is controlled by a cable operated throttle blade located in the base of the throttle body. The throttle body itself provides the chamber for metering atomizing and distributing fuel through out the air entering the engine.

Fuel Injector

The fuel injector is an electric solenoid powered by the power module but, controlled by the logic module. The logic module, based on ambient, mechanical, and sensor inputs, determines when and how long the power module should operate the injector. When an electric current is supplied to the injector, the armature and pintle move a short distance against a spring, opening a small orifice. Fuel is supplied to the inlet of the injector by the fuel pump, then passes through the injector, around the pintle, and out the orifice. Since the fuel is under high pressure a fine spray is developed in the shape of a hollow cone. The injector, through this spraying action, atomizes the fuel and distributes it into the air entering the throttle body.

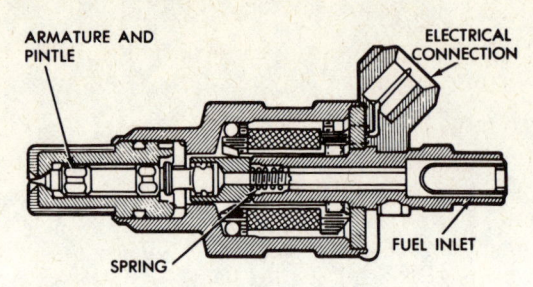

Fuel injector—cross-section

Fuel Pressure Regulator.

The pressure regulator is a mechanical device located downstream of the fuel injector on the throttle body. Its function is to maintain a constant 250kPa (36psi) across the fuel injector tip. The regulator uses a spring loaded rubber diaphragm to uncover a fuel return port. When the fuel pump becomes operational, fuel flows past the injector into the regulator, and is restricted from flowing any further by the blocked return port. When fuel pressure reaches 250kPa (36psi) it pushes on the diaphragm, compressing the spring, and uncovers the fuel return port. The diaphragm and spring will constantly move from an open to closed position to keep the fuel pressure constant. An assist to the spring loaded diaphragm comes from vacuum in the throttle body above the throttle blade. As venturi vacuum increases less pressure is required to supply the same amount of fuel into the air flow. The vacuum assists in opening the fuel port during high vacuum conditions. This fine

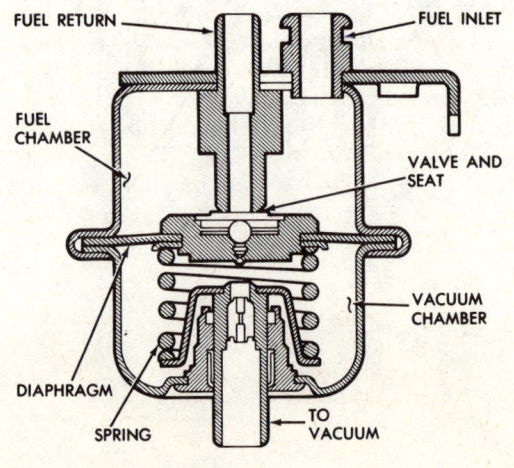

Fuel pressure regulator

EMISSION CONTROLS AND FUEL SYSTEM

tunes the fuel pressure for all operating conditions.

Throttle Position Sensor (TPS)

The throttle position sensor (TPS) is an electric resistor which is activated by the movement of the throttle shaft. It is mounted on the throttle body and senses the angle of the throttle blade opening. The voltage that the sensor produces increases or decreases according to the throttle blade opening. This voltage is transmitted to the logic module where it is used along with data from other sensors to adjust the air-fuel ratio to varying conditions and during accerleration, deceleration, idle, and wide open throttle operations.

Automatic Idle Speed (AIS) Motor

The automatic idle speed motor (AIS) is operated by the logic module. Data from the throttle position sensor, speed sensor, coolant temperature sensor, and various switch operations, (electric backlite, air conditioning, safety/neutral, brake) are used by the logic module to adjust engine idle to an optimum during all idle conditions. The AIS adjusts the air portion of the air/fuel mixture through an air bypass on the back of the throttle body. Basic (no load) idle is determined by the minimum air flow through the throttle body. The AIS opens or closes off the air bypass as an increase or decrease is needed due to engine loads or ambient conditions. The logic module senses an air/fuel change and increases or decreases fuel proportionally to change engine idles. Deceleration die out is also prevented by increasing engine idle when the throttle is closed quickly after driving (speed) condition.

Fuel Pump

The fuel pump used in this system is a positive displacement, roller vane immersible pump with a permanent magnet electric motor. The fuel is drawn in through a filter sock and pushed through the electric motor to the outlet. The pump contains two check valves. One valve is used to relieve internal fuel pump pressure and regulate maximum pump output. The other check valve, located near the pump outlet, restricts fuel movement in either direction when

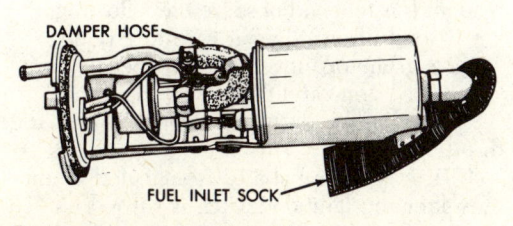

Fuel pump assembly (in-tank)

the pump is not operational. Voltage to operat the pump is supplied through the auto shut down relay.

On-Car Service

NOTE: *Experience has shown that mos complaints that may occur with EFI can b traced to poor wiring or hose connections. visual check will help spot these most com mon faults and save unnecessary test and d agnosis time.*

ON BOARD DIAGNOSTICS

The logic module has been programmed t monitor several different circuits of the fuel in jection system. This monitoring is called O Board Diagnosis. If a problem is sensed with monitored circuit, often enough to indicate a actual problem, its fault code is stored in the logic module for eventual display to the servic technician. If the problem is repaired or cease to exist, the logic module cancels the fault cod after 30 ignition key on/off cycles

Fault Codes

When a fault code appears (either by flashes o the light emitting diode or by watching the di agnostic read-out—Tool C-4805 or equivalent it indicates that the logic module has recog nized an abnormal signal in the system. Faul codes indicate the results of a failure but do no always identify the failed component.

CODE 11 means a problem in the distribu tor circuit. This code appears when the logi module has not seen a distributor signal since the battery was reconnected.

CODE 12 indicates a problem in the stand by memory circuit. This code appears if direc battery feed to the logic module is interrupted.

CODE 13 means a problem exists in the MAI sensor pneumatic system. This code appears the MAP sensor vacuum level does not change between start and start/run transfer speed (500–600 rpm).

CODE 14 means a problem exists in the MAI sensor electrical system. This code appears the MAP sensor signal is either too low (belov .02 volts) or too high (above 4.9 volts).

CODE 15 means a problem exists in the ve hicle Speed Sensor circuit. This code appear if engine speed is above 1468 rpm and speed sensor indicates less than 2 mph. This code i valid only if it is sensed while vehicle is mov ing.

CODE 21 indicates a problem in the O_2 sen sor circuit. This code appears if there has been no O_2 signal for more than 5 seconds.

CODE 22 means a problem exists in the coolant temperature sensor circuit. This code

EMISSION CONTROLS AND FUEL SYSTEM

appears if the temperature sensor circuit indicates an incorrect temperature or a temperature that change too fast to be real.

CODE 24 means a problem exists in the throttle position sensor circuit. This code appears if the sensor signal is either below 0.16 volts or above 4.7 volts.

CODE 25 means a problem in the automatic idle speed (AIS) control circuit. This code appears if the proper voltage from the AIS system is not present. An open harness or motor will not activate code.

CODE 31 means a problem in the canister purge solenoid circuit. This code appears when the proper voltage at the purge solenoid is not present (open or shorted system).

CODE 32 means a problem in the power loss lamp circuit. This code appears when proper voltage to the power loss lamp circuit is not present (open or shorted system).

CODE 33 means a problem in the air conditioning wide open throttle cut out relay circuit. This code appears if the proper voltage at the air conditioning wide open throttle relay circuit is not present (open or shorted).

CODE 34 means a problem in the EGR solenoid circuit. This code appears if proper voltage at the EGR solenoid circuit is not present (open or shorted system).

CODE 35 indicates a problem in the fan relay circuit. This code appears if the radiator fan is either not operating or operating at wrong time.

CODE 41 means a problem in the charging system. This code appears if battery voltage from the automatic shut down relay is below 11.75 volts.

CODE 42 means a problem in the automatic shut down relay (ASD) circuit. This code appears if during cranking, battery voltage from ASD relay is not present for at least ⅓ second after first distributor pulse or after engine stall, battery voltage is not off within 3 seconds after last distributor pulse.

CODE 43 means a problem in the interface circuit. This code appears if the anti-dwell or injector control signal is not present between the logic module and power module.

CODE 44 means a problem in the logic module. This code appears if an internal failure exists in the logic module.

CODE 51 indicates problem in the closed loop fuel system. This code appears if during closed loop conditions, the O_2 signal is either low or high for more than 2 minutes.

CODE 52 means a problem in the logic module. This code appears if an internal failure exists in the logic module.

CODE 53 means a problem in the logic module. This code appears if an internal failure exists in the logic module.

CODE 54 means a problem in the logic module. This code appears if an internal failure exists in the logic module.

CODE 55 means "end of message". This code appears as the final code after all other fault codes have been displayed and means "end of message".

CODE 88 means start of message. This code only appears on the diagnostic readout Tool C-4805 or equivalent, and means start of message.

SYSTEMS TEST

Obtaining Fault Codes

1. Connect diagnostic readout box tool C-4805 or equivalent, to the diagnostic connector located in the engine compartment near the passenger side strut tower.

2. Start the engine if possible, cycle the transmission selector and the A/C switch if applicable. Shut off the engine.

3. Turn the ignition switch on, off, on, off, on. Within 5 seconds record all the diagnostic codes shown on the diagnostic readout box tool, observe the power loss lamp on the instrument panel the lamp should light for 2 seconds then go out (bulb check).

Switch Test

After all codes have been shown and has indicated Code 55 end of message, actuate the following component switches. The digital display must change its numbers when the switch is activated and released:
- Brake pedal
- Gear shift selector park, reverse, park.
- A/C switch (if applicable)
- Electric backlite switch (if applicable).

Actuator Test Mode (ATM)

1. Removal coil wire from cap and place ¼ in. from a ground.

CAUTION: *Coil wire must be ¼ in. or less from ground or power module damage may result.*

2. Remove air cleaner hose from throttle body.

3. Press the ATM button on the diagnostic readout box tool and observe the following:
- 3 sparks from the coil wire to ground.
- 2 AIS motor movements (1 open, 1 close) you must listen carefully for AIS operation.
- 1 fuel pulse from the injector into the throttle body.

4. The ATM capability is canceled 5 minutes after the ignition switch is turned on. To

CHILTON'S
FUEL ECONOMY & TUNE-UP TIPS

Tune-up • Spark Plug Diagnosis • Emission Controls
Fuel System • Cooling System • Tires and Wheels
General Maintenance

55 WAYS TO IMPROVE FUEL ECONOMY

CHILTON'S FUEL ECONOMY & TUNE-UP TIPS

Fuel economy is important to everyone, no matter what kind of vehicle you drive. The maintenance-minded motorist can save both money and fuel using these tips and the periodic maintenance and tune-up procedures in this Repair and Tune-Up Guide.

There are more than 130,000,000 cars and trucks registered for private use in the United States. Each travels an average of 10-12,000 miles per year, and, and in total they consume close to 70 billion gallons of fuel each year. This represents nearly ⅔ of the oil imported by the United States each year. The Federal government's goal is to reduce consumption 10% by 1985. A variety of methods are either already in use or under serious consideration, and they all affect you driving and the cars you will drive. In addition to "down-sizing", the auto industry is using or investigating the use of electronic fuel delivery, electronic engine controls and alternative engines for use in smaller and lighter vehicles, among other alternatives to meet the federally mandated Corporate Average Fuel Economy (CAFE) of 27.5 mpg by 1985. The government, for its part, is considering rationing, mandatory driving curtailments and tax increases on motor vehicle fuel in an effort to reduce consumption. The government's goal of a 10% reduction could be realized — and further government regulation avoided — if every private vehicle could use just 1 less gallon of fuel per week.

How Much Can You Save?

Tests have proven that almost anyone can make at least a 10% reduction in fuel consumption through regular maintenance and tune-ups. When a major manufacturer of spark plugs sur-

TUNE-UP

1. Check the cylinder compression to be sure the engine will really benefit from a tune-up and that it is capable of producing good fuel economy. A tune-up will be wasted on an engine in poor mechanical condition.

2. Replace spark plugs regularly. New spark plugs alone can increase fuel economy 3%.

3. Be sure the spark plugs are the correct type (heat range) for your vehicle. See the Tune-Up Specifications.

Heat range refers to the spark plug's ability to conduct heat away from the firing end. It must conduct the heat away in an even pattern to avoid becoming a source of pre-ignition, yet it must also operate hot enough to burn off conductive deposits that could cause misfiring.

The heat range is usually indicated by a number on the spark plug, part of the manufacturer's designation for each individual spark plug. The numbers in bold-face indicate the heat range in each manufacturer's identification system.

Manufacturer	Typical Designation
AC	R **45** TS
Bosch (old)	WA **145** T30
Bosch (new)	HR **8** Y
Champion	RBL **15** Y
Fram/Autolite	4**15**
Mopar	P-**62** PR
Motorcraft	BRF-**42**
NGK	BP **5** ES-15
Nippondenso	W **16** EP
Prestolite	14GR **5** 2A

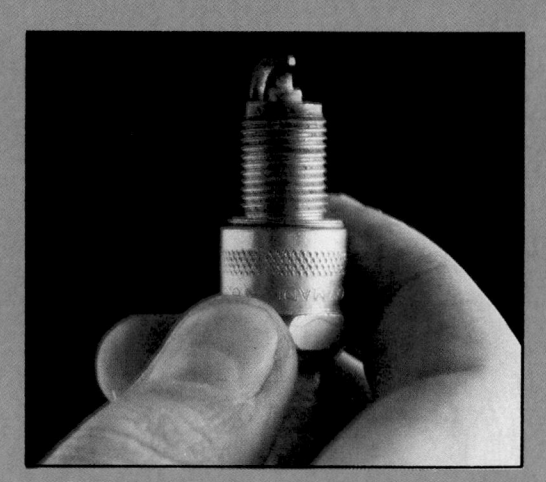

Periodically, check the spark plugs to be sure they are firing efficiently. They are excellent indicators of the internal condition of your engine.

On AC, Bosch (new), Champion, Fram/Autolite, Mopar, Motorcraft and Prestolite, a higher number indicates a hotter plug. On Bosch (old), NGK and Nippondenso, a higher number indicates a colder plug.

4. Make sure the spark plugs are properly gapped. See the Tune-Up Specifications in this book.

5. Be sure the spark plugs are firing efficiently. The illustrations on the next 2 pages show you how to "read" the firing end of the spark plug.

6. Check the ignition timing and set it to specifications. Tests show that almost all cars have incorrect ignition timing by more than 2°.

veyed over 6,000 cars nationwide, they found that a tune-up, on cars that needed one, increased fuel economy over 11%. Replacing worn plugs alone, accounted for a 3% increase. The same test also revealed that 8 out of every 10 vehicles will have some maintenance deficiency that will directly affect fuel economy, emissions or performance. Most of this mileage-robbing neglect could be prevented with regular maintenance.

Modern engines require that all of the functioning systems operate properly for maximum efficiency. A malfunction anywhere wastes fuel. You can keep your vehicle running as efficiently and economically as possible, by being aware of your vehicle's operating and performance characteristics. If your vehicle suddenly develops performance or fuel economy problems it could be due to one or more of the following:

PROBLEM	POSSIBLE CAUSE
Engine Idles Rough	Ignition timing, idle mixture, vacuum leak or something amiss in the emission control system.
Hesitates on Acceleration	Dirty carburetor or fuel filter, improper accelerator pump setting, ignition timing or fouled spark plugs.
Starts Hard or Fails to Start	Worn spark plugs, improperly set automatic choke, ice (or water) in fuel system.
Stalls Frequently	Automatic choke improperly adjusted and possible dirty air filter or fuel filter.
Performs Sluggishly	Worn spark plugs, dirty fuel or air filter, ignition timing or automatic choke out of adjustment.

Check spark plug wires on conventional point type ignition for cracks by bending them in a loop around your finger.

Be sure that spark plug wires leading to adjacent cylinders do not run too close together. (Photo courtesy Champion Spark Plug Co.)

7. If your vehicle does not have electronic ignition, check the points, rotor and cap as specified.

8. Check the spark plug wires (used with conventional point-type ignitions) for cracks and burned or broken insulation by bending them in a loop around your finger. Cracked wires decrease fuel efficiency by failing to deliver full voltage to the spark plugs. One misfiring spark plug can cost you as much as 2 mpg.

9. Check the routing of the plug wires. Misfiring can be the result of spark plug leads to adjacent cylinders running parallel to each other and too close together. One wire tends to pick up voltage from the other causing it to fire "out of time".

10. Check all electrical and ignition circuits for voltage drop and resistance.

11. Check the distributor mechanical and/or vacuum advance mechanisms for proper functioning. The vacuum advance can be checked by twisting the distributor plate in the opposite direction of rotation. It should spring back when released.

12. Check and adjust the valve clearance on engines with mechanical lifters. The clearance should be slightly loose rather than too tight.

SPARK PLUG DIAGNOSIS

Normal

APPEARANCE: This plug is typical of one operating normally. The insulator nose varies from a light tan to grayish color with slight electrode wear. The presence of slight deposits is normal on used plugs and will have no adverse effect on engine performance. The spark plug heat range is correct for the engine and the engine is running normally.
CAUSE: Properly running engine.
RECOMMENDATION: Before reinstalling this plug, the electrodes should be cleaned and filed square. Set the gap to specifications. If the plug has been in service for more than 10-12,000 miles, the entire set should probably be replaced with a fresh set of the same heat range.

Oil Deposits

APPEARANCE: The firing end of the plug is covered with a wet, oily coating.
CAUSE: The problem is poor oil control. On high mileage engines, oil is leaking past the rings or valve guides into the combustion chamber. A common cause is also a plugged PCV valve, and a ruptured fuel pump diaphragm can also cause this condition. Oil fouled plugs such as these are often found in new or recently overhauled engines, before normal oil control is achieved, and can be cleaned and reinstalled.
RECOMMENDATION: A hotter spark plug may temporarily relieve the problem, but the engine is probably in need of work.

Incorrect Heat Range

APPEARANCE: The effects of high temperature on a spark plug are indicated by clean white, often blistered insulator. This can also be accompanied by excessive wear of the electrode, and the absence of deposits.
CAUSE: Check for the correct spark plug heat range. A plug which is too hot for the engine can result in overheating. A car operated mostly at high speeds can require a colder plug. Also check ignition timing, cooling system level, fuel mixture and leaking intake manifold.
RECOMMENDATION: If all ignition and engine adjustments are known to be correct, and no other malfunction exists, install spark plugs one heat range colder.

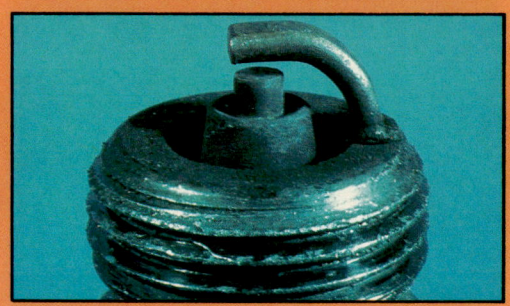

Carbon Deposits

APPEARANCE: Carbon fouling is easily identified by the presence of dry, soft, black, sooty deposits.
CAUSE: Changing the heat range can often lead to carbon fouling, as can prolonged slow, stop-and-start driving. If the heat range is correct, carbon fouling can be attributed to a rich fuel mixture, sticking choke, clogged air cleaner, worn breaker points, retarded timing or low compression. If only one or two plugs are carbon fouled, check for corroded or cracked wires on the affected plugs. Also look for cracks in the distributor cap between the towers of affected cylinders.
RECOMMENDATION: After the problem is corrected, these plugs can be cleaned and reinstalled if not worn severely.

Photos Courtesy Fram Corporation

MMT Fouled

APPEARANCE: Spark plugs fouled by MMT (Methycyclopentadienyl Maganese Tricarbonyl) have reddish, rusty appearance on the insulator and side electrode.

CAUSE: MMT is an anti-knock additive in gasoline used to replace lead. During the combustion process, the MMT leaves a reddish deposit on the insulator and side electrode.

RECOMMENDATION: No engine malfunction is indicated and the deposits will not affect plug performance any more than lead deposits (see Ash Deposits). MMT fouled plugs can be cleaned, regapped and reinstalled.

High Speed Glazing

APPEARANCE: Glazing appears as shiny coating on the plug, either yellow or tan in color.

CAUSE: During hard, fast acceleration, plug temperatures rise suddenly. Deposits from normal combustion have no chance to fluff-off; instead, they melt on the insulator forming an electrically conductive coating which causes misfiring.

RECOMMENDATION: Glazed plugs are not easily cleaned. They should be replaced with a fresh set of plugs of the correct heat range. If the condition recurs, using plugs with a heat range one step colder may cure the problem.

Ash (Lead) Deposits

APPEARANCE: Ash deposits are characterized by light brown or white colored deposits crusted on the side or center electrodes. In some cases it may give the plug a rusty appearance.

CAUSE: Ash deposits are normally derived from oil or fuel additives burned during normal combustion. Normally they are harmless, though excessive amounts can cause misfiring. If deposits are excessive in short mileage, the valve guides may be worn.

RECOMMENDATION: Ash-fouled plugs can be cleaned, gapped and reinstalled.

Detonation

APPEARANCE: Detonation is usually characterized by a broken plug insulator.

CAUSE: A portion of the fuel charge will begin to burn spontaneously, from the increased heat following ignition. The explosion that results applies extreme pressure to engine components, frequently damaging spark plugs and pistons.

Detonation can result by over-advanced ignition timing, inferior gasoline (low octane) lean air/fuel mixture, poor carburetion, engine lugging or an increase in compression ratio due to combustion chamber deposits or engine modification.

RECOMMENDATION: Replace the plugs after correcting the problem.

Photos Courtesy Champion Spark Plug Co.

EMISSION CONTROLS

13. Be aware of the general condition of the emission control system. It contributes to reduced pollution and should be serviced regularly to maintain efficient engine operation.

14. Check all vacuum lines for dried, cracked or brittle conditions. Something as simple as a leaking vacuum hose can cause poor performance and loss of economy.

15. Avoid tampering with the emission control system. Attempting to improve fuel econ-

FUEL SYSTEM

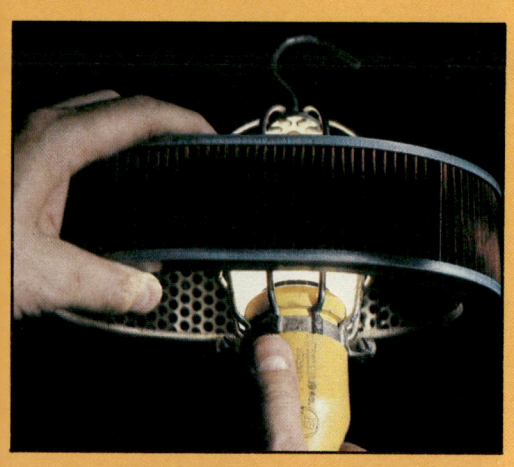

Check the air filter with a light behind it. If you can see light through the filter it can be reused.

Extremely clogged filters should be discarded and replaced with a new one.

18. Replace the air filter regularly. A dirty air filter richens the air/fuel mixture and can increase fuel consumption as much as 10%. Tests show that ⅓ of all vehicles have air filters in need of replacement.

19. Replace the fuel filter at least as often as recommended.

20. Set the idle speed and carburetor mixture to specifications.

21. Check the automatic choke. A sticking or malfunctioning choke wastes gas.

22. During the summer months, adjust the automatic choke for a leaner mixture which will produce faster engine warm-ups.

COOLING SYSTEM

29. Be sure all accessory drive belts are in good condition. Check for cracks or wear.

30. Adjust all accessory drive belts to proper tension.

31. Check all hoses for swollen areas, worn spots, or loose clamps.

32. Check coolant level in the radiator or expansion tank.

33. Be sure the thermostat is operating properly. A stuck thermostat delays engine warm-up and a cold engine uses nearly twice as much fuel as a warm engine.

34. Drain and replace the engine coolant at least as often as recommended. Rust and scale

TIRES & WHEELS

38. Check the tire pressure often with a pencil type gauge. Tests by a major tire manufacturer show that 90% of all vehicles have at least 1 tire improperly inflated. Better mileage can be achieved by over-inflating tires, but never exceed the maximum inflation pressure on the side of the tire.

39. If possible, install radial tires. Radial tires deliver as much as ½ mpg more than bias belted tires.

40. Avoid installing super-wide tires. They only create extra rolling resistance and decrease fuel mileage. Stick to the manufacturer's recommendations.

41. Have the wheels properly balanced.

omy by tampering with emission controls is more likely to worsen fuel economy than improve it. Emission control changes on modern engines are not readily reversible.

16. Clean (or replace) the EGR valve and lines as recommended.

17. Be sure that all vacuum lines and hoses are reconnected properly after working under the hood. An unconnected or misrouted vacuum line can wreak havoc with engine performance.

23. Check for fuel leaks at the carburetor, fuel pump, fuel lines and fuel tank. Be sure all lines and connections are tight.

24. Periodically check the tightness of the carburetor and intake manifold attaching nuts and bolts. These are a common place for vacuum leaks to occur.

25. Clean the carburetor periodically and lubricate the linkage.

26. The condition of the tailpipe can be an excellent indicator of proper engine combustion. After a long drive at highway speeds, the inside of the tailpipe should be a light grey in color. Black or soot on the insides indicates an overly rich mixture.

27. Check the fuel pump pressure. The fuel pump may be supplying more fuel than the engine needs.

28. Use the proper grade of gasoline for your engine. Don't try to compensate for knocking or "pinging" by advancing the ignition timing. This practice will only increase plug temperature and the chances of detonation or pre-ignition with relatively little performance gain.

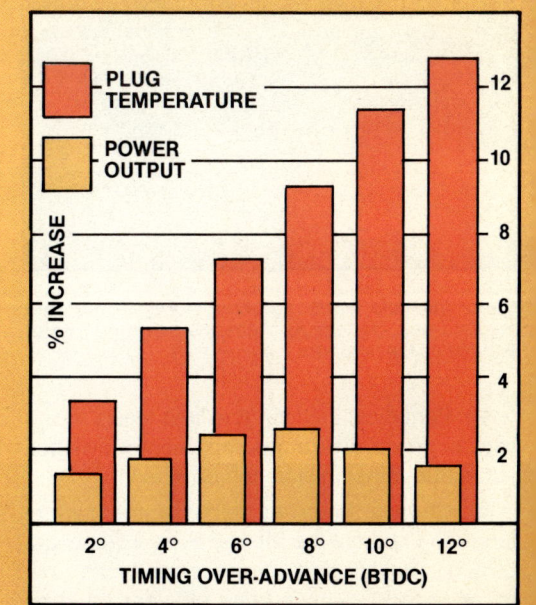

Increasing ignition timing past the specified setting results in a drastic increase in spark plug temperature with increased chance of detonation or preignition. Performance increase is considerably less. (Photo courtesy Champion Spark Plug Co.)

that form in the engine should be flushed out to allow the engine to operate at peak efficiency.

35. Clean the radiator of debris that can decrease cooling efficiency.

36. Install a flex-type or electric cooling fan, if you don't have a clutch type fan. Flex fans use curved plastic blades to push more air at low speeds when more cooling is needed; at high speeds the blades flatten out for less resistance. Electric fans only run when the engine temperature reaches a predetermined level.

37. Check the radiator cap for a worn or cracked gasket. If the cap does not seal properly, the cooling system will not function properly.

42. Be sure the front end is correctly aligned. A misaligned front end actually has wheels going in differed directions. The increased drag can reduce fuel economy by .3 mpg.

43. Correctly adjust the wheel bearings. Wheel bearings that are adjusted too tight increase rolling resistance.

Check tire pressures regularly with a reliable pocket type gauge. Be sure to check the pressure on a cold tire.

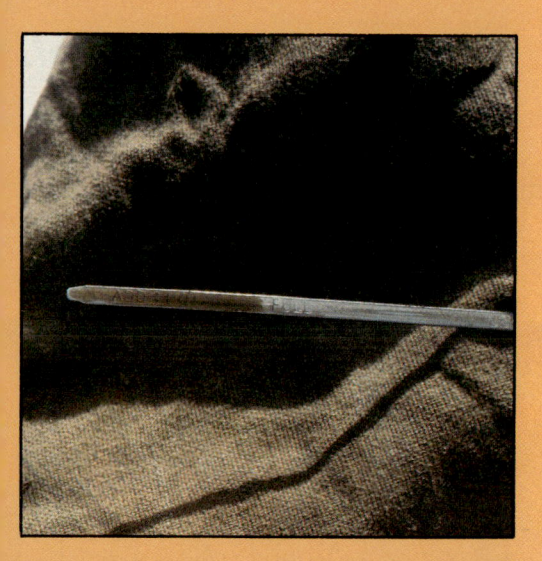

GENERAL MAINTENANCE

Check the fluid levels (particularly engine oil) on a regular basis. Be sure to check the oil for grit, water or other contamination.

A vacuum gauge is another excellent indicator of internal engine condition and can also be installed in the dash as a mileage indicator.

44. Periodically check the fluid levels in the engine, power steering pump, master cylinder, automatic transmission and drive axle.

45. Change the oil at the recommended interval and change the filter at every oil change. Dirty oil is thick and causes extra friction between moving parts, cutting efficiency and increasing wear. A worn engine requires more frequent tune-ups and gets progressively worse fuel economy. In general, use the lightest viscosity oil for the driving conditions you will encounter.

46. Use the recommended viscosity fluids in the transmission and axle.

47. Be sure the battery is fully charged for fast starts. A slow starting engine wastes fuel.

48. Be sure battery terminals are clean and tight.

49. Check the battery electrolyte level and add distilled water if necessary.

50. Check the exhaust system for crushed pipes, blockages and leaks.

51. Adjust the brakes. Dragging brakes or brakes that are not releasing create increased drag on the engine.

52. Install a vacuum gauge or miles-per-gallon gauge. These gauges visually indicate engine vacuum in the intake manifold. High vacuum = good mileage and low vacuum = poorer mileage. The gauge can also be an excellent indicator of internal engine conditions.

53. Be sure the clutch is properly adjusted. A slipping clutch wastes fuel.

54. Check and periodically lubricate the heat control valve in the exhaust manifold. A sticking or inoperative valve prevents engine warm-up and wastes gas.

55. Keep accurate records to check fuel economy over a period of time. A sudden drop in fuel economy may signal a need for tune-up or other maintenance.

© 1980 Chilton Book Company, Radnor, PA 19089

EMISSION CONTROLS AND FUEL SYSTEM

reinstate this capabilty cycle the ignition ON and OFF three times ending in the ON position.

5. When the ATM button is pressed, fault Code 42 is generated because the ASD relay is bypassed. Do not use this code for diagnostics after ATM operation.

6. The ATM test will check 3 categories of operation:
- When coil fires three times:
  a. Coil operational
  b. Logic module portion operational
  c. Power module portion operational
  d. Interface between power module and logic module is working.
- AIS is operational
- Injector fuel pulse into throttle body:
  a. Fuel injector operational
  b. Fuel pump operational
  c. Fuel lines intact

7. The electronic fuel injection system must be evaluated using all the information found in the systems test:
- Start/no start
- Fault codes
- Loss of power lamp on or off (limp in)
- ATM results:
  a. Spark yes/no
  b. Fuel yes/no
  c. AIS movement yes/no

Once this information is found, it will be easier to determine what circuit to look at for further testing.

Ignition Timing Adjustment

1. Connect a power timing light to the number one cylinder, or a magnetic timing unit to the engine. (Use a 10° offset when required).

2. Connect a tachometer to the engine and turn selector to the proper cylinder position.

3. Start engine and run until operating temperature is reached.

4. Disconnect and reconnect the water temperature sensor connector on the thermostat housing. The loss of power lamp on the dash must come on and stay on. Engine rpm should be within emission label specifications.

5. Aim power timing light at timing hole in bell housing or read the magnetic timing unit.

6. Loosen distributor and adjust timing to emission label specifications if necessary.

7. Shut engine off, disconnect and reconnect positive battery quick disconnect. Start vehicle, the loss of power lamp should be off.

8. Shut engine off, then turn ignition on, off, on, off, on. Fault codes should be clear with 88-51-55 shown.

9. Increase engine to 2000 rpm.

10. Read timing it should be approximately 40 degrees.

11. If timing advance does not reach specifications, replace logic module.

Idle Speed Adjustment

1. Before adjusting the idle on an electronic fuel injected vehicle the following items must be checked.
   a. AIS motor has been checked for operation.
   b. Engine has been checked for vacuum or EGR leaks.
   c. Engine timing has been checked and set to specifications
   d. Coolant temperature sensor has been checked for operation.

2. Connect a tachometer and timing light to engine.

3. Disconnect throttle body 6-way connector. Remove brown with white tracer AIS wire from connector and rejoin connector.

4. Connect one end of a jumper wire to AIS wire and other end to battery positive post for 5 seconds.

5. Connect a jumper to radiator fan so that it will run continuously.

6. Start and run engine for 3 minutes to allow speed to stabilize.

7. Using tool C-4804 or equivalent, turn idle speed adjusting screw to obtain 800 ± 10 rpm (Manual 725 ± 10 rpm (Automatic) with transaxle in neutral.

NOTE: *If idle will not adjust down, check for binding linkage, speed control serve cable adjustment, or throttle shaft binding.*

8. Check that timing is 8 ± 2°BTDC (Manual) 12 ± 2°BTDC (Automatic).

9. If timing is not to above specifications turn idle speed adjusting screw until correct idle speed and ignition timing are obtained.

10. Turn off engine, disconnect tachometer and timing light, reinstall AIS wire and remove jumper wire.

Relieving Fuel System Pressure

The E.F.I. fuel system is under a constant pressure of approximately 36 psi (250 kPa). Before serving the fuel tank, fuel pump, fuel lines, fuel filter, or fuel components of the throttle body the fuel pressure must be released as follows:

1. Loosen gas cap to release any in tank pressure

2. Remove wiring harness connector from injector.

3. Ground one injector terminal with a jumper.

EMISSION CONTROLS AND FUEL SYSTEM

4. Connect a jumper wire to second terminal and touch battery positive post for no longer than 10 seconds.
5. Remove jumper wires.
6. Continue fuel system service

Fuel System Pressure Test

CAUTION: *Fuel system pressure must be released each time a fuel hose is to be disconnected.*

1. Remove fuel intake hose from throttle body and connect fuel system pressure testers C-3292, and C-4749 or equivalent, between fuel filter hose and throttle body.
2. Start engine. If gauge reads 250 kPa ± 14 kPA (36 psi ± 2 psi) pressure is correct and no further testing is required. Reinstall fuel hose using a new original equipment type clamp and torque to 10 inch lbs. (1 Nm).
3. If fuel pressure is below specifications, install tester between fuel filter hose and fuel line.
4. Start engine. If pressure is now correct, replace fuel filter. If no change is observed, gently squeeze return hose. If pressure increases, replace pressure regulator. If no change is observed, problem is either a plugged pump filter sock or defective fuel pump.
5. If pressure is above specifications, remove fuel return hose from throttle body. Connect a substitute hose and place other end of hose in clean container. Start engine. If pressure is now correct, check for restricted fuel return line. If no change is observed, replace fuel regulator.

Component Removal

Mechanical malfunctions are more difficult to diagnose with the EFI system. The logic module has been programmed to compensate for some mechanical malfunctions such as incorrect cam timing, vacuum leaks, etc. If engine performance problems are encountered, and no fault codes are displayed, the problem may be mechnical rather than electrical.

THROTTLE BODY

Removal and Installation

1. Release fuel system pressure.
2. Disconnect negative battery terminal.
3. Disconnect fuel injector wiring connector and throttle body 6-way connector.
4. Remove electrical ground wire from 6-way wiring connector.
5. Remove air cleaner hose.
6. Remove throttle cable and if so equipped, the speed control and transmission kickdown cables.

7. Remove return spring.
8. Remove vacuum hoses.
9. Loosen fuel intake and return hose clamps. Wrap a shop towel around each hose, twist and pull off each hose.
10. Remove throttle body mounting screws and lift throttle body from vehicle.
11. Installation is the reverse of removal. Using a new gasket, with tabs facing forward, install throttle body and torque mounting screws to 17 ft. lbs. (23 Nm).

Disassembly

When servicing the fuel portion of the throttle body it will be necessary to bleed fuel pressure before opening any hoses. Always reassemble throttle body components with new O-rings and seals where applicable. Never use lubricants on O-rings or seals, damage may result. If assembly of components is difficult use water to aid assembly. Use care when removing fuel hoses to prevent damage to hose or hose nipple. Always use new hose clamps of the correct type when reassembling and torque hose clamps to 10 inch lbs. (1 Nm). Do not use aviation-style clamps.

NOTE: *It is not necessary to remove the throttle body from the intake manifold to perform component disassembly. If fuel system hoses are to be replaced, only hoses marked EFI/EMF may be used.*

Injector Removal

1. Perform fuel system pressure release.
2. Disconnect negative battery cable.
3. Remove 4 Torx® screws holding fuel inlet chamber to throttle body.
4. Remove vacuum tube from pressure regulator to throttle body.

CAUTION: *A shop towel around fuel inlet chamber to contain any fuel left in system.*

5. Lift fuel inlet chamber and injector off throttle body.
6. Pull injector from fuel inlet chamber.
7. Remove upper and lower O-ring from fuel injector by peeling them off.
8. Remove snap ring that retains seal and washer on injector and remove seal and washer.
9. Installation is the reverse of removal. Place new O-ring washer, and seal on injector and install snap ring.
10. Place assembly into throttle body, install 4 Torx® screws and torque these screws to 35 inch lbs. (4 Nm).

PRESSURE REGULATOR

Removal and Installation

1. Perform fuel system pressure release.
2. Disconnect negative battery cable.

EMISSION CONTROLS AND FUEL SYSTEM 101

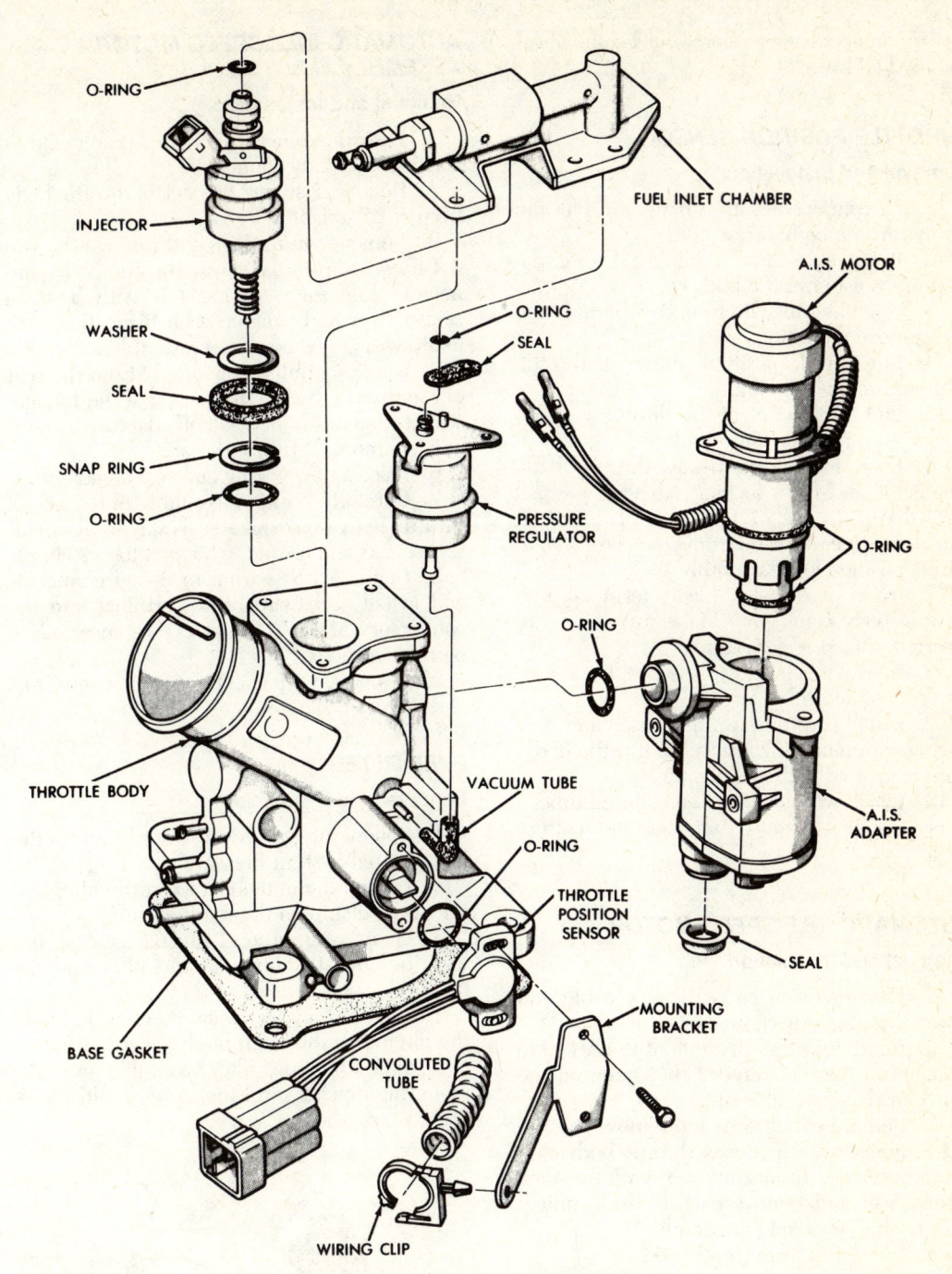

Exploded view of the throttle body

3. Remove 3 Torx® screws mounting pressure regulator to fuel inlet chamber.

CAUTION: *Place a shop towel around fuel inlet chamber to contain any fuel left in system.*

4. Remove vacuum tube from pressure regulator to throttle body.

5. Pull pressure regulator from throttle body.

6. Carefully peel O-ring off pressure regulator and remove flat seal.

7. Place new seal on pressure regulator and new O-ring.

8. Position pressure regulator on throttle body, press into place, install 3 Torx® screws and torque to 40 inch lbs. (5 Nm).

9. Install vacuum tube from pressure regulator to throttle body.

102 EMISSION CONTROLS AND FUEL SYSTEM

10. Connect battery, start vehicle, and check for any fuel leaks.

THROTTLE POSITION SENSOR
Removal and Installation

1. Disconnect negative battery cable and 6-way throttle body connector.
2. Remove 2 screws mounting throttle position sensor to throttle body.
3. Unclip wiring clip from convoluted tube and remove mounting bracket.
4. Lift throttle position sensor off throttle shaft and remove O-ring.
5. Pull the 3 wires of the throttle position sensor from the convoluted tubing.
6. Look inside the 6-way throttle body connector and lift a locking tab with a small screwdriver for each T.P.S. wire blade terminal. Remove each blade from connector. (Note wiring position for reassembly.)
7. Insert each wire blade terminal into throttle body connector. Make sure wires are inserted into correct locations.
8. Inert wires from throttle position sensor into convoluted tube.
9. Install throttle position sensor and new O-ring with mounting bracket to throttle body. Torque screws to 20 inch lbs. (2 Nm).
10. Install wiring clips to convoluted tube.
11. Connect 6-way connector and battery cable.

AUTOMATIC IDLE SPEED MOTOR
Removal and Installation

1. Disconnect negative battery cable and 6-way throttle body connector.
2. Remove screws that mount the A.I.S. to its adaptor. (Do not remove the clamp on the A.I.S. or damage will result.)
3. Remove wiring clips and remove the two A.I.S. wires from the 6-way throttle body connector. Lift each locking tab with a small screwdriver and remove each blade terminal. (Note wiring position for assembly).
4. Lift A.I.S. from its adaptor.
5. Remove the O-rings on the A.I.S. carefully.
6. Install new O-rings on A.I.S.
7. Carefully work A.I.S. into its adaptor.
8. Install 2 mounting screws and torque to 20 inch lbs. (2 Nm).
9. Route A.I.S. wiring to 6-way connector and install each wire blade terminal into the connector. Make sure wires are inserted in correct locations.
10. Connect wiring clip, 6-way connector, and battery cable.

AUTOMATIC IDLE SPEED MOTOR ASSEMBLY
Removal and Installation

1. Disconnect negative battery cable and 6-way throttle body connector.
2. Remove 2 screws on back of throttle body from A.I.S. adaptor.
3. Remove wiring clips and remove the two A.I.S. wires from the 6-way throttle body connector. Lift each locking tab with a small screwdriver and remove each blade terminal. (Note wiring position for reassembly).
4. Carefully pull the assembly from the rear of the throttle body. The O-ring at the top and seal at the bottom may fall off adaptor.
5. Remove O-ring and seal.
6. Place a new O-ring and seal on adaptor.
7. Carefully position assembly onto back of throttle body (make sure seals stay in place) insert screws and torque to 65 inch lbs. (20 Nm).
8. Route A.I.S. wiring to 6-way connector and install each wire blade terminal into the connector. Make sure wires are inserted in correct locations.
9. Connect wiring clips, 6-way connector, and battery cable.

FUEL FILTER
Removal and Installation

1. Follow the procedures listed under "Relieving Fuel System Pressure"
2. Loosen the outlet clamp on the filter and inlet hose clamp on the rear fuel tube.
3. Wrap a rag around the hoses to absorb fuel. Remove the hoses at the filter and the fuel tube.
4. Loosen the filter retaining screw and slide the filter assembly from the bracket.
5. Slide the new filter assembly into the mounting bracket until the stone shield shoulder contacts the bracket.

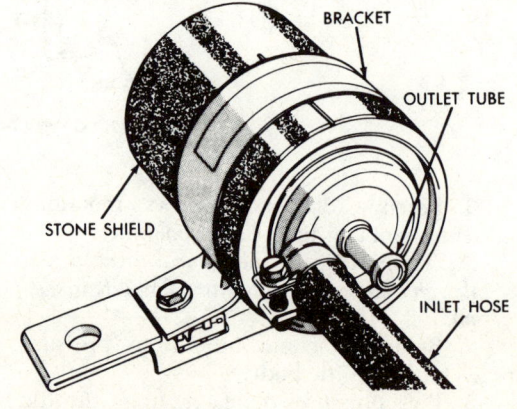

Fuel filter assembly

EMISSION CONTROLS AND FUEL SYSTEM

6. Position the filter in the bracket and tighten the filter mounting screw.
7. Install the formed outlet hose on the filter outlet fitting and tighten the clamp.
8. Install the inlet hose on the fuel tube and tighten the clamp.

FUEL PUMP
Removal and Installation

NOTE: *It is necessary to remove the fuel tank from the vehicle in order to remove the fuel pump. Follow the fuel tank removal procedure.*

1. Using a hammer and a non-metallic punch carefully tap the lock ring counter clockwise to release the pump.
2. Remove the fuel pump and O-ring seal from the tank.
3. To install: Wipe the seal area of the tank clean and place a new O-ring seal in position on the pump.
4. Before installing the pump check the condition of the filter on the end of the suction tube. Replace if necessary.
5. Position the fuel pump in the tank with the locking ring.
6. Using a hammer and a non-metallic punch drive the ring around clockwise to lock the pump in place.
CAUTION: *Use extreme care when installing the pump as overtightening could cause the pump to leak.*
7. Install the fuel tank.

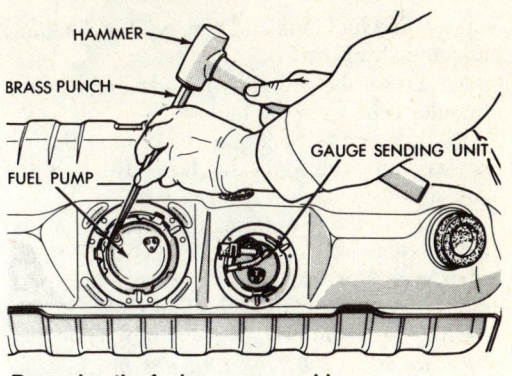

Removing the fuel pump assembly

FUEL TANK
Removal and Installation

1. Follow the procedures listed under "Relieving Fuel System Pressure".
2. Disconnect the negative battery cable.
3. Remove the fuel filler cap.
4. Remove the screws that secure the fuel filler tube to the quarter panel.
5. Raise the car and support on jackstands.
6. Remove the draft tube cap on the sending unit and connect a fuel siphon hose and siphon the fuel from the tank.
7. Disconnect the wiring and fuel lines from the tank.
NOTE: *Place rags over the lines when disconnecting to catch any fuel left in the system.*
8. Using a transmission jack or equivalent,

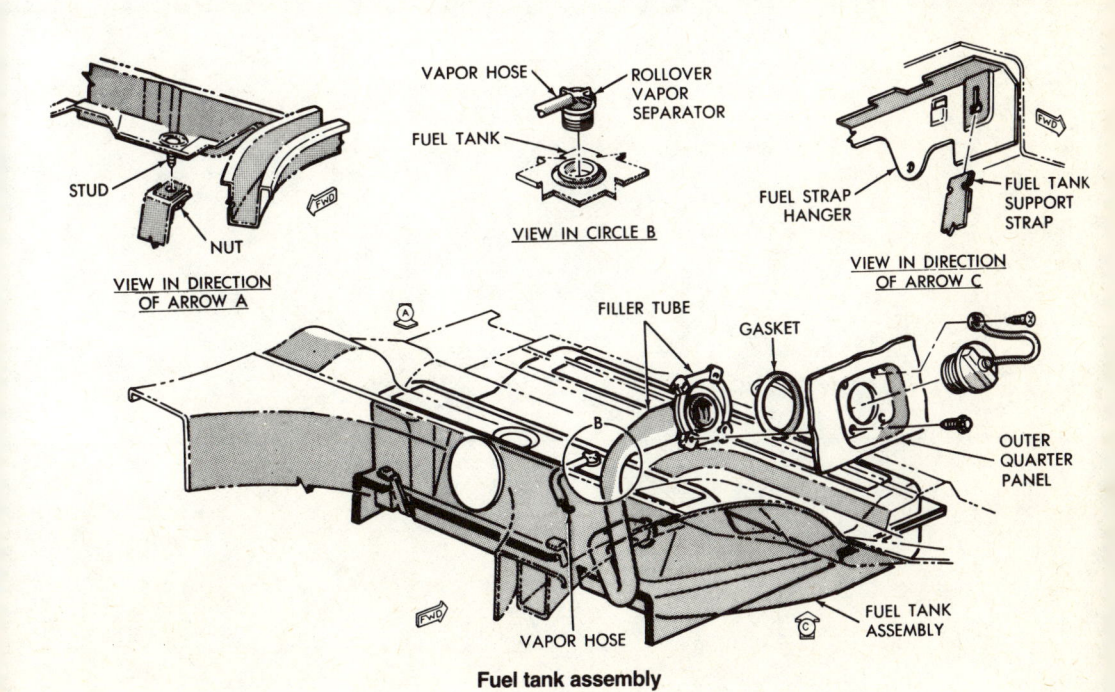

Fuel tank assembly

EMISSION CONTROLS AND FUEL SYSTEM

support the fuel tank and remove the retaining nuts and straps.

9. Lower the tank slightly and carefully work the filler tube from the tank.

10. Lower the tank and disconnect the vapor separator rollover valve hose. Remove the tank and insulator pad from the car.

11. To install: Position the fuel tank on the transmission jack or equivalent. Connect the vapor separator, roll over valve hose and position the insulator pad on the fuel tank.

CAUTION: *Be certain the vapor vent hose is clipped to the tank and not pinched between the tank and the floor pan during the installation.*

12. Raise the tank into position and carefully work the filler tube into the tank.

13. Tighten the strap nut to 250 inch lbs.

CAUTION: *Be certain the straps are not twisted or bent before or after tightening the strap nuts.*

14. Connect the lines, draft tube cap, and wiring. Use new hose clamps.

15. Lower the car and tighten the filler tube to quarter panel.

16. Fill the fuel tank, connect the battery. Start and run the car.

17. Check for any leaks at the hose connections.

Chassis Electrical
5

UNDERSTANDING AND TROUBLESHOOTING ELECTRICAL SYSTEMS

For any electrical system to operate, it must make a complete circuit. This simply means that the power flow from the battery must make a complete circle. When an electrical component is operating, power flows from the battery to the component, passes through the component causing it to perform its function (lighting a light bulb), and then returns to the battery through the ground of the circuit. This ground is usually (but not always) the metal part of the car or truck on which the electrical component is mounted.

Perhaps the easiest way to visualize this is to think of connecting a light bulb with two wires attached to it and the battery. If one of the two wires attached to the light bulb were attached to the negative post of the battery and the other were attached to the positive post of the battery, you would have a complete circuit. Current from the battery would flow to the light bulb, causing it to light, and return to the negative post of the battery.

The normal automotive circuit differs from this simple example in two ways. First, instead of having a return wire from the bulb to the battery, the light bulb returns the current to the battery through the chassis of the vehicle. Since the negative battery cable is attached to the chassis and the chassis is made of electrically conductive metal, the chassis of the vehicle can serve as ground wire to complete the circuit. Secondly, most automotive circuits contain switches to turn components on and off as required.

Every complete circuit from a power source must include a component which is using the power from the power source. If you were to disconnect the light bulb from the wires and touch the two wires together (don't do this) the power supply wire to the component would be grounded before the normal ground connection for the circuit.

Because grounding a wire from a power source makes a complete circuit—less the required component to use the power—this phenomenon is called a short circuit. Common causes are: broken insulation (exposing the metal wire to a metal part of the car or truck), or a shorted switch.

Some electrical components which require a large amount of current to operate also have a relay in their circuit. Since these circuits carry a large amount of current, the thickness of the wire in the circuit (gauge size) is also greater. If this large wire were connected from the component to the control switch on the instrument panel, and then back to the component, a voltage drop would occur in the circuit. To prevent this potential drop in voltage, an electromagnetic switch (relay) is used. The large wires in the circuit are connected from the battery to one side of the relay, and from the opposite side of the relay to the component. The relay is normally open, preventing current from passing through the circuit. An additional, smaller, wire is connected from the relay to the control switch for the circuit. When the control switch is turned on, it grounds the smaller wire from the relay and completes the circuit. This closes the relay and allows current to flow from the battery to the component. The horn, headlight, and starter circuits are three which use relays.

It is possible for larger surges of current to pass through the electrical system of your car or truck. If this surge of current were to reach an electrical component, it could burn it out. To prevent this, fuses, circuit breakers or fusible links are connected into the current supply wires of most of the major electrical systems. When an electrical current of excessive power

CHASSIS ELECTRICAL

passes throughout the component's fuse, the fuse blows out and breaks the circuit, saving the component from destruction.

A circuit breaker is basically a self-repairing fuse. The circuit breaker opens the circuit the same way a fuse does. However, when either the short is removed from the circuit or the surge subsides, the circuit breaker resets itself and does not have to be replaced as a fuse does.

A fuse link is a wire that acts as a fuse. It is normally connected between the starter relay and the main wiring harness. This connection is usually under the hood. The fuse link (if installed) protects all the chassis electrical components, and is the probable cause of trouble when none of the electrical components function, unless the battery is disconnected or dead.

Electrical problems generally fall into one of three areas:

1. The component that is not functioning is not receiving current.
2. The component itself is not functioning.
3. The component is not properly grounded.

The electrical system can be checked with a test light and a jumper wire. A test light is a device that looks like a pointed screwdriver with a wire attached to it and has a light bulb in its handle. A jumper wire is a piece of insulated wire with an alligator clip attached to each end.

If a component is not working, you must follow a systematic plan to determine which of the three causes is the villain.

1. Turn on the switch that controls the inoperable component.
2. Disconnect the power supply wire from the component.
3. Attach the ground wire on the test light to a good metal ground.
4. Touch the probe end of the test light to the end of the power supply wire that was disconnected from the component. If the component is receiving current, the test light will go on.

NOTE: *Some components work only when the ignition switch is turned on.*

If the test light does not go on, then the problem is in the circuit between the battery and the component. This includes all the switches, fuses and relays in the system. Follow the wire that runs back to the battery. The problem is an open circuit between the battery and the component. If the fuse is blown and, when replaced, immediately blows again, there is a short circuit in the system which must be located and repaired. If there is a switch in the system, bypass it with a jumper wire. This is done by connecting one end of the jumper wire to the power supply wire into the switch and the other end of the jumper wire to the wire coming out of the switch. If the test light lights with the jumper wire installed, the switch or whatever was bypassed is defective.

NOTE: *Never substitute the jumper wire for the component, since it is required to use the power from the power source.*

5. If the bulb in the test light goes on, then the current is getting to the component that is not working. This eliminates the first of the three possible causes. Connect the power supply wire and connect a jumper wire from the component to a good metal ground. Do this with the switch which controls the component turned on, and also the ignition switch turned on if it is required for the component to work. If the component works with the jumper wire installed, then it has a bad ground. This is usually caused by the metal area on the chassis being coated with some type of foreign matter.

6. If neither test located the source of the trouble, then the component itself is defective. Remember that for any electrical system to work, all connections must be clean and tight.

HEATER

Heater Assembly
REMOVAL AND INSTALLATION

1. Disconnect the negative battery cable and drain the radiator.
2. Disconnect the wiring connector from the blower motor.
3. Reach under the heater unit, depress the tab on the mode door and temperature control cables, pull the flags out from the receivers, and remove the self-adjust clip from the crank arm.
4. Remove the glovebox assembly.
5. Disconnect and plug the heater hoses on the engine side of the fire wall.
6. Remove the screw attaching the hanger strap to the heater assembly through the glovebox opening.
7. Remove the nut attaching the hanger strap to the dash panel and remove the hanger strap.
8. Remove the two screws attaching the demister adapter to the top of the heater assembly.
9. Remove the two nuts on the engine side of the firewall fastening the heater assembly to the dash panel.
10. Flex the outside bottom of the instrument panel and slide the heater assembly out of the car.
11. To install reverse the removal procedures.

CHASSIS ELECTIRCAL 107

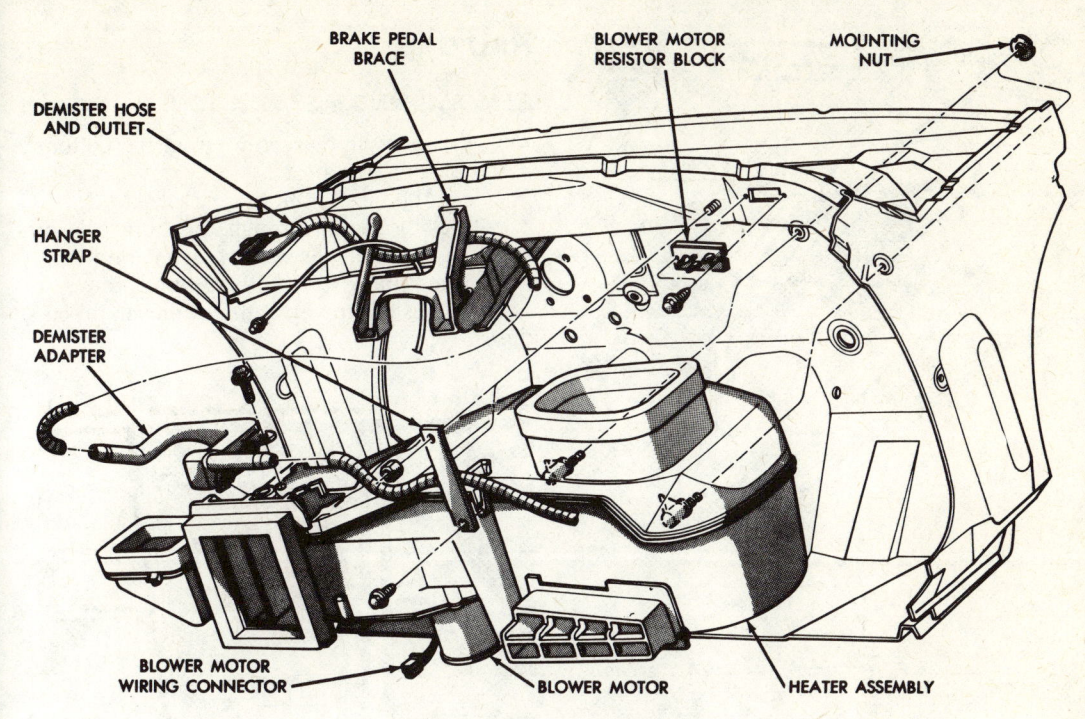

Laser/Daytona heater assembly

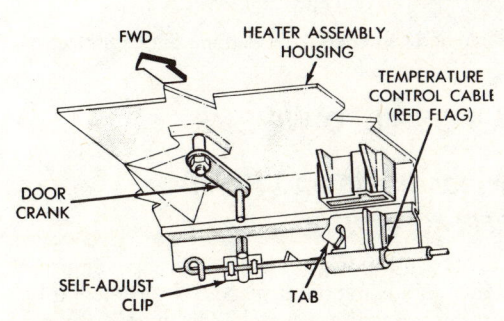

Removing the control cables from the heater assembly

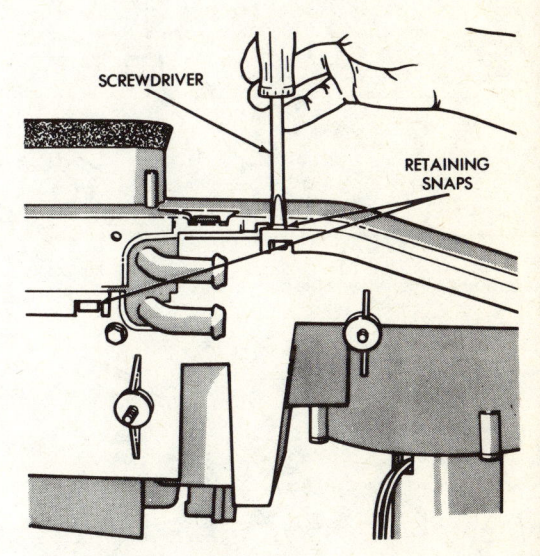

Disengaging the retaining snaps

DISASSEMBLY—CORE AND BLOWER REMOVAL

1. Follow the previous procedures and remove the heater assembly from the vehicle.
2. Remove the padding from around the heater core outlets and remove the upper core mounting screw.
3. Using a suitable tool, pry loose the retaining snaps from around the edge of the housing cover.
   NOTE: *Should a retaining snap break, the housing cover has provisions for mounting screws.*
4. Slide the heater core out of the housing.
5. Remove the nut attaching the door crank arm to the temperature control door and remove the crank.
6. Remove the door actuator arm by squeezing it off its mounting shaft.
   NOTE: *DO NOT pry the clips apart or possible breakage could occur.*
7. Remove the mode door from the heater unit.
8. Remove the temperature control door.
9. Remove the five blower mounting screws and remove the blower motor and wheel.
10. Remove the retaining clamp from the hub

108 CHASSIS ELECTRICAL

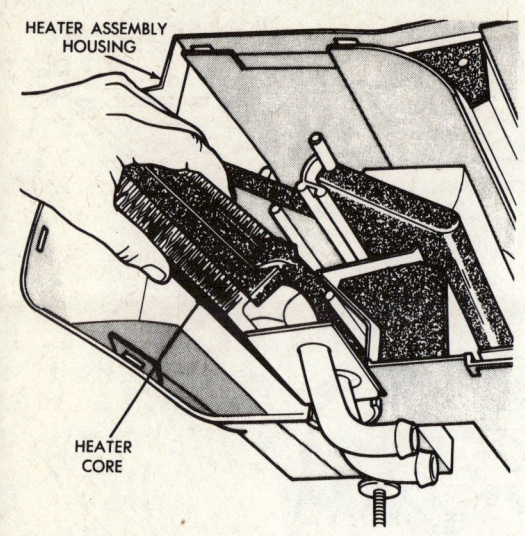

Removing the heater core

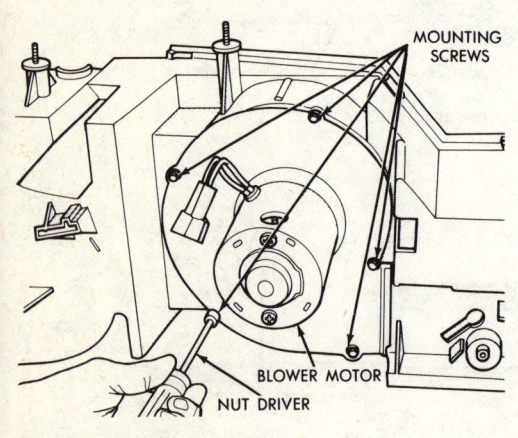

Removing the blower motor

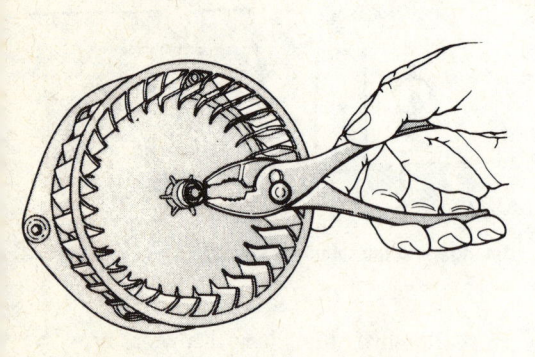

Removing or installing the blower wheel

of the blower wheel and slide the fan off the shaft.

11. Remove the two mounting nuts to separate the blower motor from the plate.

12. To assemble, reverse the disassembly procedures.

RADIO

REMOVAL AND INSTALLATION

1. Remove the two screws from the bottom of the console trim bezel.
2. Lift the bezel from the console.
3. Pull the radio through the front face of the console, then disconnect the wiring connector, antenna lead, and the ground strap.
4. To install, reverse the removal procedures.

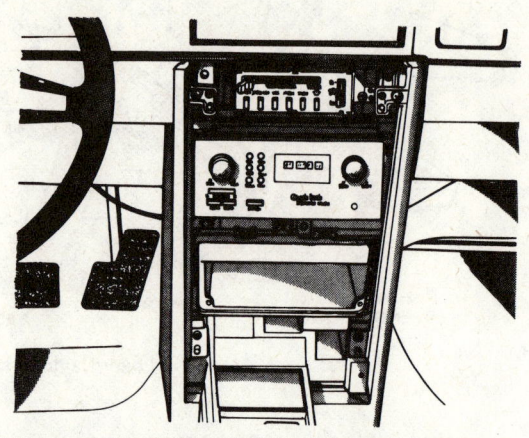

Radio and center console with the bezel removed

WINDSHIELD WIPERS

Wiper Blade and Refill

REPLACEMENT

1. Turn the wiper switch "On," position the blades in a convenient place to be removed by turning the ignition switch "On" and "Off" momentarily.
2. Lift the wiper arm to raise the blade off the glass.
3. Remove the blade from the arm by lifting the release tab on the center bridge pivot.
4. To remove the wiper refill element from the blade assembly, move the refill blade into a slight reverse bow and slide the blade element out of the end bridge claws.
5. When installing the new element, check

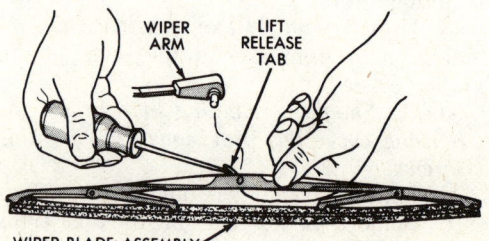

Removing the blade assembly from the arm

CHASSIS ELECTIRCAL 109

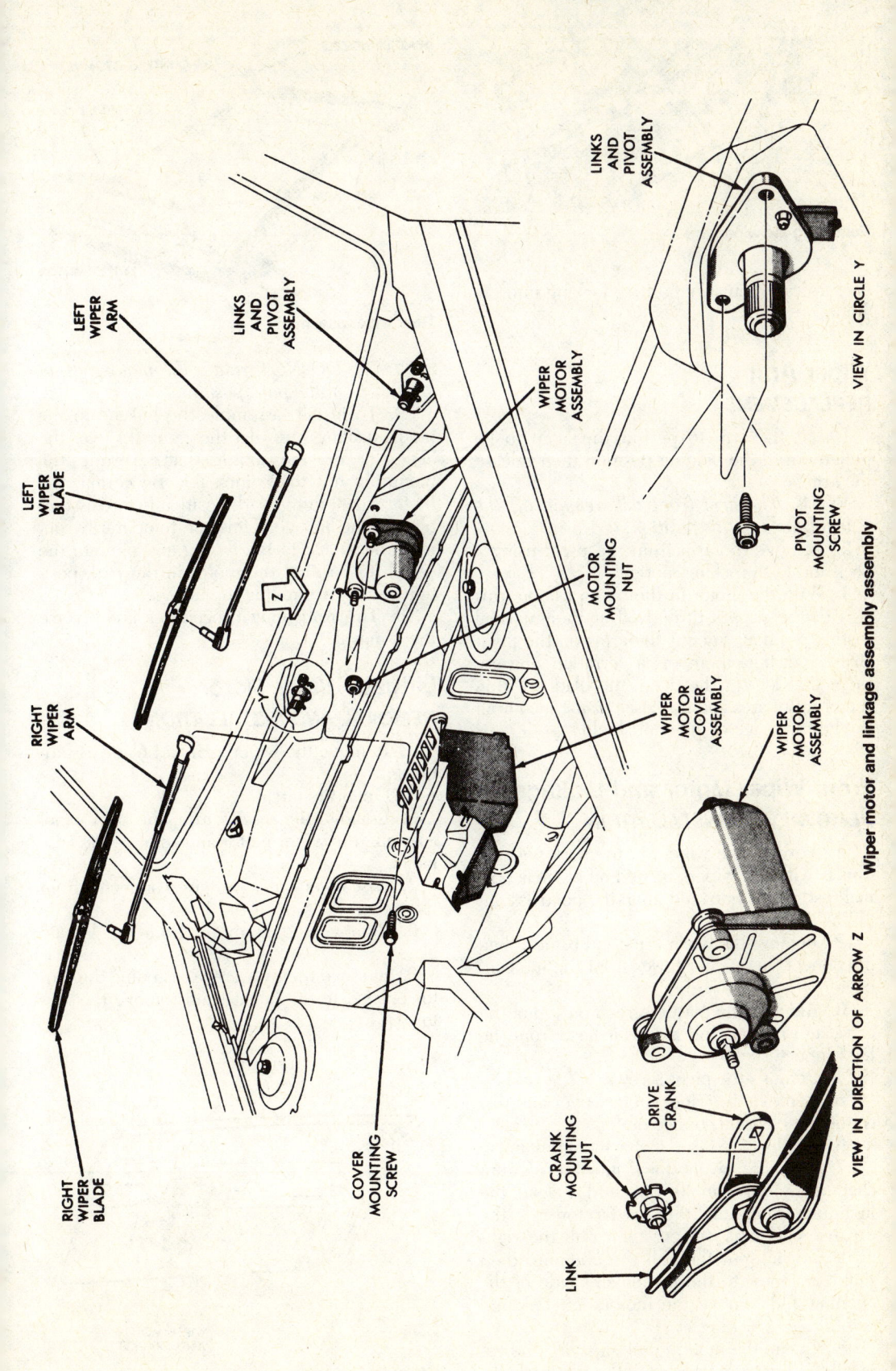

Wiper motor and linkage assembly assembly

110 CHASSIS ELECTRICAL

Removing the wiper arm

Rear wiper assembly

each release point for positive locking into position.

Wiper Arm
REPLACEMENT

1. Lift the arm to permit the latch to be pulled out to the holding position then release the arm.
   NOTE: *The arm front will remain off the windshield in this position.*
2. Remove the arm from the pivot using a back and forth rocking motion.
3. With the motor in the park position (this is with the wipers turned off at their normal resting position), mount the arms on the pivot shafts, position them on a serration engagement that locates the tip of the blades within the blackout area and no closer than 1 inch from the bottom edge of the windshield.

Front Wiper Motor and Linkage
REMOVAL AND INSTALLATION

1. Position the wipers in the park position (this is with the wipers turned off at their normal resting position) and open the hood assembly.
2. Remove the wiper arms and blades, then disconnect the washer hoses from the tee connector.
3. Remove the plastic screen on top of the cowl, and remove the reservoir hose from the tee connector.
4. Remove the pivot screws.
5. Remove the wiper motor cover and disconnect the wiring connector.
6. Remove the three motor mounting nuts.
7. Push the pivots down into the plenum chamber, pull the motor out until it clears the mounting studs and then as far towards the driver's side as it will go, then pull the right pivot and link out through the opening, then shift the motor to the passenger's side of the opening and remove the motor, left link and pivot.
8. Clamp the motor crank in a vise and remove the nut from the end of the motor shaft.

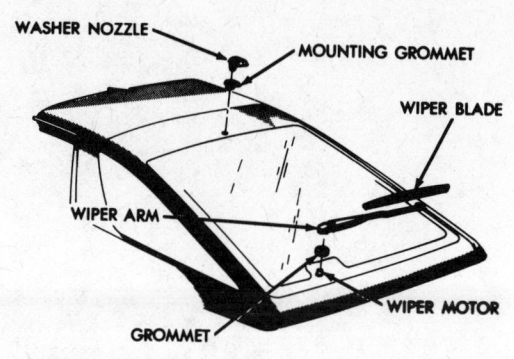

NOTE: *DO NOT rotate the motor output shaft from the park position.*

9. To install, assemble the linkage to the motor making sure that the crank fits over the "D" slot on the motor shaft. Torque the mounting nut to 95 inch lbs. Be certain the motor is still in the park position before assembling to the linkage, if it is not, temporarily connect the motor to the wiring and operate the switch to position the motor in the park position before assembling the linkage.
10. The remaining procedures are reverse the removal.

Liftgate Wiper Motor
REMOVAL AND INSTALLATION

1. Remove the wiper arm and blade assemblies.
2. Open the liftgate.
3. Remove the screws from the trim panel covering the wiper motor and remove the trim panel.
4. Disconnect the feedwire connector from the motor.
5. Remove the grommet from the liftgate glass.
6. Remove the two screws fastening the motor bracket to the liftgate and remove the motor.

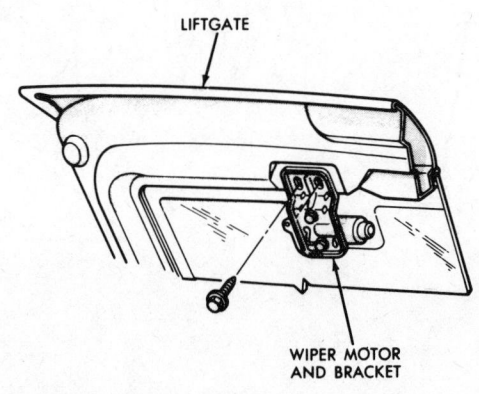

Liftgate wiper motor mounting

CHASSIS ELECTIRCAL 111

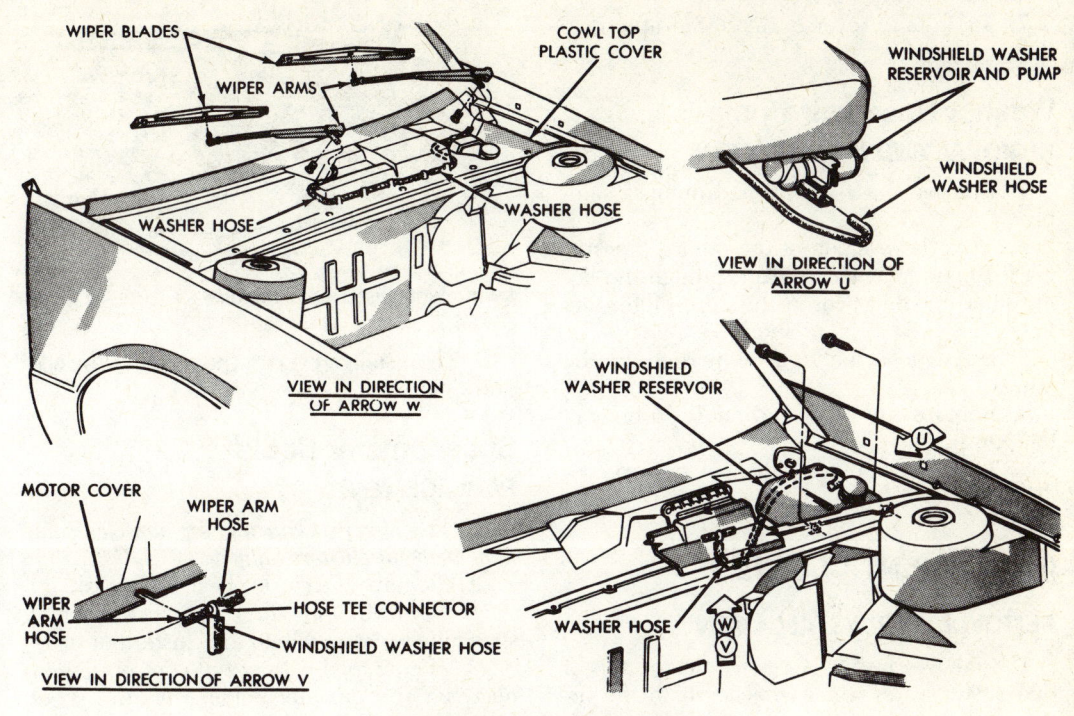

Front windshield washer system

7. To install, reverse the removal procedures and be sure to use a new grommet in the liftgate glass.

Windshield Washer Reservoir
REMOVAL AND INSTALLATION
Front

1. Open and support the hood with the prop rod.
2. Disconnect the wiper arm washer hoses from the tee connector.
3. Remove the plastic screen from the top of the cowl and disconnect the washer hose from the bottom of the tee connector.
4. Remove the two sheetmetal screws attaching the reservoir to the plenum.
5. Lift the reservoir out of the car.
6. Disconnect the wiring connector from the reservoir pump.
7. Disconnect the washer hose from the reservoir and cap the outlet to prevent washer fluid from running out while removing the reservoir.
8. To install, reverse the removal procedure.

Rear

1. Open the liftgate.
2. Remove the right rear quarter panel inside trim to gain access to the reservoir.

3. Remove the two reservoir attaching screws.
4. Disconnect the wiring connector and the filler tube from the reservoir and the pump assembly.
5. Disconnect the washer hose from the reservoir and cap the outlet to prevent washer fluid from running out while removing the reservoir.
6. Remove the reservoir and pump assembly from the rear quarter panel.

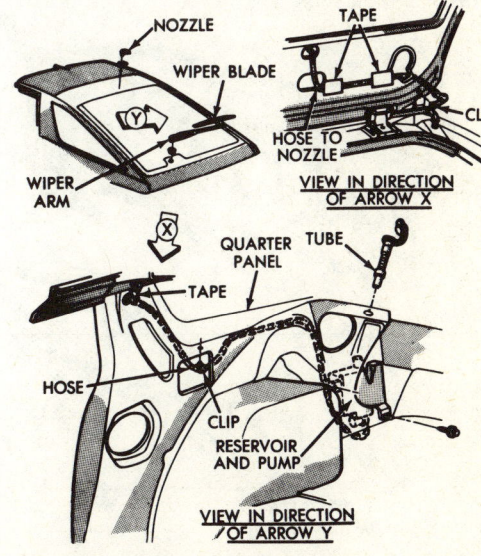

Rear liftgate window washer system

112 CHASSIS ELECTRICAL

7. To install, reverse the removal procedure.

Washer Reservoir Pump
REMOVAL AND INSTALLATION

1. Remove the reservoir and pump assembly.
2. Note the position of the pump, then using a 19mm or ¾ inch socket through the liquid filler opening, loosen the pump filter and nut.
3. Disconnect the outside portion of the pump.
4. Remove the inner and outer portions of the pump.
5. To install, reverse the removal procedure.

INSTRUMENT CLUSTER
REMOVAL AND INSTALLATION

1. Remove the five screws from the top of the cluster bezel which attaches it to the instrument panel.
2. Pull the bezel rearward to disengage the three clips on the bottom of the bezel and remove it.
3. Remove the four screws attaching the cluster housing to the base panel.
4. Pull the cluster assembly rearward, then reaching under disconnect the speedometer cable and wiring harness.
NOTE: *On Electronic clusters it is not necessary to remove the speedometer cable.*
5. Remove the cluster assembly from the car.

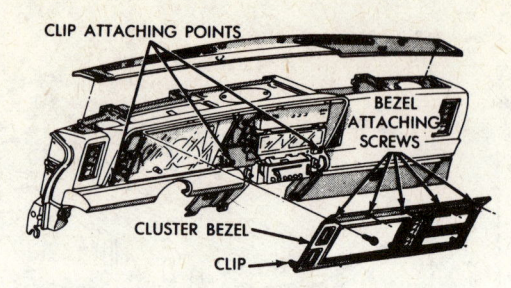

Instrument cluster bezel removal

6. To install, reverse the removal procedure.

Speedometer Cable
REPLACEMENT

NOTE: *This procedure is for non-electronic instrument clusters only.*

1. Remove the cluster bezel and mask.
2. Remove the three screws attaching speedometer assembly to the cluster housing.
3. If equipped with speed control, disconnect the speedometer cable from the speed control servo unit in the engine compartment.
4. Pull the speedometer rearward and disconnect it from the speedometer cable.
5. Disconnect the speedometer cable from the transmission, distance sensor, lower cable or speed control servo.
6. Push the lower ferrule end of the speedometer cable and grommet through the dash panel into the passenger compartment.
7. Remove the cable by pulling the upper end out from under the instrument panel.
8. To install, route the speedometer cable.

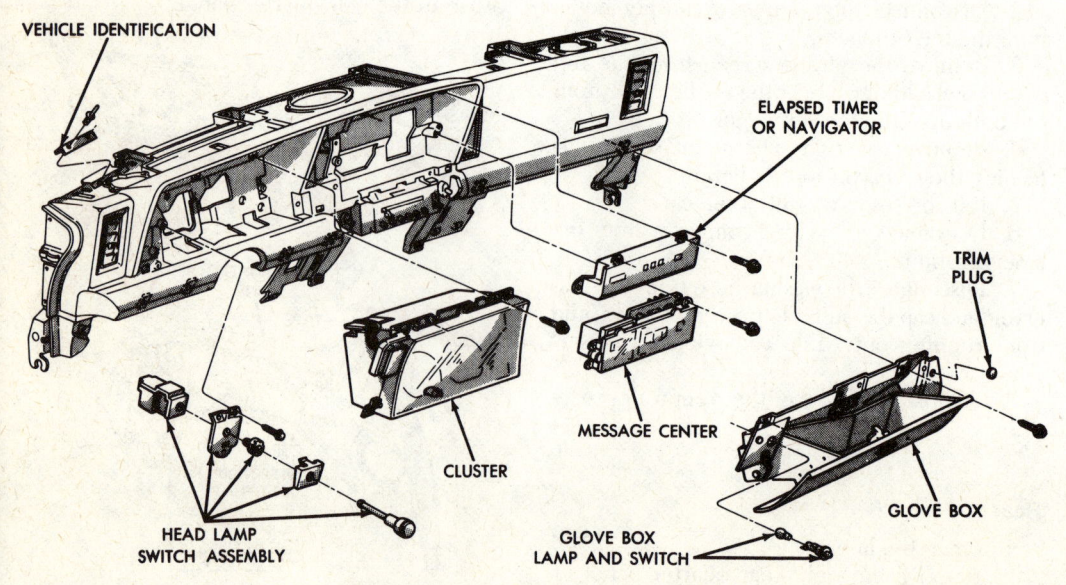

Instrument panel and cluster assembly

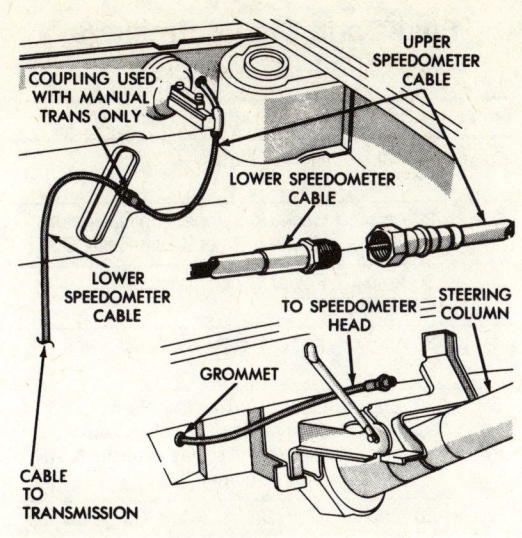

CHASSIS ELECTIRCAL 113

Speedometer cable routing

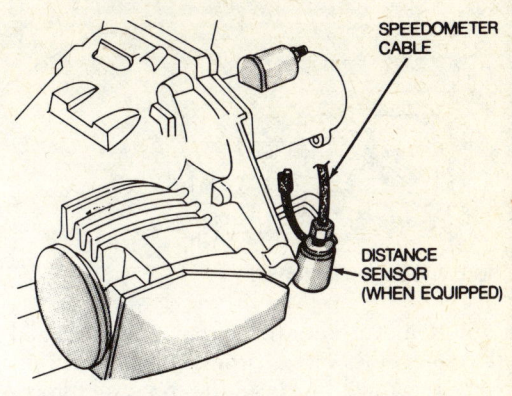

Speedometer cable—transmission attachment

Headlight assembly

NOTE: *While routing the cable be sure to keep it free of kinks and sharp bends.*

9. Connect the cable to the transmission, distance sensor, lower cable or speed control servo.

NOTE: *Tighten the cable connections to 15 inch lbs. Over–tightening the cable connections may cause improper cable operation.*

10. Position the upper cable and grommet.
11. Install the speedometer and cluster bezel and mask.

Ignition Switch
REMOVAL AND INSTALLATION

See Chapter 7 for Ignition Switch replacement.

LIGHTING

Headlights
REMOVAL AND INSTALLATION

1. Remove the screws from the headlamp bezel and remove the bezel.
2. Remove the screws from the interior retaining ring, and remove the ring.

NOTE: *DO NOT disturb the headlight adjusting screws.*

3. Pull the sealed beam unit out of the seat and unplug the wiring connector, pulling it straight off.
4. Install the new sealed beam unit.
5. Install the unit retaining ring.
6. Install the headlight bezel.

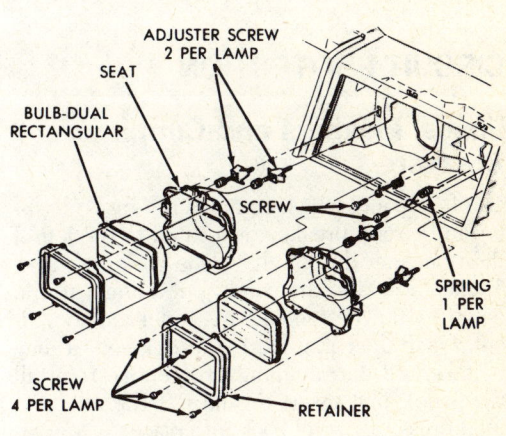

Headlight Switch
REMOVAL AND INSTALLATION

1. Reach under the instrument panel and disconnect the headlamp switch knob and shaft by pressing the button on the switch lower surface.
2. Remove the knob and shaft from the switch.
3. Remove the four screws from the left bezel and remove the bezel.
4. Remove the headlight switch mounting screws.

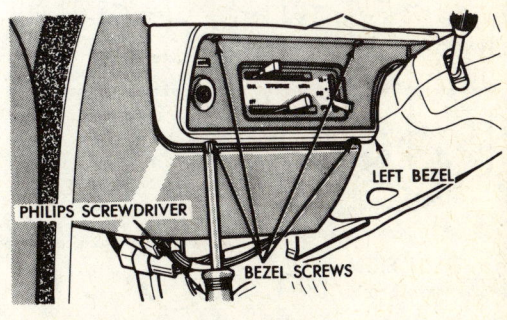

Left bezel—attachment locations

114   CHASSIS ELECTRICAL

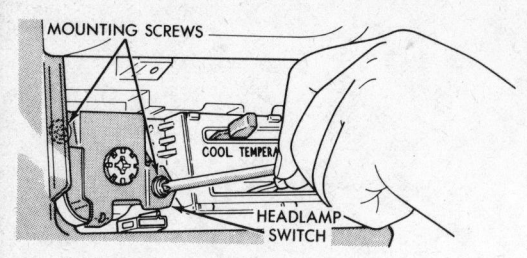

Headlight switch mounting

5. Remove the switch from the panel and disconnect the wiring harness connector.
6. To install, reverse the removal procedures.

CIRCUIT PROTECTION

Fuses, Flashers and Circuit Breakers

The fuse panel which contains the fuses, flashers and circuit breakers is located to the left of the steering column, above the parking brake. To gain access to the panel, put a finger in the notch to the bottom of the panel and pull it out. Once the panel has been removed, it may be taken off the retaining bracket. To reinstall the panel, first insert the tabs at the top, and then press the panel back into place.

CAUTION: *When replacing a blown fuse, always use a fuse of the correct amperage rating. Using a piece of wire, aluminum foil, or a fuse of a higher amperage could cause a dangerous electrical system overload. If the proper amperage rated fuse continues to blow, it indicates a problem in the electrical system that must be corrected.*

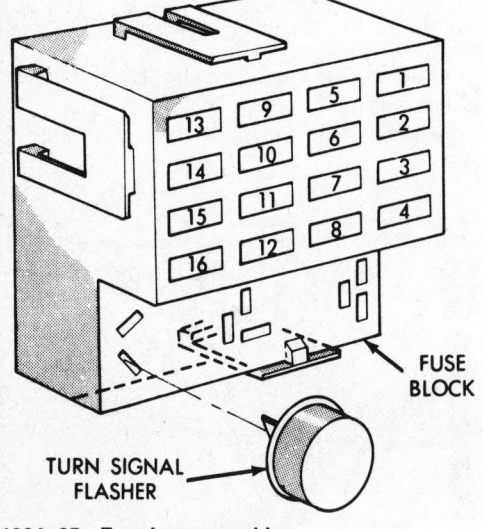

1984–85—Fuse box assembly

Fuses and Circuit Breakers 1984–85 Models

Cavity	Fuse	Item Fused
1	20 Amp Yellow	Hazard Flasher
2	20 Amp Yellow	Back-Up Lamps, Trip Navigator, Elapsed Timer & Fan Relay Coil
3	30 Amp C/BRKR	Power Window Motors
4	30 Amp Green	A/C or Heater Blower Motor
5	20 Amp Yellow	Cavity 12 (Cluster), Park, Tail, Side Marker & License Lamps, Electronic Display Intensity & Tail Lamp Outage
6	20 Amp Yellow	Stop, Dome, Map & Cargo Lamps; Time Delay Relay, Electronic Visual Message Center Electronic Voice Alert, Brake Sense, Power Mirror Motors & Illuminated Entry Coil & Lamp
7	20 Amp Yellow	Glove Box Lamp; Cigar Lighter, Memory for Radio & Elapsed Timer-Trip Navigator, Electronic Voice Alert, Chimes, Fuel Filler Door, Horn & Relay
8	30 Amp C/BRKR	Air Horns & Relay, Power Seat Motor & Power Door Locks
9	5 Amp Tan	Radio & Front Door Speaker Lamps
10	20 Amp Yellow	Turn Signal Lamps, Heated Rear Window Relay & A/C Clutch
11	20 Amp Yellow	Front Windshield Wiper & Washer
12	5 Amp Tan	Illumination Lamps (Dimmable) & V.F. Display Dimming
13	5 Amp Tan	Cluster Printed Circuit Board Gauges & Warning Lamps, Chimes, Speed Control Servo, Incandescent Message Center, Electronic Voice Alert, Electronic Visual Message Center & Illuminated Entry Seat Belt Lamp
14	6 Amp C/BRKR	Rear Wash Wipe & Liftgate Release Solenoid

WIRING DIAGRAMS

Wiring diagrams have been left out of this book. As cars have become more complex and available with longer and longer option lists, wiring diagrams have grown in size and complexity also. It has become virtually impossible to provide a readable reproduction in a reasonable number of pages.

Clutch and Transaxle 6

MANUAL TRANSAXLE

Identification

The Laser and Daytona models both use the Chrysler A525 close ratio 5-spd. manual transaxle.

The transmission identification number (TIN) is stamped on a boss that is located on the transaxle housing when the transaxles are installed into the vehicles during production.

In addition to the transaxle identification number, each transaxle carries an assembly part number which must be referenced when ordering parts for the transaxle. On the A525 manual transaxle, the assembly part number is located on a metal tag attached to the front side of the transaxle. See Chapter 1 for further information.

SHIFT LINKAGE ADJUSTMENT

1. From the left side of the car, remove the lockpin from the transaxle selector shaft housing.
2. Reverse the lockpin and insert it in the same threaded hole while pushing the selector

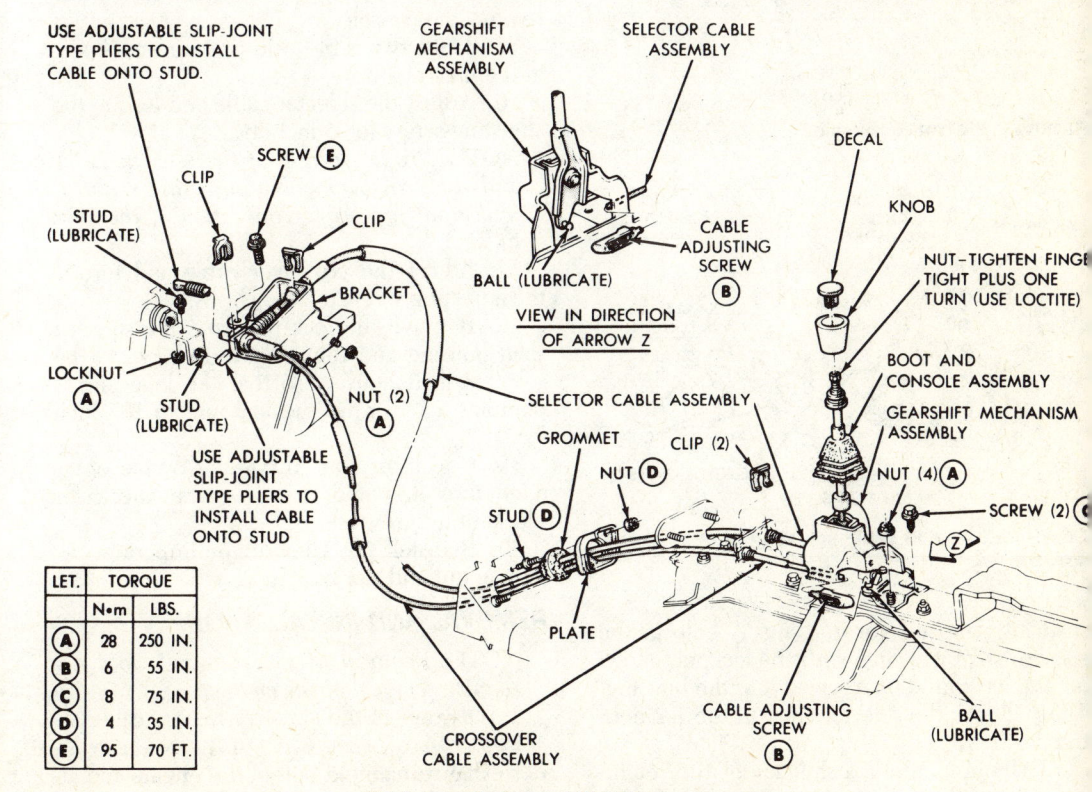

LET.	TORQUE	
	N•m	LBS.
A	28	250 IN.
B	6	55 IN.
C	8	75 IN.
D	4	35 IN.
E	95	70 FT.

Cable operated gearshift linkage assembly

CLUTCH AND TRANSAXLE

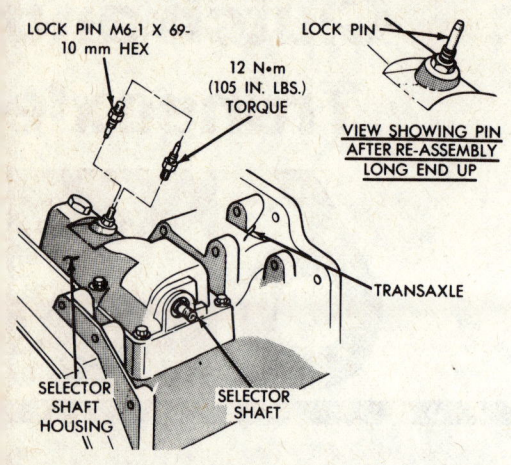

Transaxle pinned in the first-to-second neutral position

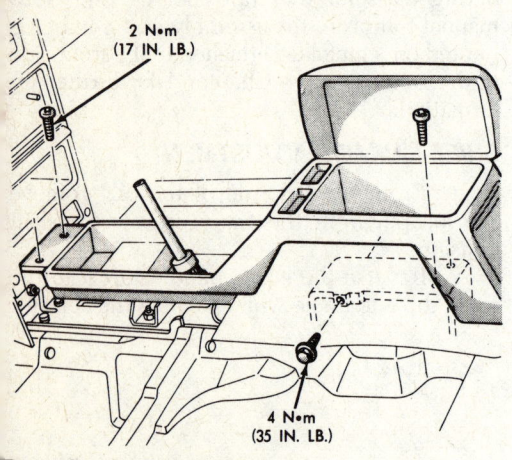

Removing the center console

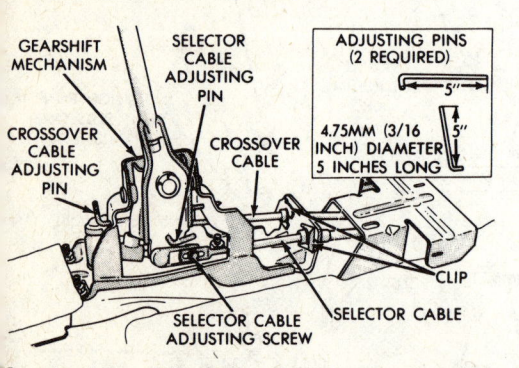

Construct two shift cable adjusting pins as shown above

shaft into the selector housing. A hole in the selector shaft will align with the lockpin, allowing the lockpin to be screwed into the housing. This will lock the selector shaft in the 1-2 neutral position.

3. Remove the gearshift knob, the retaining nut and the pull-up ring.

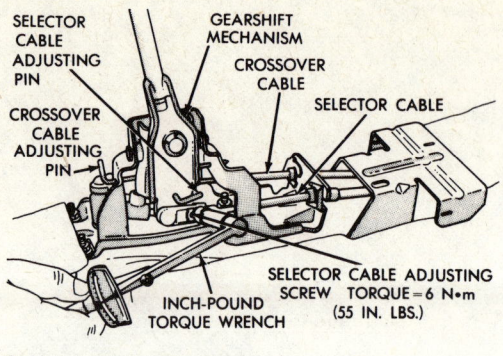

Selector cable adjustment

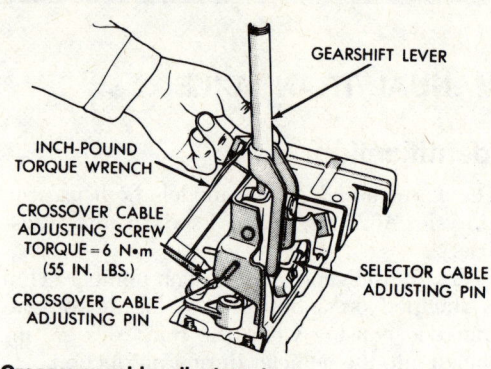

Crossover cable adjustment

4. Remove the console attaching screws and remove the console.
5. Make two cable adjusting pins as shown in the illustration.
6. Adjust the selector cable and torque the adjusting screw to 55 inch lbs.

NOTE: *Proper torque of the selector cable and the crossover cable adjusting screw is important for proper operation of the shift linkage.*

7. Adjust the crossover cable and torque the adjusting screw to 55 inch lbs.
8. Remove the lock pin from the selector shaft housing and reinstall the lock pin to the selector shaft housing so that the long end is pointing up. Torque the lock pin to 105 inch lbs.
9. Check the shift linkage for proper operation into first and reverse. Also check for blockout into reverse.
10. Reinstall the console, pull-up ring, retaining nut and the gearshift knob.

REMOVAL AND INSTALLATION

NOTE: *Removal of the transaxle does not require removal of the engine.*

1. Disconnect the negative battery cable.
2. Install a "lifting eye" on the No. 4 cylinder exhaust manifold bolt of the engine and attach it to an engine supporting fixture.

Engine supporting fixture

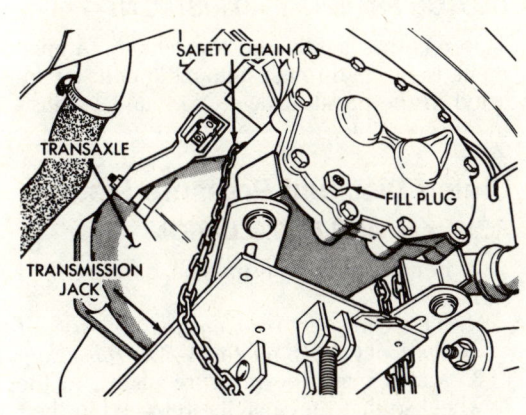

Transaxle being supported by transmission jack

3. Disconnect the gearshift lever from the selector shaft.
NOTE: *When reinstalling the operating lever, install a NEW prevailing-torque nut and torque it to 21 ft. lbs.*
4. Remove both front wheels.
5. Remove the left front splash shield.
6. Follow the procedures under "Halfshaft Removal and Installation."
7. The removal of the unit is the same as that for the automatic transaxle, except that no torque converter is used.
8. Installation is the reverse of removal procedure.
NOTE: *When installing the transaxle, it may be necessary to use two locating pins in place of the top two transaxle to engine bolts. Make the two locating pins from two stock (transaxle case to engine block) bolts as follows. Take a hacksaw and remove the bolt heads, cut a slot in the end of the bolts for a screwdriver, and remove the burrs with a grinding wheel. Install the locating pins into the engine block and proceed with the transaxle installation. After the transaxle has been positioned in place install the bolts and remove the locating pins and replace with the bolts before removing the transmission jack.*

CLUTCH AND TRANSAXLE 117

Halfshaft
REMOVAL AND INSTALLATION
Manual and Automatic Transaxle Models

The inboard CV joints are retained by circlips in the differential side gears. The circlip tangs are located on a machined surface on the inner end of the stub shaft.

1. With the car on the ground, remove the cotter pin and lock, loosen the hub nut, which has been torqued to 200 ft. lbs.
2. Raise the car and support it on jackstands.
3. Remove the hub nut, washer, wheel and tire assembly.
4. To remove the right-hand driveshaft, disconnect the speedometer cable and remove the cable and pinion gear before removing the driveshaft.
5. Remove the clamp bolt from the ball stud and steering knuckle.
6. Separate the ball joint stud from the steering knuckle, by prying against the knuckle leg and control arm.
7. Separate the outer CV joint splined shaft

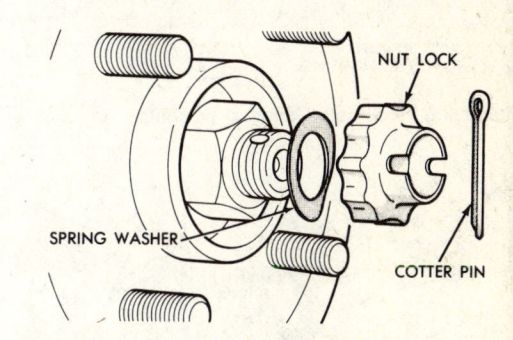

Cotter pin, nut lock and spring washer

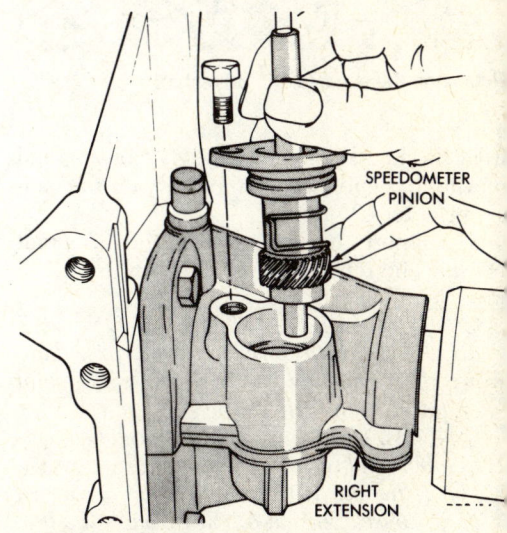

Speedometer pinion and cable removal

CLUTCH AND TRANSAXLE

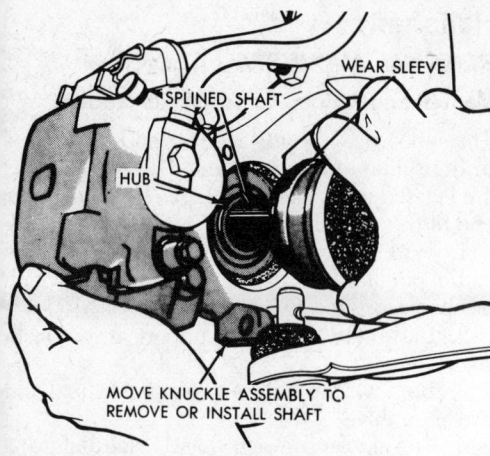

Separating the outer CV joint from the hub

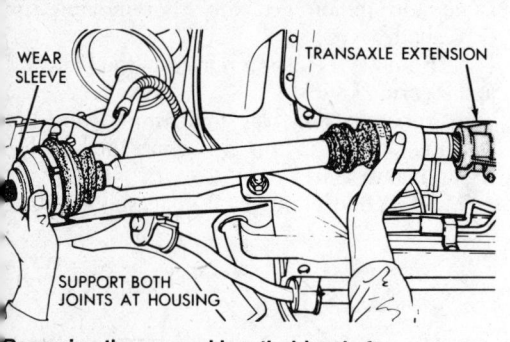

Removing the unequal length driveshaft

Removing the equal length driveshaft

from the hug by holding the CV housing and moving the hub away. Do not pry on the slinger or outer CV joint.

8. Support the assembly at the CV joint housing and remove by pulling outward on the inner joint housing.
CAUTION: *DO NOT PULL ON THE SHAFT. DO NOT pry on or otherwise damage the slinger on the right inner CV joint on the equal length system.*
NOTE: *The driveshaft, when installed, acts as a bolt and secures the hub/bearing assembly. If the car is to be supported or moved on its wheels, install a bolt through the hub to keep the hub bearing from loosening.*

9. Installation is the reverse of removal. Be sure the circlip tangs are positioned against the flattened end of the shaft before installing the shaft. A quick thrust will lock the circlip in the groove. Tighten the hub nut with the wheels on the ground to 180 ft. lbs. Install the lock, spring washer and a NEW cotter pin.

CLUTCH

The clutch is a single dry disc unit, with no adjustment for wear provided in the clutch itself.

CLUTCH FREEPLAY ADJUSTMENT

This unit has a self-adjusting clutch. Adjustment is made through automatic adjuster located in the pedal linkage. No manual adjustment is possible.

Clutch Disc and Pressure Plate
REMOVAL AND INSTALLATION

1. Remove the transmission as described earlier.
NOTE: *Chrysler recommends the use of special tool C-4676 for the A-525 transaxle.*
2. Match mark the pressure plate and the flywheel so that they may be replaced in their relative original positions if they are not being replaced.
3. Loosen the flywheel-to-pressure plate bolts diagonally, one or two turns at a time to avoid warpage.
4. Remove the pressure plate and clutch disc from the flywheel.
5. The flywheel and pressure plate surfaces should be cleaned thoroughly with a safe solvent.
6. Remove the clutch release shaft and slide the release bearing assembly off the input shaft seal retainer.
7. It is false economy to replace either the clutch disc or pressure plate separately, since this will only lead to premature failure of the other component. In order to reuse any of the components, the following conditions should be met:
   a. There should be no oil leakage through the rear main oil seal or transmission front oil seal.
   b. The friction surface of the pressure plate should have a uniform appearance over the entire surface contact area. The pressure plate may be improperly mounted or sprung if a heavy wear pattern occurs directly opposite a light wear pattern.
   c. The friction face of the flywheel should be free from discoloration, burned areas, cracks or grooves. Frequently the face of the

CLUTCH AND TRANSAXLE 119

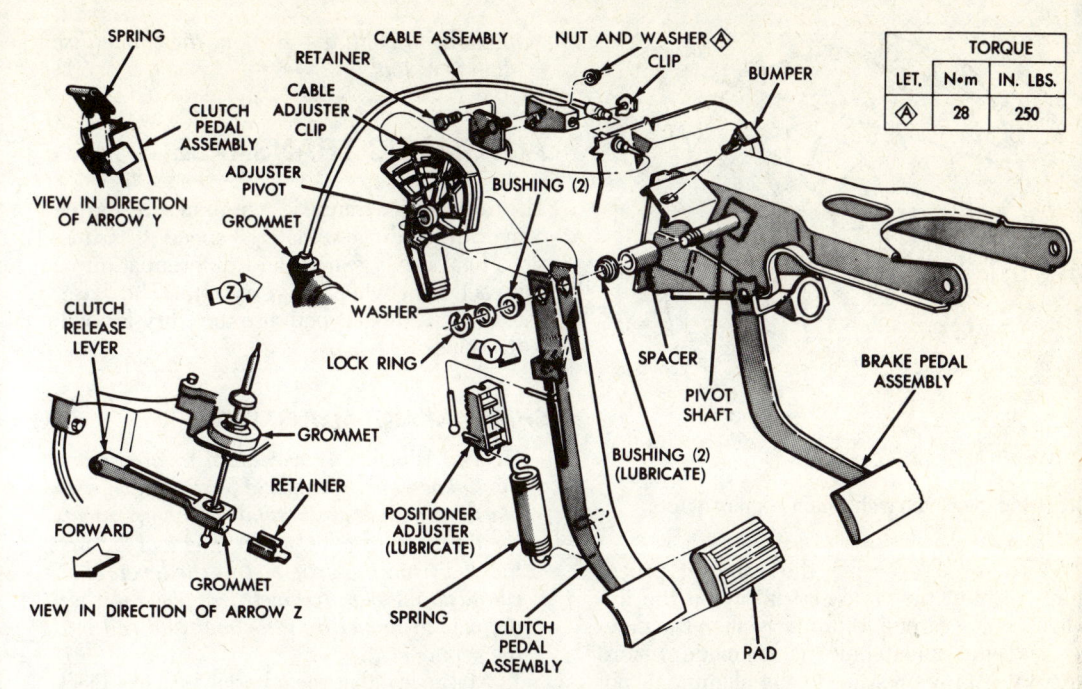

Clutch pedal assembly and self-adjusting mechanism

flywheel must be machined smooth before installing a new clutch.

d. The disc should be free of oil or grease. If it is worn to within less 0.015 in. of the rivet heads, replace the disc.

e. Check the pressure plate for flatness. It should be flat within 0.020 in. across the friction area, and be free from cracks, burns, grooves or ridges.

f. Inspect the cover outer mounting flange for flatness, burns, nicks, or dents.

g. The 2 dowels in the flywheel should be tight and undamaged.

h. Inspect the center of the release plate for cracks or heavy wear. Wear up to 0.010 in. is acceptable.

If the clutch assembly does not meet these conditions, it should be replaced.

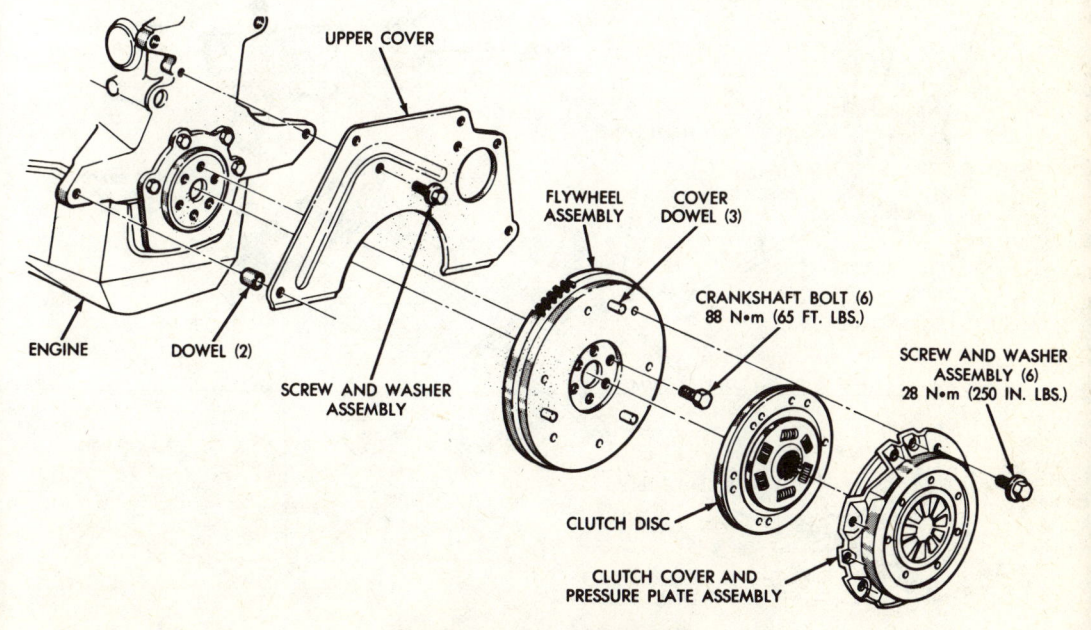

Clutch assembly—exploded view

120 CLUTCH AND TRANSAXLE

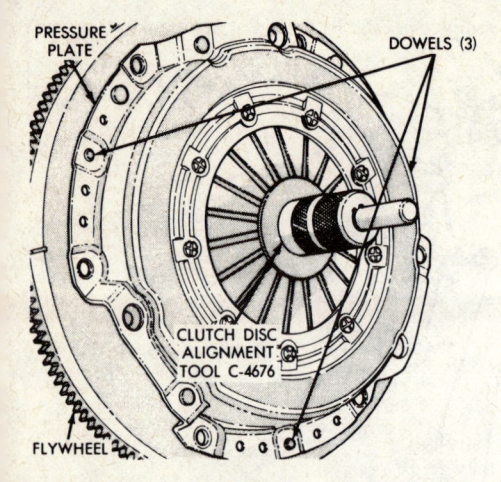

Centering the clutch with clutch alignment tool

8. To install, reverse the removal procedures. Mount the clutch assembly on the flywheel, being careful to properly align the dowels and the alignment marks made before removal. Apply pressure to the alignment tool to center the tip of the tool into the crankshaft and the sliding cone into the clutch fingers while tightening the clutch attaching bolts sufficiently to hold the disc into position.

NOTE: *To avoid distortion of the clutch cover, the bolt should be tightened a few turns until they are all seated. Torque the attaching bolts to 21 ft. lbs. Remove the clutch disc alignment tool.*

AUTOMATIC TRANSAXLE

The automatic transaxle combines a torque converter, fully automatic 3-speed transmission, final drive gearing and differential into a compact front wheel drive system. The Laser and Daytona models both use the Chrysler built A413 transaxle.

SHIFT LINKAGE ADJUSTMENT

NOTE: *When it is necessary to disconnect the linkage cable from the lever, which uses plastic grommets as retainers, the grommets should be replaced. Use a prying tool to force the rod from the grommet in the lever, then cut away the old grommet. Use pliers to snap the new grommet into the liver and rod into the grommet.*

1. Make sure that the adjustable swivel block is free to slide on the shift cable.
2. Place the shift lever in Park. Loosen the clamp bolt on the gearshift cable bracket.
3. With the linkage assembled, and the swivel lock bolt loose, move the shift arm on the transaxle into the "Park" position.
4. Hold the shift arm in position with a force

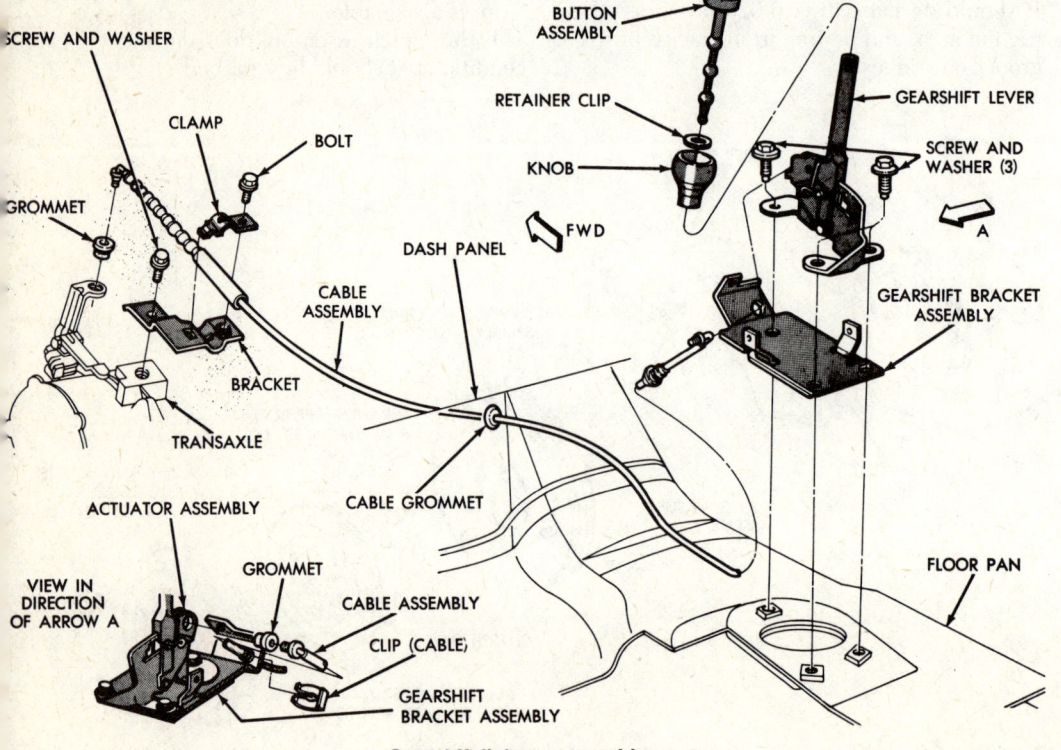

Gearshift linkage assembly

CLUTCH AND TRANSAXLE

of about 10 lbs. and tighten the adjuster swivel lock bolt to 8 ft. lbs.

BAND ADJUSTMENTS

NOTE: *Chrysler recommends that the band be adjusted at each fluid change. The adjusting screw is located on the left side of the case.*

Front (Kickdown) Band

1. Loosen the lock nut and back off the nut approximately five full turns. Check the adjusting screw to see if it's turning freely in the transaxle.
2. Using Chrysler tool C-3880-A and adapter tool C-3705, tighten the band adjusting screw to 47–50 inch pounds. If adapter tool C-3705 is not used, tighten the adjusting screw to 72 inch lbs.
3. Back off the adjusting screw exactly 21/2 turns.
4. Hold the adjusting screw and tighten the locknut to 35 ft. lbs.

Rear (Low-Reverse) Band

1. Loosen the lock nut and back off the nut approximately five full turns. Check the adjusting screw to see if it's turning free in the transaxle.
2. Using an inch-lb. torque wrench, tighten the adjusting screw to 41 inch lbs.
3. Back off the adjusting screw exactly 31/2 turns.
4. Hold the adjusting screw and tighten the locknut to 35 ft. lb.

NEUTRAL START AND BACK-UP LIGHT SWITCH

Replacement

The neutral start circuit is the center contact of the three-terminal switch located in the transmission case. It provides the ground for the starter solenoid circuit through the selector lever in only the PARK or NEUTRAL positions.

1. Remove the wiring connector and test for continuity between the center pin and case. Continuity should exist only in Park and Neutral.
2. Remove the switch and check that the operating lever fingers are centered in the switch opening.
3. Install the switch and a new seal and tighten to 24 ft. lbs. Retest with a lamp.
4. Replace the lost transmission fluid.
5. If shift linkage adjustment is correct and the switch still malfunctions, replace the switch.

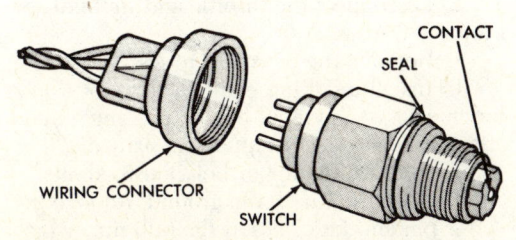

PAN REMOVAL AND INSTALLATION, FLUID AND FILTER CHANGE

NOTE: *RTV silicone sealer is used in place of a pan gasket.*

Chrysler recommends no fluid or filter

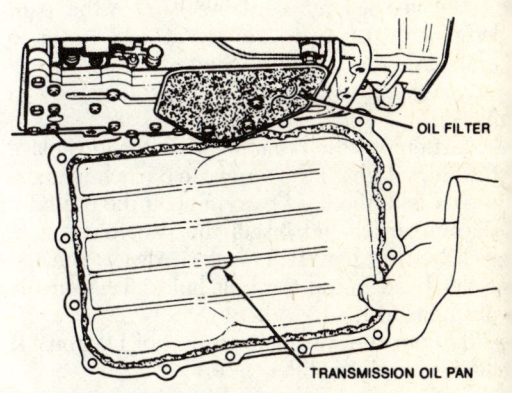

Removing transmission oil pan

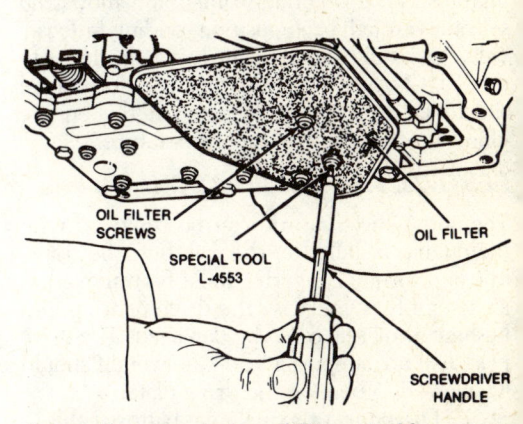

Automatic transmission oil filter attaching screws

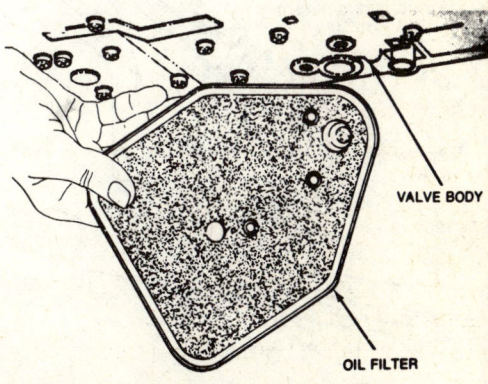

Neutral start and back-up light switch assembly

Removing automatic transmission filter

CLUTCH AND TRANSAXLE

changes during the normal service life of the car. Severe usage requires a fluid and filter change every 15,000 miles. Severe usage is defined as:

    a. more than 50% heavy city traffic during 90°F weather.

    b. police, taxi or commercial operation or trailer towing.

When changing the fluid, only Dexron® or Dexron® II fluid should be used. A filter change should be performed at every fluid change.

1. Raise the vehicle and support it on jackstands.
2. Place a large container under the pan, loosen the pan bolts and tap at one corner to brake it loose. Drain the fluid.
3. When the fluid is drained remove the pan bolts.
4. Remove the retaining screws and replace the filter. Tighten the screws to 35 inch pounds.
5. Clean the fluid pan, peel off the old RTV silicone sealer and install the pan, using a 1/8 inch bead of new RTV sealer. Always run the sealer bead inside the bolt holes. Tighten the pan bolts to 10–12 ft. lbs.
6. Pour the specified amount of Dexron® II fluid through the filler tube.
7. Start the engine and idle it for at least 2 minutes. set the parking brake and move the selector through each position, ending in Park.
8. Add sufficient fluid to bring the level to the FULL mark on the dipstick. The level should be checked in Park, with the engine idling at normal operating temperature.

REMOVAL AND INSTALLATION

The automatic transaxle can be removed with the engine installed in the car, but, the transaxle and torque converter must be removed as an assembly. Otherwise the drive plate, pump bushing or oil seal could be damaged. The drive plate will not support a load—no weight should be allowed to bear on the drive plate.

1. Disconnect the negative battery cable.

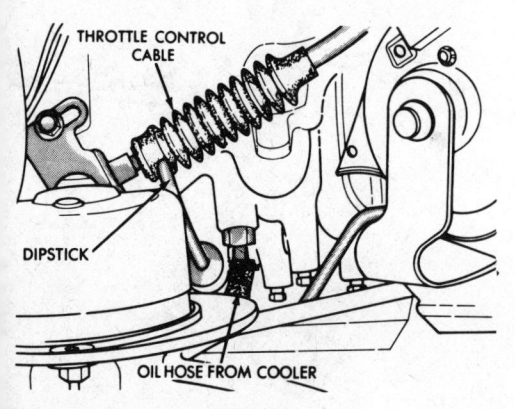

Removing the oil cooler hoses

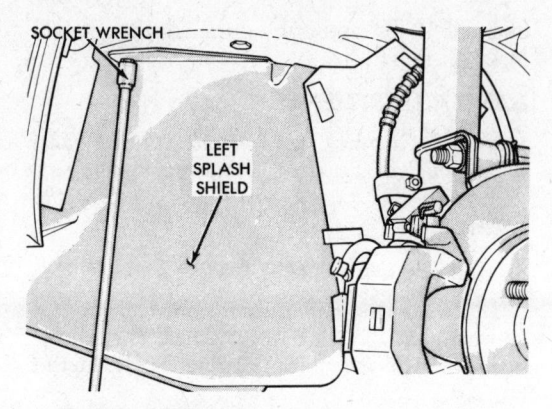

Removing the left splash shield

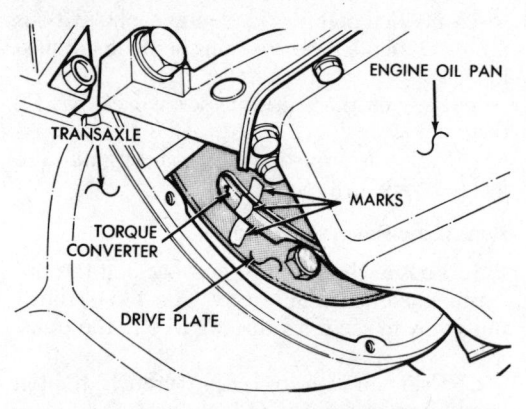

Match-mark the torque converter and the drive plate

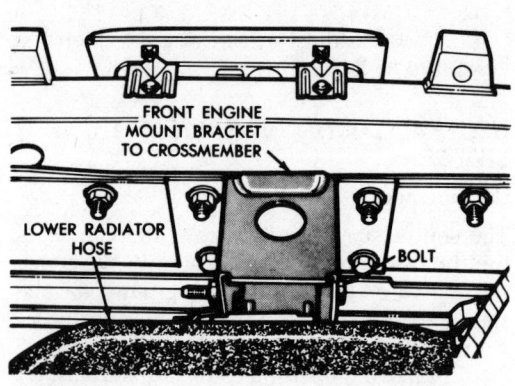

Remove the engine mount bracket from the front crossmember

2. Disconnect the throttle and shift linkage from the transaxle.
3. Remove the oil cooler hoses.
4. Install a "lifting eye" on the No. 4 cylinder exhaust manifold bolt of the engine and attach it to an engine supporting fixture.
5. Remove the upper bell housing bolts.
6. With the car on the ground, remove the cotter pin and lock, loosen the hub nut, which has been torqued to 200 ft. lbs.

CLUTCH AND TRANSAXLE

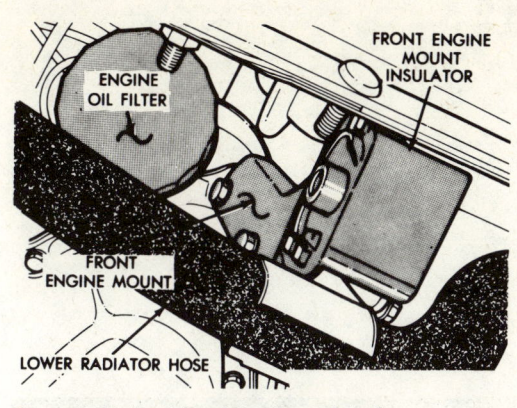

Remove the front insulator through-bolt

7. Raise the car and support on jackstands, remove the front wheels.

8. Refer to "Halfshaft Removal and Installation" to remove or install the halfshafts.

9. Remove the dust cover and matchmark the torque converter and drive plate. Remove the torque converter mounting bolts. Remove the access plug in the right splash shield to rotate the engine.

10. Remove the lower cooler tube and the wire to the neutral safety switch.

11. Remove the engine mount bracket from the front crossmember.

12. Remove the front mount insulator through bolts and the bell housing bolts.

13. Support the transmission with a transmission jack.

14. Remove the long through-bolt from the left-hand engine mount.

15. Raise the transaxle and pry it away from the engine.

16. Installation is the reverse of removal. Fill the differential with Dexron® II automatic transmission fluid before lowering the car. Form a new gasket from RTV sealant when installing the differential cover. See Chapter 1.

Suspension and Steering

7

FRONT SUSPENSION

A MacPherson type front suspension, with vertical shock absorbers attached to the upper fender reinforcement and the steering knuckle, is used. Lower control arms, attached inboard to a cross-member and outboard to the steering knuckle through a ball joint, provide lower steering knuckle position. During steering maneuvers, the upper strut and steering knuckle turn as an assembly.

Strut
REMOVAL AND INSTALLATION

1. Raise and support the vehicle.
2. Remove the wheel and tire assembly.

NOTE: *If the original strut is to be assem-*

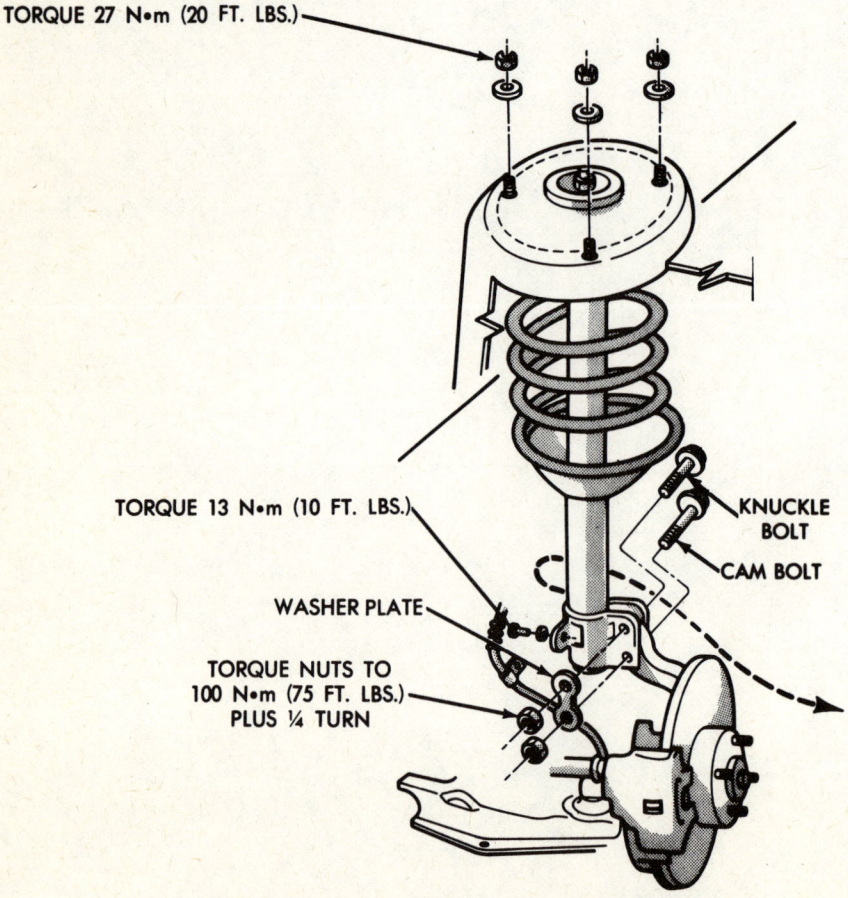

Removal and installation of the front strut assembly

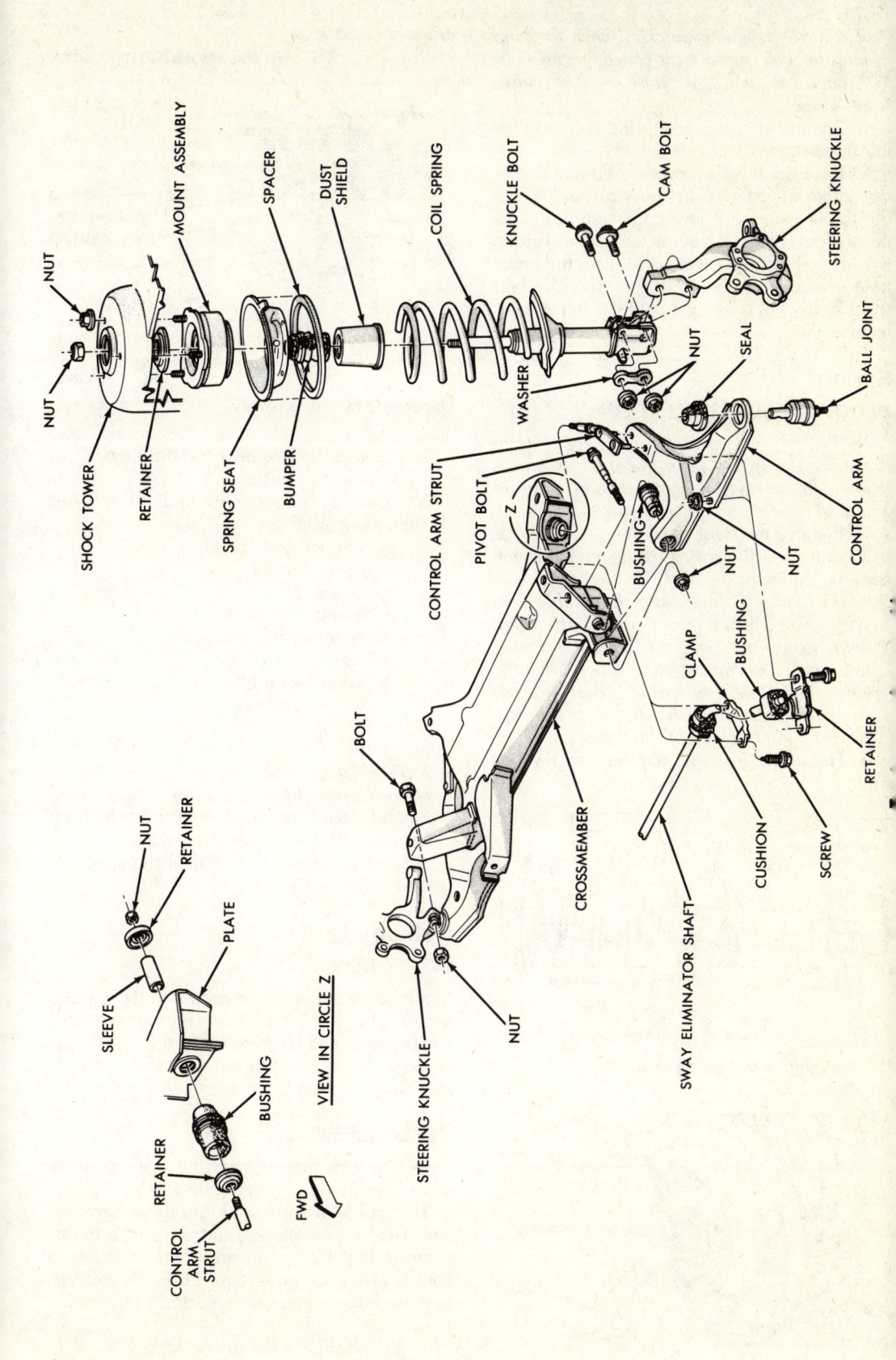

SUSPENSION AND STEERING 125

SUSPENSION AND STEERING

bled to the original knuckle, mark the cam adjusting bolt. Remove the cam adjusting bolt, through bolt and brake hose bracket retaining screw.

4. Remove the strut mounting bolts and remove the strut.
5. Installation is the reverse of removal. Position the knuckle leg in the strut and install the upper (cam) and lower through-bolts. Index the cam bolt with the match marks. Torque the strut mounting bolts to 20 ft. lbs.; the brake hose bracket screw to 10 ft. lbs.; the cam bolt to 75 ft. lbs., plus ¼ turn, and the wheel nuts to 95 ft. lbs.

Spring

REMOVAL AND INSTALLATION

NOTE: *A spring compressor is required to remove the spring from the strut. A crow's foot adaptor and torque wrench are also required.*

1. Remove the struts assembly.
2. Compress the spring, using a reliable coil spring compressor.

NOTE: *Springs are not interchangeable from side to side. During service procedures where both springs are removed, mark the spring to insure proper installation. When using the Chrysler C-4838 coil spring compressor, or equivalent be certain that five coils are captured within the jaws of the compressor.*

3. Hold the strut rod and remove the rod nut.

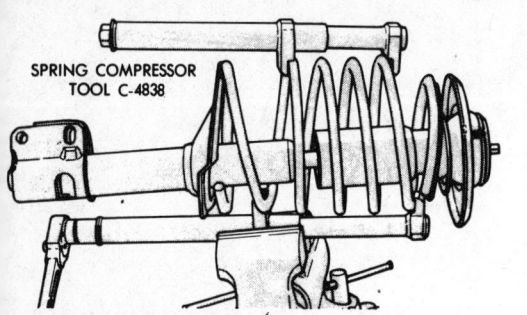

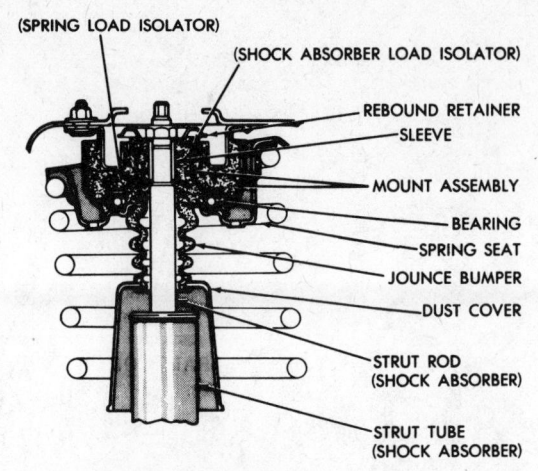

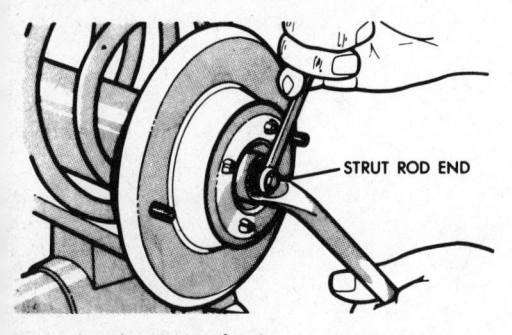

Upper strut mount assembly

4. Remove the retainers and bushings.
5. Remove the spring.
6. Assembly is the reverse of disassembly in the following order:
   - Bumper dust shield
   - Jounce bumper
   - Spacer
   - Spring seat
   - Upper spring retainer
   - Bearing
   - Mount assembly
   - Rebound bumper
   - Retainer
   - Rod nut

NOTE: *Torque rod nut to 60 ft. lbs. before removing the spring compressor. Use a crow's foot adaptor to tighten the nut while holding the rod with an open end wrench.*

Be sure the lower coil end of the spring is seated in the seat recess.

Ball Joints

INSPECTION

With the weight of the car resting on the wheels, grab hold of the grease fitting on the bottom of the ball joint and try to move it. If the ball joint is worn the grease fitting will move easily. If movement is found, replace the ball joint.

REPLACEMENT

NOTE: *This procedure requires special tools and machine shop services.*

The ball joint is pressed into the lower control arm on these models and is retained to the steering knuckle by a clamp bolt. The lower control arm must be removed from the vehicle and placed in a press in to perform this operation.

1. Pry off the rubber grease seal.
2. Position the Receiving Cup tool C-4699-

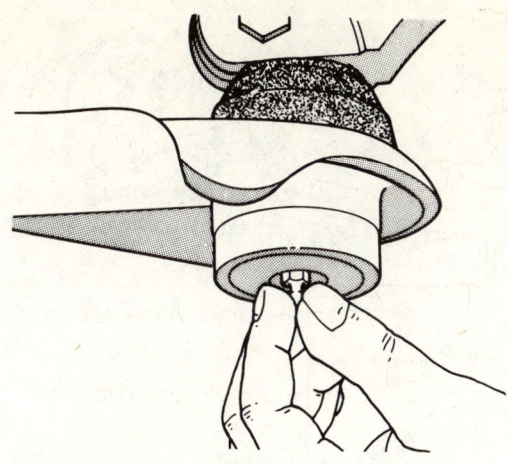

SUSPENSION AND STEERING 127

Checking ball joint wear

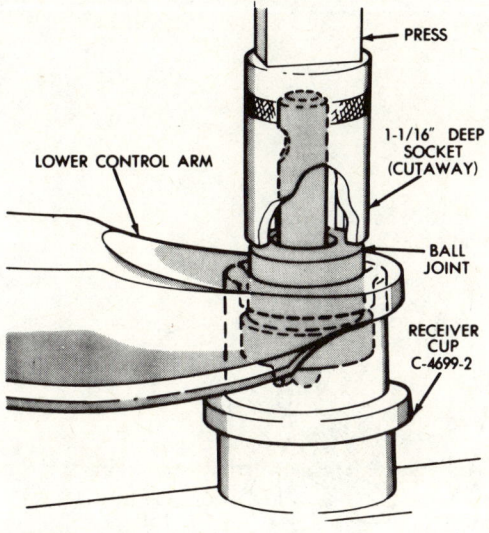

Ball joint removal

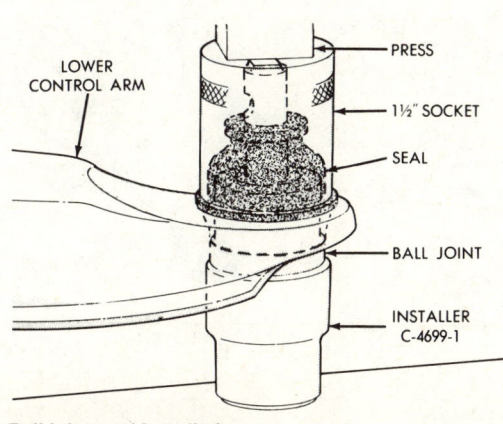

Ball joint seal installation

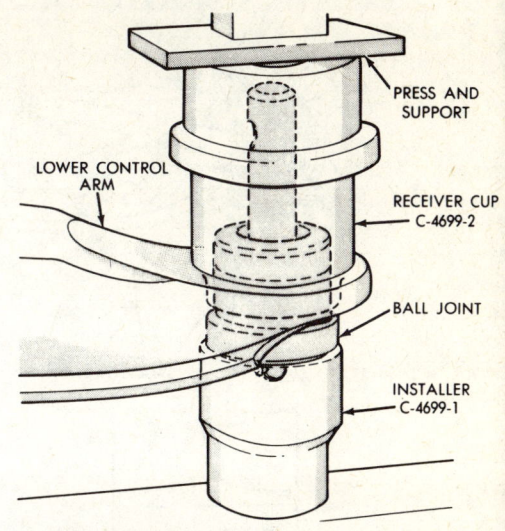

Ball joint installation

4. Apply pressure from the press to remove the joint from the arm.
5. To install, position the ball joint housing into the control arm cavity.
6. Place the assembly in the press with the installer tool C-4699-1 supporting the lower control arm.
7. Align and press the assembly until the ball joint bottoms against the control arm cavity down flange.
8. With a 1-1/2 in. socket, press the seal onto the ball joint housing so that it seats against the lower control arm.

Sway Bar
REMOVAL AND INSTALLATION

1. Raise and support the car.
2. Remove the nut from the control arm end bushing and reinforcement plates.
3. Remove the nut, retainers and insulator holding the sway bar to the crossmember linkage.
4. Remove the sway bar.
5. Inspect the sway bar for distortion or fatigue cracks in the metal. Replace any damaged or distorted bushings.
6. Installation is the reverse of removal.

Lower Control Arm
REMOVAL AND INSTALLATION

1. Raise and support the vehicle.
2. Remove the front inner pivot through bolt, the rear stub strut nut, retainer and bushing, and the ball joint-to-steering knuckle clamp bolt.
3. Separate the ball joint stud from the steering knuckle by prying between the ball

2 to support the lower control arm while receiving the ball joint assembly.
3. Install a 1-1/16 in. deep socket over the stud and against the joint upper housing.

28 SUSPENSION AND STEERING

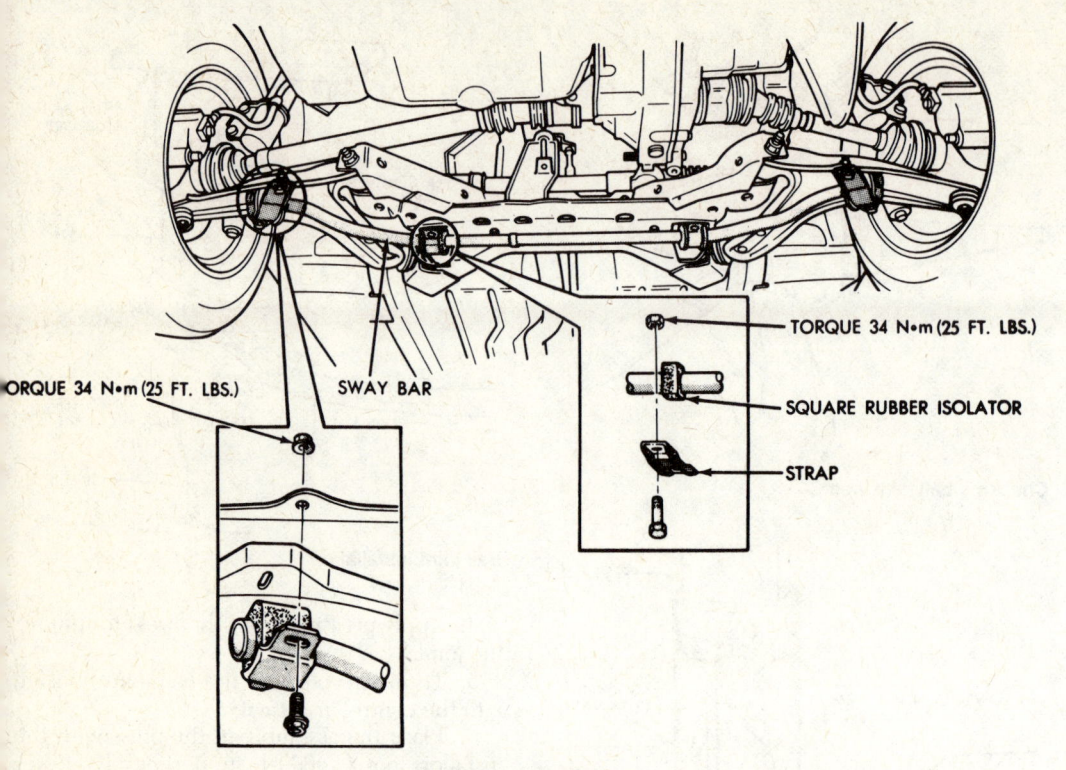

TORQUE 34 N•m (25 FT. LBS.)
SQUARE RUBBER ISOLATOR
STRAP
TORQUE 34 N•m (25 FT. LBS.)
SWAY BAR

Sway bar mounting

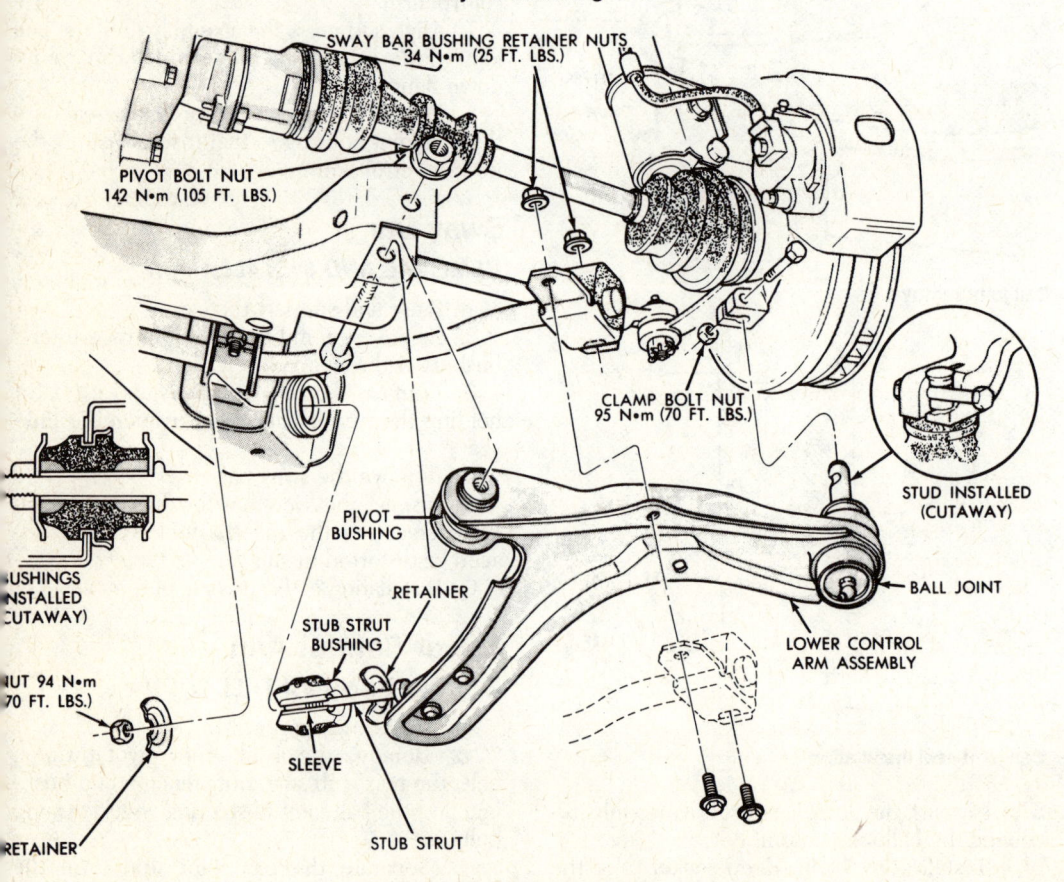

SWAY BAR BUSHING RETAINER NUTS
34 N•m (25 FT. LBS.)
PIVOT BOLT NUT
142 N•m (105 FT. LBS.)
CLAMP BOLT NUT
95 N•m (70 FT. LBS.)
STUD INSTALLED (CUTAWAY)
PIVOT BUSHING
RETAINER
STUB STRUT BUSHING
BALL JOINT
LOWER CONTROL ARM ASSEMBLY
BUSHINGS INSTALLED (CUTAWAY)
NUT 94 N•m (70 FT. LBS.)
SLEEVE
RETAINER
STUB STRUT

Lower control arm assembly

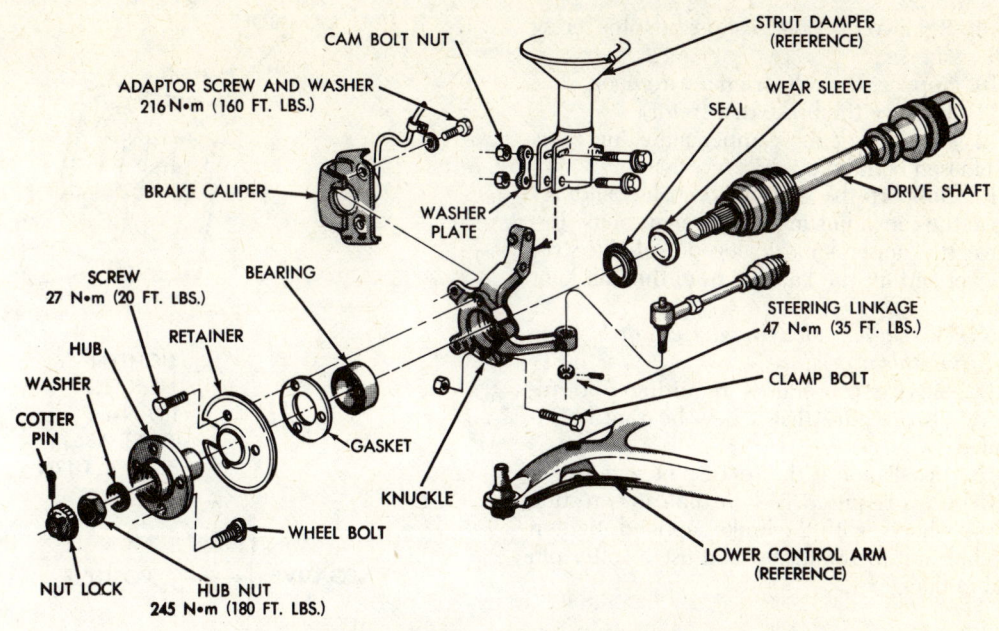

SUSPENSION AND STEERING

Steering knuckle and related components

stud retainer on the knuckle and the lower control arm.

CAUTION: *Pulling the steering knuckle out from the vehicle after releasing it from the ball joint can separate the inner C/V joint.*

4. Remove the sway bar-to-control arm nut and reinforcement and rotate the control arm over the sway bar. Remove the rear stub strut bushing, sleeve and retainer.

NOTE: *The substitution of fasteners other than those of the grade originally used is not recommended.*

5. Install the retainer, bushing and sleeve on the stub strut.
6. Position the control arm over the sway bar and install the rear stub strut and front pivot into the crossmember.
7. Install the front pivot bolt and loosely install the nut.
8. Install the stub strut bushing and retainer and loosely assemble the nut.
9. Position the sway bar bracket and stud through the control arm and install the retainer and nut. Tighten the nut to 25 ft. lbs.
10. Install the ball joint stud into the steering knuckle and install the clamp bolt. Torque the clamp bolt to 70 ft. lbs.
11. Lower the vehicle, with the suspension supporting the weight of the vehicle torque the front pivot bolt to 105 ft. lbs. and the strut nut to 70 ft. lbs.

Steering Knuckle

REMOVAL AND INSTALLATION

Service or repair to the bearing, hub, brake dust shield or the steering knuckle itself will require removal of the knuckle. Before attempting this operation, be aware that to reassemble the components it is necessary to torque the front hub nut to at least 180 ft. lbs. You will need a large torque wrench to read that high and a great deal of strength to attain that much torque on the nut.

1. Remove the cotter pin nut-lock and spring washer.
2. Loosen the hub nut while the car is resting on the wheels with the brakes applied.

NOTE: *The hub and driveshaft are splines together through the knuckle and retained by the hub nut.*

3. Raise and support the car.
4. Remove the wheel and tire.
5. Remove the hub nut. Be sure the splines driveshaft is free to separate from the spline in hub when the knuckle is removed.
6. Disconnect the tie rod end from the steering arm.
7. Disconnect the brake hose retainer from the strut.
8. Remove the clamp bolt holding the ball joint stud in the steering knuckle.

SUSPENSION AND STEERING

9. Remove the brake caliper adaptor screw and washers.
10. Support the caliper on a wire hook.
11. Remove the brake disc (rotor).
12. Matchmark the camber adjusting cams and loosen both bolts.
13. Support the steering knuckle and remove the cam adjusting and through-bolts. Remove the upper knuckle leg out of the strut bracket and lift the knuckle from the ball joint stud.

NOTE: *Do not allow the driveshaft to hang during this procedure.*

14. Service procedures requiring hub removal also require that a new bearing be installed.
15. Installation is the reverse of removal. A new hub is required. When the car is resting in the wheels, with the brakes applied, tighten the hub nut to 180 ft. lbs. and use a cotter pin and nutlock.

Wheel Alignment

Wheel alignment requires the use of fairly sophisticated equipment to accurately measure the geometry of the front end. The information is given here so that the owner will be aware of what is involved, not so that he can do the work himself.

Before the wheels are aligned, the following checks should be made, since these are factors that will influence the wheel alignment settings.

1. All tires should be of the same size and up to the recommended pressures.
2. Check the lower ball joints and steering linkage.
3. Check the struts for extremely stiff or spongy operation.
4. Check for broken or sagged springs.
5. The wheel alignment should be made with a full tank of gas, and no passenger or luggage compartment load.

CAMBER

Camber angle is the number of degrees which the centerline of the wheel is inclined from the vertical. Camber reduces loading of the outer wheel bearing and improves the tire contact patch while cornering.

Camber is adjusted by loosening the cam and through-bolts on each side. Rotate the upper cam bolt to move the top of the wheel in or out to the specified camber.

CASTER

Caster angle is the number of degrees in which a line drawn through the steering knuckle pivots is inclined from the vertical, toward the front or rear of the car. Positive caster improves directional stability and decreases susceptibility to crosswinds or road surface deviations. Other than the replacement of damaged suspension components, caster is not adjustable.

TOE-OUT

The front wheels on the Laser and Daytona are set with a slight toe-out, as on most front wheel drive cars, to counteract the tendency of the driving wheels to toe-in excessively. Toe out is the amount, measured in inches, that the wheels are closer together at the rear than at the front. Toe is checked with the wheels straight ahead.

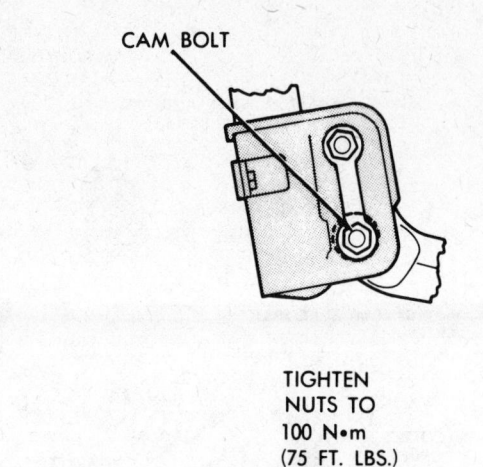

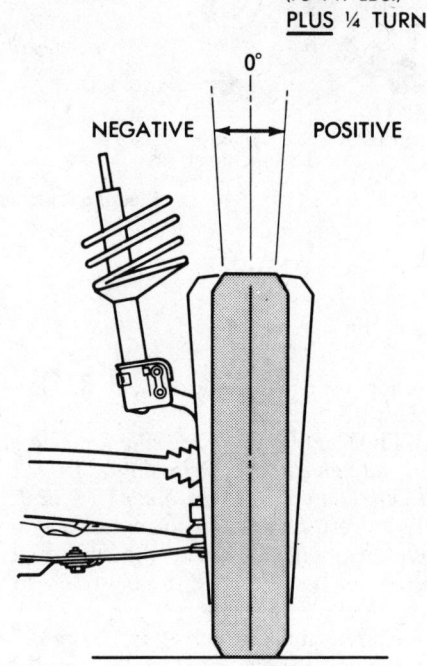

Front suspension—Camber adjustment

SUSPENSION AND STEERING 131

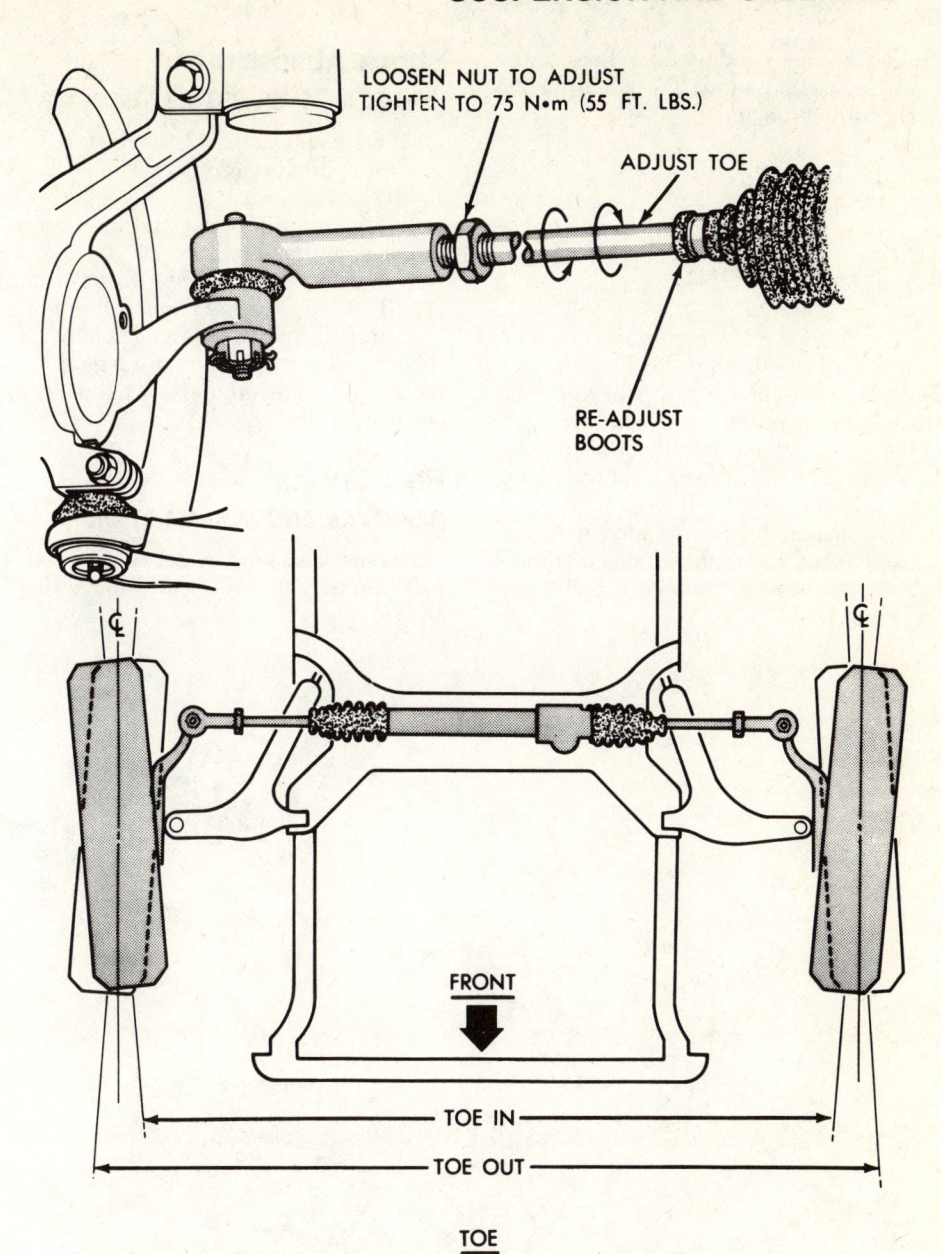

Toe adjustment and front suspension geometry

Wheel Alignment Specifications
(caster is not adjustable)

Year	Front Camber Range (deg)	Front Camber Preferred	Toe-Out (in.) Front	Toe-Out (in.) Rear	Rear Camber Range (deg)	Rear Camber Preferred
'84–'85	¼N to ¾P	5/16P	7/32 out to 1/8 in	3/16 out to 3/16 in	1N to 0	½N

132 SUSPENSION AND STEERING

The tie-rod linkage is adjustable. Loosen the nuts and clamps and adjust the length of the tie-rod for correct toe out.

REAR SUSPENSION

A trailing, independent arm assembly, with integral sway bar is used. The wheel spindles are attached to two trailing arms which extend rearward from mounting pints on the body where they are attached with shock absorbing, oval bushings. The trailing arms and coil spring seats are welded directly to the channel.

The rear suspension is equipped with coil springs and vertically mounted shock absorbers. All the suspension mounting points are rubber isolated.

Shock Absorber
REMOVAL AND INSTALLATION

1. Raise and support the vehicle.
2. Support the axle and remove the wheel and tire.
3. Remove the upper and lower shock absorber mounting bolt.
4. Remove the shock absorber assembly.
5. Installation is the reverse of removal.

Torque the upper mounting bolt to 40 ft. lbs., then install the wheel and tire assembly. Lower the vehicle to the ground and tighten the lower nut to 40 ft. lbs

Rear Spring
REMOVAL AND INSTALLATION

1. Raise and support the vehicle.
2. Support the axle and remove the wheel and tire.

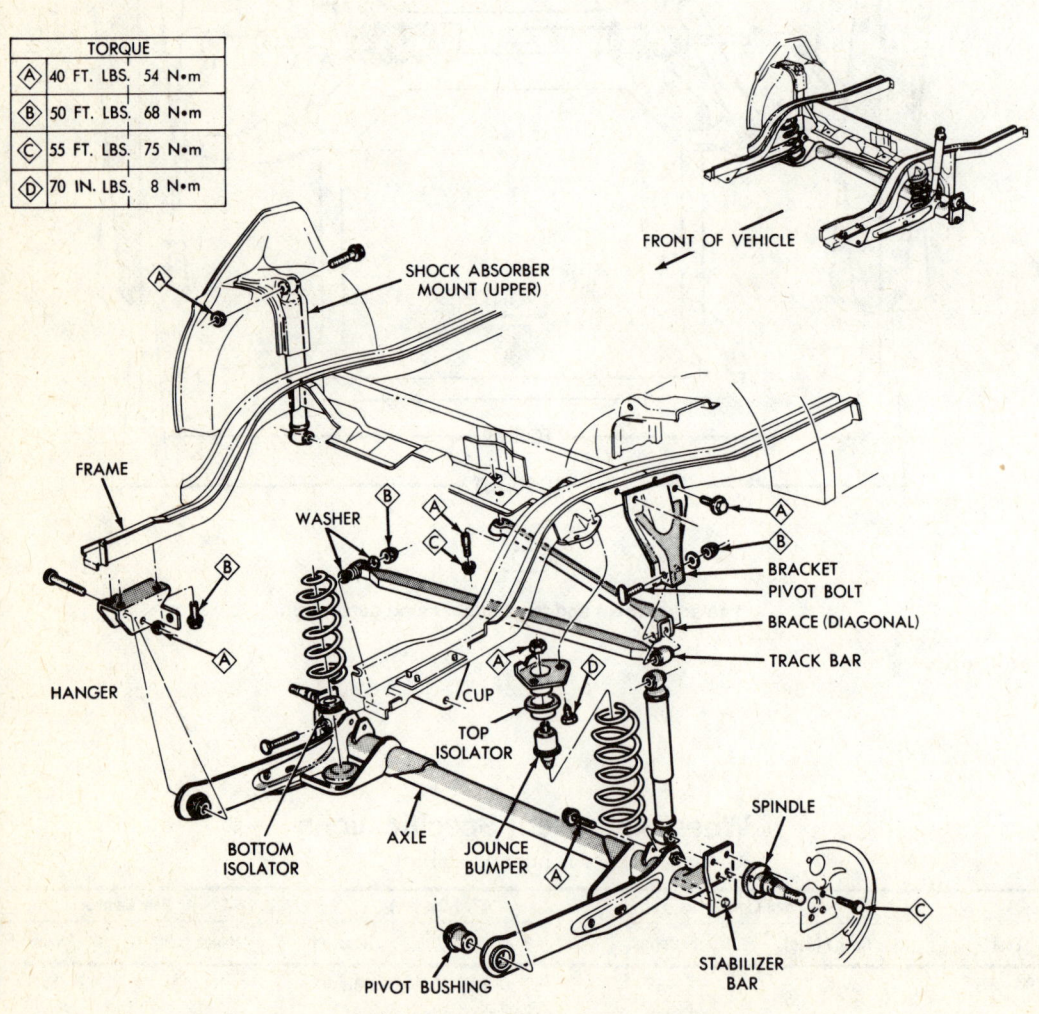

TORQUE		
A	40 FT. LBS.	54 N•m
B	50 FT. LBS.	68 N•m
C	55 FT. LBS.	75 N•m
D	70 IN. LBS.	8 N•m

Trailing arm rear suspension assembly

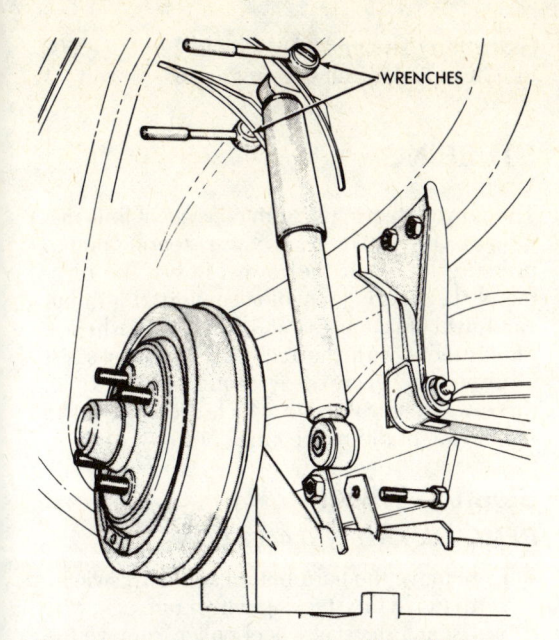

SUSPENSION AND STEERING

Rear Wheel Alignment

Due to the design of the rear suspension, it is possible to adjust both the camber and toe-in of the rear wheels. Alignment is controlled by inserting 0.010 in. shim stock between the spindle mounting surface and the spindle mounting plate. Each 0.010 in. shim stock changes wheel alignment by approximately 0.3°. Be sure to adjust the rear wheel bearings.

INSTALLATION OF REAR ALIGNMENT SHIMS

1. Block the front wheels so the vehicle will not move.
2. Release the parking brake, raise and support the rear of the car on jackstands so that the rear suspension is in the full rebound position.
3. Remove the wheel and tire assembly.
4. Pry off the grease cap and remove the cotter pin, castle lock and the adjusting nut.
5. Remove the brake drum assembly.
6. Loosen the four brake assembly and spindle mounting bolts enough to allow clearance for the shims to be installed.
NOTE: *DO NOT remove the mounting bolts.*
7. Install the shims as shown in the illus-

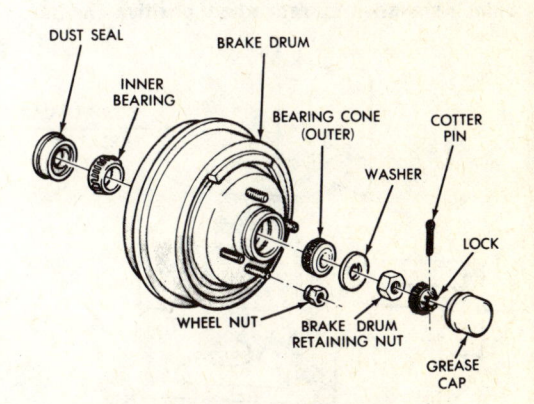

Rear shock absorber—removal and installation

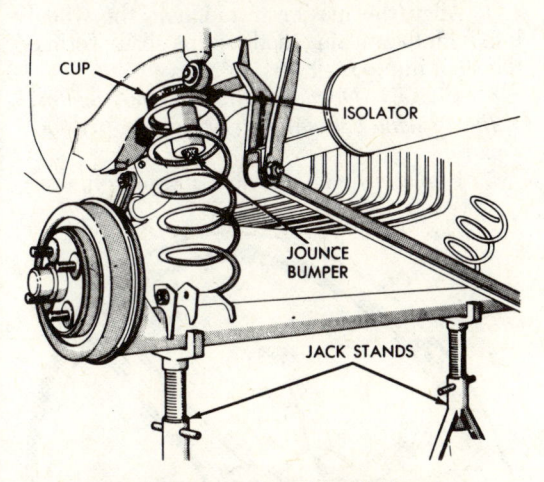

Rear coil spring—removal and installation

3. Remove both lower shock absorber mounting bolts.
4. Lower the axle assembly until the spring and its upper isolator can be removed.
NOTE: *Be careful not to stretch the brake hose.*
5. Remove the two screws which hold the cup to the rail and remove the assembly.
6. To install, reverse the removal procedure. Tighten the cup attaching screws to 6 ft. lbs. and the shock absorber bolts to 40 ft. lbs.

Rear Wheel Bearings

Please refer to Chapter 1 for rear wheel bearing service procedures.

Removing and installing the brake drum

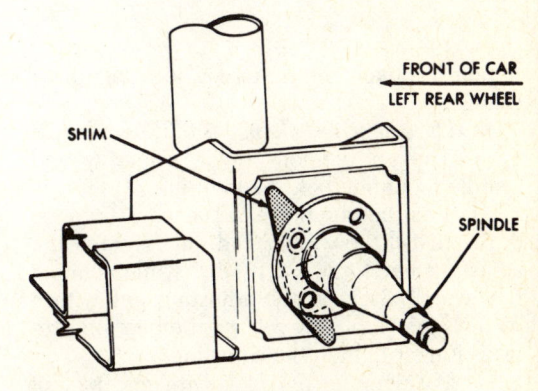

Shim installation for rear wheel toe-out

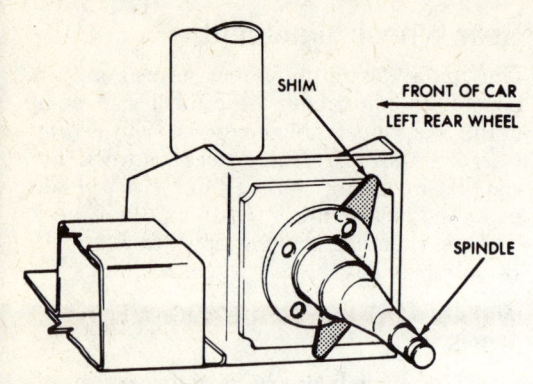

134   SUSPENSION AND STEERING

Shim installation for rear wheel toe-in

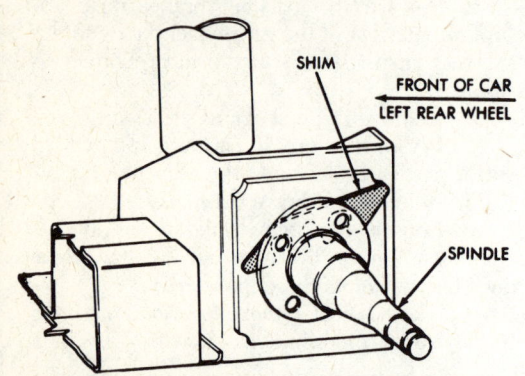

Shim installation for rear wheel positive camber

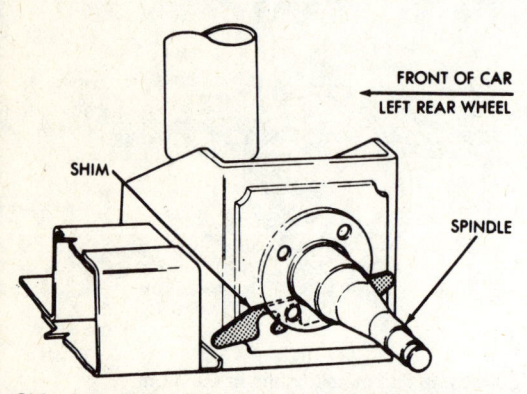

Shim installation for rear wheel negative camber

tration to obtain the desired wheel alignment change.
NOTE: *The wheel change is 0.3° per shim.*
8. Tighten the four brake assembly and spindle mounting bolts to 45 ft. lbs.
9. Reinstall the brake drum.
10. Install the washer and nut. Tighten the adjusting nut to 20–25 ft. lbs. while rotating the wheel. Back off the adjusting nut with a wrench to completely release the bearing preload. Finger tighten the adjusting nut.
11. Position the nut lock with one pair of slots in line with the cotter pin hole. Install the

cotter pin. The end play should be .001–.003 in. Clean and install the grease cap.

STEERING

The power steering system consists of four major parts: the power gear, power steering pump, pressure hose and the return hose. The turning of the steering wheel is converted into linear travel through the meshing of the helical pinion teeth with the rack teeth. Power assist is provided by an open center, rotary type, three-way control valve which directs fluid to either side of the rack control piston.

Steering Wheel
REMOVAL AND INSTALLATION
1. Remove the horn button and horn switch.
2. Remove the steering wheel nut.
3. Using a steering wheel puller, remove the steering wheel.
4. Align the master serration in the wheel hub with the missing tooth on the shaft. Torque the shaft nut to 60 ft. lbs.
  CAUTION: *Do not torque the nut against the steering column lock or damage will occur.*
5. Replace the horn switch and button.

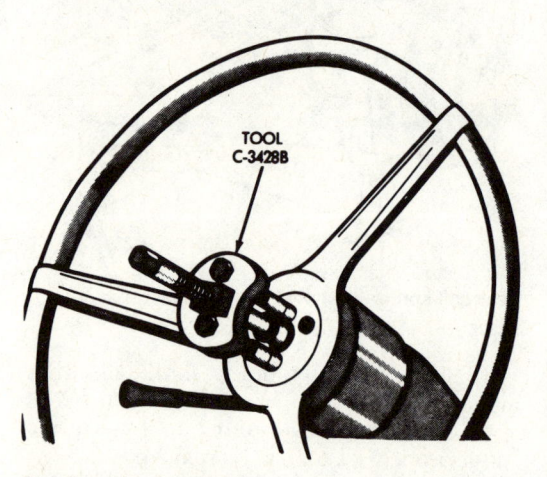

Steering wheel removal

Turn Signal Switch
REMOVAL AND INSTALLATION
1. Disconnect the negative battery cable in the engine compartment.
2. Remove the steering wheel as described earlier using special tool C-3428B or equivalent.
3. If so equipped, remove the lower column sound deadening insulation panel.

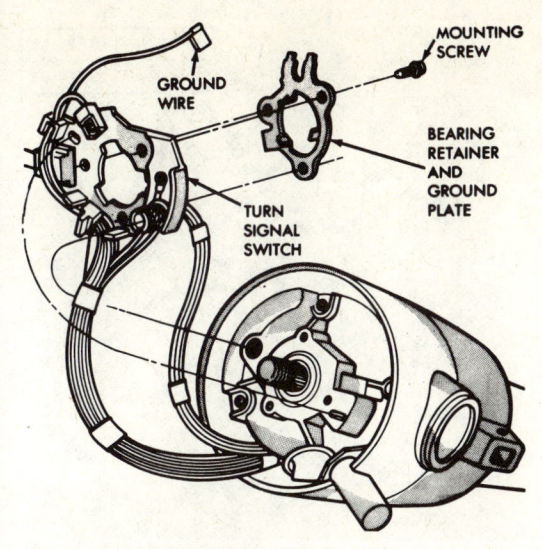

SUSPENSION AND STEERING 135

Turn signal switch removal

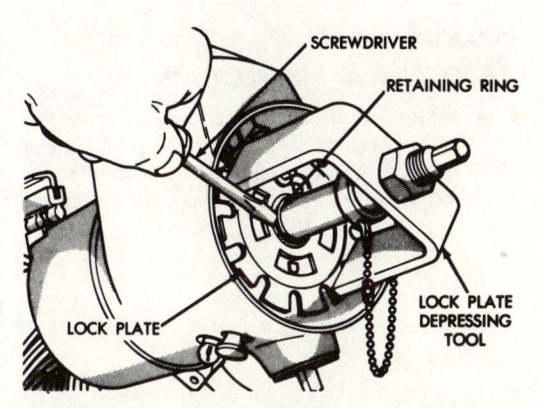

Removing the lock plate retaining ring with tool C-4156

4. Remove the lower instrument panel bezel.
5. Remove the wiring trough by prying out the plastic retainer buttons.
6. On the standard column, position the gearshift lever to its full clockwise position. On the tilt column, position the gearshift lever to its midpoint position.
7. Disconnect the turn signal switch at the wiring connector.
8. Using the following procedures, disassemble the steering column for switch removal.
   a. Standard Steering Column: Remove the screw holding the wiper-washer switch to the turn signal switch pivot. Leave the entire turn signal lever (control stalk) in its installed position. Remove the three screws attaching turn signal switch to the upper bearing housing.
   b. Tilt Steering Column: Remove the plastic cover (if so equipped) from the lock plate. Depress the lock plate with tool C-4156 or an equivalent and pry the retaining ring out of the groove with a screwdriver.
   NOTE: *The full load of the upper bearing spring should not be relieved. If it is, the retaining ring will turn too easily, making the removal more difficult.*
   Remove the lock plate, cancelling cam, and upper bearing spring.
   Place the turn signal switch in the right turn position. Remove the screw which attaches the link between the turn signal switch and the wiper-washer switch pivot. Remove the screw which attaches the hazard warning switch knob. Remove the three screws attaching the turn signal switch to the steering column. Remove the switch assembly by gently pulling the switch up from the column while straightening and guiding the wires up through the column opening.
9. Installation is the reverse of the removal procedure.

Ignition Switch
REMOVAL AND INSTALLATION

Due to the complexity of the ignition switch removal procedure and the necessity of special tools, it is recommended that the switch be replaced by a qualified repair shop.

Tie Rod End
REPLACEMENT

1. Loosen the jam nut which connects the tie rod end to the knuckle. Mark the tie rod position on the threads.
2. Using a ball joint separator, remove the tie rod end from the knuckle.
3. Install a new tie rod end in reverse of removal. Torque the end nut to 50 ft. lbs.; the locknut to 55 ft. lbs.
4. Check alignment.

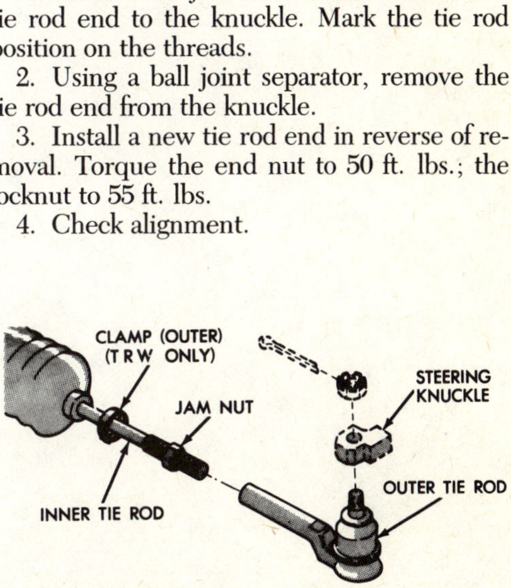

Tie-rod end replacement

136 SUSPENSION AND STEERING

Power Steering Pump
REMOVAL AND INSTALLATION

NOTE: *All the fasteners on the power steering pump and mounting brackets are metric.*

1. Remove the adjusting bolt and slip off the power steering pump drive belt.
2. Raise the vehicle and support on jackstands. Disconnect the return hose from the gear tube and drain the fluid from the pump through the open end of the hose.
3. Remove the right side splash shield.
4. Disconnect both power steering hoses from the pump. Cap all the hose openings at the pump and steering gear to prevent dirt from entering the system.
5. Remove the lower stud and pivot screw from the pump.
6. Lower the vehicle.
7. Move the pump toward the rear of the vehicle to clear the mounting bracket and remove the adjusting bracket.
8. Rotate the pump clockwise so the pump pulley faces the rear of the vehicle and pull upwards to remove the pump from the vehicle.
9. Installation is the reverse of removal. Adjust the belt to specifications. See Chapter 1.

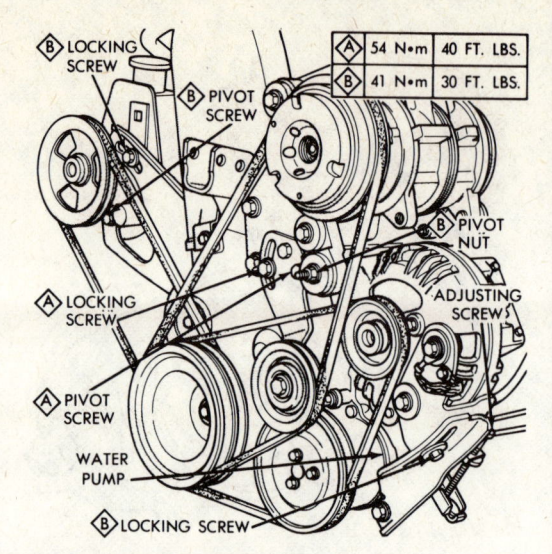

Power steering pump mounting

Steering Gear
REMOVAL AND INSTALLATION

Due to the complexity of the ignition switch removal procedure and the necessity of special tools, it is recommended that the switch be replaced by a qualified repair shop.

Brakes

BRAKE SYSTEM

A conventional front disc/rear drum setup is used. The front discs are single piston caliper types; the rear drums are activated by a conventional top mounted wheel cylinder. Disc brakes require no adjustments, the drum brakes are self adjusting by means of the parking brake cable. The only variance in the system from those found on the majority of vehicles are that the system is diagonally balanced, that is, the front left and right rear are on one system and the front right and left rear on the other. No proportioning valve is used.

CAUTION: *When servicing brake assemblies or components, DO NOT create dust by sanding, grinding or by cleaning brake parts with a dry brush or with compressed air. A water dampened cloth should be used. Many brake components contain asbestos fibers which can become airborne if dust is created during the service operations. Breathing dust which contains asbestos fibers can cause serious bodily harm.*

Adjustment

All disc brakes are inherently self-adjusting. No adjustment is possible. Even though the drum brakes are self-adjusting in normal use, there are times when a manual adjustment is required, such as after installing new shoes or if it is required to back the shoes off the drum. A star wheel with screw type adjusters is provided for these occasions.

1. Remove the access slot plug from the backing plate.
2. Using a brake adjusting spoon pry downward (left side) or upward (right side) on the end of the tool (starwheel teeth moving up) to tighten the brakes. The opposite applies to loosen the brakes.

NOTE: *It will be necessary to use a small

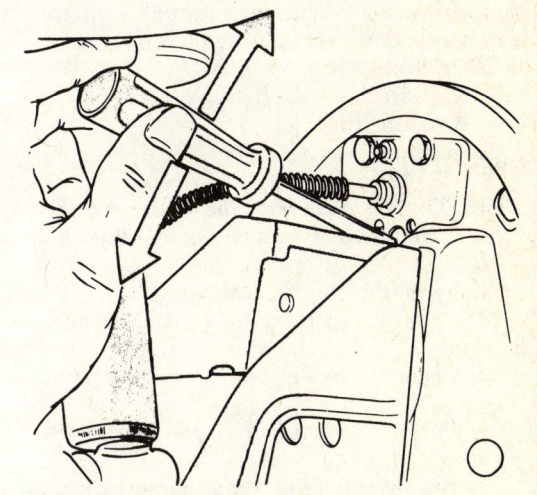

Adjusting rear brakes

screwdriver to hold the adjusting lever away from the starwheel. Be careful not to bend the adjusting lever.*

3. When the brakes are tight almost to the point of being locked, back off on the starwheel 10 clicks. The starwheel on each set of brakes must be backed off the same number of turns to prevent brake pull from side to side.
4. When all brakes are adjusted, check brake pedal travel and then make several stops, while backing the car up, to equalize all the wheels.

TESTING THE ADJUSTER

1. Raise the vehicle on a hoist, with a helper in the car, to apply the brakes.
2. Loosen the brakes by holding the adjusting lever away from the starwheel and backing off the starwheel approximately 30 notches.
3. Spin the wheel and brake drum in reverse and apply the brakes. The movement of the secondary shoe should pull the adjuster lever up, when the brakes are released the lever should snap down and turn the starwheel.

138 BRAKES

4. If the automatic adjuster doesn't work, the drum must be removed and the adjuster components inspected carefully for breakage, wear, or improper installation.

Master Cylinder

REMOVAL AND INSTALLATION

1. Disconnect the primary and secondary brake lines from the master cylinder. Plug the openings.
2. Remove the nuts attaching the cylinder to the power brake booster.
3. Slide the master cylinder straight out, away from the booster.
4. Position the master cylinder over the studs on the booster, align the pushrod with the master cylinder piston and tighten the nuts to 16–25 ft. lbs.
5. Connect the brake lines.
6. Bleed the brakes.

OVERHAUL

CAUTION: *Do not hone the master cylinder bore. Honing will remove the anodized finish.*

1. Clean the housing reservoir.
2. Remove the reservoir caps and empty the fluid.
3. Clamp the master cylinder in a soft-jawed vise.
4. Pull the reservoir from the master cylinder housing.
5. Remove the reservoir grommets.
6. Use needle nose pliers to remove the secondary piston pin from inside the housing.
7. Remove the snap-ring from the outer end of the housing.
8. Slide the primary piston out of the master cylinder bore.
9. Tap the open end of the cylinder on the bench to remove the secondary piston. If it sticks in the bore, it can be removed with light air pressure.

NOTE: *If air pressure is used to remove the piston, new cups must be installed.*

10. Note the position of the rubber cups and remove all except the primary cup.

NOTE: *Do not remove the primary cup from the primary piston. If the cup is worn, the entire primary piston assembly should be replaced.*

11. If the brass tube seats are not reusable, replace them using a suitable tool.
12. Wash the entire housing in clean brake fluid and inspect for pitting or scratches. If any are found, replace the housing. If the pistons are corroded, they should be replaced. Discard all used rubber parts and replace piston cups and seals.
13. Before assembly, dip all parts in clean brake fluid.
14. Install the check flow washer.
15. Install the secondary piston into the master cylinder bore. Be sure the cup lips enter the bore evenly. Keep well lubricated with brake fluid.
16. Center the primary piston spring retainer on the secondary piston and push the piston assemblies into the bore up to the primary piston cup.
17. Work the cup into the bore and push the piston in up to the secondary seal. Work

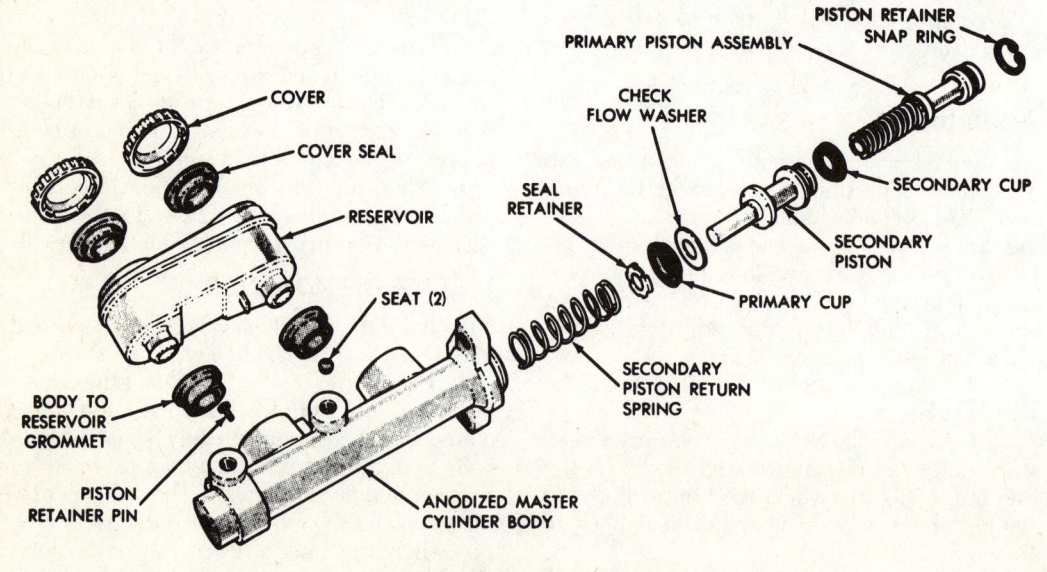

Master cylinder exploded view

the cup into the bore and push on the piston until fully seated.

18. Depress the piston and install the snapring.

19. Tap the secondary piston retainer pin into the housing.

20. Install new tube seats.

21. Install the reservoir grommets in the housing. Lubricate the area with clean brake fluid and install the reservoir. All the lettering should be properly read from the left side of the reservoir when it is properly installed. Make sure the bottom of the reservoir touches the top of the grommet.

Power Booster

REMOVAL AND INSTALLATION

1. Remove the nuts attaching the cylinder to the power brake booster.

2. Disconnect the lines between the master cylinder and the valve assembly.

3. Remove the master cylinder.

4. On manual transmission models, remove the clutch cable mounting bracket. Pull the wiring harness up and away from the strut tower.

5. Disconnect the vacuum hose from the booster.

6. Under the instrument panel, pry the retainer clip center tang over the end of the brake pedal pin and pull the retainer clip from the pin. Discard the clip.

7. Remove the stop lamp switch and striker plate.

8. Remove the four booster attaching nuts.

9. Remove the booster from the vehicle.

10. To install, position the booster on the firewall.

11. Torque the mounting nuts to 20 ft. lbs.

12. Install the stop lamp switch and striker plate.

13. Coat the bearing surface of the pedal pin with Lubriplate® or equivalent. Connect the push rod to the pedal pin and install a new retainer clip.

14. Carefully position the master cylinder on the booster.

15. Install the mounting nuts and torque them to 20 ft. lbs.

16. Connect the vacuum hose to the booster.

17. Reconnect the brake lines between the master cylinder and the valve assembly. Torque the nuts to 12 ft. lbs.

18. Reposition the wiring harness into its original position and attach it to the strut tower.

19. On manual transmission models, install the clutch cable mounting bracket.

20. Bleed the brakes. Check the stoplight operation. With vacuum applied to the power brake unit and pressure applied to the pedal, the master cylinder should vent (force a jet of fluid through the front chamber vent port).

CAUTION: *Do not attempt to disassemble the power brake unit, since the booster is serviced as a complete assembly only.*

Pressure Differential Valve and Warning Light Switch

The brake system is split diagonally. That means that the right rear and left front brakes are connected to the same reservoir. Both systems are routed through, but separated by, the pressure differential valve, which also contains the warning switch. The function of the valve is to activate the switch in the event of brake system malfunction. The warning light switch is the latching type. It will automatically recenter itself after the repair is made and the brake pedal is depressed.

The bulb can be checked each time the ignition switch is turned to the ON position or each time the parking brake is set.

Bleeding The Brake System

Anytime a brake line has been disconnected the hydraulic system should be bled. The brakes should also be bled when the pedal travel becomes unusually long ("soft pedal") or the car pulls to one side during braking. The proper bleeding sequence is: right rear wheel, left rear wheel, right front caliper, and left front caliper. You'll need a helper to pump the brake pedal while you open the bleeding valves.

NOTE: *If the system has been drained, first refill it with fresh brake fluid. Following the above sequence, open each bleeder valve to ½ to ¾ of a turn and pump the brake pedal until fluid runs out of the valve. Proceed with the bleeding as outlined below.*

1. Remove the bleeder valve dust cover and install a rubber bleeder hose.

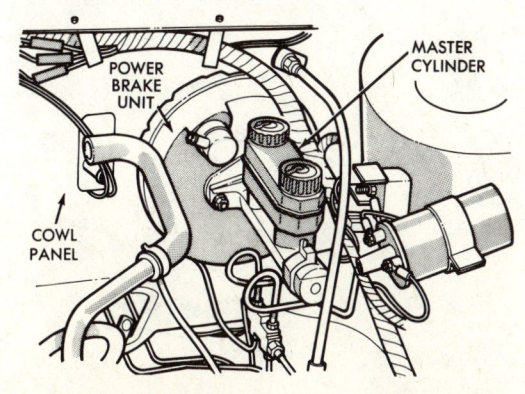

Power brake booster and master cylinder assembly

140 BRAKES

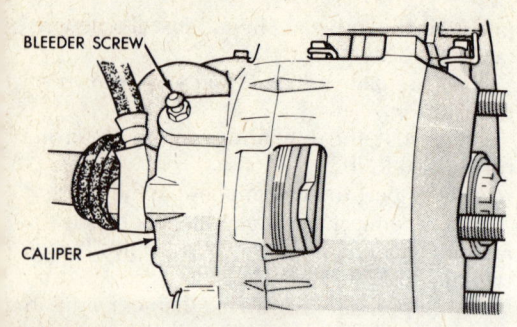

Caliper bleeder screw location

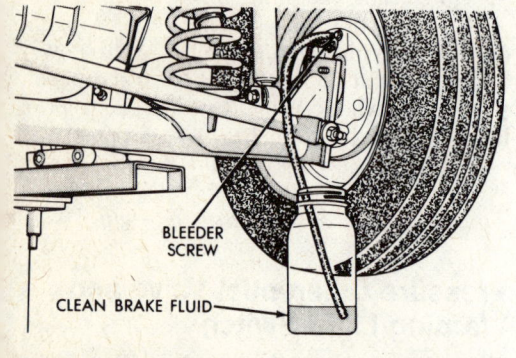

Place the bleeder hose in a jar of clean brake fluid

2. Insert the other end of the hose into a container about ⅓ full of clean brake fluid.
3. Have an assist pump the brake pedal several times until the pedal pressure increases.
4. Hold the pedal under pressure and then start to open the bleeder valve about ¼ to ¾ of a turn. At this point, have your assistant depress the pedal all the way and then quickly close the valve. The helper should allow the pedal to return slowly.

NOTE: *Keep a close check on the brake fluid in the reservoir and top it up as necessary throughout the bleeding process.*

5. Keep repeating this procedure until no more air bubbles can be seen coming from the hose in the brake fluid.
6. Remove the bleeder hose and install the dust cover.
7. Continue the bleeding at each wheel in sequence.

NOTE: *Don't splash any brake fluid on the paintwork. Brake fluid is very corrosive and will eat paint away. Any fluid accidentally spilled on the body should be immediately flushed off with water.*

FRONT DISC BRAKES

Disc Brake Pads
INSPECTON

Disc pads (lining and shoe assemblies) should be replaced in axle sets (both wheels) when the thickness of the shoe and lining is less than 5/16 inch.

NOTE: *State inspection specifications take precedence over these general recommendations.*

Note that disc pads in floating caliper type brakes may wear at an angle, and the measurement should be made at the narrow end of the taper. Tapered linings should be replaced if the taper exceeds ⅛ in. from end to end (the difference between the thickest points).

Always replace both sets on each wheel whenever one pad needs replacing.

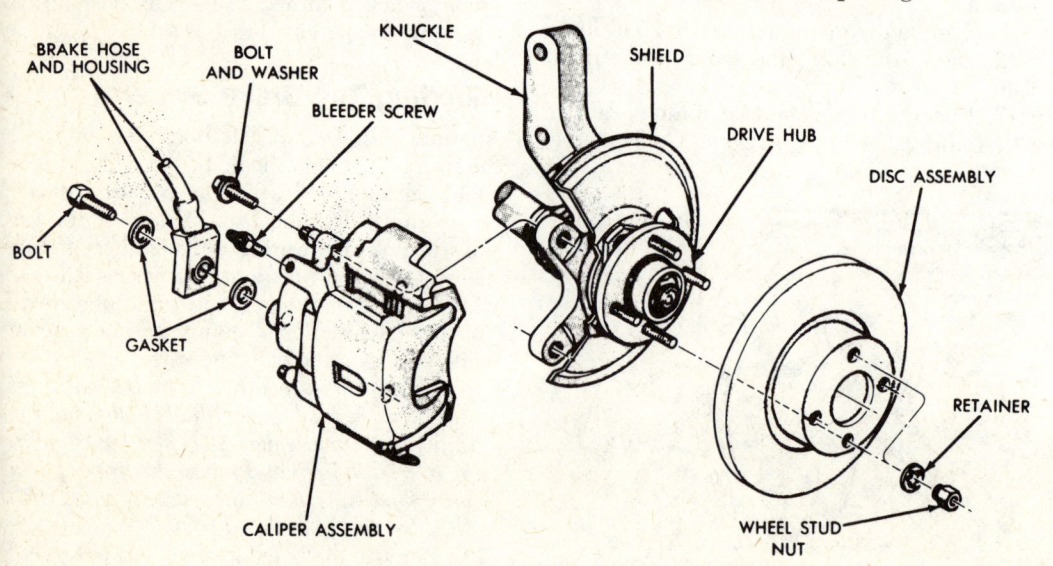

Exploded view of the disc brake components—typical

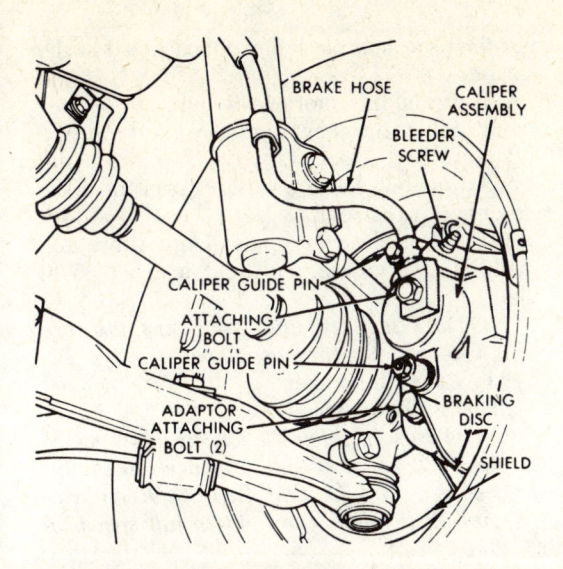

BRAKES 141

Front caliper attaching points

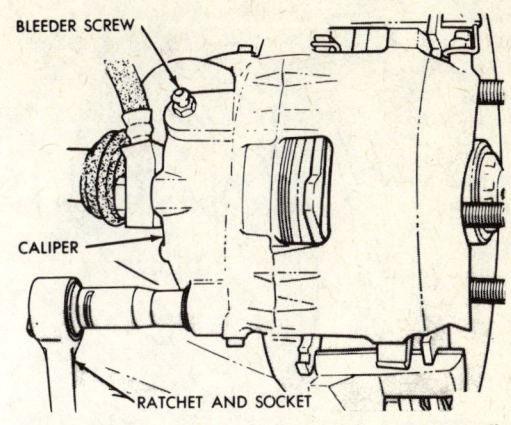

Removing the caliper guide pin—Kelsey Hayes caliper

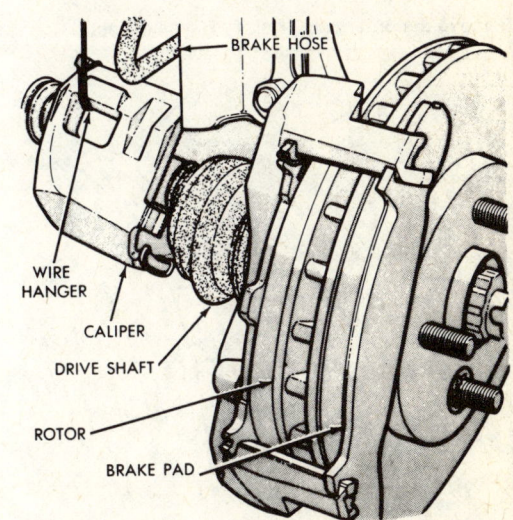

Remove the caliper and support with wire—Kelsey Hayes caliper

REMOVAL AND INSTALLATION

Kelsey-Hayes Floating Caliper

1. Remove half of the brake fluid from the master cylinder reservoir.
2. Raise and support the car on jackstands. Remove the wheels.
3. Remove the caliper guide pins and anti-rattle springs.
4. Remove the caliper by slowly sliding the caliper off the brake disc. Hang the caliper by a piece of stiff wire. Do not allow it to hang by the brake line.
5. Remove the outboard brake pad, the disc and the inboard brake pad.

NOTE: *There are three hold-down springs on the Kelsey-Hayes caliper. One spring is*

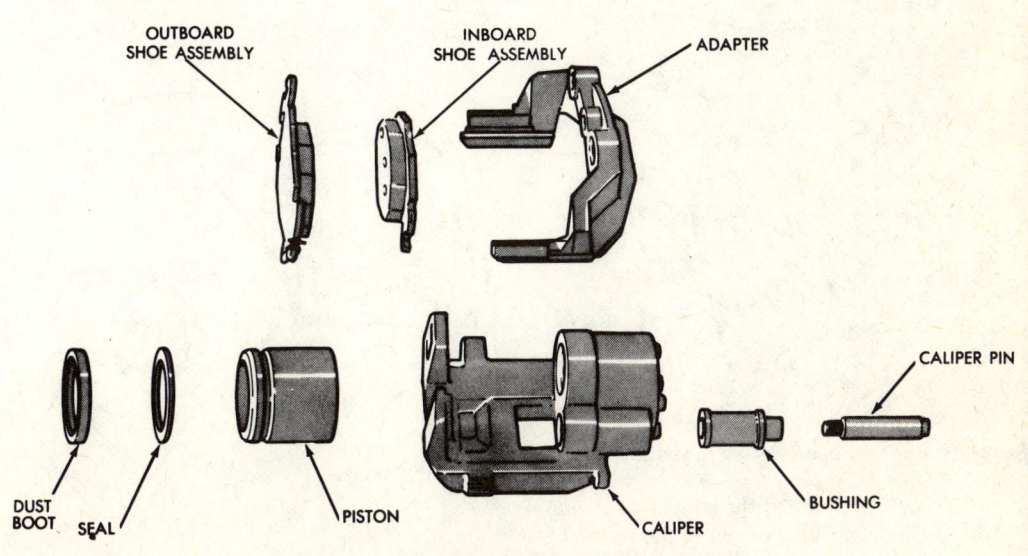

Kelsey Hayes caliper assembly—exploded view

142 BRAKES

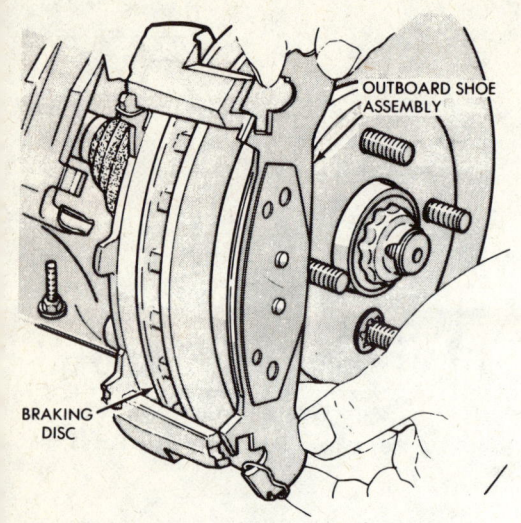

Remove the outer pad—Kelsey Hayes caliper

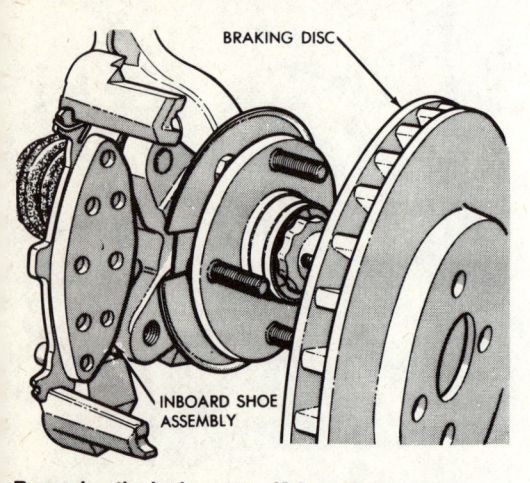

Removing the brake rotor—Kelsey Hayes caliper

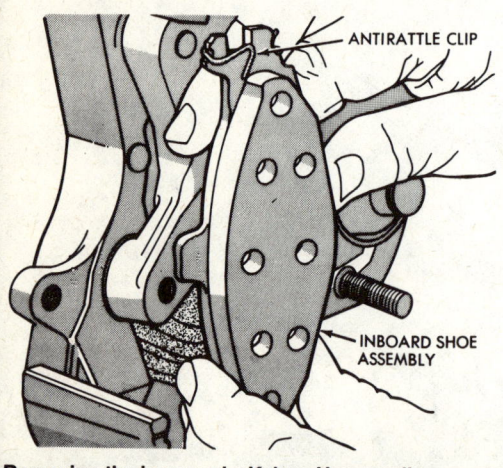

Removing the inner pad—Kelsey Hayes caliper

on top outboard side of the caliper assembly. One spring is on the bottom of the outboard lining, and one spring is on the top of the outboard lining.

6. To install, place new inboard pad in the adaptor.
7. Install the rotor on the hub.
8. Slide the new outboard pad on the adaptor.
9. Carefully lower the caliper over the brake rotor and pad assembly.
10. Install the guide pins (lightly lubricated with silicone grease) and tighten to 25–35 ft. lbs.

NOTE: *When installing guide pins, use care not to cross the threads.*

11. Bleed the brakes.
12. Install the wheels.

CAUTION: *Tighten the wheels in an every-other-nut rotation until all wheels are tightened to ½ specification. Repeat the sequence until all lug nuts are tight to full specification.*

After assembly, pump the pedal several times to remove clearance between pads and rotors.

ATE Floating Caliper

1. Remove half of the brake fluid from the master cylinder reservoir.
2. Raise and support the car on jackstands. Remove the wheels.
3. Remove the hold-down spring from the caliper assembly by pushing in at the middle of the spring and pushing it outward.
4. Remove the caliper guide pins.
5. Remove the caliper by slowly sliding the caliper off the brake disc. The inboard shoe assembly will remain with the caliper. Hang the caliper by a piece of stiff wire. Do not allow it to hang by the brake line.
6. Remove the inboard shoe from the caliper by pulling the shoe and lining assembly away from the piston.

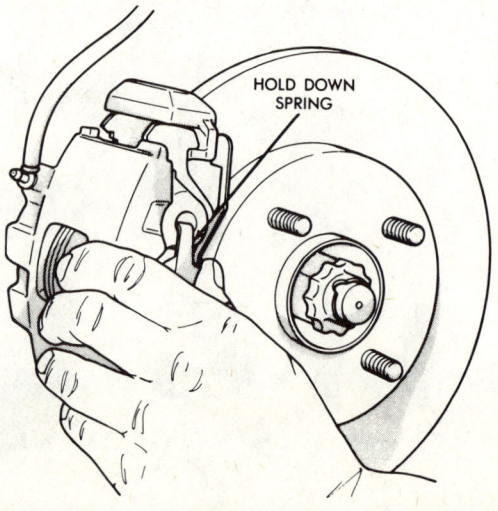

Removing the hold-down spring—A.T.E. caliper assembly

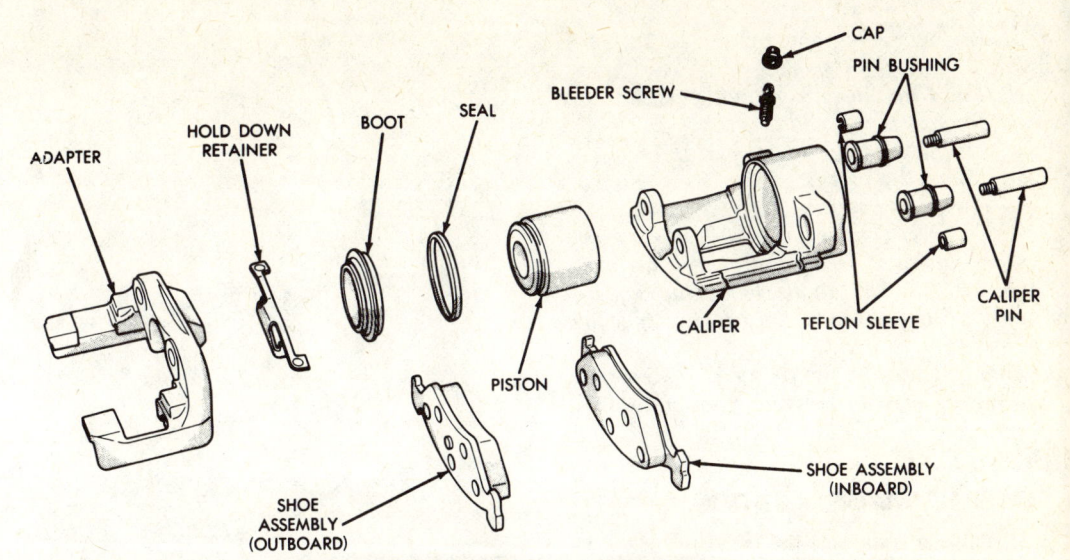

BRAKES 143

A.T.E. caliper assembly—exploded view

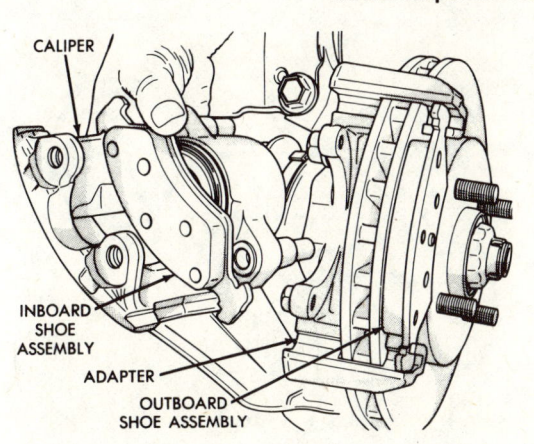

Removing the caliper and inner pad—A.T.E. caliper

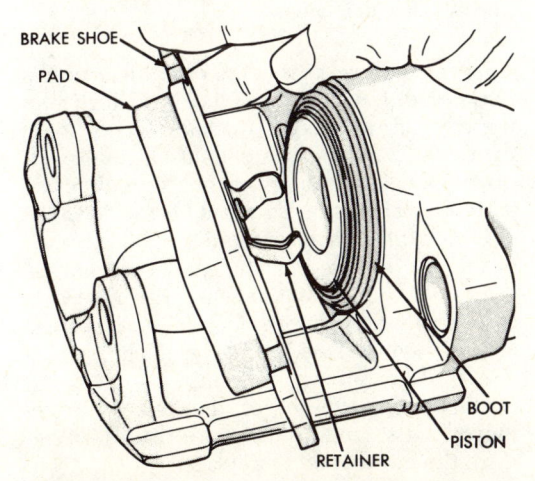

Removing the inner pad from the caliper—A.T.E. caliper

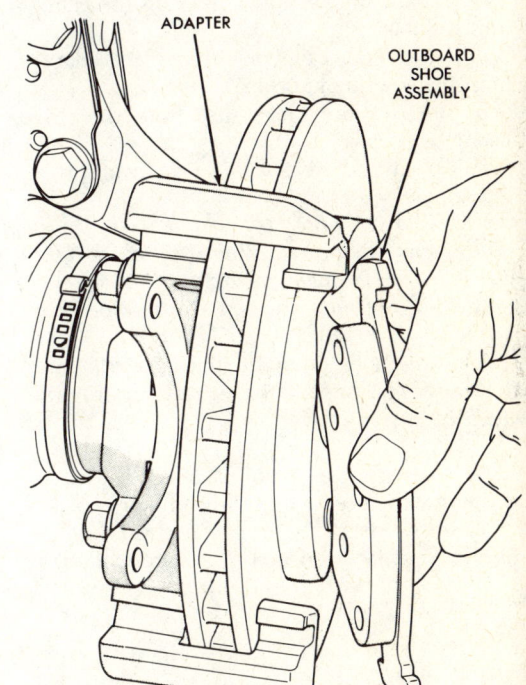

Removing the outboard pad from the adapter—A.T.E. caliper

bore in the piston. Position the outboard pad assembly on the adaptor.

9. Loosen the rear cap of the master cylinder reservoir and slowly push the caliper pistons back into the housing.

CAUTION: *Be sure the reservoir does not overflow, especially onto painted surfaces.*

10. Hold the outboard lining in position and carefully slide the caliper into position on the adaptor.

7. Remove the outboard brake pad from the adaptor.

8. To install the pads, place a new inboard pad in the caliper entering the retainer into the

11. Install the guide pins (lightly lubricated

144 BRAKES

with silicone grease) and tighten to 18–22 ft. lbs.

NOTE: *When installing guide pins, use care not to cross the threads.*

12. Install the hold-down spring.
13. Bleed the brakes.
14. Install the wheels.

CAUTION: *Tighten the wheels in an every-other-nut rotation until all wheels are tightened to ½ specification. Repeat the sequence until all lug nuts are tight to full specification.*

After assembly, pump the pedal several times to remove clearance between pads and rotors.

Brake Disc

REMOVAL AND INSTALLATION

1. Raise and support the car.
2. Remove the wheels.
3. Remove the caliper. Suspend the caliper from a hook.
4. On A.T.E. calipers, remove the adaptor from the steering knuckle.
5. Remove the brake disc from the drive flange studs.
6. To install, reverse the removal procedures.

CAUTION: *Tighten the wheels in an every-other-nut rotation until all wheels are tightened to ½ specification. Repeat the sequence until all lug nuts are tight to full specification.*

After assembly, pump the pedal several times to remove clearance between pads and rotors.

INSPECTION

Light scoring is acceptable. Heavy scoring or warping will necessitate refinishing or replacement of the disc. The brake disc must be replaced if cracks or burned marks are evident.

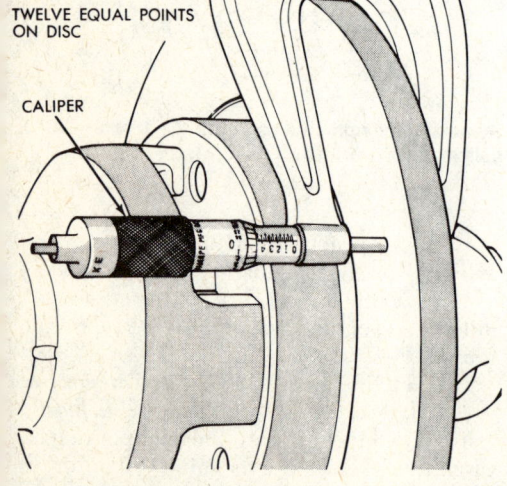

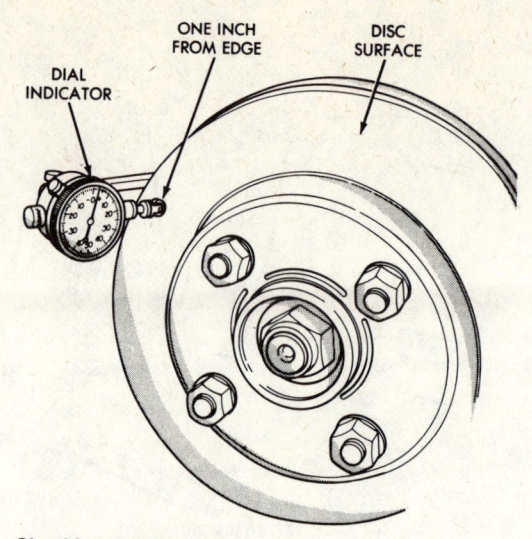

Checking the disc runout

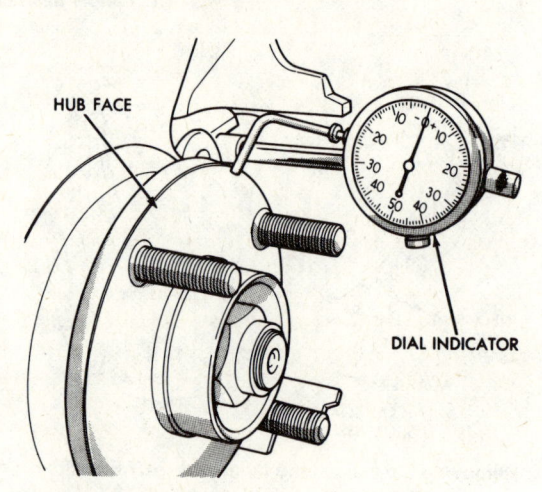

Checking the hub runout

Checking the disc thickness

Check the thickness of the disc. Measure the thickness of 12 equally spaced points 1-inch from the edge of the disc. If thickness varies more than 0.0005 in. the disc should be refinished, provided equal amounts are out from each side and the thickness does not fall below 0.882 in.

Check the run-out of the disc. Total run-out of the disc installed on the car should not exceed 0.0005 in. The disc can be resurfaced to correct minor variations as long as equal amounts are cut from each side and the thickness is at least 0.912 in. after resurfacing.

Check the run-out of the hub (disc removed). It should not be more than 0.003 in. If so, the hub should be replaced.

Caliper

REMOVAL AND INSTALLATION

1. Raise and support the car.
2. Remove the wheels.

BRAKES 149

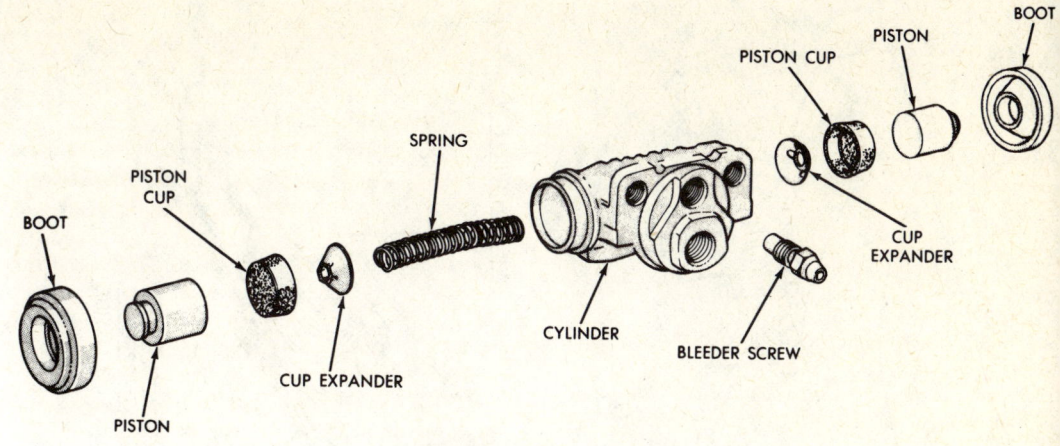

Rear wheel cylinder assembly

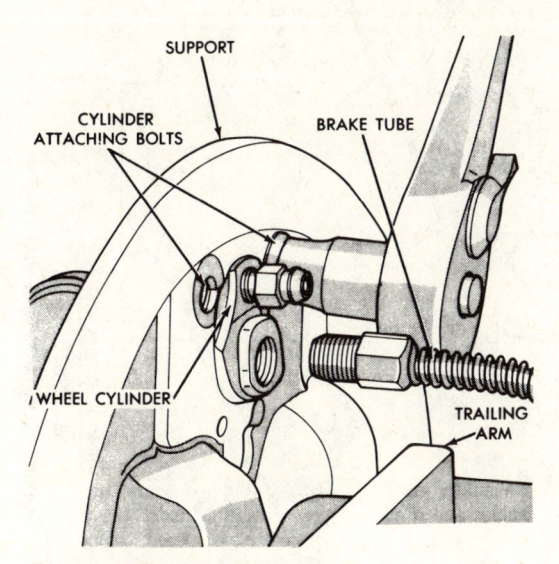

Disconnecting the rear brake line

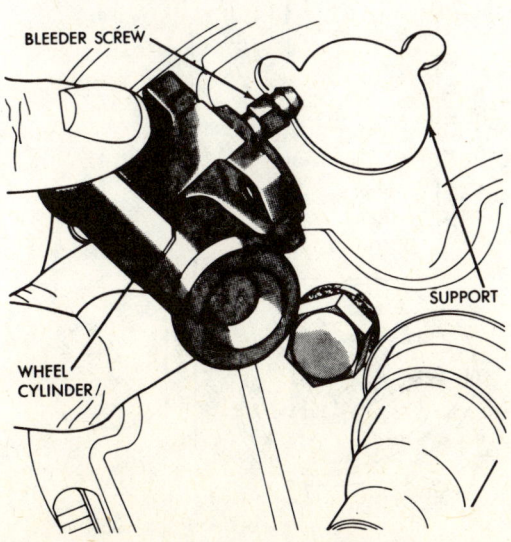

Rear wheel cylinder removal and installation

8. Install the expansion spring with the cup expanders.

9. Install the cups in each end of the cylinder with the open ends facing each other.

10. Assemble new boots on the piston and slide them into the cylinder bore.

11. Press the boot over the wheel cylinder until seated.

12. Install the wheel cylinder.

PARKING BRAKE

ADJUSTMENT

The cable operated parking brake is adjusted at the equalizer (connector) under the car.

1. Adjust the service brakes.
2. Release the parking brake lever and back off the parking brake cable until there is slack in the cable.
3. Clean and lubricate the adjuster threads.
4. Use a brake spoon to turn the starwheel adjuster until there is light shoe-to-drum contact. Back off the starwheel until the wheel rotates freely with no brake drag.
5. Tighten the parking brake adjustment until a slight drag is felt while rotating the wheels.
6. Loosen the cable adjusting nut until both rear wheels can be rotated freely, then back the cable adjuster nut off 2 full turns.
7. Test the parking brake. The rear wheels should rotate freely without dragging.

Front Brake Cable
REMOVAL AND INSTALLATION

1. Raise and support the car.
2. Loosen the cable adjusting nut under the car and disengage the front cable from the equalizer bracket.

150 BRAKES

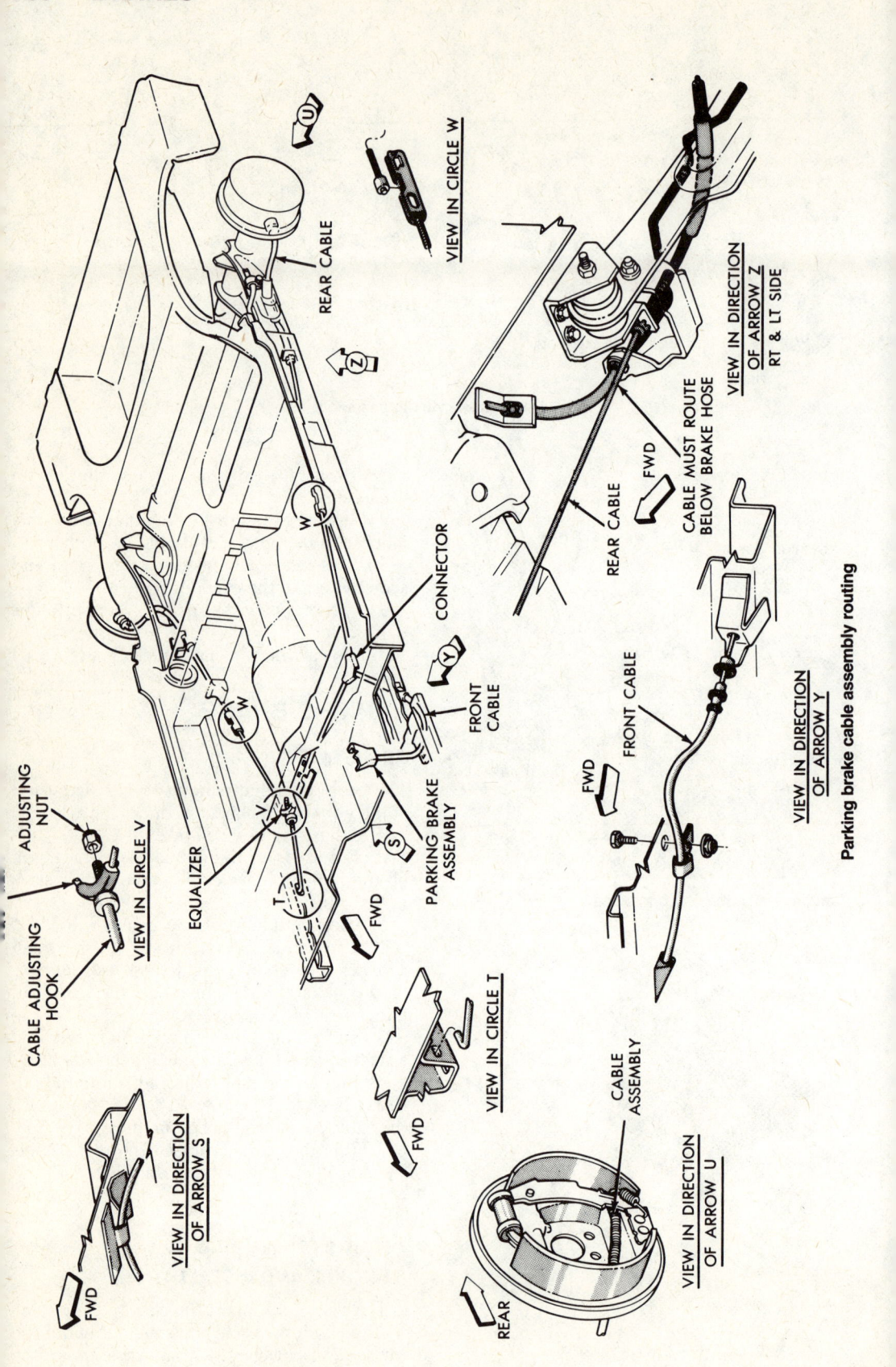

Parking brake cable assembly routing

BRAKES 151

3. Lift the floor mat for access to the floor pan and remove the floor pan seal panel.
4. Pull the cable end foreward and disconnect it from the clevis.
5. Pull the cable assembly through the hole.
6. Installation is the reverse of removal. Adjust the parking and service brakes and test the operation of both.

Rear Brake Cable
REMOVAL AND INSTALLATION

1. Raise and support the car.
2. Remove the rear wheels and brake drums.
3. Disconnect the brake cable from the connector.
4. Disconnect the cable from the brake shoe lever.
5. Using an aircraft type hose clamp and a screwdriver, compress the retainer on the end of the cable and start the housing out of the support plate. Remove the clamp when the cable is free.
6. Pull the cable assembly out from the rear axle.
7. Installation is the reverse of removal. Adjust the service and parking brakes and test the operation of both.

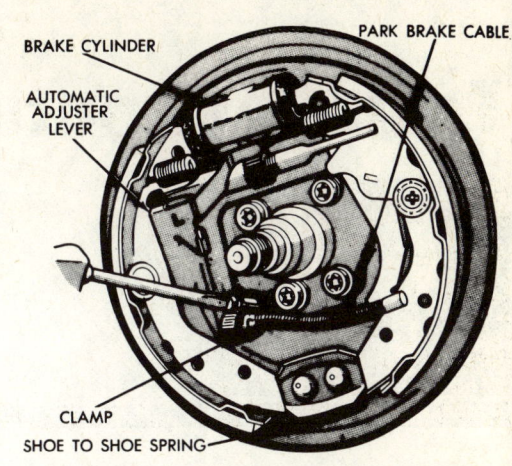

Removing the brake cable from the support plate

Brake Specifications
All measurements given are (in.) unless noted

Model	Lug Nut Torque (ft./lb.)	Master Cylinder Bore	Brake Disc Minimum Thickness	Brake Disc Maximum Run-Out	Brake Drum Diameter	Brake Drum Max Machine O/S	Brake Drum Max Wear Limit	Minimum Lining Thickness Front	Minimum Lining Thickness Rear
1984–85	95	0.827	0.882	0.005	8.661	8.691	8.691	①	5/16

NOTE: *Minimum lining thickness is as recommended by the manufacturer. Because of variations in state inspection regulations, the minimum allowable thickness may be different than recommended by the manufacturer.*
① 5/16 in.—minimum thickness of lining and backing plate at any point.

Troubleshooting 19

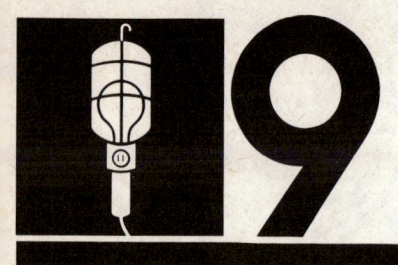

This section is designed to aid in the quick, accurate diagnosis of automotive problems. While automotive repairs can be made by many people, accurate troubleshooting is a rare skill for the amateur and professional alike.

In its simplest state, troubleshooting is an exercise in logic. It is essential to realize that an automobile is really composed of a series of systems. Some of these systems are interrelated; others are not. Automobiles operate within a framework of logical rules and physical laws, and the key to troubleshooting is a good understanding of all the automotive systems.

This section breaks the car or truck down into its component systems, allowing the problem to be isolated. The charts and diagnostic road maps list the most common problems and the most probable causes of trouble. Obviously it would be impossible to list every possible problem that could happen along with every possible cause, but it will locate MOST problems and eliminate a lot of unnecessary guesswork. The systematic format will locate problems within a given system, but, because many automotive systems are interrelated, the solution to your particular problem may be found in a number of systems on the car or truck.

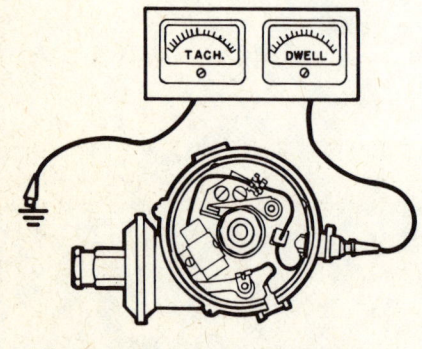

USING THE TROUBLESHOOTING CHARTS

This book contains all of the specific information that the average do-it-yourself mechanic needs to repair and maintain his or her car or truck. The troubleshooting charts are designed to be used in conjunction with the specific procedures and information in the text. For instance, troubleshooting a point-type ignition system is fairly standard for all models, but you may be directed to the text to find procedures for troubleshooting an individual type of electronic ignition. You will also have to refer to the specification charts throughout the book for specifications applicable to your car or truck.

TOOLS AND EQUIPMENT

The tools illustrated in Chapter 1 (plus two more diagnostic pieces) will be adequate to troubleshoot most problems. The two other tools needed are a voltmeter and an ohmmeter. These can be purchased separately or in combination, known as a VOM meter.

In the event that other tools are required, they will be noted in the procedures.

Tach-dwell hooked-up to distributor

TROUBLESHOOTING

Troubleshooting Engine Problems

See Chapters 2, 3, 4 for more information and service procedures.

Index to Systems

System	To Test	Group
Battery	Engine need not be running	1
Starting system	Engine need not be running	2
Primary electrical system	Engine need not be running	3
Secondary electrical system	Engine need not be running	4
Fuel system	Engine need not be running	5
Engine compression	Engine need not be running	6
Engine vacuum	Engine must be running	7
Secondary electrical system	Engine must be running	8
Valve train	Engine must be running	9
Exhaust system	Engine must be running	10
Cooling system	Engine must be running	11
Engine lubrication	Engine must be running	12

Index to Problems

Problem: Symptom	Begin at Specific Diagnosis, Number
Engine Won't Start:	
Starter doesn't turn	1.1, 2.1
Starter turns, engine doesn't	2.1
Starter turns engine very slowly	1.1, 2.4
Starter turns engine normally	3.1, 4.1
Starter turns engine very quickly	6.1
Engine fires intermittently	4.1
Engine fires consistently	5.1, 6.1
Engine Runs Poorly:	
Hard starting	3.1, 4.1, 5.1, 8.1
Rough idle	4.1, 5.1, 8.1
Stalling	3.1, 4.1, 5.1, 8.1
Engine dies at high speeds	4.1, 5.1
Hesitation (on acceleration from standing stop)	5.1, 8.1
Poor pickup	4.1, 5.1, 8.1
Lack of power	3.1, 4.1, 5.1, 8.1
Backfire through the carburetor	4.1, 8.1, 9.1
Backfire through the exhaust	4.1, 8.1, 9.1
Blue exhaust gases	6.1, 7.1
Black exhaust gases	5.1
Running on (after the ignition is shut off)	3.1, 8.1
Susceptible to moisture	4.1
Engine misfires under load	4.1, 7.1, 8.4, 9.1
Engine misfires at speed	4.1, 8.4
Engine misfires at idle	3.1, 4.1, 5.1, 7.1, 8.4

Sample Section

Test and Procedure	Results and Indications	Proceed to
4.1—Check for spark: Hold each spark plug wire approximately ¼" from ground with gloves or a heavy, dry rag. Crank the engine and observe the spark.	→ If no spark is evident:	→4.2
	→ If spark is good in some cases:	→4.3
	→ If spark is good in all cases:	→4.6

154　TROUBLESHOOTING

Specific Diagnosis

This section is arranged so that following each test, instructions are given to proceed to another, until a problem is diagnosed.

Section 1—Battery

Test and Procedure	Results and Indications	Proceed to
1.1—Inspect the battery visually for case condition (corrosion, cracks) and water level.	If case is cracked, replace battery:	1.4
	If the case is intact, remove corrosion with a solution of baking soda and water (**CAUTION**: *do not get the solution into the battery*), and fill with water:	1.2

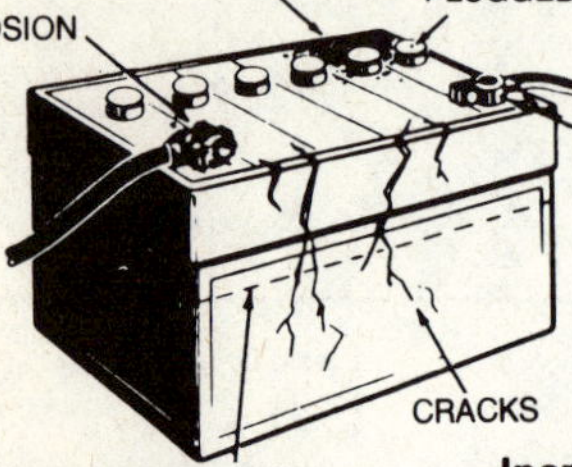

Inspect the battery case

1.2—Check the battery cable connections: Insert a screwdriver between the battery post and the cable clamp. Turn the headlights on high beam, and observe them as the screwdriver is gently twisted to ensure good metal to metal contact.	If the lights brighten, remove and clean the clamp and post; coat the post with petroleum jelly, install and tighten the clamp:	1.4
	If no improvement is noted:	1.3

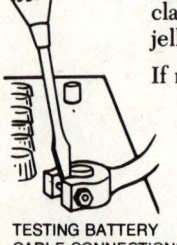

TESTING BATTERY CABLE CONNECTIONS USING A SCREWDRIVER

1.3—Test the state of charge of the battery using an individual cell tester or hydrometer.	If indicated, charge the battery. **NOTE:** *If no obvious reason exists for the low state of charge (i.e., battery age, prolonged storage), proceed to:*	1.4

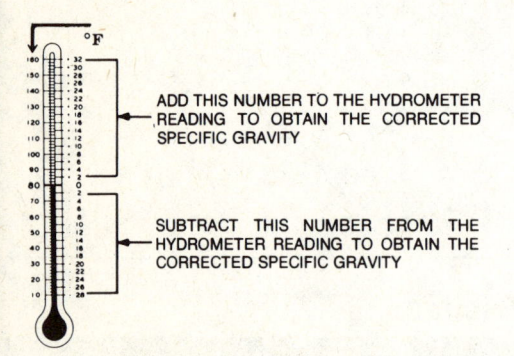

ADD THIS NUMBER TO THE HYDROMETER READING TO OBTAIN THE CORRECTED SPECIFIC GRAVITY

SUBTRACT THIS NUMBER FROM THE HYDROMETER READING TO OBTAIN THE CORRECTED SPECIFIC GRAVITY

Specific Gravity (@ 80° F.)

Minimum	Battery Charge
1.260	100% Charged
1.230	75% Charged
1.200	50% Charged
1.170	25% Charged
1.140	Very Little Power Left
1.110	Completely Discharged

The effects of temperature on battery specific gravity (left) and amount of battery charge in relation to specific gravity (right)

1.4—Visually inspect battery cables for cracking, bad connection to ground, or bad connection to starter.	If necessary, tighten connections or replace the cables:	2.1

TROUBLESHOOTING 155

Section 2—Starting System
See Chapter 3 for service procedures

Test and Procedure	Results and Indications	Proceed to
Note: Tests in Group 2 are performed with coil high tension lead disconnected to prevent accidental starting.		
2.1—Test the starter motor and solenoid: Connect a jumper from the battery post of the solenoid (or relay) to the starter post of the solenoid (or relay).	If starter turns the engine normally:	2.2
	If the starter buzzes, or turns the engine very slowly:	2.4
	If no response, replace the solenoid (or relay).	3.1
	If the starter turns, but the engine doesn't, ensure that the flywheel ring gear is intact. If the gear is undamaged, replace the starter drive.	3.1
2.2—Determine whether ignition override switches are functioning properly (clutch start switch, neutral safety switch), by connecting a jumper across the switch(es), and turning the ignition switch to "start".	If starter operates, adjust or replace switch:	3.1
	If the starter doesn't operate:	2.3
2.3—Check the ignition switch "start" position: Connect a 12V test lamp or voltmeter between the starter post of the solenoid (or relay) and ground. Turn the ignition switch to the "start" position, and jiggle the key.	If the lamp doesn't light or the meter needle doesn't move when the switch is turned, check the ignition switch for loose connections, cracked insulation, or broken wires. Repair or replace as necessary:	3.1
	If the lamp flickers or needle moves when the key is jiggled, replace the ignition switch.	3.3

Checking the ignition switch "start" position

STARTER RELAY (IF EQUIPPED)

2.4—Remove and bench test the starter, according to specifications in the engine electrical section.	If the starter does not meet specifications, repair or replace as needed:	3.1
	If the starter is operating properly:	2.5
2.5—Determine whether the engine can turn freely: Remove the spark plugs, and check for water in the cylinders. Check for water on the dipstick, or oil in the radiator. Attempt to turn the engine using an 18″ flex drive and socket on the crankshaft pulley nut or bolt.	If the engine will turn freely only with the spark plugs out, and hydrostatic lock (water in the cylinders) is ruled out, check valve timing:	9.2
	If engine will not turn freely, and it is known that the clutch and transmission are free, the engine must be disassembled for further evaluation:	Chapter 3

TROUBLESHOOTING

Section 3—Primary Electrical System

Test and Procedure	Results and Indications	Proceed to
3.1—Check the ignition switch "on" position: Connect a jumper wire between the distributor side of the coil and ground, and a 12V test lamp between the switch side of the coil and ground. Remove the high tension lead from the coil. Turn the ignition switch on and jiggle the key.	If the lamp lights:	3.2
	If the lamp flickers when the key is jiggled, replace the ignition switch:	3.3
	If the lamp doesn't light, check for loose or open connections. If none are found, remove the ignition switch and check for continuity. If the switch is faulty, replace it:	3.3

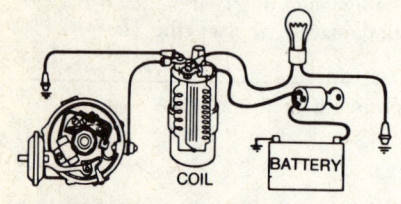

Checking the ignition switch "on" position

3.2—Check the ballast resistor or resistance wire for an open circuit, using an ohmmeter. See Chapter 3 for specific tests.	Replace the resistor or resistance wire if the resistance is zero. **NOTE:** *Some ignition systems have no ballast resistor.*	3.3

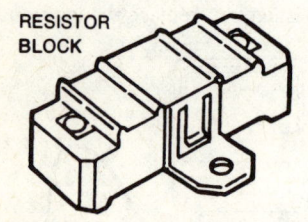

Two types of resistors

3.3—On point-type ignition systems, visually inspect the breaker points for burning, pitting or excessive wear. Gray coloring of the point contact surfaces is normal. Rotate the crankshaft until the contact heel rests on a high point of the distributor cam and adjust the point gap to specifications. On electronic ignition models, remove the distributor cap and visually inspect the armature. Ensure that the armature pin is in place, and that the armature is on tight and rotates when the engine is cranked. Make sure there are no cracks, chips or rounded edges on the armature.	If the breaker points are intact, clean the contact surfaces with fine emery cloth, and adjust the point gap to specifications. If the points are worn, replace them. On electronic systems, replace any parts which appear defective. If condition persists:	3.4

TROUBLESHOOTING 157

Test and Procedure	Results and Indications	Proceed to
3.4—On point-type ignition systems, connect a dwell-meter between the distributor primary lead and ground. Crank the engine and observe the point dwell angle. On electronic ignition systems, conduct a stator (magnetic pickup assembly) test. See Chapter 3.	On point-type systems, adjust the dwell angle if necessary. **NOTE:** *Increasing the point gap decreases the dwell angle and vice-versa.* If the dwell meter shows little or no reading; On electronic ignition systems, if the stator is bad, replace the stator. If the stator is good, proceed to the other tests in Chapter 3.	3.6 3.5

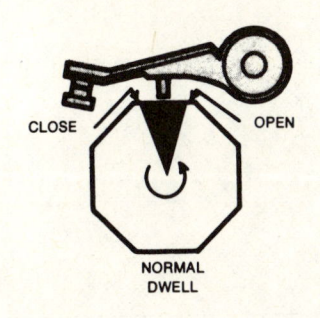

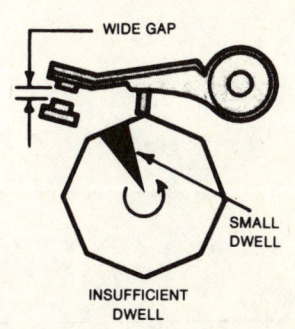

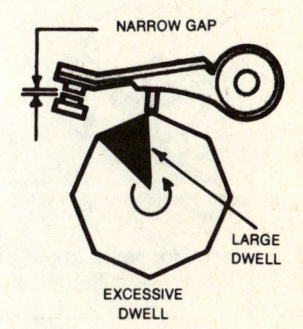

Dwell is a function of point gap

3.5—On the point-type ignition systems, check the condenser for short: connect an ohmeter across the condenser body and the pigtail lead.	If any reading other than infinite is noted, replace the condenser	3.6

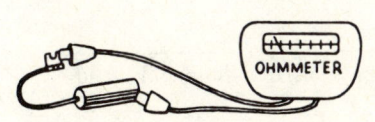

Checking the condenser for short

3.6—Test the coil primary resistance: On point-type ignition systems, connect an ohmmeter across the coil primary terminals, and read the resistance on the low scale. Note whether an external ballast resistor or resistance wire is used. On electronic ignition systems, test the coil primary resistance as in Chapter 3.	Point-type ignition coils utilizing ballast resistors or resistance wires should have approximately 1.0 ohms resistance. Coils with internal resistors should have approximately 4.0 ohms resistance. If values far from the above are noted, replace the coil.	4.1

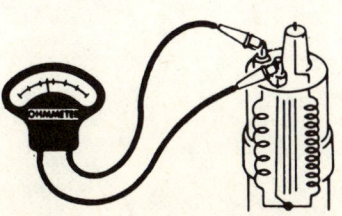

Check the coil primary resistance

158 TROUBLESHOOTING

Section 4—Secondary Electrical System
See Chapters 2–3 for service procedures

Test and Procedure	Results and Indications	Proceed to
4.1—Check for spark: Hold each spark plug wire approximately ¼" from ground with gloves or a heavy, dry rag. Crank the engine, and observe the spark.	If no spark is evident:	4.2
	If spark is good in some cylinders:	4.3
	If spark is good in all cylinders:	4.6

Check for spark at the plugs

4.2—Check for spark at the coil high tension lead: Remove the coil high tension lead from the distributor and position it approximately ¼" from ground. Crank the engine and observe spark. **CAUTION: *This test should not be performed on engines equipped with electronic ignition.***	If the spark is good and consistent:	4.3
	If the spark is good but intermittent, test the primary electrical system starting at 3.3:	3.3
	If the spark is weak or non-existent, replace the coil high tension lead, clean and tighten all connections and retest. If no improvement is noted:	4.4
4.3—Visually inspect the distributor cap and rotor for burned or corroded contacts, cracks, carbon tracks, or moisture. Also check the fit of the rotor on the distributor shaft (where applicable).	If moisture is present, dry thoroughly, and retest per 4.1:	4.1
	If burned or excessively corroded contacts, cracks, or carbon tracks are noted, replace the defective part(s) and retest per 4.1:	4.1
	If the rotor and cap appear intact, or are only slightly corroded, clean the contacts thoroughly (including the cap towers and spark plug wire ends) and retest per 4.1:	
	If the spark is good in all cases:	4.6
	If the spark is poor in all cases:	4.5

Inspect the distributor cap and rotor

TROUBLESHOOTING

Test and Procedure	Results and Indications	Proceed to
4.4—Check the coil secondary resistance: On point-type systems connect an ohmmeter across the distributor side of the coil and the coil tower. Read the resistance on the high scale of the ohmmeter. On electronic ignition systems, see Chapter 3 for specific tests.	The resistance of a satisfactory coil should be between 4,000 and 10,000 ohms. If resistance is considerably higher (i.e., 40,000 ohms) replace the coil and retest per 4.1. **NOTE:** *This does not apply to high performance coils.*	

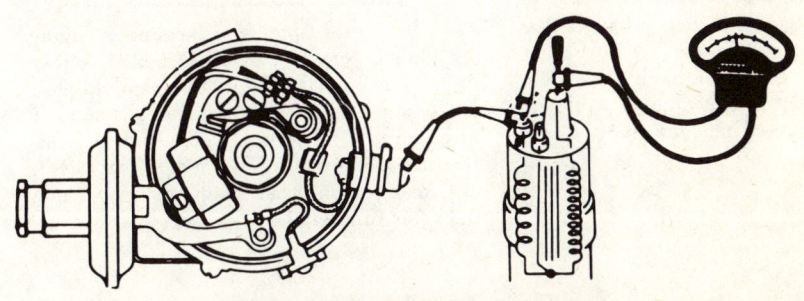

Testing the coil secondary resistance

4.5—Visually inspect the spark plug wires for cracking or brittleness. Ensure that no two wires are positioned so as to cause induction firing (adjacent and parallel). Remove each wire, one by one, and check resistance with an ohmmeter.	Replace any cracked or brittle wires. If any of the wires are defective, replace the entire set. Replace any wires with excessive resistance (over 8000 Ω per foot for suppression wire), and separate any wires that might cause induction firing.	4.6

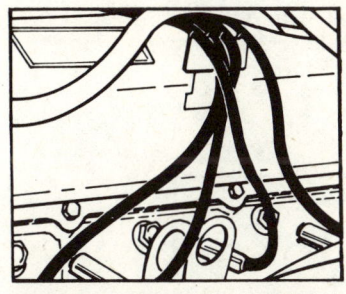

Misfiring can be the result of spark plug leads to adjacent, consecutively firing cylinders running parallel and too close together

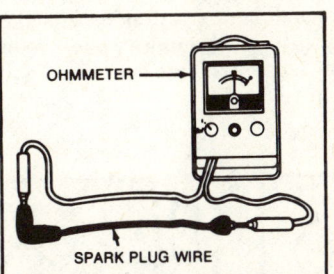

On point-type ignition systems, check the spark plug wires as shown. On electronic ignitions, do not remove the wire from the distributor cap terminal; instead, test through the cap

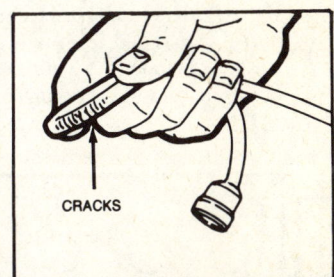

Spark plug wires can be checked visually by bending them in a loop over your finger. This will reveal any cracks, burned or broken insulation. Any wire with cracked insulation should be replaced

4.6—Remove the spark plugs, noting the cylinders from which they were removed, and evaluate according to the color photos in the middle of this book.	See following.	See following.

160 TROUBLESHOOTING

Test and Procedure	Results and Indications	Proceed to
4.7—Examine the location of all the plugs.	The following diagrams illustrate some of the conditions that the location of plugs will reveal.	4.8

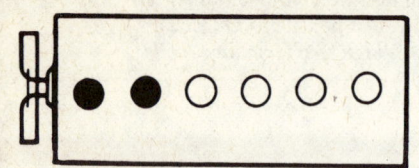

Two adjacent plugs are fouled in a 6-cylinder engine, 4-cylinder engine or either bank of a V-8. This is probably due to a blown head gasket between the two cylinders

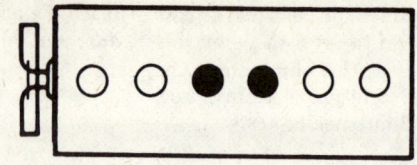

The two center plugs in a 6-cylinder engine are fouled. Raw fuel may be "boiled" out of the carburetor into the intake manifold after the engine is shut-off. Stop-start driving can also foul the center plugs, due to overly rich mixture. Proper float level, a new float needle and seat or use of an insulating spacer may help this problem

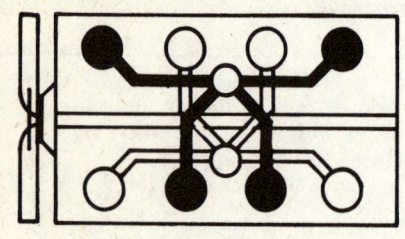

An unbalanced carburetor is indicated. Following the fuel flow on this particular design shows that the cylinders fed by the right-hand barrel are fouled from overly rich mixture, while the cylinders fed by the left-hand barrel are normal

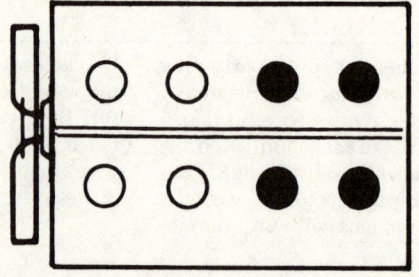

If the four rear plugs are overheated, a cooling system problem is suggested. A thorough cleaning of the cooling system may restore coolant circulation and cure the problem

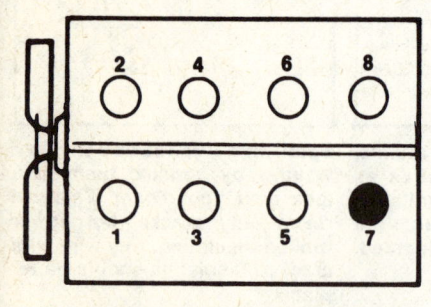

Finding one plug overheated may indicate an intake manifold leak near the affected cylinder. If the overheated plug is the second of two adjacent, consecutively firing plugs, it could be the result of ignition cross-firing. Separating the leads to these two plugs will eliminate cross-fire

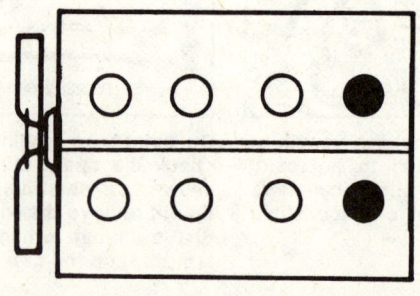

Occasionally, the two rear plugs in large, lightly used V-8's will become oil fouled. High oil consumption and smoky exhaust may also be noticed. It is probably due to plugged oil drain holes in the rear of the cylinder head, causing oil to be sucked in around the valve stems. This usually occurs in the rear cylinders first, because the engine slants that way

TROUBLESHOOTING 161

Test and Procedure	Results and Indications	Proceed to
4.8—Determine the static ignition timing. Using the crankshaft pulley timing marks as a guide, locate top dead center on the compression stroke of the number one cylinder.	The rotor should be pointing toward the No. 1 tower in the distributor cap, and, on electronic ignitions, the armature spoke for that cylinder should be lined up with the stator.	4.8
4.9—Check coil polarity: Connect a voltmeter negative lead to the coil high tension lead, and the positive lead to ground (**NOTE:** *Reverse the hook-up for positive ground systems*). Crank the engine momentarily.	If the voltmeter reads up-scale, the polarity is correct:	5.1
	If the voltmeter reads down-scale, reverse the coil polarity (switch the primary leads):	5.1
	Checking coil polarity	

Section 5—Fuel System
See Chapter 4 for service procedures

Test and Procedure	Results and Indications	Proceed to
5.1—Determine that the air filter is functioning efficiently: Hold paper elements up to a strong light, and attempt to see light through the filter.	Clean permanent air filters in solvent (or manufacturer's recommendation), and allow to dry. Replace paper elements through which light cannot be seen:	5.2
5.2—Determine whether a flooding condition exists: Flooding is identified by a strong gasoline odor, and excessive gasoline present in the throttle bore(s) of the carburetor.	If flooding is not evident:	5.3
	If flooding is evident, permit the gasoline to dry for a few moments and restart.	
	If flooding doesn't recur:	5.7
	If flooding is persistent:	5.5
	If the engine floods repeatedly, check the choke butterfly flap	
5.3—Check that fuel is reaching the carburetor: Detach the fuel line at the carburetor inlet. Hold the end of the line in a cup (not styrofoam), and crank the engine.	If fuel flows smoothly:	5.7
	If fuel doesn't flow (**NOTE:** *Make sure that there is fuel in the tank*), or flows erratically:	5.4
	Check the fuel pump by disconnecting the output line (fuel pump-to-carburetor) at the carburetor and operating the starter briefly	

TROUBLESHOOTING

Test and Procedure	Results and Indications	Proceed to
5.4—Test the fuel pump: Disconnect all fuel lines from the fuel pump. Hold a finger over the input fitting, crank the engine (with electric pump, turn the ignition or pump on); and feel for suction.	If suction is evident, blow out the fuel line to the tank with low pressure compressed air until bubbling is heard from the fuel filler neck. Also blow out the carburetor fuel line (both ends disconnected):	5.7
	If no suction is evident, replace or repair the fuel pump: **NOTE:** *Repeated oil fouling of the spark plugs, or a no-start condition, could be the result of a ruptured vacuum booster pump diaphragm, through which oil or gasoline is being drawn into the intake manifold (where applicable).*	5.7
5.5—Occasionally, small specks of dirt will clog the small jets and orifices in the carburetor. With the engine cold, hold a flat piece of wood or similar material over the carburetor, where possible, and crank the engine.	If the engine starts, but runs roughly the engine is probably not run enough. If the engine won't start:	5.9
5.6—Check the needle and seat: Tap the carburetor in the area of the needle and seat.	If flooding stops, a gasoline additive (e.g., Gumout) will often cure the problem:	5.7
	If flooding continues, check the fuel pump for excessive pressure at the carburetor (according to specifications). If the pressure is normal, the needle and seat must be removed and checked, and/or the float level adjusted:	5.7
5.7—Test the accelerator pump by looking into the throttle bores while operating the throttle.	If the accelerator pump appears to be operating normally:	5.8
	If the accelerator pump is not operating, the pump must be reconditioned. Where possible, service the pump with the carburetor(s) installed on the engine. If necessary, remove the carburetor. Prior to removal:	5.8

Check for gas at the carburetor by looking down the carburetor throat while someone moves the accelerator

5.8—Determine whether the carburetor main fuel system is functioning: Spray a commercial starting fluid into the carburetor while attempting to start the engine.	If the engine starts, runs for a few seconds, and dies:	5.9
	If the engine doesn't start:	6.1

CHILTON'S
AUTO BODY REPAIR TIPS

EASY STEP-BY-STEP TIPS FROM PROS

Tools and Materials • Step-by-Step Illustrated Procedures
How To Repair Dents, Scratches and Rust Holes
Spray Painting and Refinishing Tips

With a little practice, basic body repair procedures can be mastered by any do-it-yourself mechanic. The step-by-step repairs shown here can be applied to almost any type of auto body repair.

TOOLS & MATERIALS

You may already have basic tools, such as hammers and electric drills. Other tools unique to body repair — body hammers, grinding attachments, sanding blocks, dent puller, half-round plastic file and plastic spreaders — are relatively inexpensive and can be obtained wherever auto parts or auto body repair parts are sold. Portable air compressors and paint spray guns can be purchased or rented.

Auto Body Repair Kits

The best and most often used products are available to the do-it-yourselfer in kit form, from major manufacturers of auto body repair products. The same manufacturers also merchandise the individual products for use by pros.

Kits are available to make a wide variety of repairs, including holes, dents and scratches and fiberglass, and offer the advantage of buying the materials you'll need for the job. There is little waste or chance of materials going bad from not being used. Many kits may also contain basic body-working tools such as body files, sanding blocks and spreaders. Check the contents of the kit before buying your tools.

BODY REPAIR TIPS

Safety

Many of the products associated with auto body repair and refinishing contain toxic chemicals. Read all labels before opening containers and store them in a safe place and manner.

• Wear eye protection (safety goggles) when using power tools or when performing any operation that involves the removal of any type of material.

• Wear lung protection (disposable mask or respirator) when grinding, sanding or painting.

Sanding

1 Sand off paint before using a dent puller. When using a non-adhesive sanding disc, cover the back of the disc with an overlapping layer or two of masking tape and trim the edges. The disc will last considerably longer.

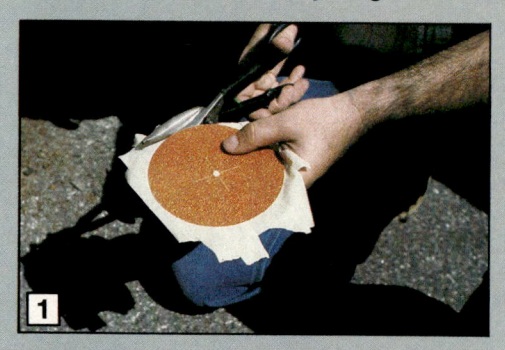

2 Use the circular motion of the sanding disc to grind *into* the edge of the repair. Grinding or sanding away from the jagged edge will only tear the sandpaper.

3 Use the palm of your hand flat on the panel to detect high and low spots. Do not use your fingertips. Slide your hand slowly back and forth.

WORKING WITH BODY FILLER

Mixing The Filler

Cleanliness and proper mixing and application are extremely important. Use a clean piece of plastic or glass or a disposable artist's palette to mix body filler.

1 Allow plenty of time and follow directions. No useful purpose will be served by adding more hardener to make it cure (set-up) faster. Less hardener means more curing time, but the mixture dries harder; more hardener means less curing time but a softer mixture.

2 Both the hardener and the filler should be thoroughly kneaded or stirred before mixing. Hardener should be a solid paste and dispense like thin toothpaste. Body filler should be smooth, and free of lumps or thick spots.

Getting the proper amount of hardener in the filler is the trickiest part of preparing the filler. Use the same amount of hardener in cold or warm weather. For contour filler (thick coats), a bead of hardener twice the diameter of the filler is about right. There's about a 15% margin on either side, but, if in doubt use less hardener.

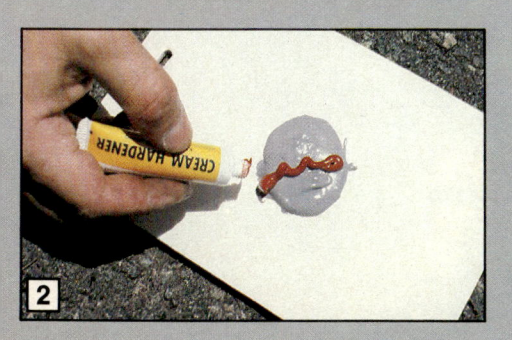

3 Mix the body filler and hardener by wiping across the mixing surface, picking the mixture up and wiping it again. Colder weather requires longer mixing times. Do not mix in a circular motion; this will trap air bubbles which will become holes in the cured filler.

Applying The Filler

1 For best results, filler should not be applied over 1/4" thick.

Apply the filler in several coats. Build it up to above the level of the repair surface so that it can be sanded or grated down.

The first coat of filler must be pressed on with a firm wiping motion.

Apply the filler in one direction only. Working the filler back and forth will either pull it off the metal or trap air bubbles.

REPAIRING DENTS

Before you start, take a few minutes to study the damaged area. Try to visualize the shape of the panel before it was damaged. If the damage is on the left fender, look at the right fender and use it as a guide. If there is access to the panel from behind, you can reshape it with a body hammer. If not, you'll have to use a dent puller. Go slowly and work the metal a little at a time. Get the panel as straight as possible before applying filler.

1 This dent is typical of one that can be pulled out or hammered out from behind. Remove the headlight cover, headlight assembly and turn signal housing.

2 Drill a series of holes ½ the size of the end of the dent puller along the stress line. Make some trial pulls and assess the results. If necessary, drill more holes and try again. Do not hurry.

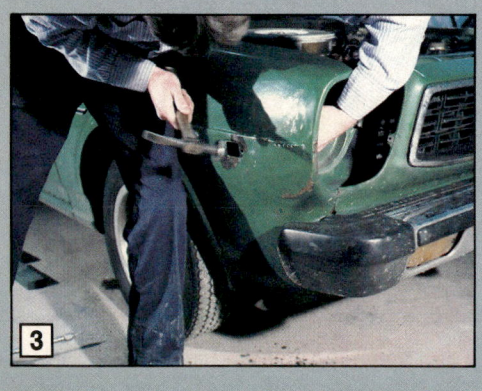

3 If possible, use a body hammer and block to shape the metal back to its original contours. Get the metal back as close to its original shape as possible. Don't depend on body filler to fill dents.

4 Using an 80-grit grinding disc on an electric drill, grind the paint from the surrounding area down to bare metal. Use a new grinding pad to prevent heat buildup that will warp metal.

5 The area should look like this when you're finished grinding. Knock the drill holes in and tape over small openings to keep plastic filler out.

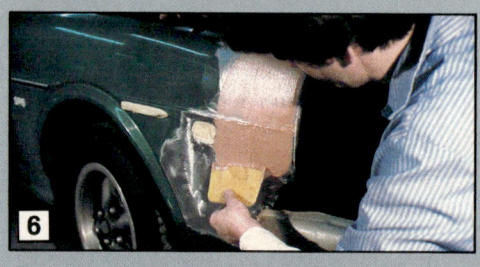

6 Mix the body filler (see Body Repair Tips). Spread the body filler evenly over the entire area (see Body Repair Tips). Be sure to cover the area completely.

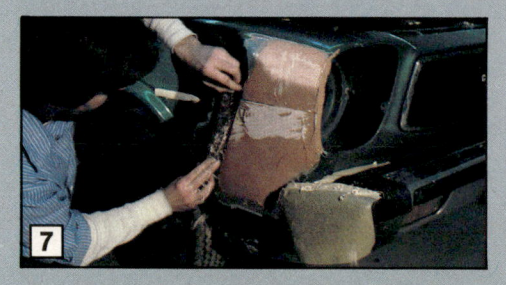

7 Let the body filler dry until the surface can just be scratched with your fingernail. Knock the high spots from the body filler with a body file ("Cheesegrater"). Check frequently with the palm of your hand for high and low spots.

8 Check to be sure that trim pieces that will be installed later will fit exactly. Sand the area with 40-grit paper.

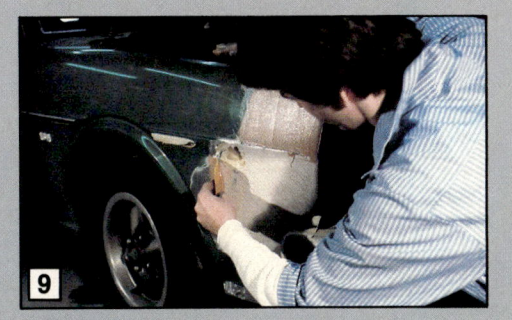

9 If you wind up with low spots, you may have to apply another layer of filler.

10 Knock the high spots off with 40-grit paper. When you are satisfied with the contours of the repair, apply a thin coat of filler to cover pin holes and scratches.

11 Block sand the area with 40-grit paper to a smooth finish. Pay particular attention to body lines and ridges that must be well-defined.

12 Sand the area with 400 paper and then finish with a scuff pad. The finished repair is ready for priming and painting (see Painting Tips).

Materials and photos courtesy of Ritt Jones Auto Body, Prospect Park, PA.

REPAIRING RUST HOLES

There are many ways to repair rust holes. The fiberglass cloth kit shown here is one of the most cost efficient for the owner because it provides a strong repair that resists cracking and moisture and is relatively easy to use. It can be used on large and small holes (with or without backing) and can be applied over contoured areas. Remember, however, that short of replacing an entire panel, no repair is a guarantee that the rust will not return.

1 Remove any trim that will be in the way. Clean away all loose debris. Cut away all the rusted metal. But be sure to leave enough metal to retain the contour or body shape.

2 Grind away all traces of rust with a 24-grit grinding disc. Be sure to grind back 3-4 inches from the edge of the hole down to bare metal and be sure all traces of paint, primer and rust are removed.

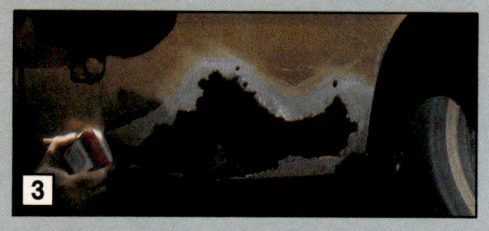

3 Block sand the area with 80 or 100 grit sandpaper to get a clear, shiny surface and feathered paint edge. Tap the edges of the hole inward with a ball peen hammer.

4 If you are going to use release film, cut a piece about 2-3" larger than the area you have sanded. Place the film over the repair and mark the sanded area on the film. Avoid any unnecessary wrinkling of the film.

5 Cut 2 pieces of fiberglass matte to match the shape of the repair. One piece should be about 1" smaller than the sanded area and the second piece should be 1" smaller than the first. Mix enough filler and hardener to saturate the fiberglass material (see Body Repair Tips).

6 Lay the release sheet on a flat surface and spread an even layer of filler, large enough to cover the repair. Lay the smaller piece of fiberglass cloth in the center of the sheet and spread another layer of filler over the fiberglass cloth. Repeat the operation for the larger piece of cloth.

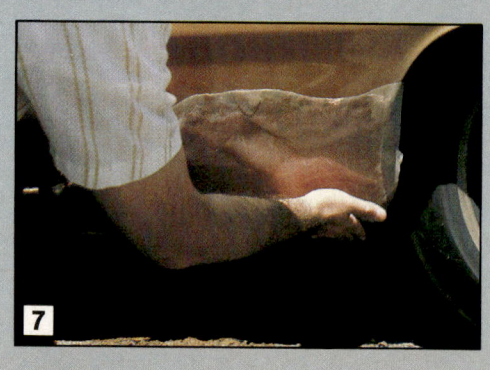

7 Place the repair material over the repair area, with the release film facing outward. Use a spreader and work from the center outward to smooth the material, following the body contours. Be sure to remove all air bubbles.

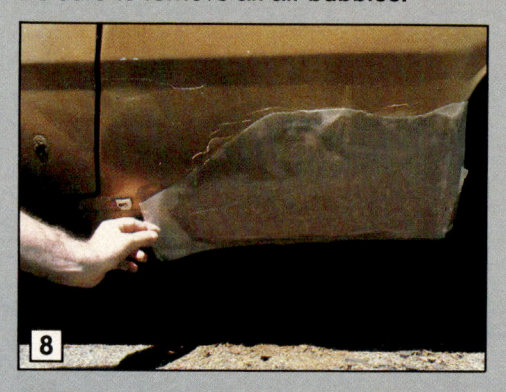

8 Wait until the repair has dried tack-free and peel off the release sheet. The ideal working temperature is 60°-90° F. Cooler or warmer temperatures or high humidity may require additional curing time. Wait longer, if in doubt.

9 Sand and feather-edge the entire area. The initial sanding can be done with a sanding disc on an electric drill if care is used. Finish the sanding with a block sander. Low spots can be filled with body filler; this may require several applications.

10 When the filler can just be scratched with a fingernail, knock the high spots down with a body file and smooth the entire area with 80-grit. Feather the filled areas into the surrounding areas.

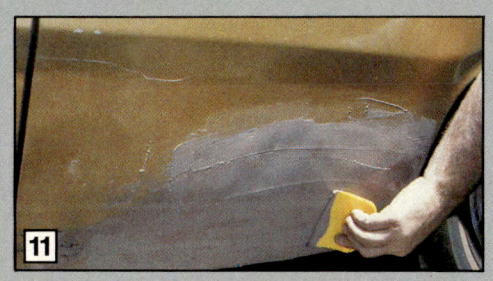

11 When the area is sanded smooth, mix some topcoat and hardener and apply it directly with a spreader. This will give a smooth finish and prevent the glass matte from showing through the paint.

12 Block sand the topcoat smooth with finishing sandpaper (200 grit), and 400 grit. The repair is ready for masking, priming and painting (see Painting Tips).

Materials and photos courtesy Marson Corporation, Chelsea, Massachusetts

PAINTING TIPS

Preparation

1 SANDING — Use a 400 or 600 grit wet or dry sandpaper. Wet-sand the area with a 1/4 sheet of sandpaper soaked in clean water. Keep the paper wet while sanding. Sand the area until the repaired area tapers into the original finish.

2 CLEANING — Wash the area to be painted thoroughly with water and a clean rag. Rinse it thoroughly and wipe the surface dry until you're sure it's completely free of dirt, dust, fingerprints, wax, detergent or other foreign matter.

3 MASKING — Protect any areas you don't want to overspray by covering them with masking tape and newspaper. Be careful not get fingerprints on the area to be painted.

4 PRIMING — All exposed metal should be primed before painting. Primer protects the metal and provides an excellent surface for paint adhesion. When the primer is dry, wet-sand the area again with 600 grit wet-sandpaper. Clean the area again after sanding.

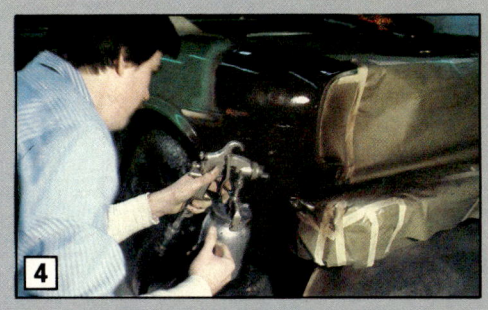

Painting Techniques

Paint applied from either a spray gun or a spray can (for small areas) will provide good results. Experiment on an old piece of metal to get the right combination before you begin painting.

SPRAYING VISCOSITY (SPRAY GUN ONLY) — Paint should be thinned to spraying viscosity according to the directions on the can. Use only the recommended thinner or reducer and the same amount of reduction regardless of temperature.

AIR PRESSURE (SPRAY GUN ONLY) — This is extremely important. Be sure you are using the proper recommended pressure.

TEMPERATURE — The surface to be painted should be approximately the same temperature as the surrounding air. Applying warm paint to a cold surface, or vice versa, will completely upset the paint characteristics.

THICKNESS — Spray with smooth strokes. In general, the thicker the coat of paint, the longer the drying time. Apply several thin coats about 30 seconds apart. The paint should remain wet long enough to flow out and no longer; heavier coats will only produce sags or wrinkles. Spray a light (fog) coat, followed by heavier color coats.

DISTANCE — The ideal spraying distance is 8"-12" from the gun or can to the surface. Shorter distances will produce ripples, while greater distances will result in orange peel, dry film and poor color match and loss of material due to overspray.

OVERLAPPING — The gun or can should be kept at right angles to the surface at all times. Work to a wet edge at an even speed, using a 50% overlap and direct the center of the spray at the lower or nearest edge of the previous stroke.

RUBBING OUT (BLENDING) FRESH PAINT — Let the paint dry thoroughly. Runs or imperfections can be sanded out, primed and repainted.

Don't be in too big a hurry to remove the masking. This only produces paint ridges. When the finish has dried for at least a week, apply a small amount of fine grade rubbing compound with a clean, wet cloth. Use lots of water and blend the new paint with the surrounding area.

WRONG
Thin coat. Stroke too fast, not enough overlap, gun too far away.

CORRECT
Medium coat. Proper distance, good stroke, proper overlap.

WRONG
Heavy coat. Stroke too slow, too much overlap, gun too close.

TROUBLESHOOTING 163

Test and Procedure	Results and Indications	Proceed to
5.9—Uncommon fuel system malfunctions: See below:	If the problem is solved: If the problem remains, remove and recondition the carburetor.	6.1

Condition	Indication	Test	Prevailing Weather Conditions	Remedy
Vapor lock	Engine will not restart shortly after running.	Cool the components of the fuel system until the engine starts. Vapor lock can be cured faster by draping a wet cloth over a mechanical fuel pump.	Hot to very hot	Ensure that the exhaust manifold heat control valve is operating. Check with the vehicle manufacturer for the recommended solution to vapor lock on the model in question.
Carburetor icing	Engine will not idle, stalls at low speeds.	Visually inspect the throttle plate area of the throttle bores for frost.	High humidity, 32–40° F.	Ensure that the exhaust manifold heat control valve is operating, and that the intake manifold heat riser is not blocked.
Water in the fuel	Engine sputters and stalls; may not start.	Pump a small amount of fuel into a glass jar. Allow to stand, and inspect for droplets or a layer of water.	High humidity, extreme temperature changes.	For droplets, use one or two cans of commercial gas line anti-freeze. For a layer of water, the tank must be drained, and the fuel lines blown out with compressed air.

Section 6—Engine Compression
See Chapter 3 for service procedures

6.1—Test engine compression: Remove all spark plugs. Block the throttle wide open. Insert a compression gauge into a spark plug port, crank the engine to obtain the maximum reading, and record.	If compression is within limits on all cylinders:	7.1
	If gauge reading is extremely low on all cylinders:	6.2
	If gauge reading is low on one or two cylinders: (If gauge readings are identical and low on two or more adjacent cylinders, the head gasket must be replaced.)	6.2

Checking compression

6.2—Test engine compression (wet): Squirt approximately 30 cc. of engine oil into each cylinder, and retest per 6.1.	If the readings improve, worn or cracked rings or broken pistons are indicated:	See Chapter 3
	If the readings do not improve, burned or excessively carboned valves or a jumped timing chain are indicated: **NOTE:** *A jumped timing chain is often indicated by difficult cranking.*	7.1

TROUBLESHOOTING

Section 7—Engine Vacuum
See Chapter 3 for service procedures

Test and Procedure	Results and Indications	Proceed to
7.1—Attach a vacuum gauge to the intake manifold beyond the throttle plate. Start the engine, and observe the action of the needle over the range of engine speeds.	See below.	See below

INDICATION: normal engine in good condition

Proceed to: 8.1

Normal engine
Gauge reading: steady, from 17–22 in./Hg.

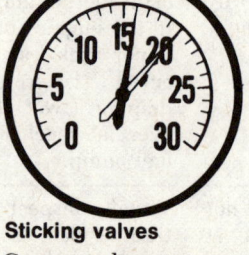

INDICATION: sticking valves or ignition miss

Proceed to: 9.1, 8.3

Sticking valves
Gauge reading: intermittent fluctuation at idle

INDICATION: late ignition or valve timing, low compression, stuck throttle valve, leaking carburetor or manifold gasket

Proceed to: 6.1

Incorrect valve timing
Gauge reading: low (10–15 in./Hg) but steady

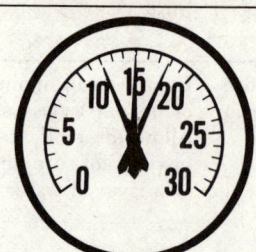

INDICATION: improper carburetor adjustment or minor intake leak.

Proceed to: 7.2

Carburetor requires adjustment
Gauge reading: drifting needle

INDICATION: ignition miss, blown cylinder head gasket, leaking valve or weak valve spring

Proceed to: 8.3, 6.1

Blown head gasket
Gauge reading: needle fluctuates as engine speed increases

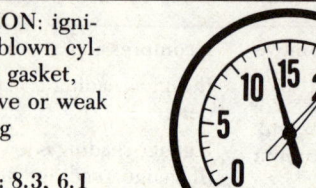

INDICATION: burnt valve or faulty valve clearance. Needle will fall when defective valve operates

Proceed to: 9.1

Burnt or leaking valves
Gauge reading: steady needle, but drops regularly

INDICATION: choked muffler, excessive back pressure in system

Proceed to: 10.1

Clogged exhaust system
Gauge reading: gradual drop in reading at idle

INDICATION: worn valve guides

Proceed to: 9.1

Worn valve guides
Gauge reading: needle vibrates excessively at idle, but steadies as engine speed increases

White pointer = steady gauge hand

Black pointer = fluctuating gauge hand

Test and Procedure	Results and Indications	Proceed to
7.2—Attach a vacuum gauge per 7.1, and test for an intake manifold leak. Squirt a small amount of oil around the intake manifold gaskets, carburetor gaskets, plugs and fittings. Observe the action of the vacuum gauge.	If the reading improves, replace the indicated gasket, or seal the indicated fitting or plug: If the reading remains low:	8.1 7.3
7.3—Test all vacuum hoses and accessories for leaks as described in 7.2. Also check the carburetor body (dashpots, automatic choke mechanism, throttle shafts) for leaks in the same manner.	If the reading improves, service or replace the offending part(s): If the reading remains low:	8.1 6.1

Section 8—Secondary Electrical System
See Chapter 2 for service procedures

Test and Procedure	Results and Indications	Proceed to
8.1—Remove the distributor cap and check to make sure that the rotor turns when the engine is cranked. Visually inspect the distributor components.	Clean, tighten or replace any components which appear defective.	8.2
8.2—Connect a timing light (per manufacturer's recommendation) and check the dynamic ignition timing. Disconnect and plug the vacuum hose(s) to the distributor if specified, start the engine, and observe the timing marks at the specified engine speed.	If the timing is not correct, adjust to specifications by rotating the distributor in the engine: (Advance timing by rotating distributor opposite normal direction of rotor rotation, retard timing by rotating distributor in same direction as rotor rotation.)	8.3
8.3—Check the operation of the distributor advance mechanism(s): To test the mechanical advance, disconnect the vacuum lines from the distributor advance unit and observe the timing marks with a timing light as the engine speed is increased from idle. If the mark moves smoothly, without hesitation, it may be assumed that the mechanical advance is functioning properly. To test vacuum advance and/or retard systems, alternately crimp and release the vacuum line, and observe the timing mark for movement. If movement is noted, the system is operating.	If the systems are functioning: If the systems are not functioning, remove the distributor, and test on a distributor tester:	8.4 8.4
8.4—Locate an ignition miss: With the engine running, remove each spark plug wire, one at a time, until one is found that doesn't cause the engine to roughen and slow down.	When the missing cylinder is identified:	4.1

TROUBLESHOOTING

Section 9—Valve Train
See Chapter 3 for service procedures

Test and Procedure	Results and Indications	Proceed to
9.1—Evaluate the valve train: Remove the valve cover, and ensure that the valves are adjusted to specifications. A mechanic's stethoscope may be used to aid in the diagnosis of the valve train. By pushing the probe on or near push rods or rockers, valve noise often can be isolated. A timing light also may be used to diagnose valve problems. Connect the light according to manufacturer's recommendations, and start the engine. Vary the firing moment of the light by increasing the engine speed (and therefore the ignition advance), and moving the trigger from cylinder to cylinder. Observe the movement of each valve.	Sticking valves or erratic valve train motion can be observed with the timing light. The cylinder head must be disassembled for repairs.	See Chapter 3
9.2—Check the valve timing: Locate top dead center of the No. 1 piston, and install a degree wheel or tape on the crankshaft pulley or damper with zero corresponding to an index mark on the engine. Rotate the crankshaft in its direction of rotation, and observe the opening of the No. 1 cylinder intake valve. The opening should correspond with the correct mark on the degree wheel according to specifications.	If the timing is not correct, the timing cover must be removed for further investigation.	See Chapter 3

Section 10—Exhaust System

Test and Procedure	Results and Indications	Proceed to
10.1—Determine whether the exhaust manifold heat control valve is operating: Operate the valve by hand to determine whether it is free to move. If the valve is free, run the engine to operating temperature and observe the action of the valve, to ensure that it is opening.	If the valve sticks, spray it with a suitable solvent, open and close the valve to free it, and retest. If the valve functions properly: If the valve does not free, or does not operate, replace the valve:	10.2 10.2
10.2—Ensure that there are no exhaust restrictions: Visually inspect the exhaust system for kinks, dents, or crushing. Also note that gases are flowing freely from the tailpipe at all engine speeds, indicating no restriction in the muffler or resonator.	Replace any damaged portion of the system:	11.1

TROUBLESHOOTING

Section 11—Cooling System
See Chapter 3 for service procedures

Test and Procedure	Results and Indications	Proceed to
11.1—Visually inspect the fan belt for glazing, cracks, and fraying, and replace if necessary. Tighten the belt so that the longest span has approximately ½" play at its midpoint under thumb pressure (see Chapter 1).	Replace or tighten the fan belt as necessary: *Checking belt tension*	11.2
11.2—Check the fluid level of the cooling system.	If full or slightly low, fill as necessary:	11.5
	If extremely low:	11.3
11.3—Visually inspect the external portions of the cooling system (radiator, radiator hoses, thermostat elbow, water pump seals, heater hoses, etc.) for leaks. If none are found, pressurize the cooling system to 14–15 psi.	If cooling system holds the pressure:	11.5
	If cooling system loses pressure rapidly, reinspect external parts of the system for leaks under pressure. If none are found, check dipstick for coolant in crankcase. If no coolant is present, but pressure loss continues:	11.4
	If coolant is evident in crankcase, remove cylinder head(s), and check gasket(s). If gaskets are intact, block and cylinder head(s) should be checked for cracks or holes.	
	If the gasket(s) is blown, replace, and purge the crankcase of coolant:	12.6
	NOTE: *Occasionally, due to atmospheric and driving conditions, condensation of water can occur in the crankcase. This causes the oil to appear milky white. To remedy, run the engine until hot, and change the oil and oil filter.*	
11.4—Check for combustion leaks into the cooling system: Pressurize the cooling system as above. Start the engine, and observe the pressure gauge. If the needle fluctuates, remove each spark plug wire, one at a time, noting which cylinder(s) reduce or eliminate the fluctuation.	Cylinders which reduce or eliminate the fluctuation, when the spark plug wire is removed, are leaking into the cooling system. Replace the head gasket on the affected cylinder bank(s). *Pressurizing the cooling system*	

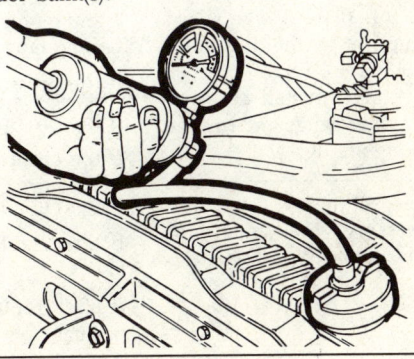

168　TROUBLESHOOTING

Test and Procedure	Results and Indications	Proceed to
11.5—Check the radiator pressure cap: Attach a radiator pressure tester to the radiator cap (wet the seal prior to installation). Quickly pump up the pressure, noting the point at which the cap releases.	If the cap releases within ± 1 psi of the specified rating, it is operating properly:	11.6
	If the cap releases at more than ± 1 psi of the specified rating, it should be replaced:	11.6

Checking radiator pressure cap

Test and Procedure	Results and Indications	Proceed to
11.6—Test the thermostat: Start the engine cold, remove the radiator cap, and insert a thermometer into the radiator. Allow the engine to idle. After a short while, there will be a sudden, rapid increase in coolant temperature. The temperature at which this sharp rise stops is the thermostat opening temperature.	If the thermostat opens at or about the specified temperature:	11.7
	If the temperature doesn't increase: (If the temperature increases slowly and gradually, replace the thermostat.)	11.7
11.7—Check the water pump: Remove the thermostat elbow and the thermostat, disconnect the coil high tension lead (to prevent starting), and crank the engine momentarily.	If coolant flows, replace the thermostat and retest per 11.6:	11.6
	If coolant doesn't flow, reverse flush the cooling system to alleviate any blockage that might exist. If system is not blocked, and coolant will not flow, replace the water pump.	

Section 12—Lubrication
See Chapter 3 for service procedures

Test and Procedure	Results and Indications	Proceed to
12.1—Check the oil pressure gauge or warning light: If the gauge shows low pressure, or the light is on for no obvious reason, remove the oil pressure sender. Install an accurate oil pressure gauge and run the engine momentarily.	If oil pressure builds normally, run engine for a few moments to determine that it is functioning normally, and replace the sender.	—
	If the pressure remains low:	12.2
	If the pressure surges:	12.3
	If the oil pressure is zero:	12.3
12.2—Visually inspect the oil: If the oil is watery or very thin, milky, or foamy, replace the oil and oil filter.	If the oil is normal:	12.3
	If after replacing oil the pressure remains low:	12.3
	If after replacing oil the pressure becomes normal:	—

Test and Procedure	Results and Indications	Proceed to
12.3—Inspect the oil pressure relief valve and spring, to ensure that it is not sticking or stuck. Remove and thoroughly clean the valve, spring, and the valve body.	If the oil pressure improves: If no improvement is noted:	— 12.4
12.4—Check to ensure that the oil pump is not cavitating (sucking air instead of oil): See that the crankcase is neither over nor underfull, and that the pickup in the sump is in the proper position and free from sludge.	Fill or drain the crankcase to the proper capacity, and clean the pickup screen in solvent if necessary. If no improvement is noted:	12.5
12.5—Inspect the oil pump drive and the oil pump:	If the pump drive or the oil pump appear to be defective, service as necessary and retest per 12.1: If the pump drive and pump appear to be operating normally, the engine should be disassembled to determine where blockage exists:	12.1 See Chapter 3
12.6—Purge the engine of ethylene glycol coolant: Completely drain the crankcase and the oil filter. Obtain a commercial butyl cellosolve base solvent, designated for this purpose, and follow the instructions precisely. Following this, install a new oil filter and refill the crankcase with the proper weight oil. The next oil and filter change should follow shortly thereafter (1000 miles).		

TROUBLESHOOTING EMISSION CONTROL SYSTEMS

See Chapter 4 for procedures applicable to individual emission control systems used on specific combinations of engine/transmission/model.

TROUBLESHOOTING THE CARBURETOR
See Chapter 4 for service procedures

Carburetor problems cannot be effectively isolated unless all other engine systems (particularly ignition and emission) are functioning properly and the engine is properly tuned.

TROUBLESHOOTING

Condition	Possible Cause
Engine cranks, but does not start	1. Improper starting procedure 2. No fuel in tank 3. Clogged fuel line or filter 4. Defective fuel pump 5. Choke valve not closing properly 6. Engine flooded 7. Choke valve not unloading 8. Throttle linkage not making full travel 9. Stuck needle or float 10. Leaking float needle or seat 11. Improper float adjustment
Engine stalls	1. Improperly adjusted idle speed or mixture **Engine hot** 2. Improperly adjusted dashpot 3. Defective or improperly adjusted solenoid 4. Incorrect fuel level in fuel bowl 5. Fuel pump pressure too high 6. Leaking float needle seat 7. Secondary throttle valve stuck open 8. Air or fuel leaks 9. Idle air bleeds plugged or missing 10. Idle passages plugged **Engine Cold** 11. Incorrectly adjusted choke 12. Improperly adjusted fast idle speed 13. Air leaks 14. Plugged idle or idle air passages 15. Stuck choke valve or binding linkage 16. Stuck secondary throttle valves 17. Engine flooding—high fuel level 18. Leaking or misaligned float
Engine hesitates on acceleration	1. Clogged fuel filter 2. Leaking fuel pump diaphragm 3. Low fuel pump pressure 4. Secondary throttle valves stuck, bent or misadjusted 5. Sticking or binding air valve 6. Defective accelerator pump 7. Vacuum leaks 8. Clogged air filter 9. Incorrect choke adjustment (engine cold)
Engine feels sluggish or flat on acceleration	1. Improperly adjusted idle speed or mixture 2. Clogged fuel filter 3. Defective accelerator pump 4. Dirty, plugged or incorrect main metering jets 5. Bent or sticking main metering rods 6. Sticking throttle valves 7. Stuck heat riser 8. Binding or stuck air valve 9. Dirty, plugged or incorrect secondary jets 10. Bent or sticking secondary metering rods. 11. Throttle body or manifold heat passages plugged 12. Improperly adjusted choke or choke vacuum break.
Carburetor floods	1. Defective fuel pump. Pressure too high. 2. Stuck choke valve 3. Dirty, worn or damaged float or needle valve/seat 4. Incorrect float/fuel level 5. Leaking float bowl

TROUBLESHOOTING

Condition	Possible Cause
Engine idles roughly and stalls	1. Incorrect idle speed 2. Clogged fuel filter 3. Dirt in fuel system or carburetor 4. Loose carburetor screws or attaching bolts 5. Broken carburetor gaskets 6. Air leaks 7. Dirty carburetor 8. Worn idle mixture needles 9. Throttle valves stuck open 10. Incorrectly adjusted float or fuel level 11. Clogged air filter
Engine runs unevenly or surges	1. Defective fuel pump 2. Dirty or clogged fuel filter 3. Plugged, loose or incorrect main metering jets or rods 4. Air leaks 5. Bent or sticking main metering rods 6. Stuck power piston 7. Incorrect float adjustment 8. Incorrect idle speed or mixture 9. Dirty or plugged idle system passages 10. Hard, brittle or broken gaskets 11. Loose attaching or mounting screws 12. Stuck or misaligned secondary throttle valves
Poor fuel economy	1. Poor driving habits 2. Stuck choke valve 3. Binding choke linkage 4. Stuck heat riser 5. Incorrect idle mixture 6. Defective accelerator pump 7. Air leaks 8. Plugged, loose or incorrect main metering jets 9. Improperly adjusted float or fuel level 10. Bent, misaligned or fuel-clogged float 11. Leaking float needle seat 12. Fuel leak 13. Accelerator pump discharge ball not seating properly 14. Incorrect main jets
Engine lacks high speed performance or power	1. Incorrect throttle linkage adjustment 2. Stuck or binding power piston 3. Defective accelerator pump 4. Air leaks 5. Incorrect float setting or fuel level 6. Dirty, plugged, worn or incorrect main metering jets or rods 7. Binding or sticking air valve 8. Brittle or cracked gaskets 9. Bent, incorrect or improperly adjusted secondary metering rods 10. Clogged fuel filter 11. Clogged air filter 12. Defective fuel pump

TROUBLESHOOTING FUEL INJECTION PROBLEMS

Each fuel injection system has its own unique components and test procedures, for which it is impossible to generalize. Refer to Chapter 4 of this Repair & Tune-Up Guide for specific test and repair procedures, if the vehicle is equipped with fuel injection.

TROUBLESHOOTING ELECTRICAL PROBLEMS

See Chapter 5 for service procedures

For any electrical system to operate, it must make a complete circuit. This simply means that the power flow from the battery must make a complete circle. When an electrical component is operating, power flows from the battery to the component, passes through the component causing it to perform its function (lighting a light bulb), and then returns to the battery through the ground of the circuit. This ground is usually (but not always) the metal part of the car or truck on which the electrical component is mounted.

Perhaps the easiest way to visualize this is to think of connecting a light bulb with two wires attached to it to the battery. If one of the two wires attached to the light bulb were attached to the negative post of the battery and the other were attached to the positive post of the battery, you would have a complete circuit. Current from the battery would flow to the light bulb, causing it to light, and return to the negative post of the battery.

The normal automotive circuit differs from this simple example in two ways. First, instead of having a return wire from the bulb to the battery, the light bulb returns the current to the battery through the chassis of the vehicle. Since the negative battery cable is attached to the chassis and the chassis is made of electrically conductive metal, the chassis of the vehicle can serve as a ground wire to complete the circuit. Secondly, most automotive circuits contain switches to turn components on and off as required.

Every complete circuit from a power source must include a component which is using the power from the power source. If you were to disconnect the light bulb from the wires and touch the two wires together (don't do this) the power supply wire to the component would be grounded before the normal ground connection for the circuit.

Because grounding a wire from a power source makes a complete circuit—less the required component to use the power—this phenomenon is called a short circuit. Common causes are: broken insulation (exposing the metal wire to a metal part of the car or truck), or a shorted switch.

Some electrical components which require a large amount of current to operate also have a relay in their circuit. Since these circuits carry a large amount of current, the thickness of the wire in the circuit (gauge size) is also greater. If this large wire were connected from the component to the control switch on the instrument panel, and then back to the component, a voltage drop would occur in the circuit. To prevent this potential drop in voltage, an electromagnetic switch (relay) is used. The large wires in the circuit are connected from the battery to one side of the relay, and from the opposite side of the relay to the component. The relay is normally open, preventing current from passing through the circuit. An additional, smaller, wire is connected from the relay to the control switch for the circuit. When the control switch is turned on, it grounds the smaller wire from the relay and completes the circuit. This closes the relay and allows current to flow from the battery to the component. The horn, headlight, and starter circuits are three which use relays.

It is possible for larger surges of current to pass through the electrical system of your car or truck. If this surge of current were to reach an electrical component, it could burn it out. To prevent this, fuses, circuit breakers or fusible links are connected into the current supply wires of most of the major electrical systems. When an electrical current of excessive power passes through the component's fuse, the fuse blows out and breaks the circuit, saving the component from destruction.

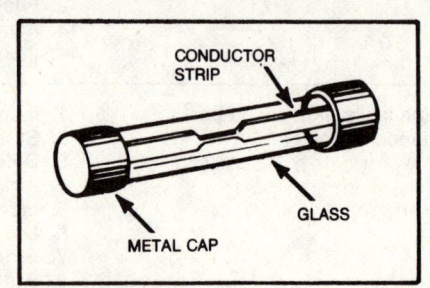

Typical automotive fuse

A circuit breaker is basically a self-repairing fuse. The circuit breaker opens the circuit the same way a fuse does. However, when either the short is removed from the circuit or the surge subsides, the circuit breaker resets itself and does not have to be replaced as a fuse does.

A fuse link is a wire that acts as a fuse. It is normally connected between the starter relay and the main wiring harness. This connection is usually under the hood. The fuse link (if installed) protects all the

TROUBLESHOOTING

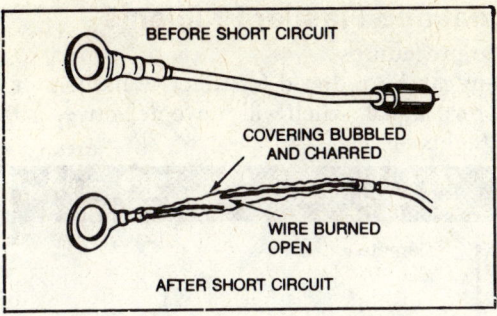

Most fusible links show a charred, melted insulation when they burn out

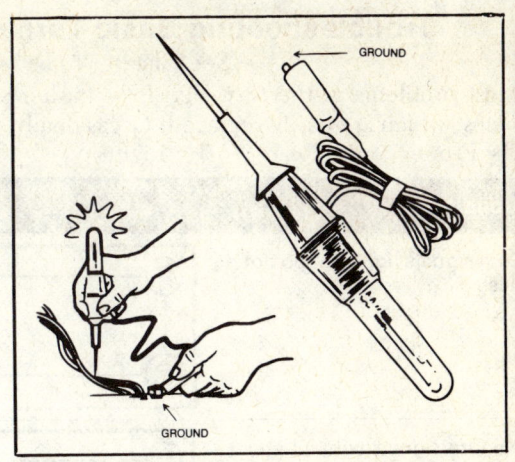

The test light will show the presence of current when touched to a hot wire and grounded at the other end

chassis electrical components, and is the probable cause of trouble when none of the electrical components function, unless the battery is disconnected or dead.

Electrical problems generally fall into one of three areas:

1. The component that is not functioning is not receiving current.
2. The component itself is not functioning.
3. The component is not properly grounded.

The electrical system can be checked with a test light and a jumper wire. A test light is a device that looks like a pointed screwdriver with a wire attached to it and has a light bulb in its handle. A jumper wire is a piece of insulated wire with an alligator clip attached to each end.

If a component is not working, you must follow a systematic plan to determine which of the three causes is the villain.

1. Turn on the switch that controls the inoperable component.
2. Disconnect the power supply wire from the component.
3. Attach the ground wire on the test light to a good metal ground.
4. Touch the probe end of the test light to the end of the power supply wire that was disconnected from the component. If the component is receiving current, the test light will go on.

NOTE: *Some components work only when the ignition switch is turned on.*

If the test light does not go on, then the problem is in the circuit between the battery and the component. This includes all the switches, fuses, and relays in the system. Follow the wire that runs back to the battery. The problem is an open circuit between the battery and the component. If the fuse is blown and, when replaced, immediately blows again, there is a short circuit in the system which must be located and repaired. If there is a switch in the system, bypass it with a jumper wire. This is done by connecting one end of the jumper wire to the power supply wire into the switch and the other end of the jumper wire to the wire coming out of the switch. If the test light lights with the jumper wire installed, the switch or whatever was bypassed is defective.

NOTE: *Never substitute the jumper wire for the component, since it is required to use the power from the power source.*

5. If the bulb in the test light goes on, then the current is getting to the component that is not working. This eliminates the first of the three possible causes. Connect the power supply wire and connect a jumper wire from the component to a good metal ground. Do this with the switch which controls the component turned on, and also the ignition switch turned on if it is required for the component to work. If the component works with the jumper wire installed, then it has a bad ground. This is usually caused by the metal area on which the component mounts to the chassis being coated with some type of foreign matter.

6. If neither test located the source of the trouble, then the component itself is defective. Remember that for any electrical system to work, all connections must be clean and tight.

TROUBLESHOOTING

Troubleshooting Basic Turn Signal and Flasher Problems
See Chapter 5 for service procedures

Most problems in the turn signals or flasher system can be reduced to defective flashers or bulbs, which are easily replaced. Occasionally, the turn signal switch will prove defective.

F = Front   R = Rear   ● = Lights off   ○ = Lights on

Condition		Possible Cause
Turn signals light, but do not flash	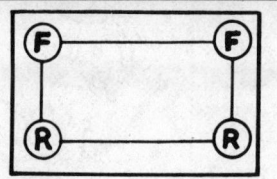	Defective flasher
No turn signals light on either side	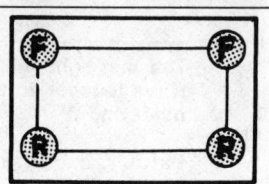	Blown fuse. Replace if defective. Defective flasher. Check by substitution. Open circuit, short circuit or poor ground.
Both turn signals on one side don't work	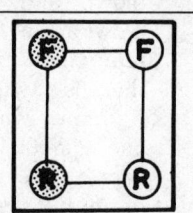	Bad bulbs. Bad ground in both (or either) housings.
One turn signal light on one side doesn't work	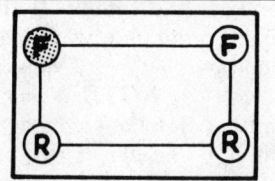	Defective bulb. Corrosion in socket. Clean contacts. Poor ground at socket.
Turn signal flashes too fast or too slowly	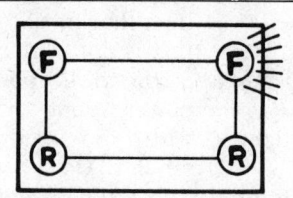	Check any bulb on the side flashing too fast. A heavy-duty bulb is probably installed in place of a regular bulb. Check the bulb flashing too slowly. A standard bulb was probably installed in place of a heavy-duty bulb. Loose connections or corrosion at the bulb socket.
Indicator lights don't work in either direction		Check if the turn signals are working. Check the dash indicator lights. Check the flasher by substitution.
One indicator light doesn't light		On systems with one dash indicator: See if the lights work on the same side. Often the filaments have been reversed in systems combining stoplights with taillights and turn signals. Check the flasher by substitution. On systems with two indicators: Check the bulbs on the same side. Check the indicator light bulb. Check the flasher by substitution.

TROUBLESHOOTING

Troubleshooting Lighting Problems

See Chapter 5 for service procedures

Condition	Possible Cause
One or more lights don't work, but others do	1. Defective bulb(s) 2. Blown fuse(s) 3. Dirty fuse clips or light sockets 4. Poor ground circuit
Lights burn out quickly	1. Incorrect voltage regulator setting or defective regulator 2. Poor battery/alternator connections
Lights go dim	1. Low/discharged battery 2. Alternator not charging 3. Corroded sockets or connections 4. Low voltage output
Lights flicker	1. Loose connection 2. Poor ground. (Run ground wire from light housing to frame) 3. Circuit breaker operating (short circuit)
Lights "flare"—Some flare is normal on acceleration—If excessive, see "Lights Burn Out Quickly"	High voltage setting
Lights glare—approaching drivers are blinded	1. Lights adjusted too high 2. Rear springs or shocks sagging 3. Rear tires soft

Troubleshooting Dash Gauge Problems

Most problems can be traced to a defective sending unit or faulty wiring. Occasionally, the gauge itself is at fault. See Chapter 5 for service procedures.

Condition	Possible Cause
COOLANT TEMPERATURE GAUGE	
Gauge reads erratically or not at all	1. Loose or dirty connections 2. Defective sending unit. 3. Defective gauge. To test a bi-metal gauge, remove the wire from the sending unit. Ground the wire for an instant. If the gauge registers, replace the sending unit. To test a magnetic gauge, disconnect the wire at the sending unit. With ignition ON gauge should register COLD. Ground the wire; gauge should register HOT.
AMMETER GAUGE—TURN HEADLIGHTS ON (DO NOT START ENGINE). NOTE REACTION	
Ammeter shows charge Ammeter shows discharge Ammeter does not move	1. Connections reversed on gauge 2. Ammeter is OK 3. Loose connections or faulty wiring 4. Defective gauge

TROUBLESHOOTING

Condition	Possible Cause

OIL PRESSURE GAUGE

Gauge does not register or is inaccurate	1. On mechanical gauge, Bourdon tube may be bent or kinked. 2. Low oil pressure. Remove sending unit. Idle the engine briefly. If no oil flows from sending unit hole, problem is in engine. 3. Defective gauge. Remove the wire from the sending unit and ground it for an instant with the ignition ON. A good gauge will go to the top of the scale. 4. Defective wiring. Check the wiring to the gauge. If it's OK and the gauge doesn't register when grounded, replace the gauge. 5. Defective sending unit.

ALL GAUGES

All gauges do not operate All gauges read low or erratically All gauges pegged	1. Blown fuse 2. Defective instrument regulator 3. Defective or dirty instrument voltage regulator 4. Loss of ground between instrument voltage regulator and frame 5. Defective instrument regulator

WARNING LIGHTS

Light(s) do not come on when ignition is ON, but engine is not started	1. Defective bulb 2. Defective wire 3. Defective sending unit. Disconnect the wire from the sending unit and ground it. Replace the sending unit if the light comes on with the ignition ON.
Light comes on with engine running	4. Problem in individual system 5. Defective sending unit

Troubleshooting Clutch Problems

It is false economy to replace individual clutch components. The pressure plate, clutch plate and throwout bearing should be replaced as a set, and the flywheel face inspected, whenever the clutch is overhauled. See Chapter 6 for service procedures.

Condition	Possible Cause
Clutch chatter	1. Grease on driven plate (disc) facing 2. Binding clutch linkage or cable 3. Loose, damaged facings on driven plate (disc) 4. Engine mounts loose 5. Incorrect height adjustment of pressure plate release levers 6. Clutch housing or housing to transmission adapter misalignment 7. Loose driven plate hub
Clutch grabbing	1. Oil, grease on driven plate (disc) facing 2. Broken pressure plate 3. Warped or binding driven plate. Driven plate binding on clutch shaft
Clutch slips	1. Lack of lubrication in clutch linkage or cable (linkage or cable binds, causes incomplete engagement) 2. Incorrect pedal, or linkage adjustment 3. Broken pressure plate springs 4. Weak pressure plate springs 5. Grease on driven plate facings (disc)

TROUBLESHOOTING

Troubleshooting Clutch Problems (cont.)

Condition	Possible Cause
Incomplete clutch release	1. Incorrect pedal or linkage adjustment or linkage or cable binding 2. Incorrect height adjustment on pressure plate release levers 3. Loose, broken facings on driven plate (disc) 4. Bent, dished, warped driven plate caused by overheating
Grinding, whirring grating noise when pedal is depressed	1. Worn or defective throwout bearing 2. Starter drive teeth contacting flywheel ring gear teeth. Look for milled or polished teeth on ring gear.
Squeal, howl, trumpeting noise when pedal is being released (occurs during first inch to inch and one-half of pedal travel)	Pilot bushing worn or lack of lubricant. If bushing appears OK, polish bushing with emery cloth, soak lube wick in oil, lube bushing with oil, apply film of chassis grease to clutch shaft pilot hub, reassemble. NOTE: Bushing wear may be due to misalignment of clutch housing or housing to transmission adapter
Vibration or clutch pedal pulsation with clutch disengaged (pedal fully depressed)	1. Worn or defective engine transmission mounts 2. Flywheel run out. (Flywheel run out at face not to exceed 0.005″) 3. Damaged or defective clutch components

Troubleshooting Manual Transmission Problems
See Chapter 6 for service procedures

Condition	Possible Cause
Transmission jumps out of gear	1. Misalignment of transmission case or clutch housing. 2. Worn pilot bearing in crankshaft. 3. Bent transmission shaft. 4. Worn high speed sliding gear. 5. Worn teeth or end-play in clutch shaft. 6. Insufficient spring tension on shifter rail plunger. 7. Bent or loose shifter fork. 8. Gears not engaging completely. 9. Loose or worn bearings on clutch shaft or mainshaft. 10. Worn gear teeth. 11. Worn or damaged detent balls.
Transmission sticks in gear	1. Clutch not releasing fully. 2. Burred or battered teeth on clutch shaft, or sliding sleeve. 3. Burred or battered transmission mainshaft. 4. Frozen synchronizing clutch. 5. Stuck shifter rail plunger. 6. Gearshift lever twisting and binding shifter rail. 7. Battered teeth on high speed sliding gear or on sleeve. 8. Improper lubrication, or lack of lubrication. 9. Corroded transmission parts. 10. Defective mainshaft pilot bearing. 11. Locked gear bearings will give same effect as stuck in gear.
Transmission gears will not synchronize	1. Binding pilot bearing on mainshaft, will synchronize in high gear only. 2. Clutch not releasing fully. 3. Detent spring weak or broken. 4. Weak or broken springs under balls in sliding gear sleeve. 5. Binding bearing on clutch shaft, or binding countershaft. 6. Binding pilot bearing in crankshaft. 7. Badly worn gear teeth. 8. Improper lubrication. 9. Constant mesh gear not turning freely on transmission mainshaft. Will synchronize in that gear only.

TROUBLESHOOTING

Condition	Possible Cause
Gears spinning when shifting into gear from neutral	1. Clutch not releasing fully. 2. In some cases an extremely light lubricant in transmission will cause gears to continue to spin for a short time after clutch is released. 3. Binding pilot bearing in crankshaft.
Transmission noisy in all gears	1. Insufficient lubricant, or improper lubricant. 2. Worn countergear bearings. 3. Worn or damaged main drive gear or countergear. 4. Damaged main drive gear or mainshaft bearings. 5. Worn or damaged countergear anti-lash plate.
Transmission noisy in neutral only	1. Damaged main drive gear bearing. 2. Damaged or loose mainshaft pilot bearing. 3. Worn or damaged countergear anti-lash plate. 4. Worn countergear bearings.
Transmission noisy in one gear only	1. Damaged or worn constant mesh gears. 2. Worn or damaged countergear bearings. 3. Damaged or worn synchronizer.
Transmission noisy in reverse only	1. Worn or damaged reverse idler gear or idler bushing. 2. Worn or damaged mainshaft reverse gear. 3. Worn or damaged reverse countergear. 4. Damaged shift mechanism.

TROUBLESHOOTING AUTOMATIC TRANSMISSION PROBLEMS

Keeping alert to changes in the operating characteristics of the transmission (changing shift points, noises, etc.) can prevent small problems from becoming large ones. If the problem cannot be traced to loose bolts, fluid level, misadjusted linkage, clogged filters or similar problems, you should probably seek professional service.

Transmission Fluid Indications

The appearance and odor of the transmission fluid can give valuable clues to the overall condition of the transmission. Always note the appearance of the fluid when you check the fluid level or change the fluid. Rub a small amount of fluid between your fingers to feel for grit and smell the fluid on the dipstick.

If the fluid appears:	It indicates:
Clear and red colored	Normal operation
Discolored (extremely dark red or brownish) or smells burned	Band or clutch pack failure, usually caused by an overheated transmission. Hauling very heavy loads with insufficient power or failure to change the fluid often result in overheating. Do not confuse this appearance with newer fluids that have a darker red color and a strong odor (though not a burned odor).
Foamy or aerated (light in color and full of bubbles)	1. The level is too high (gear train is churning oil) 2. An internal air leak (air is mixing with the fluid). Have the transmission checked professionally.
Solid residue in the fluid	Defective bands, clutch pack or bearings. Bits of band material or metal abrasives are clinging to the dipstick. Have the transmission checked professionally.
Varnish coating on the dipstick	The transmission fluid is overheating

TROUBLESHOOTING DRIVE AXLE PROBLEMS

First, determine when the noise is most noticeable.

Drive Noise: Produced under vehicle acceleration.

Coast Noise: Produced while coasting with a closed throttle.

Float Noise: Occurs while maintaining constant speed (just enough to keep speed constant) on a level road.

External Noise Elimination

It is advisable to make a thorough road test to determine whether the noise originates in the rear axle or whether it originates from the tires, engine, transmission, wheel bearings or road surface. Noise originating from other places cannot be corrected by servicing the rear axle.

ROAD NOISE

Brick or rough surfaced concrete roads produce noises that seem to come from the rear axle. Road noise is usually identical in Drive or Coast and driving on a different type of road will tell whether the road is the problem.

TIRE NOISE

Tire noise can be mistaken as rear axle noise, even though the tires on the front are at fault. Snow tread and mud tread tires or tires worn unevenly will frequently cause vibrations which seem to originate elsewhere; *temporarily, and for test purposes only,* inflate the tires to 40–50 lbs. This will significantly alter the noise produced by the tires, but will not alter noise from the rear axle. Noises from the rear axle will normally cease at speeds below 30 mph on coast, while tire noise will continue at lower tone as speed is decreased. The rear axle noise will usually change from drive conditions to coast conditions, while tire noise will not. Do not forget to lower the tire pressure to normal after the test is complete.

ENGINE/TRANSMISSION NOISE

Determine at what speed the noise is most pronounced, then stop in a quiet place. With the transmission in Neutral, run the engine through speeds corresponding to road speeds where the noise was noticed. Noises produced with the vehicle standing still are coming from the engine or transmission.

FRONT WHEEL BEARINGS

Front wheel bearing noises, sometimes confused with rear axle noises, will not change when comparing drive and coast conditions. While holding the speed steady, lightly apply the footbrake. This will often cause wheel bearing noise to lessen, as some of the weight is taken off the bearing. Front wheel bearings are easily checked by jacking up the wheels and spinning the wheels. Shaking the wheels will also determine if the wheel bearings are excessively loose.

REAR AXLE NOISES

Eliminating other possible sources can narrow the cause to the rear axle, which normally produces noise from worn gears or bearings. Gear noises tend to peak in a narrow speed range, while bearing noises will usually vary in pitch with engine speeds.

Noise Diagnosis

The Noise Is:	Most Probably Produced By:
1. Identical under Drive or Coast	Road surface, tires or front wheel bearings
2. Different depending on road surface	Road surface or tires
3. Lower as speed is lowered	Tires
4. Similar when standing or moving	Engine or transmission
5. A vibration	Unbalanced tires, rear wheel bearing, unbalanced driveshaft or worn U-joint
6. A knock or click about every two tire revolutions	Rear wheel bearing
7. Most pronounced on turns	Damaged differential gears
8. A steady low-pitched whirring or scraping, starting at low speeds	Damaged or worn pinion bearing
9. A chattering vibration on turns	Wrong differential lubricant or worn clutch plates (limited slip rear axle)
10. Noticed only in Drive, Coast or Float conditions	Worn ring gear and/or pinion gear

TROUBLESHOOTING

Troubleshooting Steering & Suspension Problems

Condition	Possible Cause
Hard steering (wheel is hard to turn)	1. Improper tire pressure 2. Loose or glazed pump drive belt 3. Low or incorrect fluid 4. Loose, bent or poorly lubricated front end parts 5. Improper front end alignment (excessive caster) 6. Bind in steering column or linkage 7. Kinked hydraulic hose 8. Air in hydraulic system 9. Low pump output or leaks in system 10. Obstruction in lines 11. Pump valves sticking or out of adjustment 12. Incorrect wheel alignment
Loose steering (too much play in steering wheel)	1. Loose wheel bearings 2. Faulty shocks 3. Worn linkage or suspension components 4. Loose steering gear mounting or linkage points 5. Steering mechanism worn or improperly adjusted 6. Valve spool improperly adjusted 7. Worn ball joints, tie-rod ends, etc.
Veers or wanders (pulls to one side with hands off steering wheel)	1. Improper tire pressure 2. Improper front end alignment 3. Dragging or improperly adjusted brakes 4. Bent frame 5. Improper rear end alignment 6. Faulty shocks or springs 7. Loose or bent front end components 8. Play in Pitman arm 9. Steering gear mountings loose 10. Loose wheel bearings 11. Binding Pitman arm 12. Spool valve sticking or improperly adjusted 13. Worn ball joints
Wheel oscillation or vibration transmitted through steering wheel	1. Low or uneven tire pressure 2. Loose wheel bearings 3. Improper front end alignment 4. Bent spindle 5. Worn, bent or broken front end components 6. Tires out of round or out of balance 7. Excessive lateral runout in disc brake rotor 8. Loose or bent shock absorber or strut
Noises (see also "Troubleshooting Drive Axle Problems")	1. Loose belts 2. Low fluid, air in system 3. Foreign matter in system 4. Improper lubrication 5. Interference or chafing in linkage 6. Steering gear mountings loose 7. Incorrect adjustment or wear in gear box 8. Faulty valves or wear in pump 9. Kinked hydraulic lines 10. Worn wheel bearings
Poor return of steering	1. Over-inflated tires 2. Improperly aligned front end (excessive caster) 3. Binding in steering column 4. No lubrication in front end 5. Steering gear adjusted too tight
Uneven tire wear (see "How To Read Tire Wear")	1. Incorrect tire pressure 2. Improperly aligned front end 3. Tires out-of-balance 4. Bent or worn suspension parts

TROUBLESHOOTING

HOW TO READ TIRE WEAR

The way your tires wear is a good indicator of other parts of the suspension. Abnormal wear patterns are often caused by the need for simple tire maintenance, or for front end alignment.

Excessive wear at the center of the tread indicates that the air pressure in the tire is consistently too high. The tire is riding on the center of the tread and wearing it prematurely. Occasionally, this wear pattern can result from outrageously wide tires on narrow rims. The cure for this is to replace either the tires or the wheels.

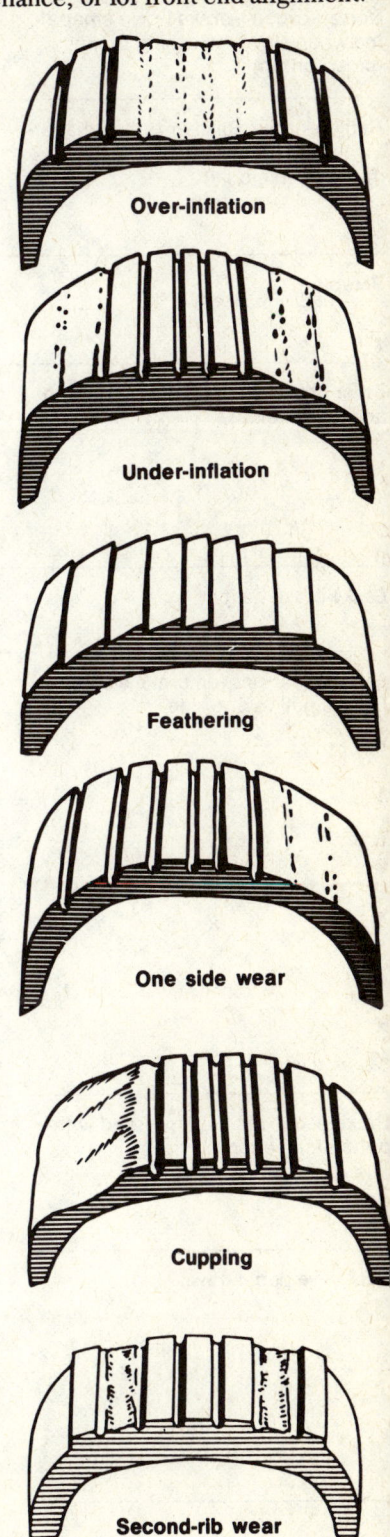

Over-inflation

This type of wear usually results from consistent under-inflation. When a tire is under-inflated, there is too much contact with the road by the outer treads, which wear prematurely. When this type of wear occurs, and the tire pressure is known to be consistently correct, a bent or worn steering component or the need for wheel alignment could be indicated.

Under-inflation

Feathering is a condition when the edge of each tread rib develops a slightly rounded edge on one side and a sharp edge on the other. By running your hand over the tire, you can usually feel the sharper edges before you'll be able to see them. The most common causes of feathering are incorrect toe-in setting or deteriorated bushings in the front suspension.

Feathering

When an inner or outer rib wears faster than the rest of the tire, the need for wheel alignment is indicated. There is excessive camber in the front suspension, causing the wheel to lean too much putting excessive load on one side of the tire. Misalignment could also be due to sagging springs, worn ball joints, or worn control arm bushings. Be sure the vehicle is loaded the way it's normally driven when you have the wheels aligned.

One side wear

Cups or scalloped dips appearing around the edge of the tread almost always indicate worn (sometimes bent) suspension parts. Adjustment of wheel alignment alone will seldom cure the problem. Any worn component that connects the wheel to the suspension can cause this type of wear. Occasionally, wheels that are out of balance will wear like this, but wheel imbalance usually shows up as bald spots between the outside edges and center of the tread.

Cupping

Second-rib wear is usually found only in radial tires, and appears where the steel belts end in relation to the tread. It can be kept to a minimum by paying careful attention to tire pressure and frequently rotating the tires. This is often considered normal wear but excessive amounts indicate that the tires are too wide for the wheels.

Second-rib wear

TROUBLESHOOTING

Troubleshooting Disc Brake Problems

Condition	Possible Cause
Noise—groan—brake noise emanating when slowly releasing brakes (creep-groan)	Not detrimental to function of disc brakes—no corrective action required. (This noise may be eliminated by slightly increasing or decreasing brake pedal efforts.)
Rattle—brake noise or rattle emanating at low speeds on rough roads, (front wheels only).	1. Shoe anti-rattle spring missing or not properly positioned. 2. Excessive clearance between shoe and caliper. 3. Soft or broken caliper seals. 4. Deformed or misaligned disc. 5. Loose caliper.
Scraping	1. Mounting bolts too long. 2. Loose wheel bearings. 3. Bent, loose, or misaligned splash shield.
Front brakes heat up during driving and fail to release	1. Operator riding brake pedal. 2. Stop light switch improperly adjusted. 3. Sticking pedal linkage. 4. Frozen or seized piston. 5. Residual pressure valve in master cylinder. 6. Power brake malfunction. 7. Proportioning valve malfunction.
Leaky brake caliper	1. Damaged or worn caliper piston seal. 2. Scores or corrosion on surface of cylinder bore.
Grabbing or uneven brake action—Brakes pull to one side	1. Causes listed under "Brakes Pull". 2. Power brake malfunction. 3. Low fluid level in master cylinder. 4. Air in hydraulic system. 5. Brake fluid, oil or grease on linings. 6. Unmatched linings. 7. Distorted brake pads. 8. Frozen or seized pistons. 9. Incorrect tire pressure. 10. Front end out of alignment. 11. Broken rear spring. 12. Brake caliper pistons sticking. 13. Restricted hose or line. 14. Caliper not in proper alignment to braking disc. 15. Stuck or malfunctioning metering valve. 16. Soft or broken caliper seals. 17. Loose caliper.
Brake pedal can be depressed without braking effect	1. Air in hydraulic system or improper bleeding procedure. 2. Leak past primary cup in master cylinder. 3. Leak in system. 4. Rear brakes out of adjustment. 5. Bleeder screw open.
Excessive pedal travel	1. Air, leak, or insufficient fluid in system or caliper. 2. Warped or excessively tapered shoe and lining assembly. 3. Excessive disc runout. 4. Rear brake adjustment required. 5. Loose wheel bearing adjustment. 6. Damaged caliper piston seal. 7. Improper brake fluid (boil). 8. Power brake malfunction. 9. Weak or soft hoses.

Troubleshooting Disc Brake Problems (cont.)

Condition	Possible Cause
Brake roughness or chatter (pedal pumping)	1. Excessive thickness variation of braking disc. 2. Excessive lateral runout of braking disc. 3. Rear brake drums out-of-round. 4. Excessive front bearing clearance.
Excessive pedal effort	1. Brake fluid, oil or grease on linings. 2. Incorrect lining. 3. Frozen or seized pistons. 4. Power brake malfunction. 5. Kinked or collapsed hose or line. 6. Stuck metering valve. 7. Scored caliper or master cylinder bore. 8. Seized caliper pistons.
Brake pedal fades (pedal travel increases with foot on brake)	1. Rough master cylinder or caliper bore. 2. Loose or broken hydraulic lines/connections. 3. Air in hydraulic system. 4. Fluid level low. 5. Weak or soft hoses. 6. Inferior quality brake shoes or fluid. 7. Worn master cylinder piston cups or seals.

Troubleshooting Drum Brakes

Condition	Possible Cause
Pedal goes to floor	1. Fluid low in reservoir. 2. Air in hydraulic system. 3. Improperly adjusted brake. 4. Leaking wheel cylinders. 5. Loose or broken brake lines. 6. Leaking or worn master cylinder. 7. Excessively worn brake lining.
Spongy brake pedal	1. Air in hydraulic system. 2. Improper brake fluid (low boiling point). 3. Excessively worn or cracked brake drums. 4. Broken pedal pivot bushing.
Brakes pulling	1. Contaminated lining. 2. Front end out of alignment. 3. Incorrect brake adjustment. 4. Unmatched brake lining. 5. Brake drums out of round. 6. Brake shoes distorted. 7. Restricted brake hose or line. 8. Broken rear spring. 9. Worn brake linings. 10. Uneven lining wear. 11. Glazed brake lining. 12. Excessive brake lining dust. 13. Heat spotted brake drums. 14. Weak brake return springs. 15. Faulty automatic adjusters. 16. Low or incorrect tire pressure.

TROUBLESHOOTING

Condition	Possible Cause
Squealing brakes	1. Glazed brake lining. 2. Saturated brake lining. 3. Weak or broken brake shoe retaining spring. 4. Broken or weak brake shoe return spring. 5. Incorrect brake lining. 6. Distorted brake shoes. 7. Bent support plate. 8. Dust in brakes or scored brake drums. 9. Linings worn below limit. 10. Uneven brake lining wear. 11. Heat spotted brake drums.
Chirping brakes	1. Out of round drum or eccentric axle flange pilot.
Dragging brakes	1. Incorrect wheel or parking brake adjustment. 2. Parking brakes engaged or improperly adjusted. 3. Weak or broken brake shoe return spring. 4. Brake pedal binding. 5. Master cylinder cup sticking. 6. Obstructed master cylinder relief port. 7. Saturated brake lining. 8. Bent or out of round brake drum. 9. Contaminated or improper brake fluid. 10. Sticking wheel cylinder pistons. 11. Driver riding brake pedal. 12. Defective proportioning valve. 13. Insufficient brake shoe lubricant.
Hard pedal	1. Brake booster inoperative. 2. Incorrect brake lining. 3. Restricted brake line or hose. 4. Frozen brake pedal linkage. 5. Stuck wheel cylinder. 6. Binding pedal linkage. 7. Faulty proportioning valve.
Wheel locks	1. Contaminated brake lining. 2. Loose or torn brake lining. 3. Wheel cylinder cups sticking. 4. Incorrect wheel bearing adjustment. 5. Faulty proportioning valve.
Brakes fade (high speed)	1. Incorrect lining. 2. Overheated brake drums. 3. Incorrect brake fluid (low boiling temperature). 4. Saturated brake lining. 5. Leak in hydraulic system. 6. Faulty automatic adjusters.
Pedal pulsates	1. Bent or out of round brake drum.
Brake chatter and shoe knock	1. Out of round brake drum. 2. Loose support plate. 3. Bent support plate. 4. Distorted brake shoes. 5. Machine grooves in contact face of brake drum (Shoe Knock). 6. Contaminated brake lining. 7. Missing or loose components. 8. Incorrect lining material. 9. Out-of-round brake drums. 10. Heat spotted or scored brake drums. 11. Out-of-balance wheels.

TROUBLESHOOTING

Troubleshooting Drum Brakes (cont.)

Condition	Possible Cause
Brakes do not self adjust	1. Adjuster screw frozen in thread. 2. Adjuster screw corroded at thrust washer. 3. Adjuster lever does not engage star wheel. 4. Adjuster installed on wrong wheel.
Brake light glows	1. Leak in the hydraulic system. 2. Air in the system. 3. Improperly adjusted master cylinder pushrod. 4. Uneven lining wear. 5. Failure to center combination valve or proportioning valve.

Mechanic's Data

General Conversion Table

Multiply By	To Convert	To	
LENGTH			
2.54	Inches	Centimeters	.3937
25.4	Inches	Millimeters	.03937
30.48	Feet	Centimeters	.0328
.304	Feet	Meters	3.28
.914	Yards	Meters	1.094
1.609	Miles	Kilometers	.621
VOLUME			
.473	Pints	Liters	2.11
.946	Quarts	Liters	1.06
3.785	Gallons	Liters	.264
.016	Cubic inches	Liters	61.02
16.39	Cubic inches	Cubic cms.	.061
28.3	Cubic feet	Liters	.0353
MASS (Weight)			
28.35	Ounces	Grams	.035
.4536	Pounds	Kilograms	2.20
—	To obtain	From	Multiply by

Multiply By	To Convert	To	
AREA			
.645	Square inches	Square cms.	.155
.836	Square yds.	Square meters	1.196
FORCE			
4.448	Pounds	Newtons	.225
.138	Ft./lbs.	Kilogram/meters	7.23
1.36	Ft./lbs.	Newton-meters	.737
.112	In./lbs.	Newton-meters	8.844
PRESSURE			
.068	Psi	Atmospheres	14.7
6.89	Psi	Kilopascals	.145
OTHER			
1.104	Horsepower (DIN)	Horsepower (SAE)	.9861
.746	Horsepower (SAE)	Kilowatts (KW)	1.34
1.60	Mph	Km/h	.625
.425	Mpg	Km/1	2.35
—	To obtain	From	Multiply by

Tap Drill Sizes

National Coarse or U.S.S.

Screw & Tap Size	Threads Per Inch	Use Drill Number
No. 5	40	39
No. 6	32	36
No. 8	32	29
No. 10	24	25
No. 12	24	17
1/4	20	8
5/16	18	F
3/8	16	5/16
7/16	14	U
1/2	13	27/64
9/16	12	31/64
5/8	11	17/32
3/4	10	21/32
7/8	9	49/64

National Coarse or U.S.S.

Screw & Tap Size	Threads Per Inch	Use Drill Number
1	8	7/8
1 1/8	7	63/64
1 1/4	7	1 7/64
1 1/2	6	1 11/32

National Fine or S.A.E.

Screw & Tap Size	Threads Per Inch	Use Drill Number
No. 5	44	37
No. 6	40	33
No. 8	36	29
No. 10	32	21

National Fine or S.A.E.

Screw & Tap Size	Threads Per Inch	Use Drill Number
No. 12	28	15
1/4	28	3
6/16	24	1
3/8	24	Q
7/16	20	W
1/2	20	29/64
9/16	18	33/64
5/8	18	37/64
3/4	16	11/16
7/8	14	13/16
1 1/8	12	1 3/64
1 1/4	12	1 11/64
1 1/2	12	1 27/64

MECHANIC'S DATA

Drill Sizes In Decimal Equivalents

Inch	Decimal	Wire	mm	Inch	Decimal	Wire	mm	Inch	Decimal	Wire & Letter	mm	Inch	Decimal	Letter	mm	Inch	Decimal	mm
1/64	.0156		.39		.0730	49			.1614		4.1		.2717		6.9		.4331	11.0
	.0157		.4		.0748		1.9		.1654		4.2		.2720	I		7/16	.4375	11.11
	.0160	78			.0760	48			.1660	19			.2756		7.0		.4528	11.5
	.0165		.42		.0768		1.95		.1673		4.25		.2770	J		29/64	.4531	11.51
	.0173		.44	5/64	.0781		1.98		.1693		4.3		.2795		7.1	15/32	.4688	11.90
	.0177		.45		.0785	47			.1695	18			.2810	K			.4724	12.0
	.0180	77			.0787		2.0	11/64	.1719		4.36	9/32	.2812		7.14	31/64	.4844	12.30
	.0181		.46		.0807		2.05		.1730	17			.2835		7.2		.4921	12.5
	.0189		.48		.0810	46			.1732		4.4		.2854		7.25	1/2	.5000	12.70
	.0197		.5		.0820	45			.1770	16			.2874		7.3		.5118	13.0
	.0200	76			.0827		2.1		.1772		4.5		.2900	L		33/64	.5156	13.09
	.0210	75			.0846		2.15		.1800	15			.2913		7.4	17/32	.5312	13.49
	.0217		.55		.0860	44			.1811		4.6		.2950	M			.5315	13.5
	.0225	74			.0866		2.2		.1820	14			.2953		7.5	35/64	.5469	13.89
	.0236		.6		.0886		2.25		.1850	13		19/64	.2969		7.54		.5512	14.0
	.0240	73			.0890	43			.1850		4.7		.2992		7.6	9/16	.5625	14.28
	.0250	72			.0906		2.3		.1870		4.75		.3020	N			.5709	14.5
	.0256		.65		.0925		2.35	3/16	.1875		4.76		.3031		7.7	37/64	.5781	14.68
	.0260	71			.0935	42			.1890		4.8		.3051		7.75		.5906	15.0
	.0276		.7	3/32	.0938		2.38		.1890	12			.3071		7.8	19/32	.5938	15.08
	.0280	70			.0945		2.4		.1910	11			.3110		7.9	39/64	.6094	15.47
	.0292	69			.0960	41			.1929		4.9		.3125		7.93		.6102	15.5
	.0295		.75		.0965		2.45		.1935	10			.3150		8.0	5/8	.6250	15.87
	.0310	68			.0980	40			.1960	9			.3160	O			.6299	16.0
1/32	.0312		.79		.0981		2.5		.1969		5.0		.3189		8.1	41/64	.6406	16.27
	.0315		.8		.0995	39			.1990	8			.3228		8.2		.6496	16.5
	.0320	67			.1015	38			.2008		5.1		.3230	P		21/32	.6562	16.66
	.0330	66			.1024		2.6		.2010	7			.3248		8.25		.6693	17.0
	.0335		.85		.1040	37		13/64	.2031		5.16		.3268		8.3	43/64	.6719	17.06
	.0350	65			.1063		2.7		.2040	6		21/64	.3281		8.33	11/16	.6875	17.46
	.0354		.9		.1065	36			.2047		5.2		.3307		8.4		.6890	17.5
	.0360	64			.1083		2.75		.2055	5			.3320	Q		45/64	.7031	17.85
	.0370	63		7/64	.1094		2.77		.2067		5.25		.3346		8.5		.7087	18.0
	.0374		.95		.1100	35			.2087		5.3		.3386		8.6	23/32	.7188	18.25
	.0380	62			.1102		2.8		.2090	4			.3390	R			.7283	18.5
	.0390	61			.1110	34			.2126		5.4		.3425		8.7	47/64	.7344	18.65
	.0394		1.0		.1130	33			.2130	3		11/32	.3438		8.73		.7480	19.0
	.0400	60			.1142		2.9		.2165		5.5		.3445		8.75	3/4	.7500	19.05
	.0410	59			.1160	32		7/32	.2188		5.55		.3465		8.8	49/64	.7656	19.44
	.0413		1.05		.1181		3.0		.2205		5.6		.3480	S			.7677	19.5
	.0420	58			.1200	31			.2210	2			.3504		8.9	25/32	.7812	19.84
	.0430	57			.1220		3.1		.2244		5.7		.3543		9.0		.7874	20.0
	.0433		1.1	1/8	.1250		3.17		.2264		5.75		.3580	T		51/64	.7969	20.24
	.0453		1.15		.1260		3.2		.2280	1			.3583		9.1		.8071	20.5
3/64	.0465	56			.1280		3.25		.2283		5.8	23/64	.3594		9.12	13/16	.8125	20.63
	.0469		1.19		.1285	30			.2323		5.9		.3622		9.2		.8268	21.0
	.0472		1.2		.1299		3.3		.2340	A			.3642		9.25	53/64	.8281	21.03
	.0492		1.25		.1339		3.4	15/64	.2344		5.95		.3661		9.3	27/32	.8438	21.43
	.0512		1.3		.1360	29			.2362		6.0		.3680	U			.8465	21.5
	.0520	55			.1378		3.5		.2380	B			.3701		9.4	55/64	.8594	21.82
	.0531		1.35		.1405	28			.2402		6.1		.3740		9.5		.8661	22.0
	.0550	54		9/64	.1406		3.57		.2420	C		3/8	.3750		9.52	7/8	.8750	22.22
	.0551		1.4		.1417		3.6		.2441		6.2		.3770	V			.8858	22.5
	.0571		1.45		.1440	27			.2460	D			.3780		9.6	57/64	.8906	22.62
	.0591		1.5		.1457		3.7		.2461		6.25		.3819		9.7		.9055	23.0
	.0595	53			.1470	26			.2480		6.3		.3839		9.75	29/32	.9062	23.01
	.0610		1.55		.1476		3.75	1/4	.2500	E	6.35		.3858		9.8	59/64	.9219	23.41
1/16	.0625		1.59		.1495	25			.2520		6.		.3860	W			.9252	23.5
	.0630		1.6		.1496		3.8		.2559		6.5		.3898		9.9	15/16	.9375	23.81
	.0635	52			.1520	24			.2570	F		25/64	.3906		9.92		.9449	24.0
	.0650		1.65		.1535		3.9		.2598		6.6		.3937		10.0	61/64	.9531	24.2
	.0669		1.7		.1540	23			.2610	G			.3970	X			.9646	24.5
	.0670	51		5/32	.1562		3.96		.2638		6.7		.4040	Y		31/64	.9688	24.6
	.0689		1.75		.1570	22		17/64	.2656		6.74	13/32	.4062		10.31		.9843	25.0
	.0700	50			.1575		4.0		.2657		6.75		.4130	Z		63/64	.9844	25.0
	.0709		1.8		.1590	21			.2660	H			.4134		10.5	1	1.0000	25.4
	.0728		1.85		.1610	20			.2677		6.8	27/64	.4219		10.71			

Index

A

Air cleaner, 7
Air conditioning
    Sight glass inspection, 12
Alternator, 38
Automatic transmission
    Adjustment, 120
    Filter change, 23
    Pan removal, 23, 121

B

Ball joints, 126
Battery
    Jump starting, 29
    Maintenance, 9, 41
Belt tension adjustment, 10
Brakes
    Adjustment, 137
    Bleeding, 139
    Caliper, 144
    Fluid level, 25
    Fluid recommendations, 25
    Front brakes, 140
    Master cylinder, 138
    Parking brake, 149
    Power Booster, 139
    Rear brakes, 146

C

Camber, 130
Camshaft and bearings, 58
Capacities, 20
Caster, 130
Catalytic converter, 72
Chassis lubrication, 26
Clutch
    Adjustment, 118
    Replacement, 118
Compression, 53
Control arm, 127
Cooling system, 23
Crankcase ventilation (PCV), 8
Crankshaft, 65
Cylinder head
    Removal and installation, 49

D

Distributor, 37

E

Electrical
    Chassis, 105
    Engine, 37
Emission controls, 72
Engine
    Camshaft, 58
    Exhaust manifold, 45
    Identification, 6
    Intake manifold, 45
    Oil recommendations, 18
    Pistons and rings, 63
    Rebuilding, 50
    Removal and installation, 43
    Rocker arm (or shaft), 45
    Specifications, 42
    Timing belt (or gears), 58
    Tune-up, 32
Evaporative canister, 8
Exhaust manifold, 45
Exhaust system, 70

F

Firing order, 35
Fluid level checks
    Battery, 9
    Coolant, 23
    Engine oil, 18
    Master cylinder, 25
    Power steering pump, 25
    Transmission, 21
Fluid recommendations, 18
Front suspension, 124
    Ball joints, 126
    lower control arm, 127
Fuel injection, 81, 92
Fuel filter, 18, 90, 102
Fuel pump, 103
Fuel system, 81
Fuel tank, 91, 103
Fuses and flashers, 114

G

Gearshift linkage adjustment
    Automatic, 120
    Manual, 115

H

Halfshaft, 117
Hand brake, 149
Headlights, 113
Heater, 106
Hoses, 13

I

Identification
    Vehicle, 6
    Engine, 6
    Transmission, 6, 115
Idle speed and mixture, 36, 88, 99
Ignition switch, 113, 135
Instrument cluster, 112
Intake manifold, 45

INDEX

J
Jacking points, 31
Jump starting, 29

L
Lower control arm, 127
Lubrication
   Chassis, 26
   Engine, 21
   Transmission, 21

M
Maintenance intervals, 18
Manifolds,
   Intake, 45·
   Exhaust, 45
Manual transmission, 115
Master cylinder, 138
Model identification, 6

N
Neutral safety switch, 121

O
Oil and fuel recommendations, 18
Oil change, 21
Oil filter (engine), 21
Oil pan, 67
Oil pump, 67
Oil level (engine), 18

P
Parking brake, 149
Pistons and rings
   Installation, 63
   Positioning, 64
PCV valve, 8
Power brakes, 139
Power steering pump, 136

R
Radiator, 68
Radio, 108
Rear suspension, 132
Regulator, 39
Rear main oil seal, 68
Rings, 64
Rocker arm (or shaft), 45

S
Safety notice, ii
Serial number location, 6
Shock absorbers, 132
Spark plugs, 33

Specifications
   Alternator and regulator, 40
   Battery and starter, 42
   Brakes, 151
   Capacities, 20
   Crankshaft and connecting rod, 42
   General engine, 42
   Piston and ring, 42
   Torque, 43
   Tune-up, 32
   Valve, 42
   Wheel alignment, 131
Speedometer cable, 112
Springs
   Front, 126
   Rear, 132
Starter, 39
Steering
   Gear, 136
   Linkage, 135
   Wheel, 134
Stripped threads, 51
Strut, 124
Sway bar, 127

T
Thermostat, 69
Tie-rod, 135
Timing (ignition), 35
Tires, 16
Tools, 2
Towing, 31
Transmission
   Automatic, 120
   Manual, 115
   Fluid change, 23
Troubleshooting, 152
Tune-up
   Procedures, 32
   Specifications, 32
Turbocharger, 47
Turn signal switch, 134

V
Valves
   Adjustment, 36
   Service, 55
Vehicle identification, 6

W
Water pump, 68
Wheel alignment, 130, 133
Wheel bearings, 28
Wheel cylinders, 148
Windshield wipers
   Arm, 110
   Blade, 15
   Linkage, 108
   Motor, 110

Chilton's Repair & Tune-Up Guides

The Complete line covers domestic cars, imports, trucks, vans, RV's and 4-wheel drive vehicles.

IMPORTANT

- All vehicles are listed alphabetically by individual model names rather than by manufacturer.
- Numerical model names follow the alphabetical model name listing.

Model Name	RTUG Title	Part No.
Accord	Honda 1973–84	6980
Alliance	Renault 1975–85	7165
AMX	AMC 1975–82	7199
Aries 1981–82	Chrysler K-Car 1981–82	7163
Arrow	Champ/Arrow/Sapporo 1978–83	7041
Arrow Pick-Ups	D-50/Arrow Pick-Up 1979–82	7032
Aspen 1976–80	Aspen/Volare 1976–80	6637
Astre 1975–77	GM Subcompact 1971–80	6935
Barracuda 1965–72	Barracuda/Challenger 1965–72	5807
Bavaria	BMW 1970–82	6844
Bel Air 1968–75	Chevrolet 1968–83	7135
Belvedere 1968–70	Roadrunner/Satellite/Belvedere/GTX 1968–73	5821
Biscayne 1968–71	Chevrolet 1968–83	7135
Blazer 1969–82	Blazer/Jimmy 1969–82	6931
Bobcat 1975–80	Pinto/Bobcat 1971–80	7027
Bonneville 1975–83	Buick/Olds/Pontiac 1975–83	7308
BRAT	Subaru 1970–84	6982
Bronco 1966–83	Ford Bronco 1966–83	7140
Bronco II 1984	Ford Bronco II 1984	7408
Brookwood 1968–72	Chevrolet 1968–83	7135
Brougham 1974–75	Valiant/Duster 1968–76	6326
B-210 1974–78	Datsun 1200, etc. 1973–84	7197
Caballero 1964–82	Chevrolet Mid-Size 1964–84	6840
Camaro 1967–81	Camaro 1967–81	6735
Camaro 1982–83	Camaro 1982–83	7317
Camry 1983–84	Toyota Corona, etc. 1970–84	7004
Capri 1970–77	Capri 1970–77	6695
Capri 1979–83	Mustang/Capri 1979–83	6963
Caprice 1975–83	Chevrolet 1968–83	7135
Caravan 1984–85	Caravan/Voyager 1984–85	7482
Carina 1972–73	Toyota Corolla, etc. 1970–84	7036
Catalina 1975–83	Buick/Olds/Pontiac 1975–83	7308
Cavalier 1982	GM J-Car 1982	7059
Celebrity 1982–83	GM A-Body 1982–83	7309
Celica 1971–83	Toyota Celica/Supra 1971–83	7043
Century, front wheel drive 1982–83	GM A-Body 1982–83	7309
Century, rear wheel drive 1975–83	Century/Regal 1975–83	7307
Challenger 1965–72	Barracuda/Challenger 1965–72	5807
Challenger 1977–83	Colt/Challenger/Vista 1971–83	7037
Champ	Champ/Arrow/Sapporo 1978–83	7041
Charger 2.2 1982–84	Omni/Horizon 1978–84	6845
Cherokee 1974–84	Jeep Wagoneer, etc. 1962–84	6739
Chevelle 1964–77	Chevrolet Mid-Size 1964–84	6840
Chevette 1976–84	Chevette/T-1000 1976–84	6836
Chevy Pick-Ups 1970–84	Chevrolet/GMC Pick-Ups/Suburban 1970–84	6936
Chevy Vans 1967–84	Chevy/GMC Vans 1967–84	6930
Chevy II 1962–68	Chevy II/Nova 1962–79	6841
Cimarron 1982	GM J-Car 1982	7059
Citation 1980–83	GM X-Body 1980–83	7049
Civic	Honda 1973–84	6980
Colt	Colt/Challenger/Vista 1971–83	7037
Comet 1971–77	Maverick/Comet 1971–77	6634
Commando 1971–73	Jeep Wagoneer, Commando, Cherokee, Truck 1962–84	6739
Concord	AMC 1975–82	7199
Continental 1982–85	Ford/Mercury Mid-Size 1971–85	6696
Corolla 1968–70	Toyota 1966–70	5795
Corolla 1970–84	Toyota Corolla, etc. 1970–84	7036
Corona 1966–70	Toyota 1966–70	5795
Corona 1970–81	Toyota Corona, etc. 1970–84	7004
Corsa	Corvair 1960–69	6691
Corvair 1960–69	Corvair 1960–69	6691
Corvette 1953–62	Corvette 1953–62	6576
Corvette 1963–84	Corvette 1963–84	6843
Cosmo	Mazda 1971–84	6981
Cougar 1967–71	Mustang/Cougar 1965–73	6542
Cougar 1972–85	Ford/Mercury Mid-Size 1971–85	6696
Country Sedan 1968–81	Ford/Mercury/Lincoln 1968–85	6842
Country Squire 1968–83	Ford/Mercury/Lincoln 1968–85	6842
Courier 1972–82	Ford Courier 1972–82	6983
Cressida 1978–84	Toyota Corona, etc. 1970–84	7004
Crown 1966–70	Toyota 1966–70	5795
Crown 1970–72	Toyota Corona, etc. 1970–84	7004
Crown Victoria 1981–85	Ford/Mercury/Lincoln 1968–85	6842
Cutlass 1970–82	Cutlass 1970–82	6933
Cutlass Ciera 1982–83	GM A-Body 1982–83	7309
Dart 1968–76	Dart/Demon 1968–76	6324
Dasher	VW Front Wheel Drive 1974–83	6962
Datsun Pick-Ups 1961–72	Datsun 1961–72	5790
Datsun Pick-Ups 1970–83	Datsun Pick-Ups 1970–83	6816
Demon 1971–76	Dart/Demon 1968–76	6324
deVille 1967–84	Cadillac 1967–84	7462
Dodge Pick-Ups 1967–84	Dodge/Plymouth Trucks 1967–84	7459
Dodge Vans	Dodge/Plymouth Trucks 1967–84	6934
Duster 1970–76	Valiant/Duster 1968–76	6326
D-50 Pick-Up 1979–81	D-50/Arrow Pick-Ups 1979–82	7032
Eagle	AMC 1975–82	7199
El Camino 1964–82	Chevrolet Mid-Size 1964–84	6840
Eldorado 1967–84	Cadillac 1967–84	7462
Electra 1975–84	Buick/Olds/Pontiac 1975–83	7308
Elite 1974–76	Ford/Mercury Mid-Size 1971–85	6696
Encore	Renault 1975–85	7165
Escort, EXP 1981–85	Ford/Mercury Front Wheel Drive 1981–85	7055
Fairlane 1962–70	Fairlane 1962–75	6320
Fairmont 1978–83	Fairmont/Zephyr 1978–83	6965
FF-1	Subaru 1970–84	6982
Fiat, all models	Fiat 1969–81	7042
Fiesta	Fiesta 1978–80	6846
Firebird 1967–81	Firebird 1967–81	5996
Firebird 1982–83	Firebird 1982–83	7345
Firenza 1982	GM J-Car 1982	7059
Fleetwood 1967–84	Cadillac 1967–84	7462
Ford Pick-Ups 1965–84	Ford Pick-Ups 1965–84	6913
Ford Vans	Ford Vans 1961–84	6849
Fuego	Renault 1975–85	7165
Fury 1968–76	Plymouth 1968–76	6552
F-10 1977–78	Datsun F-10, etc. 1977–82	7196
F-85 1970–72	Cutlass 1970–82	6933
Galaxie 1968–81	Ford/Mercury/Lincoln 1968–85	6842
GLC	Mazda 1971–84	6981
GMC Pick-Ups 1970–84	Chevrolet/GMC Pick-Ups/Suburban 1970–84	6936
GMC Vans	Chevrolet/GMC Vans 1967–84	6930
Gordini	Renault 1975–85	7165
Granada 1975–82	Granada/Monarch 1975–82	6937
Grand Coupe, Gran Fury, Gran Sedan	Plymouth 1968–76	6552
Grand Am 1974–80	Pontiac Mid-Size 1974–83	7346
Grand Prix 1974–83	Pontiac Mid-Size 1974–83	7346
Grand Safari 1975–83	Buick/Olds/Pontiac 1975–83	7308
Grand Ville 1975–83	Buick/Olds/Pontiac 1975–83	7308
Greenbriar	Corvair 1960–69	6691
Gremlin	AMC 1975–82	7199
GTO 1968–73	Tempest/GTO/LeMans 1968–73	5905
GTO 1974	Pontiac Mid-Size 1974–83	7346
GTX 1968–71	Roadrunner/Satellite/Belvedere/GTX 1968–73	5821
GT6	Triumph 1969–73	5910
G.T.350, G.T.500	Mustang/Cougar 1965–73	6542
Horizon 1978–84	Omni/Horizon 1978–84	6845
Hornet	AMC 1975–82	7199
Impala 1968–78	Chevrolet 1968–83	7135
Jeep CJ	Jeep CJ 1945–84	6817
Jeep Pick-Ups	Jeep Wagoneer, Commando, Cherokee, Truck 1962–84	6739
Jeepster 1966–70	Jeep Wagoneer, Commando, Cherokee, Truck 1962–84	6739
Jetta	VW Front Wheel Drive 1974–83	6962
Jimmy 1970–82	Blazer/Jimmy 1969–82	6931
Kingswood 1968–81	Chevrolet 1968–83	7135
Lakewood	Corvair 1960–69	6691
Lancer	Champ/Arrow/Sapporo 1977–83	7041
Land Cruiser 1966–70	Toyota 1966–70	5795
Land Cruiser 1970–83	Toyota Trucks 1970–83	7035
LeBaron 1982	Chrysler K-Car 1981–82	7163
LeCar	Renault 1975–85	7165
LeMans 1968–73	Tempest/GTO/LeMans 1968–73	5905
LeMans, Grand LeMans 1974–83	Pontiac Mid-Size 1974–83	7346
LeSabre 1975–85	Buick/Olds/Pontiac 1975–85	7308
Lincoln 1968–85	Ford/Mercury/Lincoln 1968–85	6842
LTD 1968–81	Ford/Mercury/Lincoln 1968–85	6842
LTD II 1977–79	Ford/Mercury Mid-Size 1971–85	6696
LUV 1972–81	Chevrolet LUV 1972–81	6815
Lynx, LN-7 1981–85	Ford/Mercury Front Wheel Drive 1981–85	7055
Mach 1 1968–73	Mustang/Cougar 1965–73	6542
Malibu	Chevrolet Mid-Size 1964–84	6840
Matador	AMC 1975–82	7199
Maverick 1970–77	Maverick/Comet 1970–77	6634
Maxima 1980–84	Datsun 200SX, etc. 1973–84	7170
Mercury (Full-Size) 1968–85	Ford/Mercury/Lincoln 1968–85	6842
MG	MG 1961–81	6780
Mk.II 1969–70	Toyota 1966–70	5795
Mk.II 1970–76	Toyota Corona, etc. 1970–84	7004
Monaco 1968–77	Dodge 1968–77	6554
Monarch 1975–80	Granada/Monarch 1975–82	6937
Monte Carlo 1970–84	Chevrolet Mid-Size 1964–84	6840
Montego 1971–78	Ford/Mercury Mid-Size 1971–85	6696
Monza 1960–69	Corvair 1960–69	6691
Monza 1975–80	GM Subcompact 1971–80	6935
Mustang 1965–73	Mustang/Cougar 1965–73	6542
Mustang 1979–83	Mustang/Capri 1979–83	6963
Mustang II 1974–78	Mustang II 1974–78	6812
Nova	Chevy II/Nova 1962–79	6841
Omega 1980–81	GM X-Body 1980–83	7049
Omni 1978–84	Omni/Horizon 1978–84	6845
Opel	Opel 1964–70	5792
Opel	Opel 1971–75	6575
Pacer	AMC 1975–82	7199
Patrol 1961–72	Datsun 1961–72	5790
Peugeot	Peugeot 1970–74	5982
Phoenix 1980–83	GM X-Body 1980–83	7049
Pinto 1971–80	Pinto/Bobcat 1971–80	7027

continued on next page

Model Name	RTUG Title	Part No.
Plymouth Vans 1974–84	Dodge/Plymouth Vans 1967–84	6934
Polara 1968–77	Dodge 1968–77	6554
Prelude	Honda 1973–84	6980
PV-444, 544	Volvo 1956–69	6529
P-1800	Volvo 1956–69	6529
Quantum 1974–84	VW Front Wheel Drive 1974–83	6962
Rabbit	VW Front Wheel Drive 1974–84	6962
Ramcharger	Dodge/Plymouth Trucks 1967–84	7459
Ranchero 1967–70	Fairlane/Torino 1962–70	6320
Ranchero 1971–78	Ford/Mercury Mid-Size 1971–85	6696
Ranch Wagon	Ford/Mercury/Lincoln 1968–85	6842
Ranger Pick-Up 1983–84	Ford Ranger 1983–84	7338
Regal 1975–85	Century/Regal 1975–85	7307
Reliant 1981–85	Chrysler K-Car 1981–85	7163
Roadrunner 1968–73	Roadrunner/Satellite/Belvedere/GTX 1968–73	5821
RX-2, RX-3, RX-4	Mazda 1971–84	6981
RX-7	RX-7 1979–81	7031
R-12, 15, 17, 18, 18i	Renault 1975–85	7165
Sapporo 1977–83	Champ/Arrow/Saporro 1978–83	7041
Satellite 1968–73	Roadrunner/Satellite/Belvedere/GTX 1968–73	5821
Scamp 1971–76	Valiant/Duster 1968–76	6326
Scamp 1982	Omni/Horizon 1978–84	6845
Scirocco	VW Front Wheel Drive 1974–83	6962
Scout 1967–73	International Scout 1967–73	5912
Scrambler 1981–84	Jeep CJ 1981–84	6817
Sentra 1982–84	Datsun 1200, etc. 1973–84	7197
Seville 1967–84	Cadillac 1967–84	7462
Skyhawk 1975–80	GM Subcompact 1971–80	6935
Skyhawk 1982	GM J-Car 1982	7059
Skylark 1980–83	GM X-Body 1980–83	7049
Spirit	AMC 1975–82	7199
Sport Wagon	Renault 1975–85	7165
Stanza	Datsun F-10, etc. 1977–82	7196
Starfire 1975–80	GM Subcompact 1971–80	6935
Starlet 1981–84	Toyota Corolla, etc. 1970–84	7036
Suburban 1968–76	Plymouth 1968–76	6552
Suburban 1970–84	Chevy/GMC Pick-Ups/Suburban 1970–84	6936
Sunbird 1975–80	GM Subcompact 1971–80	6935
Super 90	Audi 1970–73	5902
Supra 1979–84	Toyota Celica/Supra 1971–84	7043
SX-4	AMC 1975–82	7199
S-10 Blazer, S-15 Jimmy 1982–85	Chevy S-10 Blazer/GMC S-15 Jimmy 1982–85	7383
S-10, S-15 Pick-Ups 1982–85	Chevy S-10/GMC S-15 Pick-Ups 1982–85	7310
TC-3 1978–82	Omni/Horizon/Rampage 1978–84	6845
Tempest 1968–73	Tempest/GTO/LeMans 1968–73	5905
Tempo 1984–85	Ford/Mercury Front Wheel Drive 1981–85	7055
Tercel 1980–84	Toyota Corolla, etc. 1970–84	7036
Thunderbird 1977–83	Ford/Mercury Mid-Size 1971–83	6696
Topaz 1983–85	Ford/Mercury Front Wheel Drive 1981–85	7055
Torino	Fairlane/Torino 1962–75	6320
Torino, Gran Torino 1971–76	Ford/Mercury Mid-Size 1971–83	6696
Townsman 1968–72	Chevrolet 1968–83	7135
Toyota Pick-Ups 1966–70	Toyota 1966–70	5795
Toyota Pick-Ups 1970–83	Toyota Trucks 1970–83	7035
Toyota Van 1984	Toyota Corona, etc. 1970–84	7004
Trail Duster 1974–84	Dodge/Plymouth Trucks 1967–84	7459
Triumph, all models	Triumph 1969–73	5910
Turismo 1982–84	Omni/Horizon 1978–84	6845
T-37 1971	Tempest/GTO/LeMans 1968–73	5905
Vega 1971–77	GM Subcompact 1971–80	6935
Ventura 1974–79	Pontiac Mid-Size 1974–83	7346
Versailles 1978–80	Ford/Mercury Mid-Size 1971–83	6696
VIP 1969–74	Plymouth 1968–76	6552
Vista Cruiser 1970–72	Cutlass 1970–82	6933
Volare 1976–80	Aspen/Volare 1976–80	6637
Voyager 1984	Caravan/Voyager 1984	7482
VW All models 1949–71	VW 1949–71	5796
VW Types 1, 2, 3	VW 1949–71	5796
VW 1970–81	VW 1970–81	6837
Wagoneer 1962–84	Jeep Wagoneer, Commando, Cherokee, Truck 1962–84	6739
XL 1968–75	Ford/Mercury/Lincoln 1968–83	6842
XR-7 1977–83	Ford/Mercury Mid-Size 1971–83	6696
Zephyr 1978–80	Fairmont/Zephyr 1978–83	6965
Z-28 1967–81	Camaro 1967–81	6735
Z-28 1982–83	Camaro 1982–83	7317
4-4-2 1970–80	Cutlass 1970–82	6933
024 1978–80	Omni/Horizon 1978–84	6845
3.0S, 3.0Si, 3.0CS	BMW 1970–82	6844
6.9 1978–79	Mercedes-Benz 1974–84	6809
88, 98	Buick/Olds/Pontiac 1975–83	7308
99 1969–75	SAAB 99 1969–75	5988
100 LS, 100GL	Audi 1970–73	5902
122, 122S	Volvo 1956–69	6529
142, 144, 145, 164	Volvo 1956–69	6529
	Volvo 1970–84	7040
190E, 190D 1984	Mercedes-Benz 1974–84	6809
190C, 190DC 1961–66	Mercedes-Benz 1959–70	6065
200, 200D	Mercedes-Benz 1959–70	6065
200SX 1977–84	Datsun 200SX, etc. 1973–84	7170
210 1979–81	Datsun 1200, etc. 1971–84	7197
220D, 220B, 220Sb, 220SEb	Mercedes-Benz 1959–70	6065
220/8 1968–73	Mercedes-Benz 1968–73	5907
230 1974–78	Mercedes-Benz 1974–84	6809
230S, 230SL	Mercedes-Benz 1959–70	6065
230/8 1968–69	Mercedes-Benz 1968–73	5907
240D 1974–79	Mercedes-Benz 1974–84	6809
240Z, 260Z, 280Z, 280ZX, 300ZX	Datsun Z & ZX 1970–84	6932
242, 244, 245, 262, 264, 265	Volvo 1970–84	7040
250C, 250/8	Mercedes-Benz 1968–73	5907
250S, 250SE, 250SL	Mercedes-Benz 1959–70	6065
280, 280C, 280S/8, 280SE, 280SE/8, 280SEL, 280SEL/8, 280SL	Mercedes-Benz 1968–73	5907
280, 280C, 280CE, 280E, 280S, 280SE, 300CD, 300D, 300SD	Mercedes-Benz 1974–84	6809
300SE, 1961–63	Mercedes-Benz 1959–70	6065
300SEL, 3.5, 4.5, 6.3, 300SEL/8	Mercedes-Benz 1968–73	5907
300TD 1979	Mercedes-Benz 1974–84	6809
304	Peugeot 1970–74	5982
310, 311 1962–69	Datsun 1961–72	5790
310 1979–82	Datsun F-10, etc. 1977–82	7196
320i	BMW 1970–82	6844
350SL 1972	Mercedes-Benz 1968–73	5907
380SEC, 380SL, 380SLC, 380SEL	Mercedes-Benz 1974–84	6809
400 1982	Chrysler K-Car 1981–82	7163
410, 411, 1963–68	Datsun 1961–72	5790
411, 412	VW 1970–81	7081
450SLC 1973	Mercedes-Benz 1968–73	5907
450SE, 450SEL, 450SEL 6.9, 450SL, 450SLC	Mercedes-Benz 1974–84	6809
500SEC, 500SEL	Mercedes-Benz 1974–84	6809
504	Peugeot 1970–74	5982
510 1968–71	Datsun 1961–72	5790
510 1973, 1978–80	Datsun 200SX, etc. 1973–84	7170
528i, 530i	BMW 1970–82	6844
600	Honda 1973–84	6980
610 1973–76	Datsun 200SX, etc. 1973–84	7170
626	Mazda 1971–84	6981
630 CSi, 633 CSi	BMW 1970–82	6844
710 1974–77	Datsun 200SX, etc. 1973–84	7170
733i	BMW 1970–82	6844
760, 760GLE	Volvo 1970–84	7040
808 (1300, 1600)	Mazda 1971–84	6981
810 1977–80	Datsun 200SX, etc. 1973–84	7170
900, 900 Turbo 1976–85	SAAB 900 1976–85	7572
911, 914	Porsche 1969–73	5822
924, 928	Porsche 924/928 1976–81	7048
1000 1981–84	Chevette/1000 1976–84	6836
1200 1500, 1600, 2000	Datsun 1961–72	5790
1200 1973	Datsun 1200, etc. 1973–84	7197
1400, 1600, 1800 GL/DL/GF	Subaru 1970–84	6982
1500, 1600, 1600–2, 1800	BMW 1970–82	6844
1800, 1800S	Volvo 1956–69	6529
2000, 2002, 2002Ti, 2002Tii, 2500, 2800	BMW 1970–82	6844
2000 1982	GM J-Car 1982	7059
4000, 5000	Audi 4000/5000 1978–81	7028
6000 1982–83	GM A-Body 1982–83	7309

Spanish Language Repair & Tune-Up Guides

Chevrolet/GMC Pick-ups 1970–82	Part No. 7468
Ford Pick-ups 1965–82	Part No. 7469
Toyota 1970–79	Part No. 7467
Chevrolet 1968–79	Part No. 7082
Datsun 1973–80	Part No. 7083
Ford 1968–79	Part No. 7084
Rabbit/Scirocco 1975–78	Part No. 7089
Volkswagen 1970–79	Part No. 7081

Chilton's Repair & Tune-Up Guides are available at your local retailer or by mailing a check or money order for **$11.95** plus **$1.75** to cover postage and handling to:

**Chilton Book Company
Dept. DM
Radnor, PA 19089**

NOTE: When ordering be sure to include your name & address, book part No. & title.